ドラゴン騎士団.12
DRAGON KNIGHTS 12

押上美猫

Mineko Ohkami

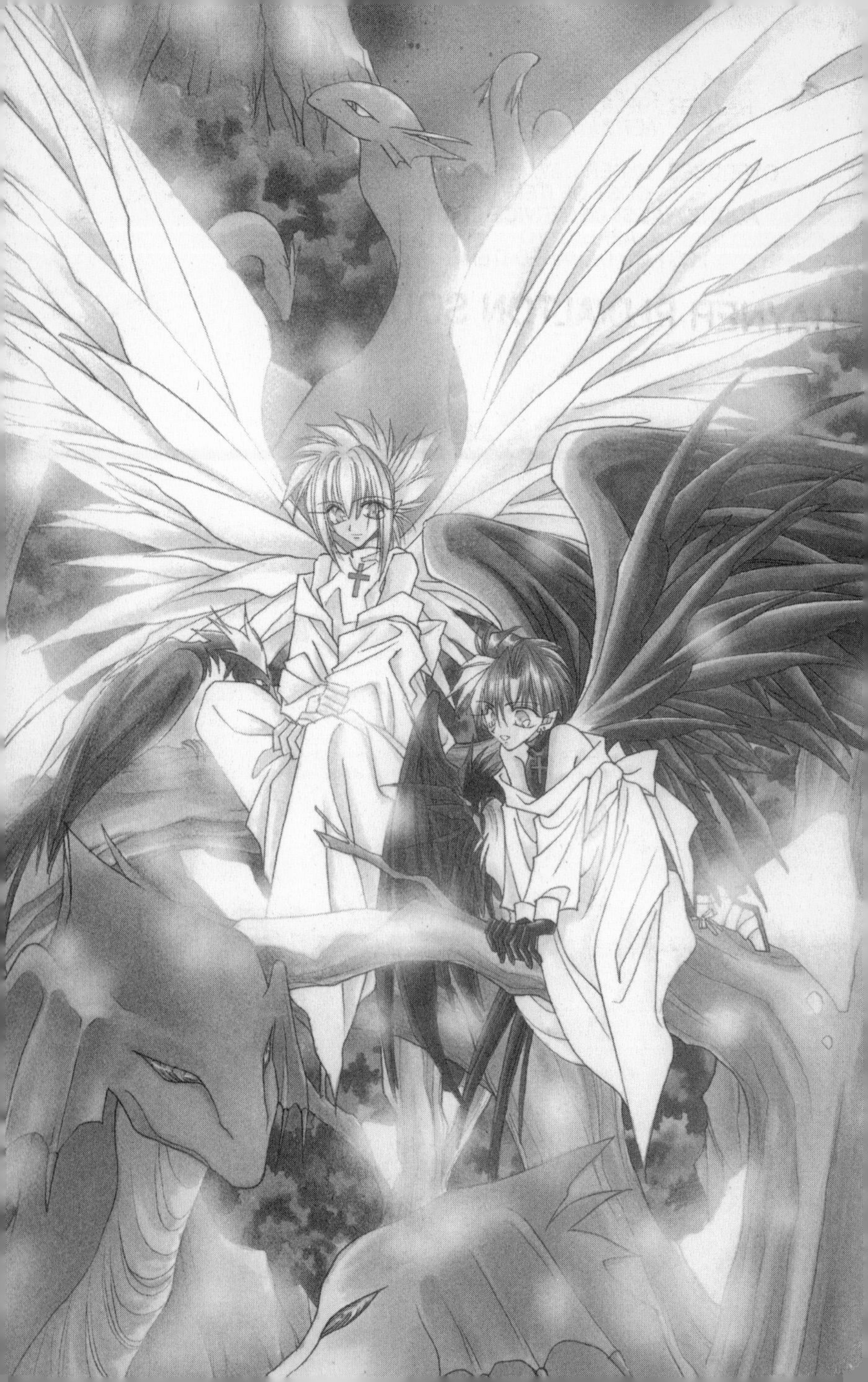

616156626

Dragon Knights

**Written and Illustrated by
Mineko Ohkami**

Volume 12

TOKYOPOP®

Los Angeles • Tokyo • London

Translator - Yuki Nakamura
English Adaptation - Stephanie Sheh
Associate Editor - Tim Beedle
Retouch and Lettering - James Lee
Cover Layout - Anna Kernbaum

Editor - Luis Reyes
Managing Editor - Jill Freshney
Production Coordinator - Antonio DePietro
Production Managers - Jennifer Miller, Mutsumi Miyazaki
Art Director - Matt Alford
Editorial Director - Jeremy Ross
VP of Production - Ron Klamert
President & C.O.O. - John Parker
Publisher & C.E.O. - Stuart Levy

Email: editor@TOKYOPOP.com
Come visit us online at www.TOKYOPOP.com

A  Manga

TOKYOPOP Inc.
5900 Wilshire Blvd. Suite 2000
Los Angeles, CA 90036

Dragon Knights Vol. 12

ISBN: 1-59182-440-0

First TOKYOPOP printing: February 2004

10 9 8 7 6 5 4 3 2 1
Printed in the USA

From the Chronicles of Dusis, the West Continent...

The Beginnings: Nadil and Lord Lykouleon

When the Yokai Nadil, the leader of the Demon Forces, kidnapped the Dragon Queen Raseleane, the Dragon Lord Lykouleon ventured to the Demon Realm to rescue her. He defeated Nadil by cutting off his head, but not before the demon leader rendered Raseleane barren, unable to give Lykouleon a child...and the Dragon Kingdom an heir. Now the Demon and Yokai forces, under the command of Shydeman and Shyrendora, plot against Draqueen, the Dragon Kingdom, and aim to retrieve their leader's head in the hopes of reviving him. Over time, other shady characters such as Kharl the Alchemist, the evil sorcerer Kirukulus, and the rogue Yokai Bierrez have also entered the contest for control of Dusis. The Dragon Officers and Lord Lykouleon have had no choice but to train the guard and prepare the Dragon Palace against an inevitable assault by Demon Forces.

The Dragon Knights: A Motley Trio

The Dragon Knights are three specially chosen warriors granted the power of the various elemental dragons for use in protecting of the Dragon Realm. The human Thatz is the Dragon Knight of Earth, and despite his former career as a thief, has proven to be one of Lykouleon's most dependable servants. The elf Rune healed the Water Dragon in a battle with the Demon Fish Varawoo, thereby unlocking its seal and becoming the Dragon Knight of Water. The half-demon Rath is the Dragon Knight of Fire. With a passion for hunting demons and a mysterious past, Rath has long been the Dragon Kingdom's most formidable warrior, feared by nearly every demon in Dusis...and more than a few members of the Dragon Tribe as well.

Besieged

After a prolonged absence, Rath returns to Draqueen acting very strangely, a matter largely ignored by the distracted Dragon Tribe. Nadil's army moves towards the Dragon Kingdom, and with the news that a large demonic presence is mysteriously amassing within the castle itself, the Dragon Tribe realizes that the day they've long feared has at last arrived—the Demon Army is attacking. However, as the Dragon Officers ready the castle's external defenses, they fail to notice that the greatest threat hides within their ranks. Possessed by a powerful demon, Rath strikes a staggering blow against the Dragon Tribe as he murders Alfeegi, the White Dragon Officer, and unleashes the Demon Fish Varawoo from within Rune's psyche. As the Dragon Officers lead the charge against the Demon Army, Lykouleon must help Rune regain control of the monstrous Varawoo. It's a feat that would have claimed the Dragon Knight of Water's life were it not for the strength provided to him by Alfeegi's Dragon Ball. However, while the Dragon Lord may take solace in Rune's triumph, the victory is bittersweet. For Lykouleon knows that only one thing would cause a Dragon Officer to release his Dragon Ball. With the forces of Nadil at the Dragon Lord's doorstep, death has come to the Dragon Tribe.

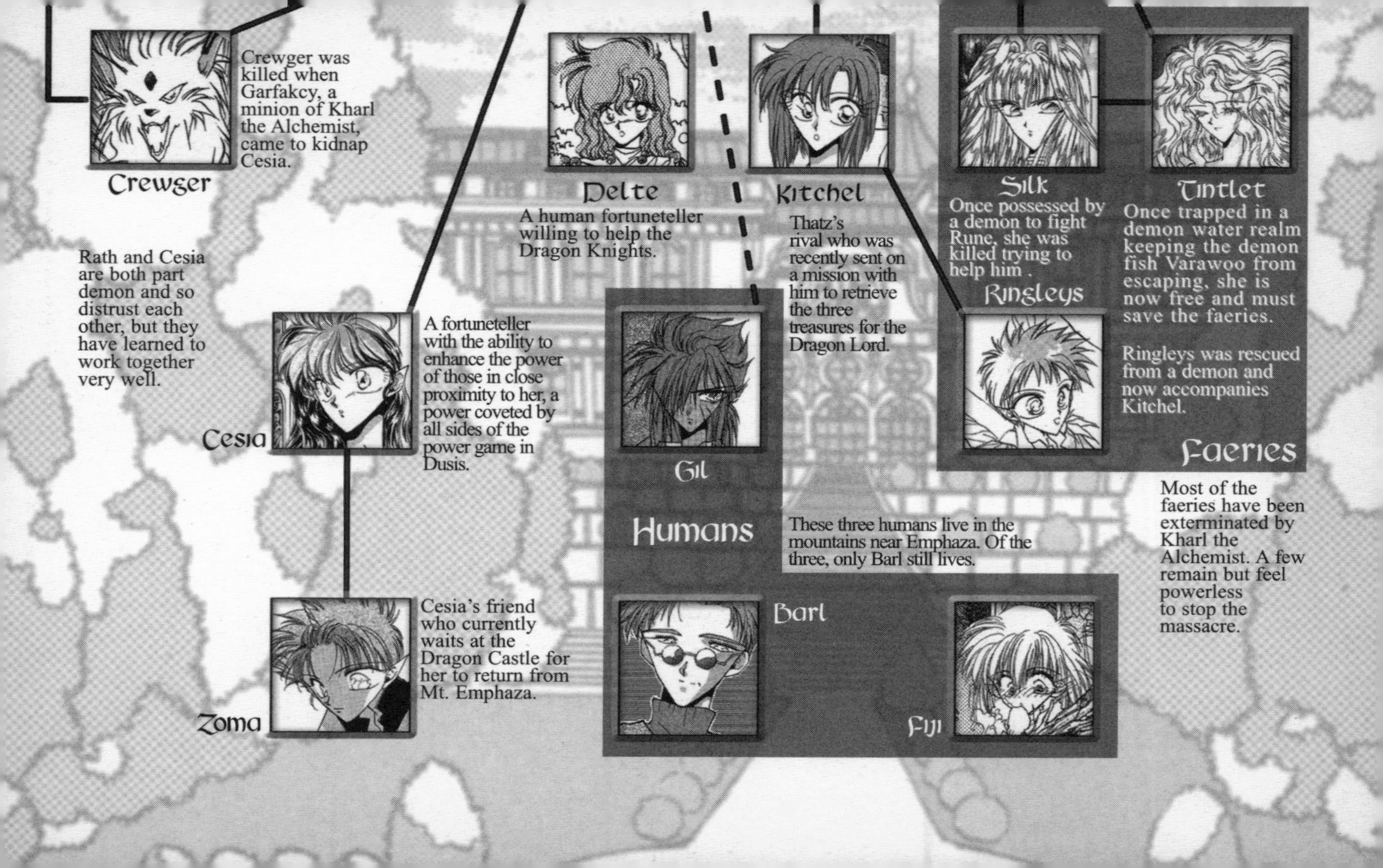

Crewger
Crewger was killed when Garfakcy, a minion of Kharl the Alchemist, came to kidnap Cesia.
Rath and Cesia are both part demon and so distrust each other, but they have learned to work together very well.
Cesia
A fortuneteller with the ability to enhance the power of those in close proximity to her, a power coveted by all sides of the power game in Dusis.
Zoma
Cesia's friend who currently waits at the Dragon Castle for her to return from Mt. Emphaza.
Delte
A human fortuneteller willing to help the Dragon Knights.
Kitchel
Thatz's rival who was recently sent on a mission with him to retrieve the three treasures for the Dragon Lord.
Humans
Gil
These three humans live in the mountains near Emphaza. Of the three, only Barl still lives.
Barl
Fiji
Silk
Once possessed by a demon to fight Rune, she was killed trying to help him .
Tintlet
Once trapped in a demon water realm keeping the demon fish Varawoo from escaping, she is now free and must save the faeries.
Ringleys
Ringleys was rescued from a demon and now accompanies Kitchel.
Faeries
Most of the faeries have been exterminated by Kharl the Alchemist. A few remain but feel powerless to stop the massacre.

The Cast of Dragon Knights

The Dragon Knights and the Dragon Officers, under the command of Lord Lykouleon, are positioning themselves to face the Demon Forces in the defense of Dusis. But they will have to rely on the help of others to see them through. This is an overview of the Dragon Clan and their allies.

Royalty

Lord Lykouleon

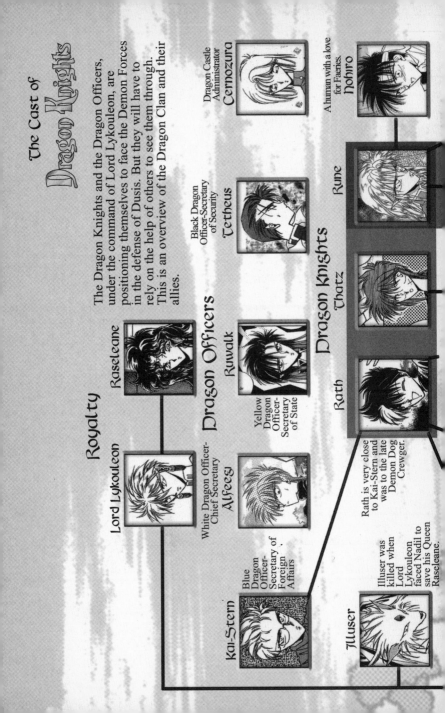

Raseleane

Dragon Officers

Alfeegi
White Dragon Officer-Chief Secretary

Ruwalk
Yellow Dragon Officer-Secretary of State

Tetheus
Black Dragon Officer-Secretary of Security

Cernozura
Dragon Castle Administrator

Dragon Knights

Rath

Thatz

Rune

Nohiro
A human with a love for Faeries.

Kai-Stern
Blue Dragon Officer-Secretary of Foreign Affairs

Illuser

Rath is very close to Kai-Stern and was to the late Demon Dog Crewger.

Illuser was killed when Lord Lykouleon faced Nadil to save his Queen Raseleane.

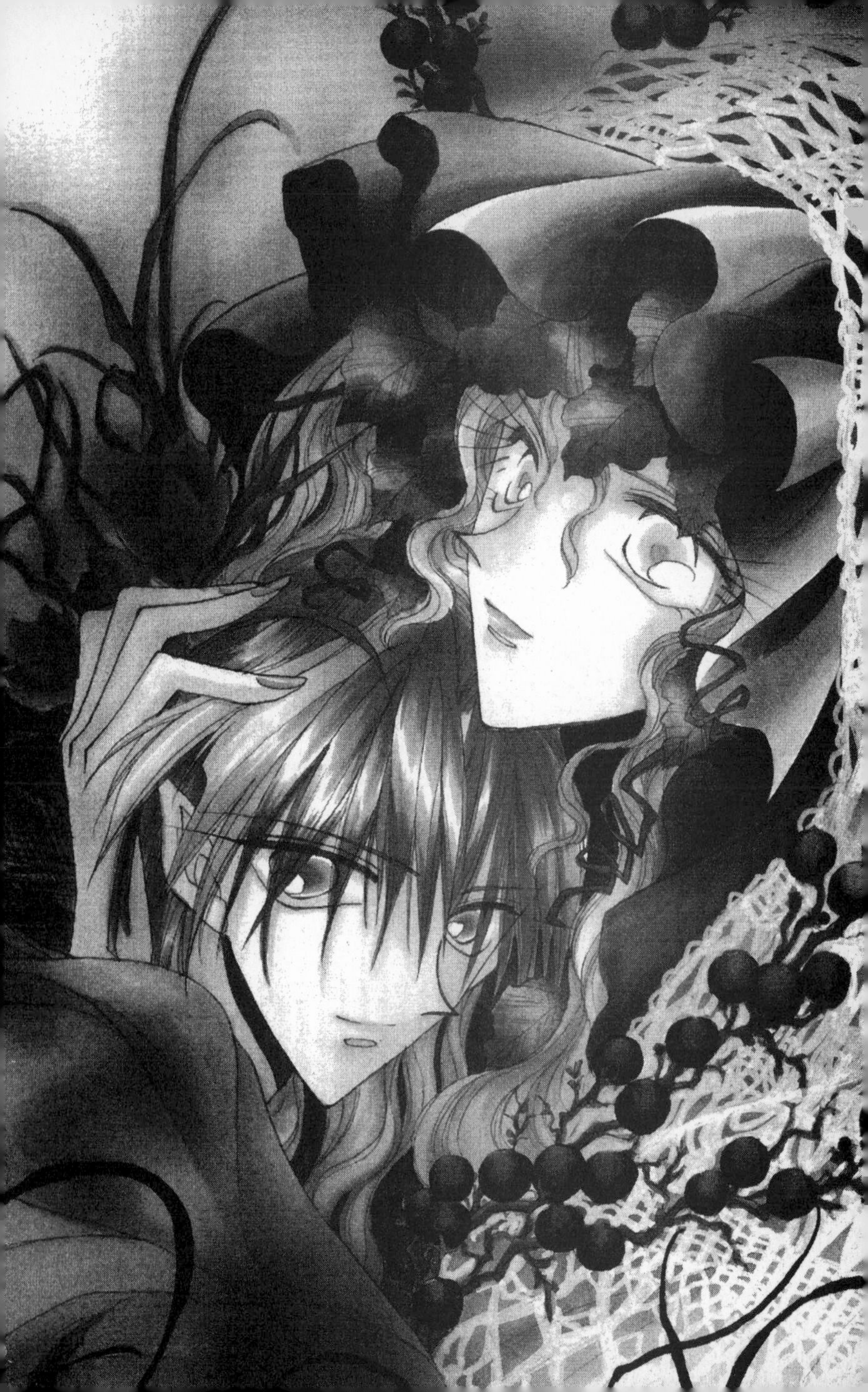

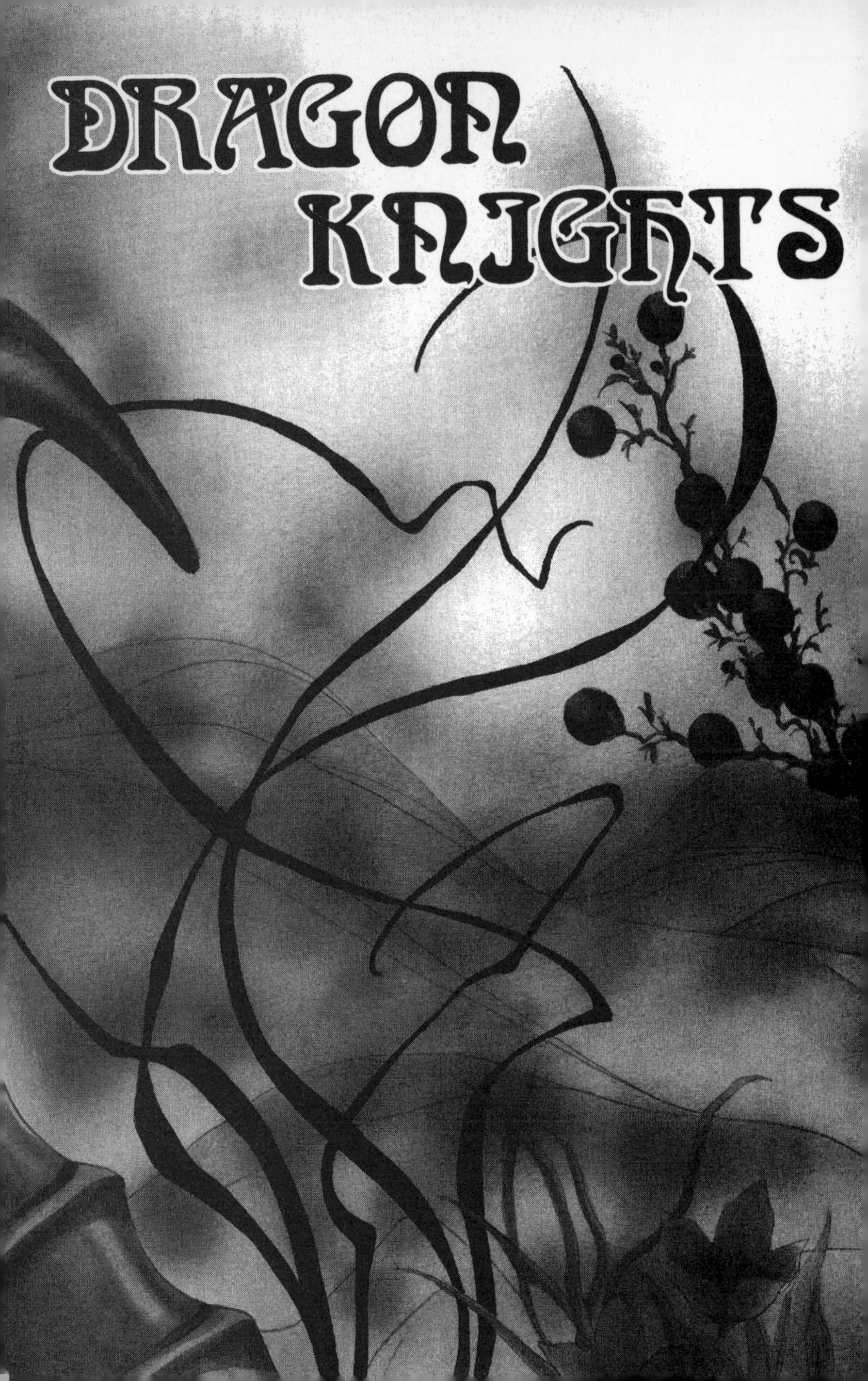
DRAGON
KNIGHTS

CONTENTS

Dragon Knights: Revival..11
Dragon Knights: Black Education...109

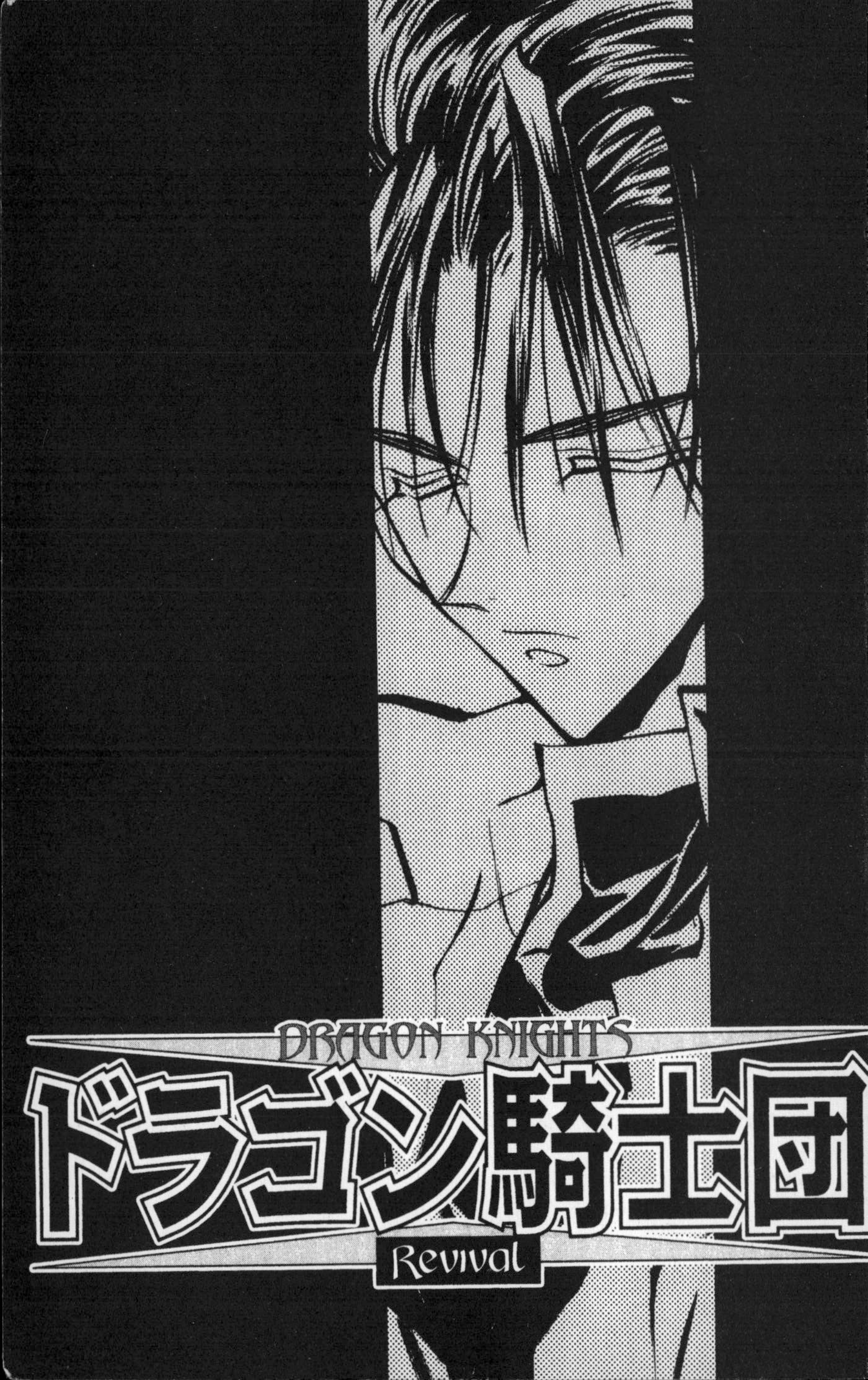
DRAGON KNIGHTS
ドラゴン騎士団
Revival

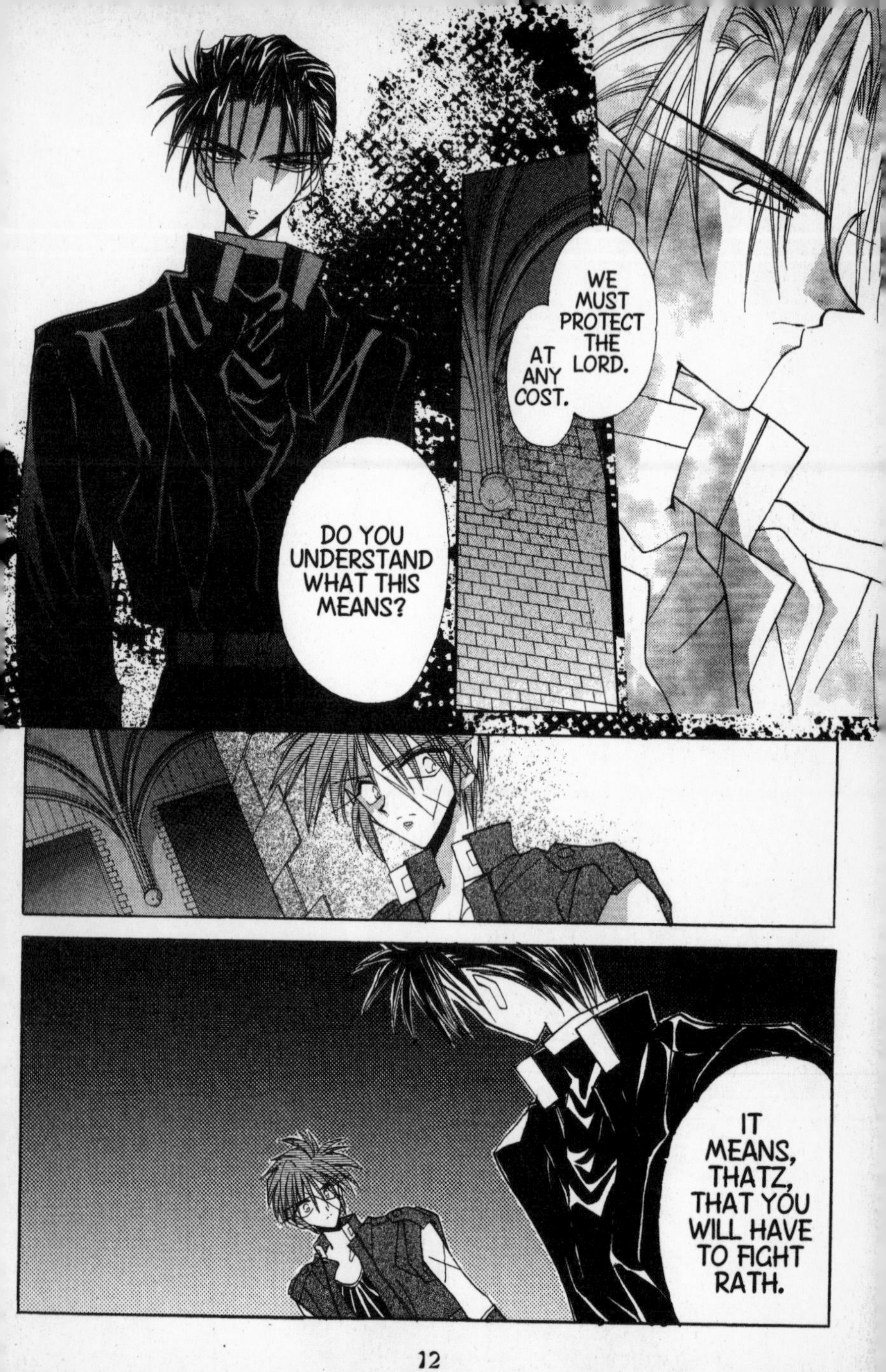
WE MUST PROTECT THE LORD.
AT ANY COST.
DO YOU UNDERSTAND WHAT THIS MEANS?
IT MEANS, THATZ, THAT YOU WILL HAVE TO FIGHT RATH.

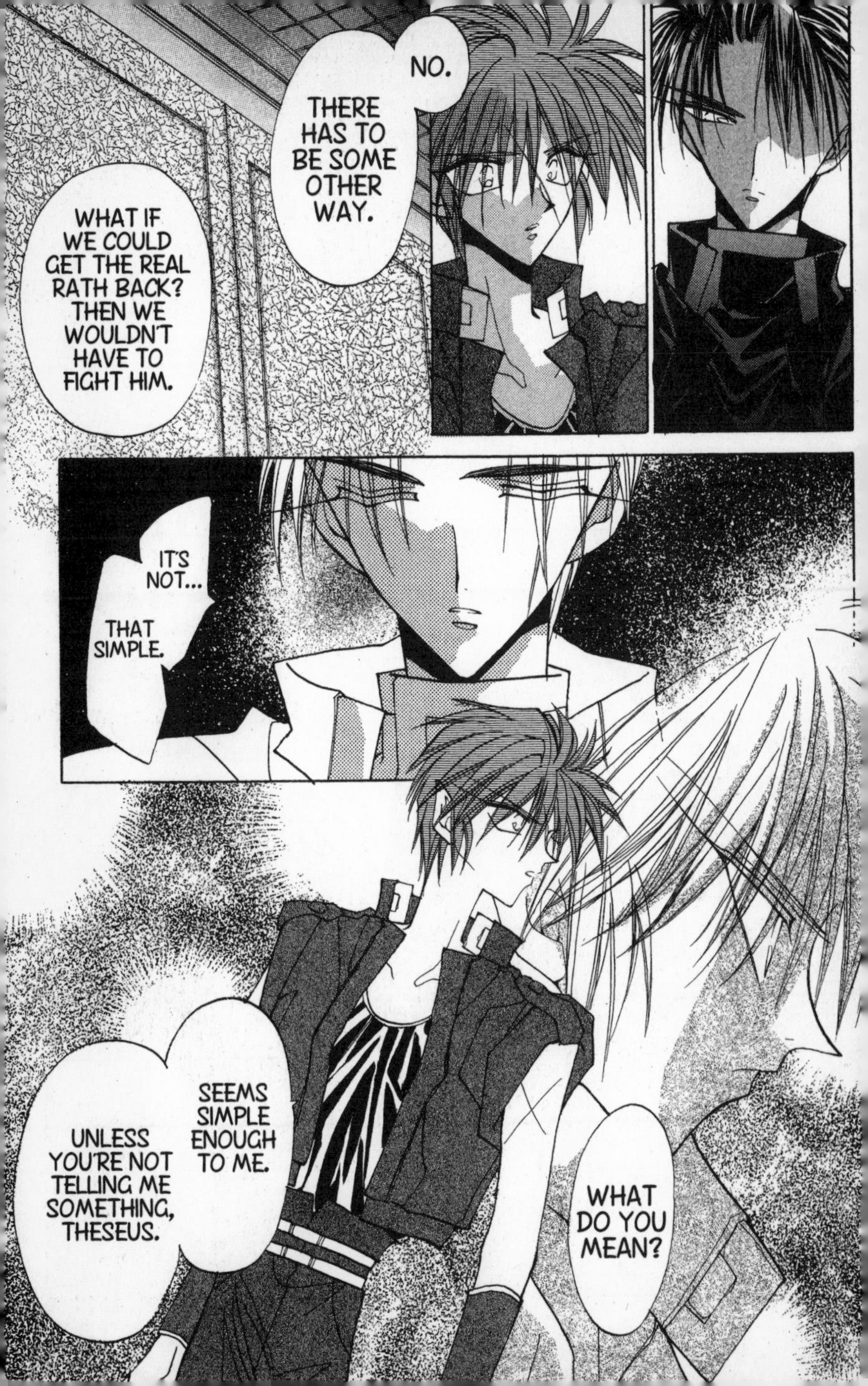
NO.
THERE HAS TO BE SOME OTHER WAY.
WHAT IF WE COULD GET THE REAL RATH BACK? THEN WE WOULDN'T HAVE TO FIGHT HIM.
IT'S NOT...
THAT SIMPLE.
SEEMS SIMPLE ENOUGH TO ME.
UNLESS YOU'RE NOT TELLING ME SOMETHING, THESEUS.
WHAT DO YOU MEAN?

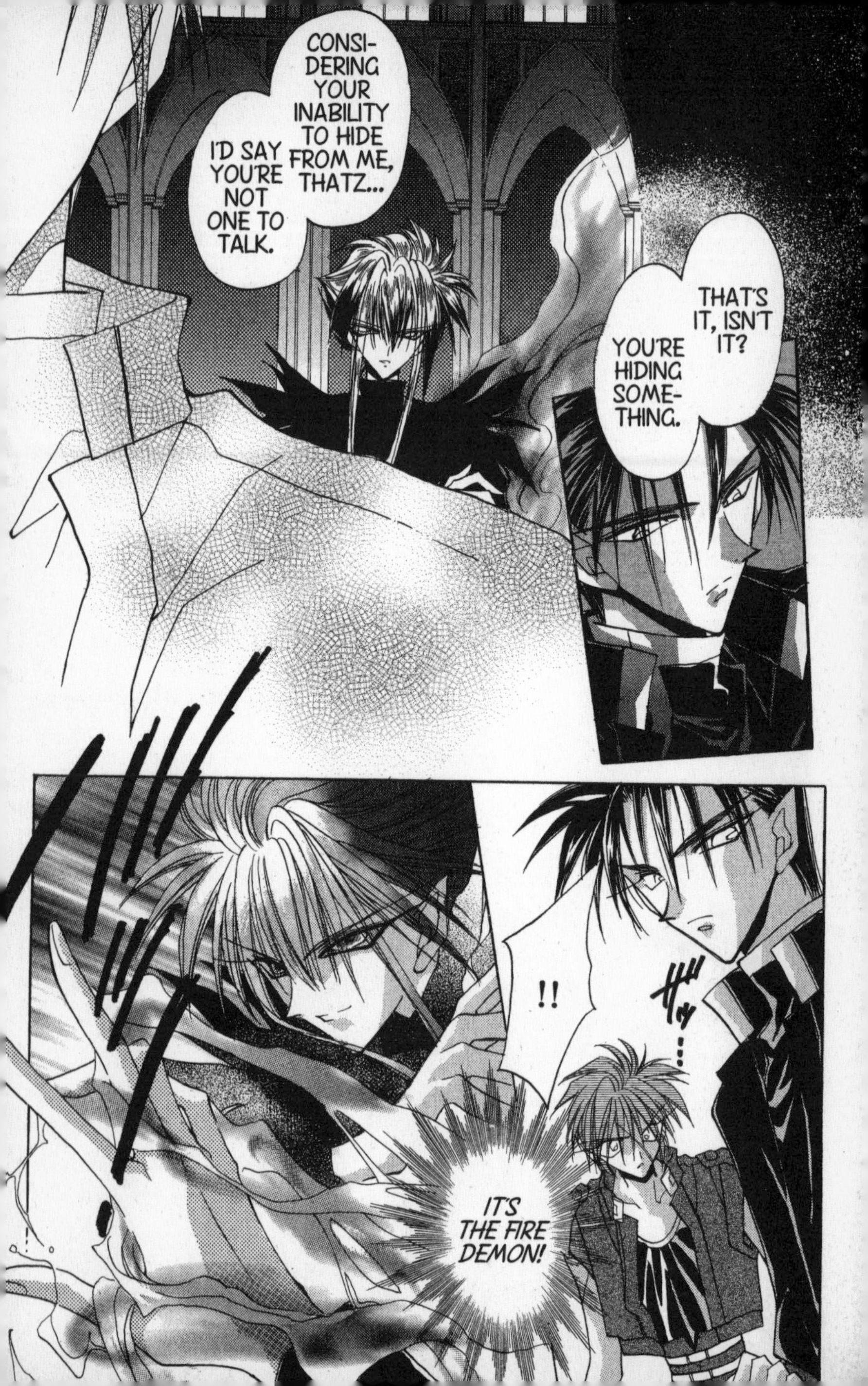
THAT'S IT, ISN'T IT?
YOU'RE HIDING SOME-THING.
CONSI-DERING YOUR INABILITY TO HIDE FROM ME, THATZ...
I'D SAY YOU'RE NOT ONE TO TALK.
!!
IT'S THE FIRE DEMON!

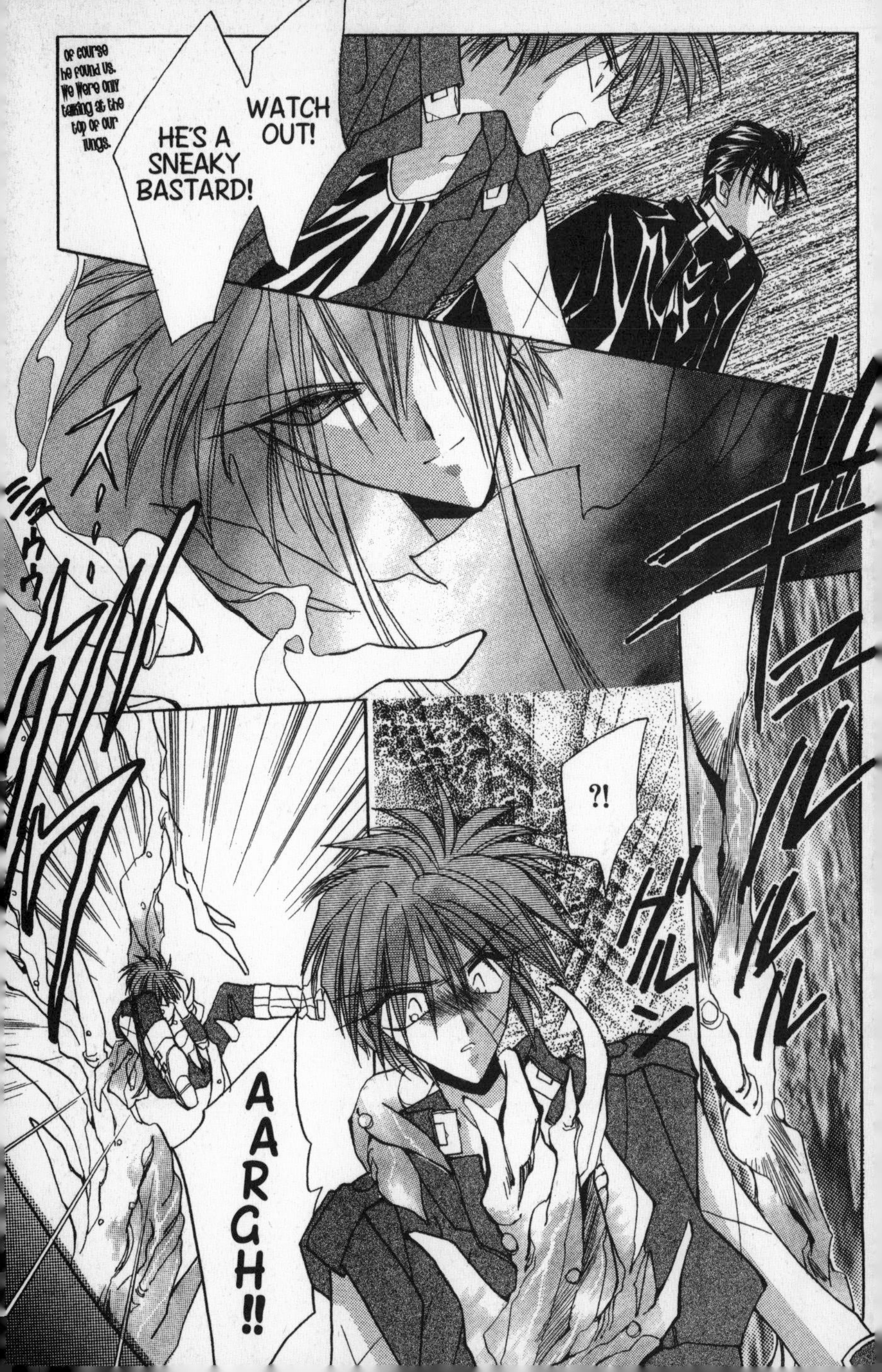
WATCH OUT!
HE'S A SNEAKY BASTARD!
Of course he found us. We were only talking at the top of our lungs.
?!
AARGH!!

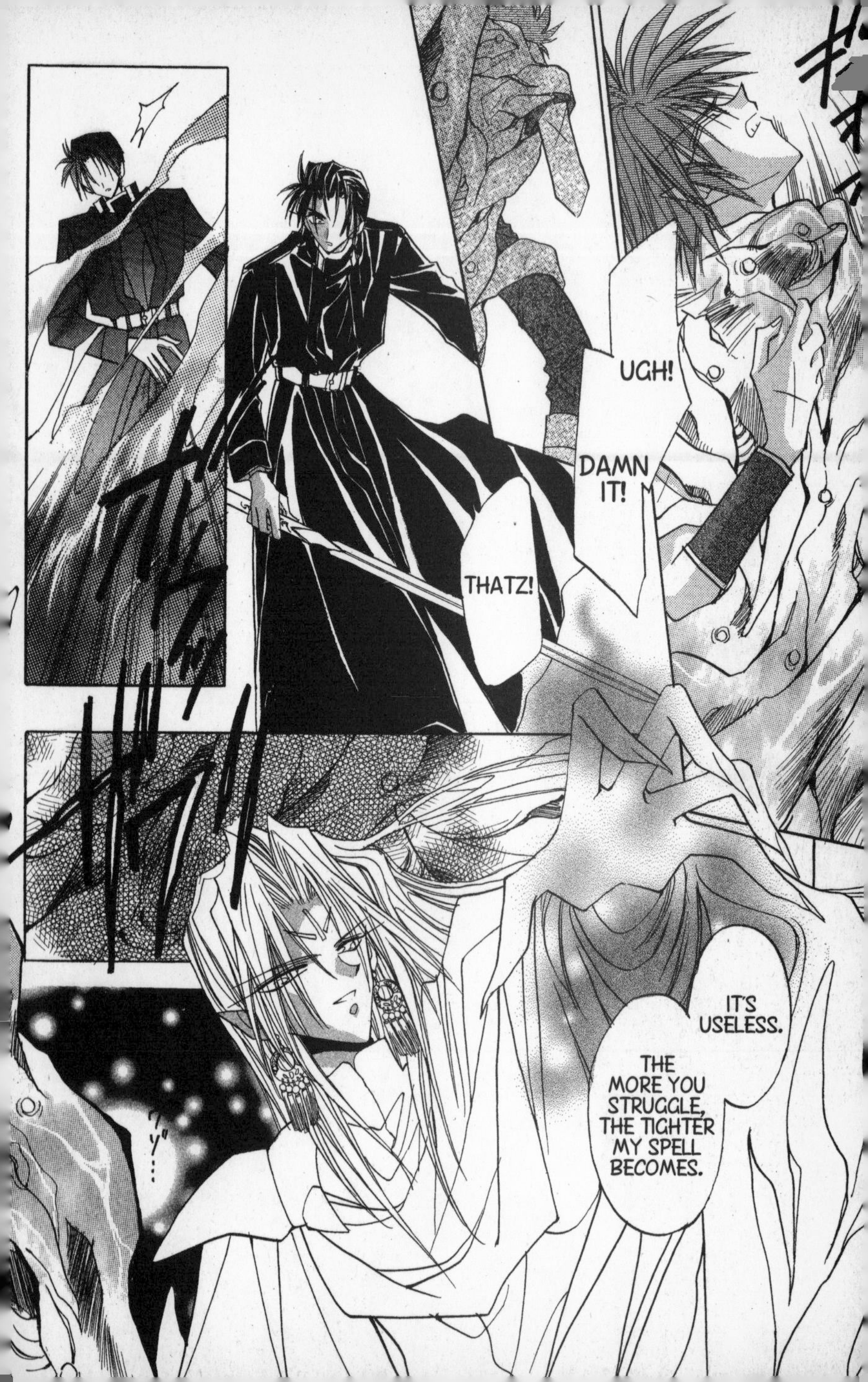
UGH!
DAMN IT!
THATZ!
IT'S USELESS.
THE MORE YOU STRUGGLE, THE TIGHTER MY SPELL BECOMES.

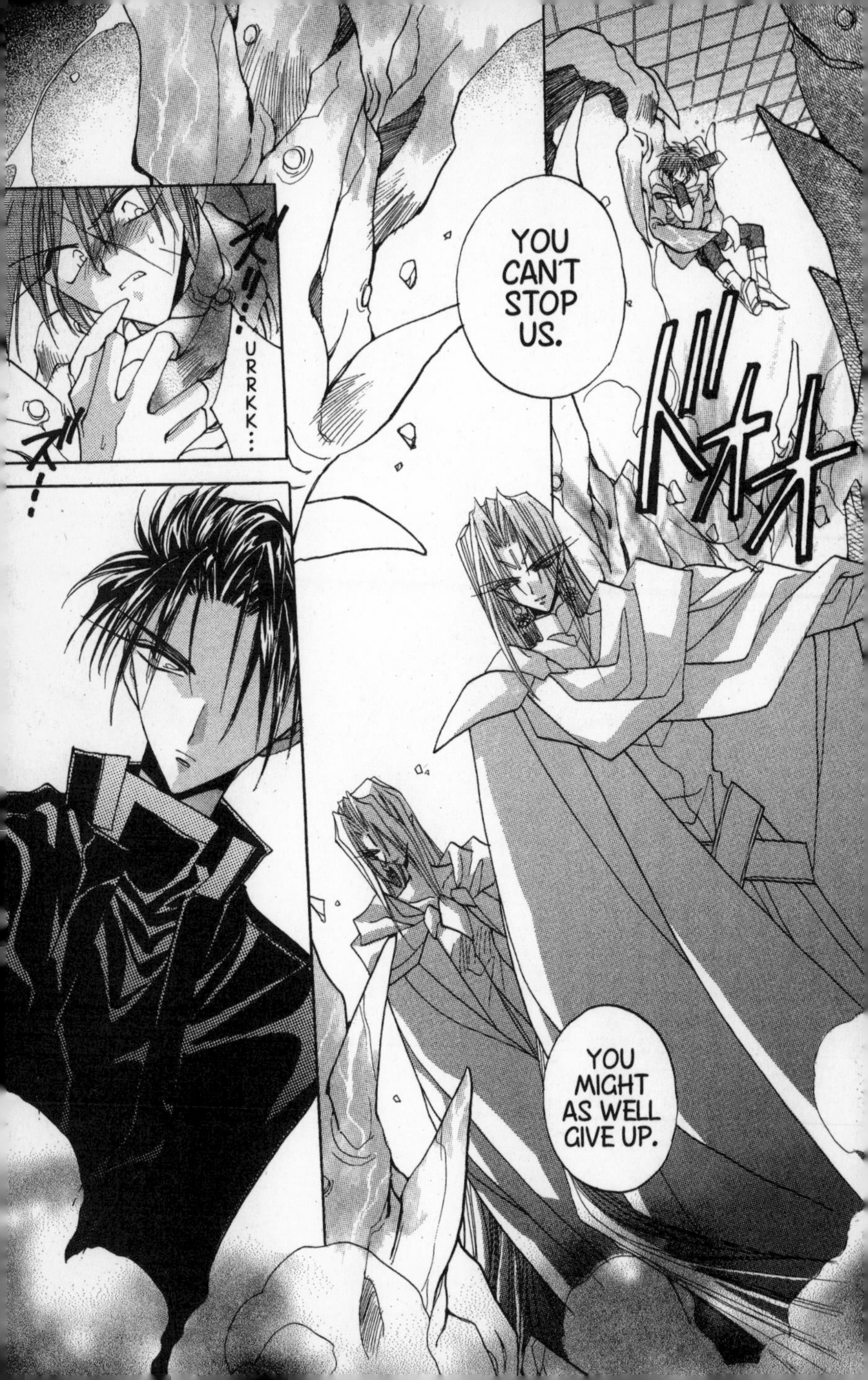
YOU CAN'T STOP US.
YOU MIGHT AS WELL GIVE UP.
URRKK...

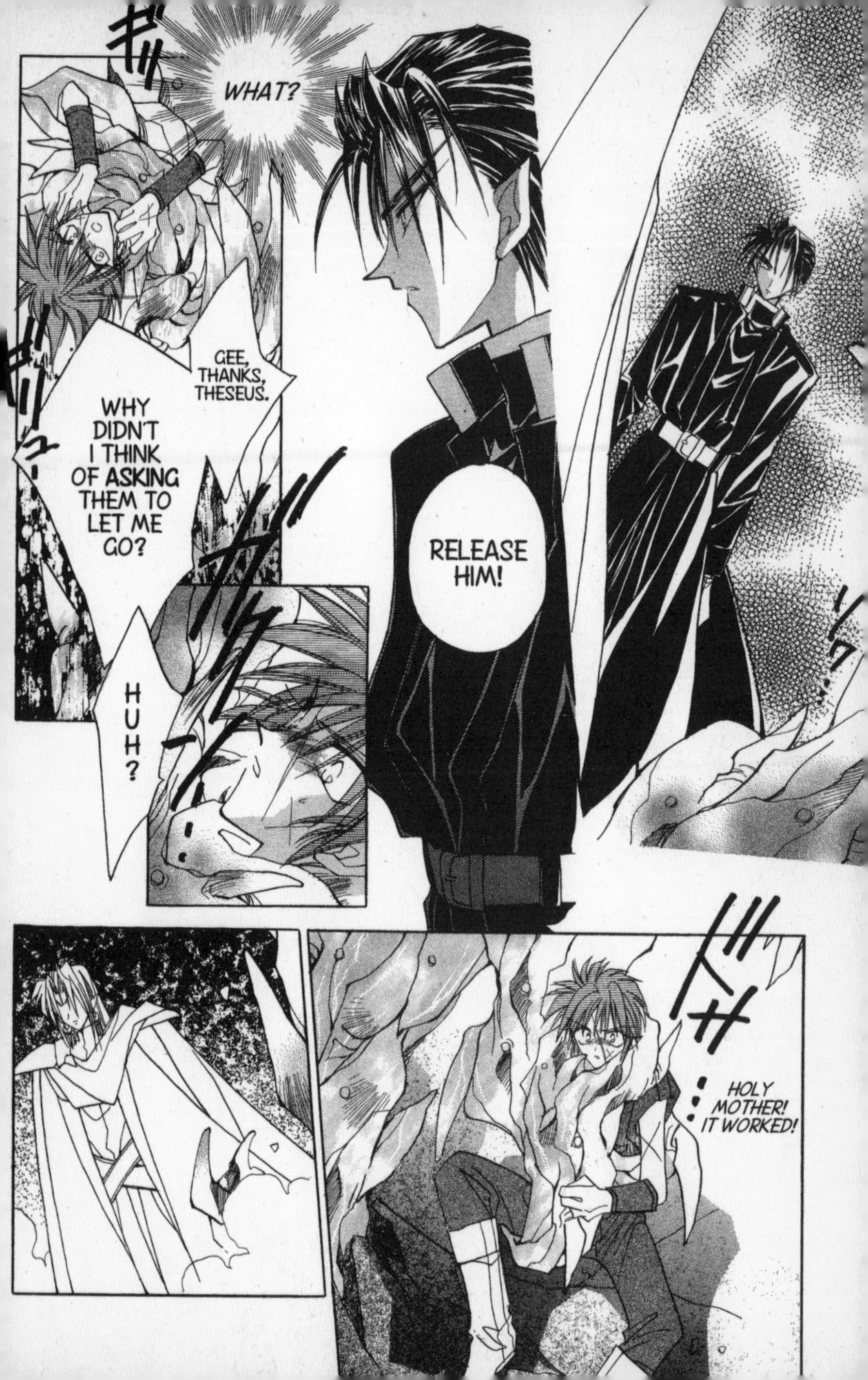
RELEASE HIM!
WHAT?
GEE, THANKS, THESEUS.
WHY DIDN'T I THINK OF ASKING THEM TO LET ME GO?
HUH?
HOLY MOTHER! IT WORKED!

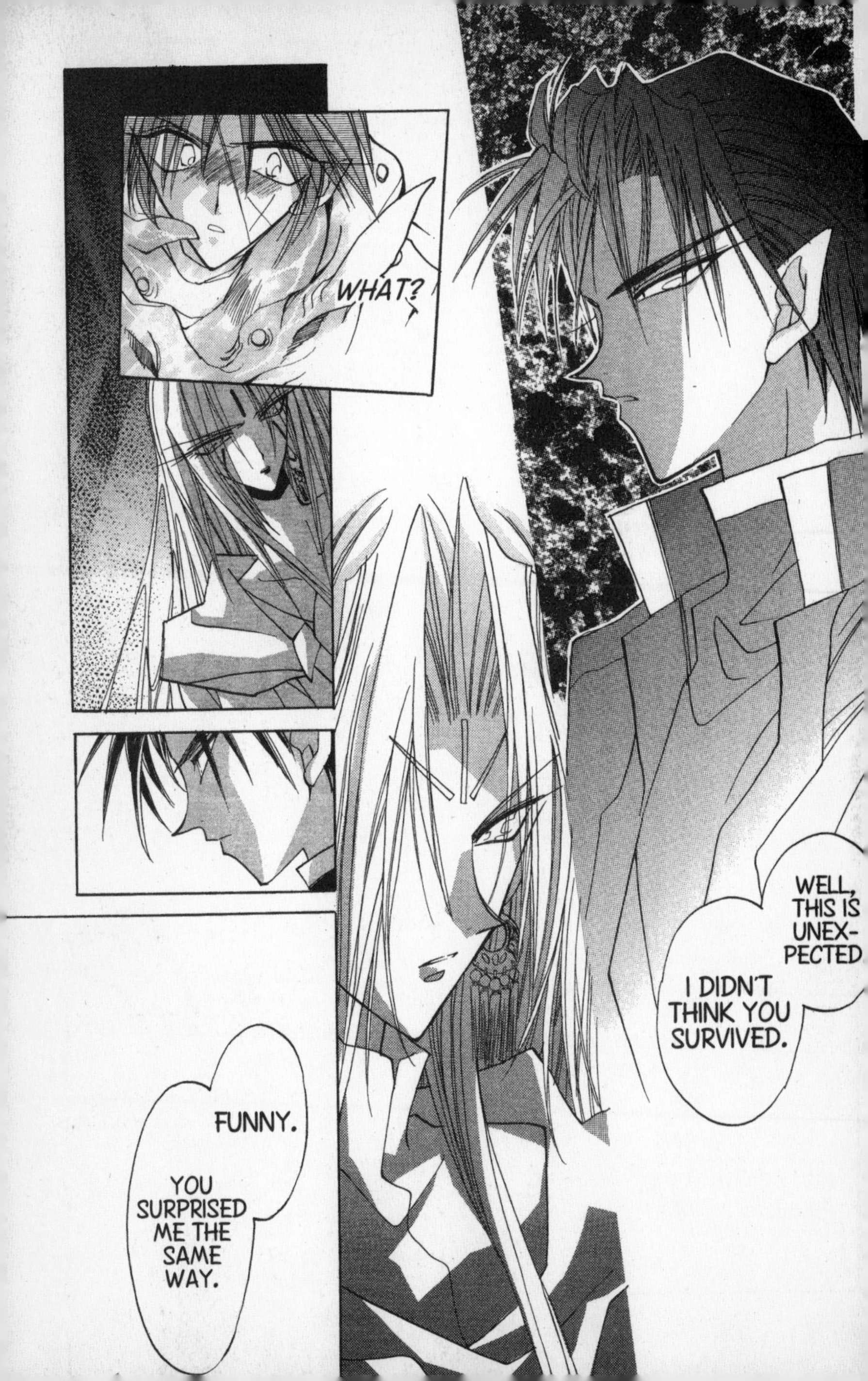
WELL, THIS IS UNEXPECTED
I DIDN'T THINK YOU SURVIVED.
WHAT?
FUNNY.
YOU SURPRISED ME THE SAME WAY.

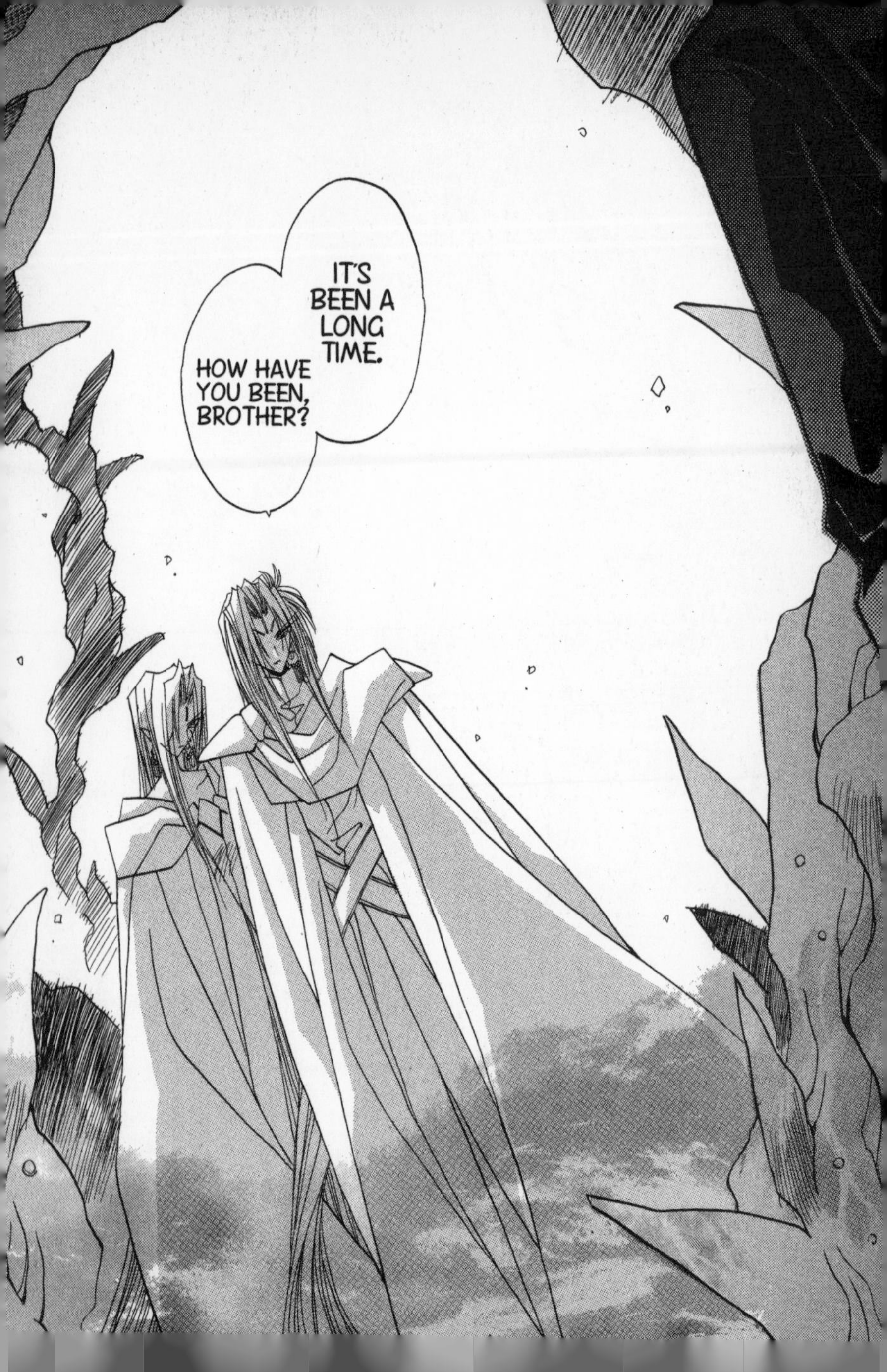
IT'S BEEN A LONG TIME.
HOW HAVE YOU BEEN, BROTHER?

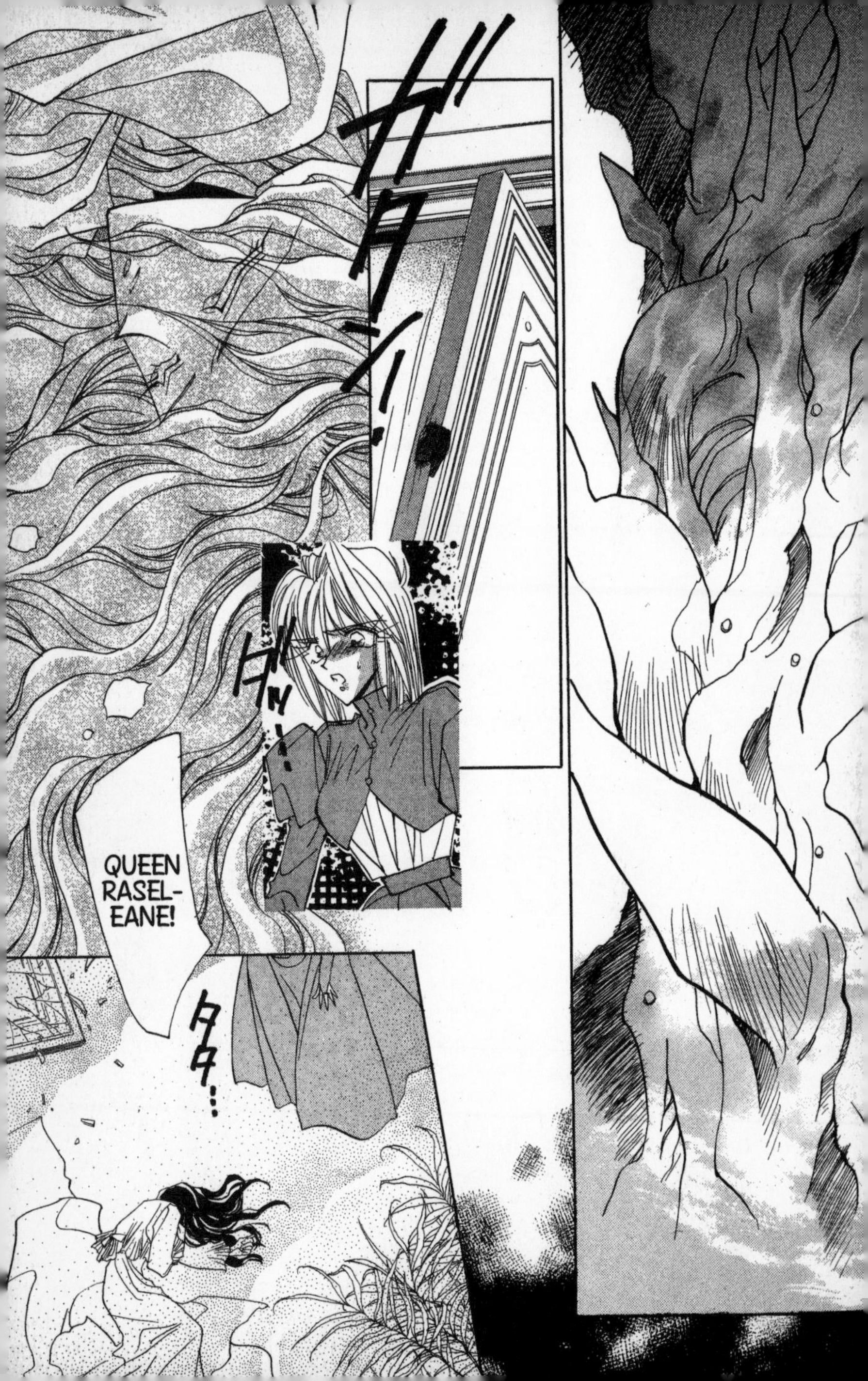
QUEEN RASEL-EANE!

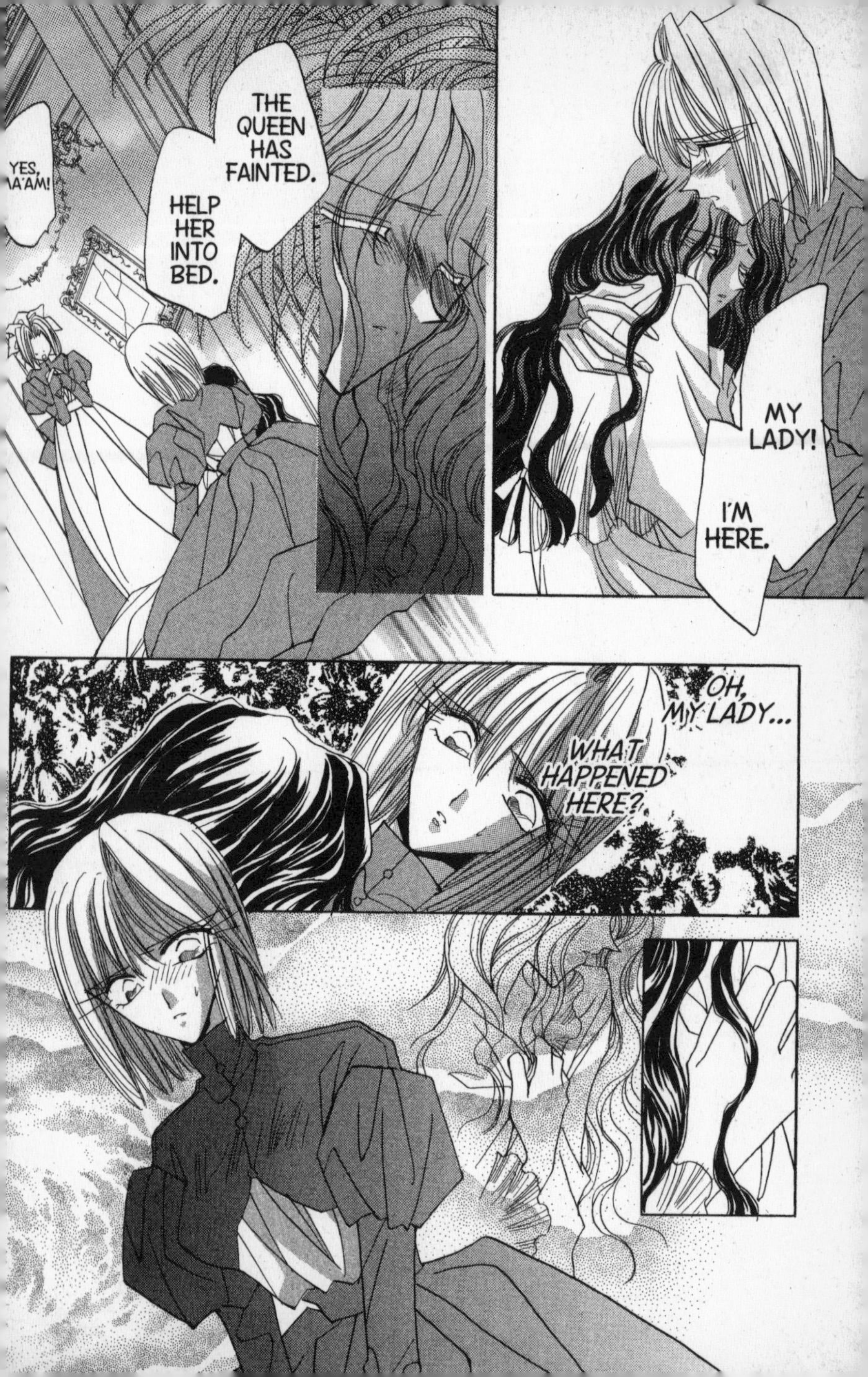
MY LADY!
I'M HERE.
THE QUEEN HAS FAINTED.
HELP HER INTO BED.
YES, MA'AM!
OH, MY LADY...
WHAT HAPPENED HERE?

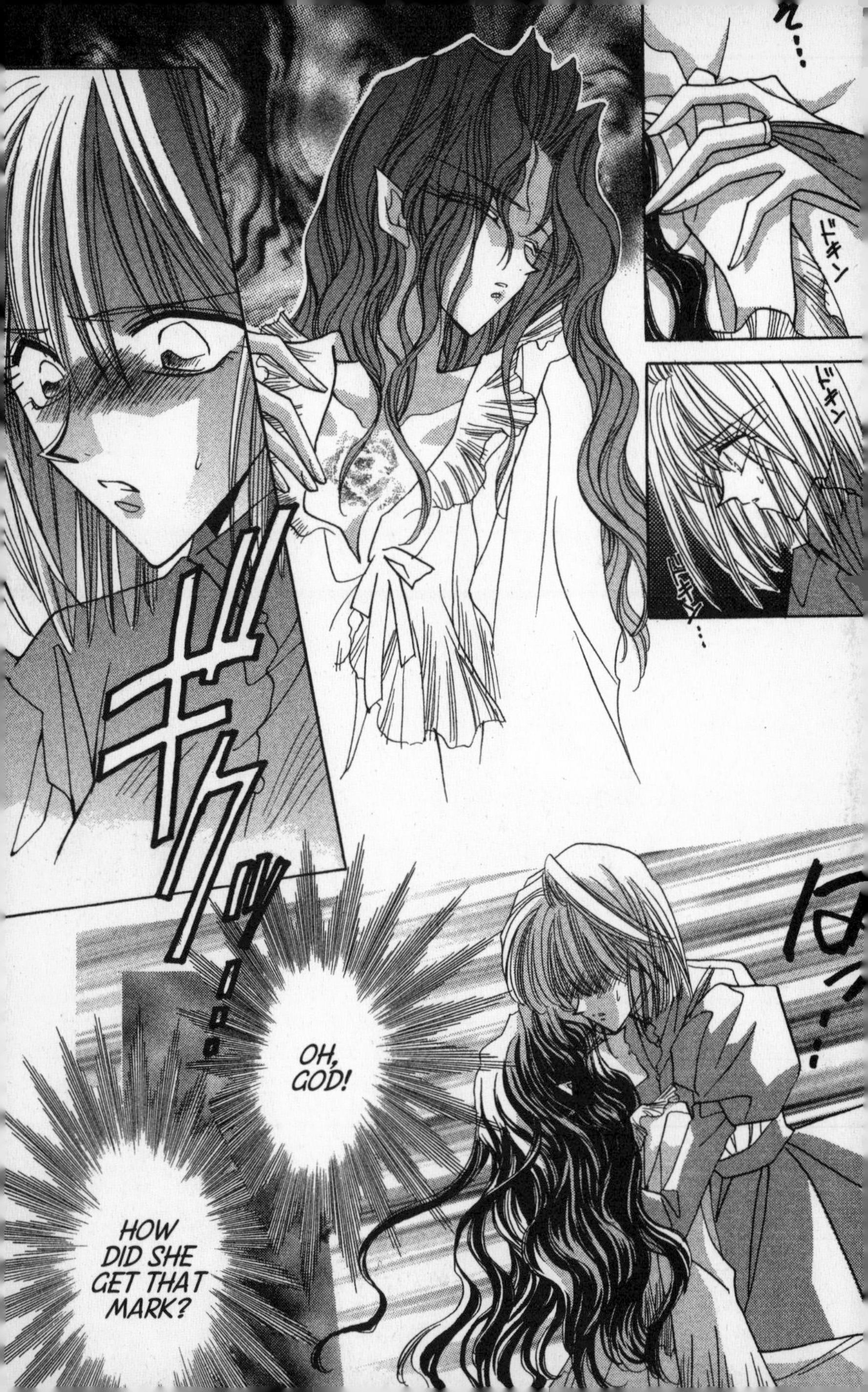
ん…
ドキン
ドキン
ドキン…
ギクッ…
はっ…
OH, GOD!
HOW DID SHE GET THAT MARK?

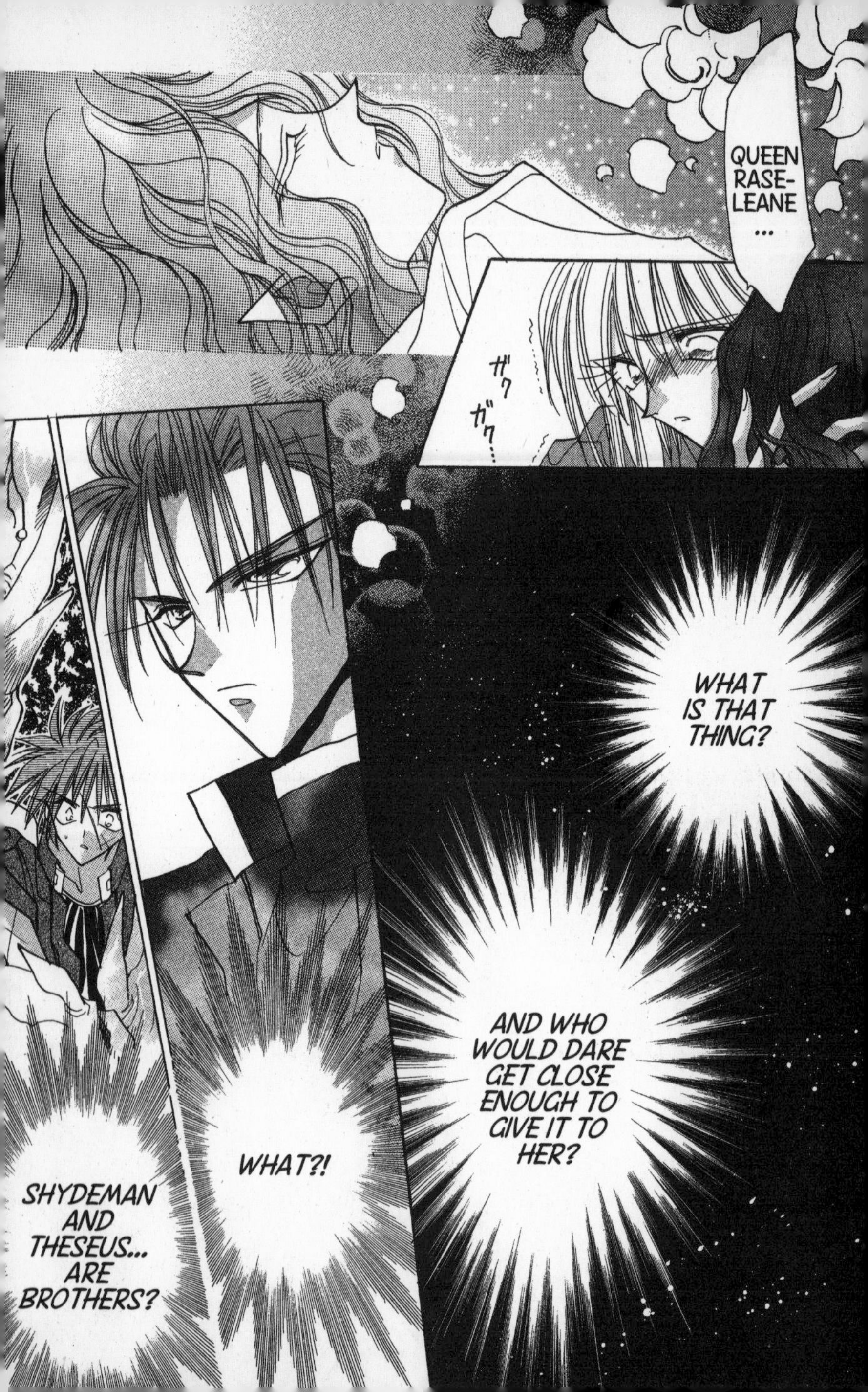
QUEEN RASE-LEANE ...
ガク ガク…
WHAT IS THAT THING?
AND WHO WOULD DARE GET CLOSE ENOUGH TO GIVE IT TO HER?
WHAT?!
SHYDEMAN AND THESEUS... ARE BROTHERS?

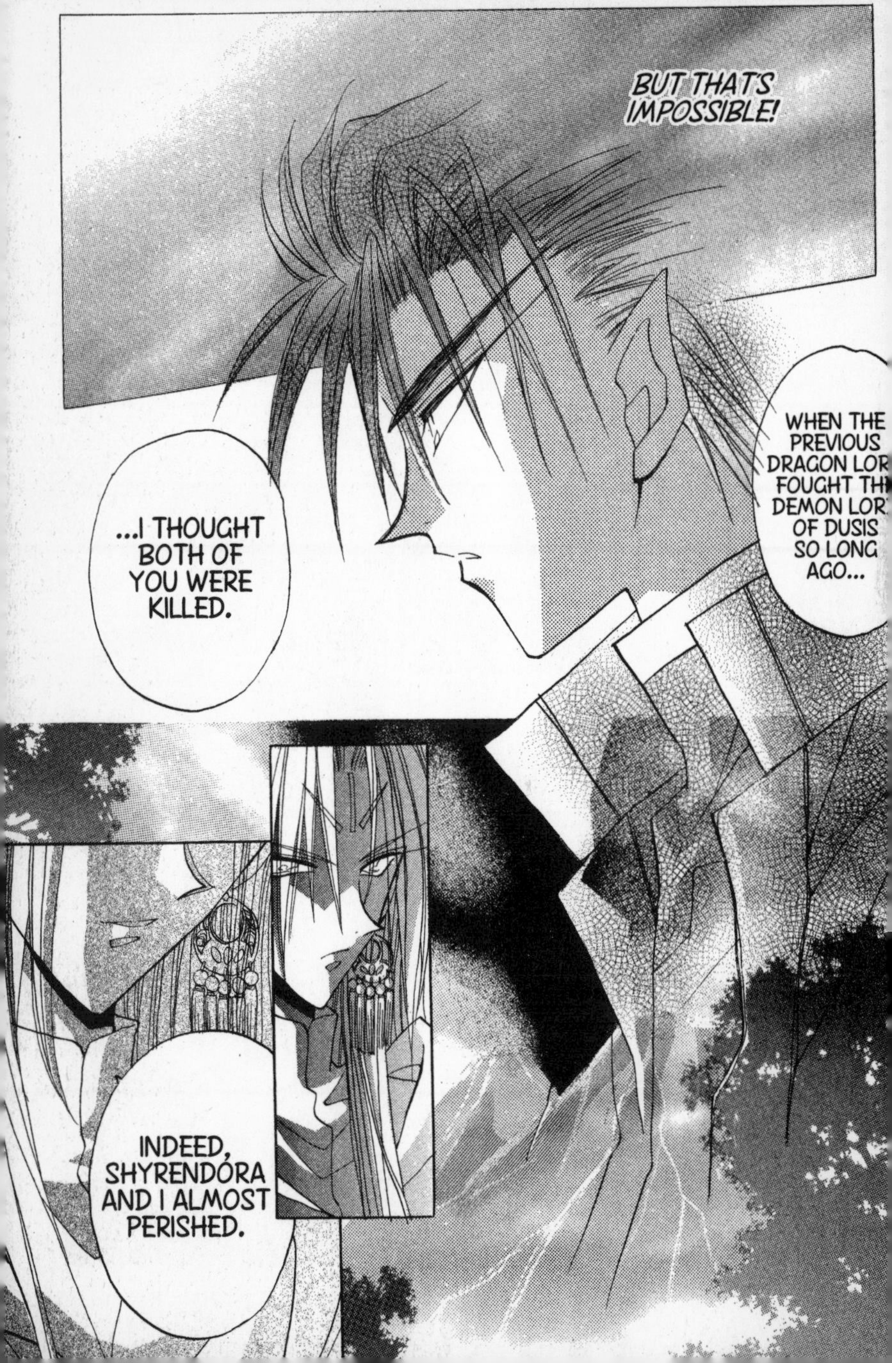
BUT THAT'S IMPOSSIBLE!
WHEN THE PREVIOUS DRAGON LOR FOUGHT TH DEMON LOR OF DUSIS SO LONG AGO...
...I THOUGHT BOTH OF YOU WERE KILLED.
INDEED, SHYRENDORA AND I ALMOST PERISHED.

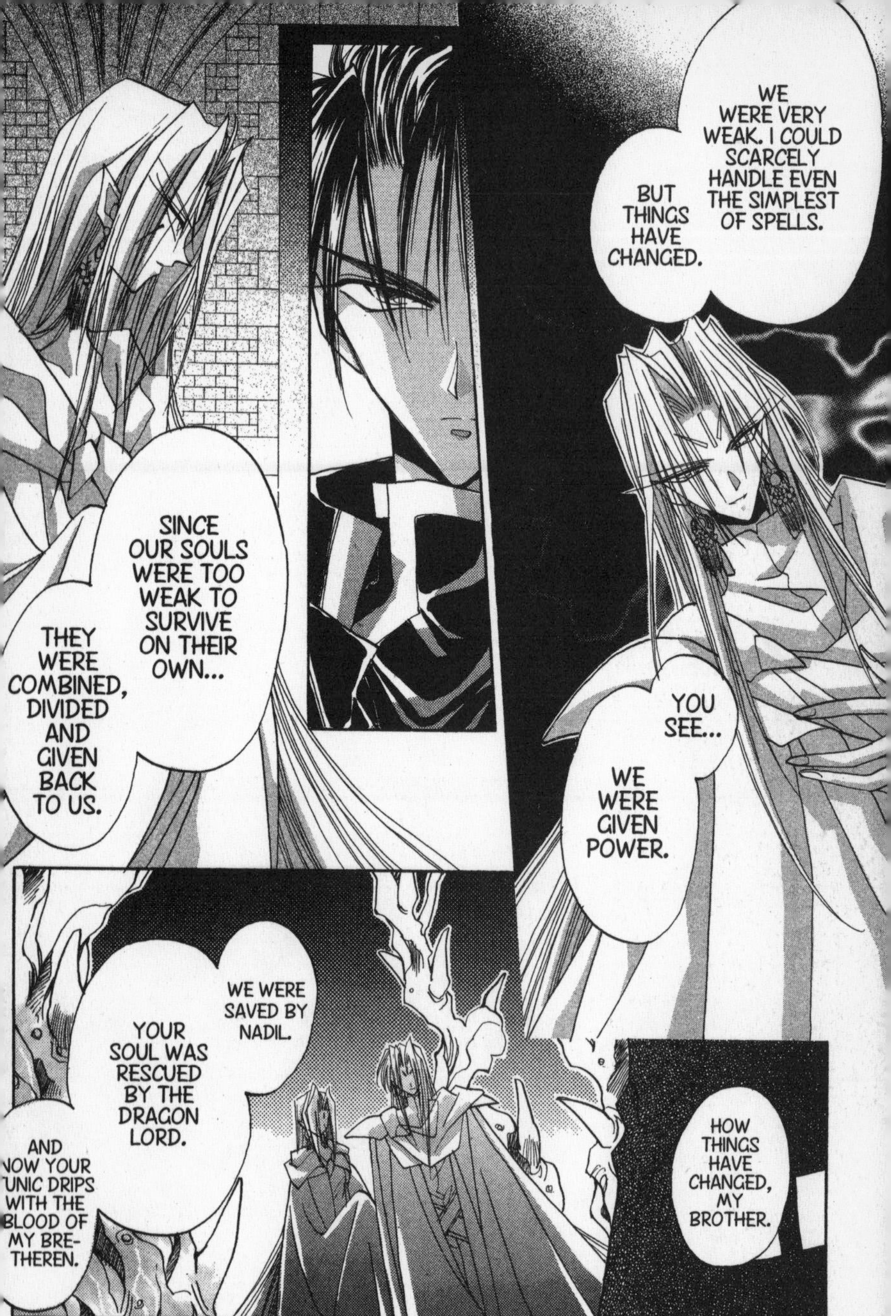
WE WERE VERY WEAK. I COULD SCARCELY HANDLE EVEN THE SIMPLEST OF SPELLS.
BUT THINGS HAVE CHANGED.
YOU SEE...
WE WERE GIVEN POWER.
SINCE OUR SOULS WERE TOO WEAK TO SURVIVE ON THEIR OWN...
THEY WERE COMBINED, DIVIDED AND GIVEN BACK TO US.
HOW THINGS HAVE CHANGED, MY BROTHER.
WE WERE SAVED BY NADIL.
YOUR SOUL WAS RESCUED BY THE DRAGON LORD.
AND NOW YOUR UNIC DRIPS WITH THE BLOOD OF MY BRE-THEREN.

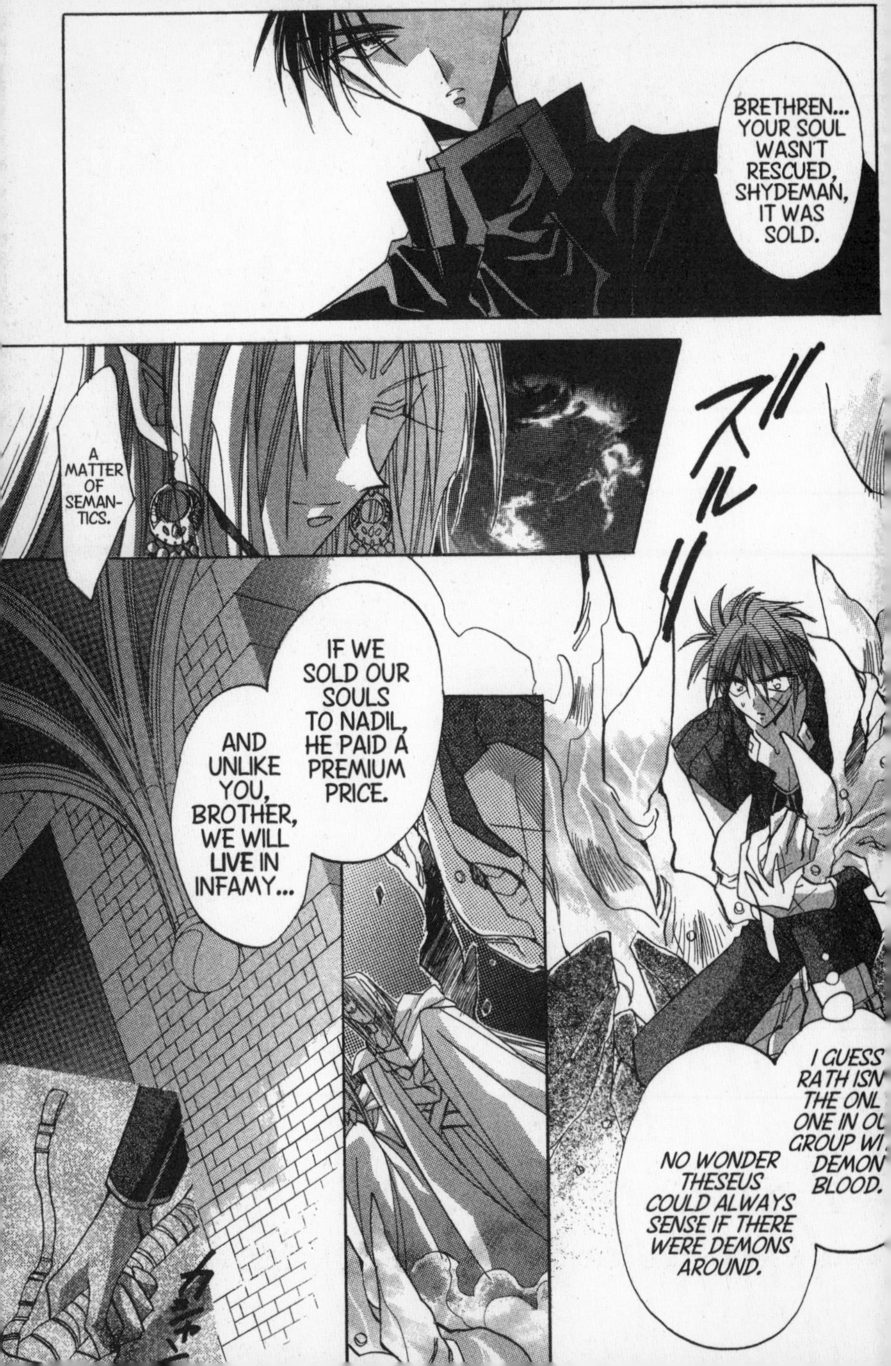
BRETHREN... YOUR SOUL WASN'T RESCUED, SHYDEMAN, IT WAS SOLD.
ズルリ
A MATTER OF SEMAN-TICS.
IF WE SOLD OUR SOULS TO NADIL, HE PAID A PREMIUM PRICE.
AND UNLIKE YOU, BROTHER, WE WILL LIVE IN INFAMY...
I GUESS RATH ISN THE ONL ONE IN OU GROUP WI DEMON BLOOD.
NO WONDER THESEUS COULD ALWAYS SENSE IF THERE WERE DEMONS AROUND.

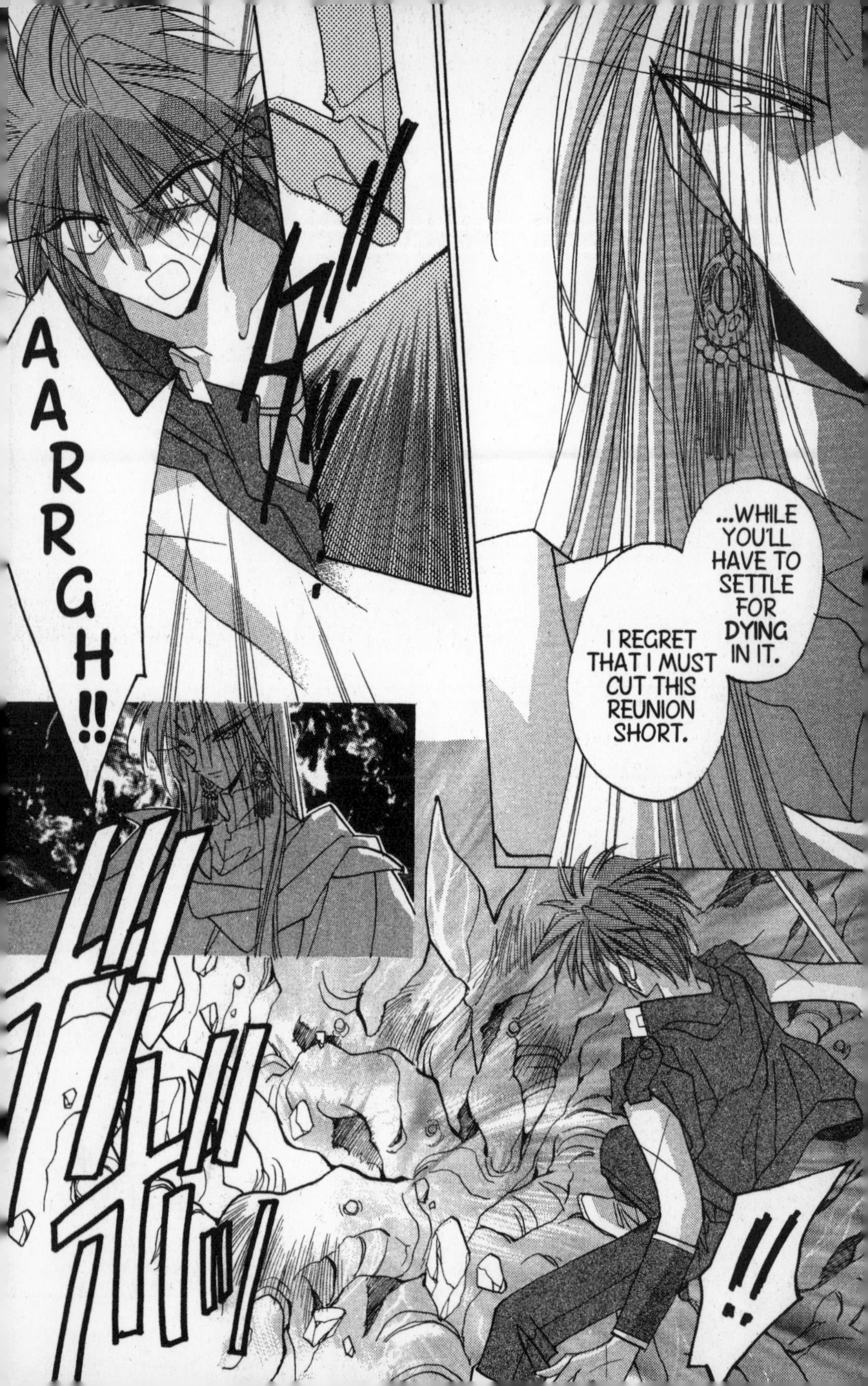
I REGRET THAT I MUST CUT THIS REUNION SHORT.
...WHILE YOU'LL HAVE TO SETTLE FOR DYING IN IT.
AARRGH!!
!!

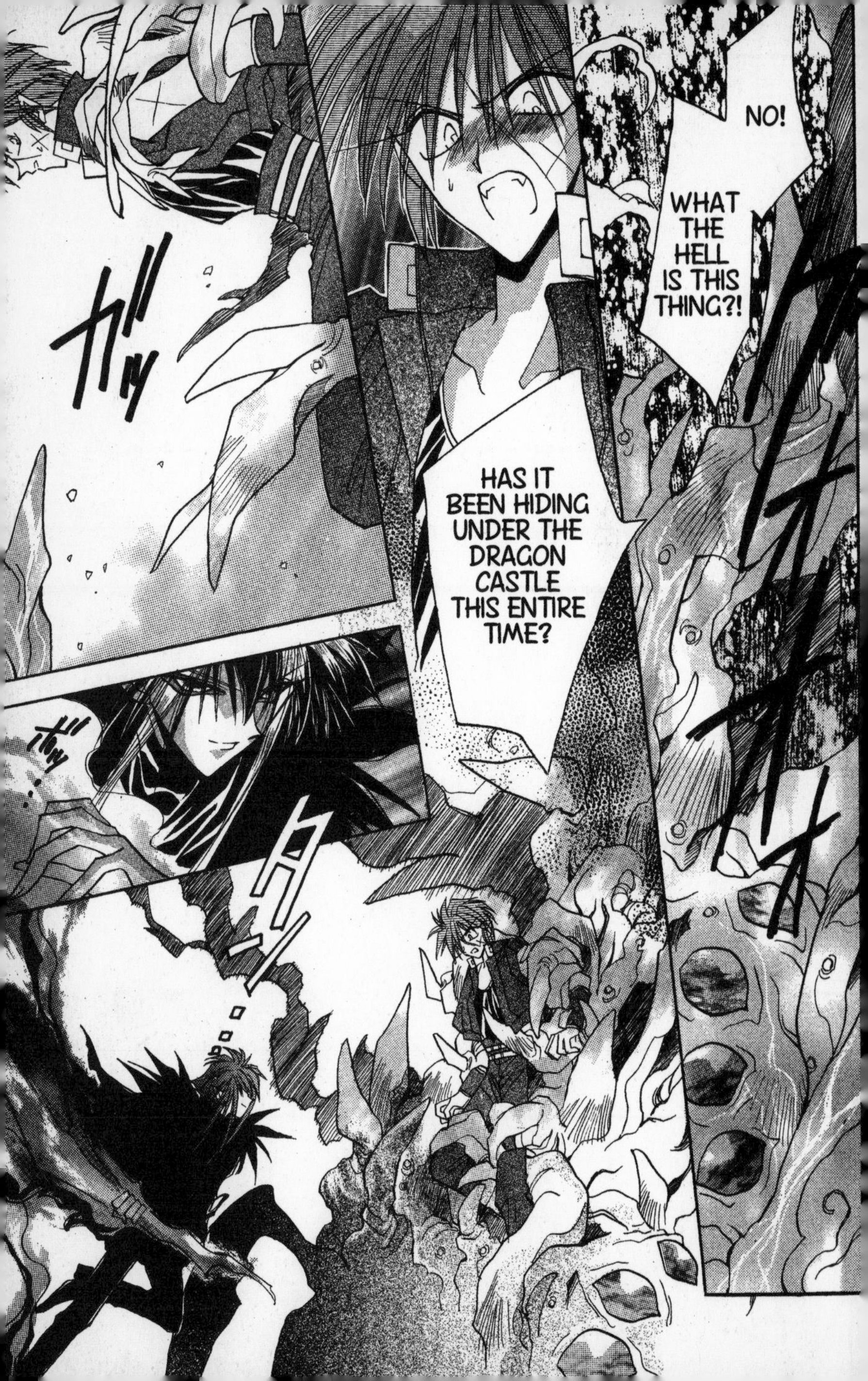
NO!
WHAT THE HELL IS THIS THING?!
HAS IT BEEN HIDING UNDER THE DRAGON CASTLE THIS ENTIRE TIME?

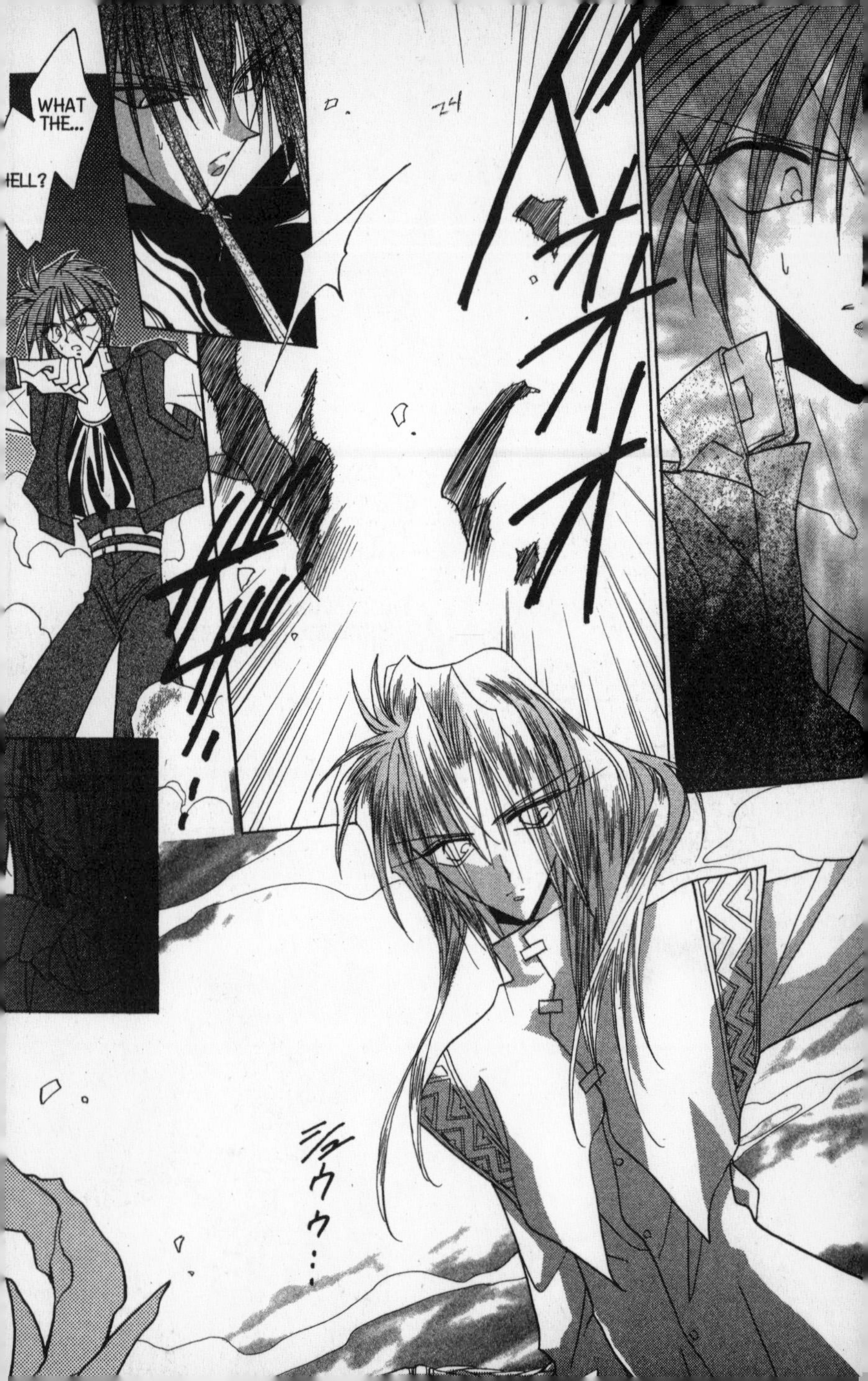
WHAT THE...
HELL?

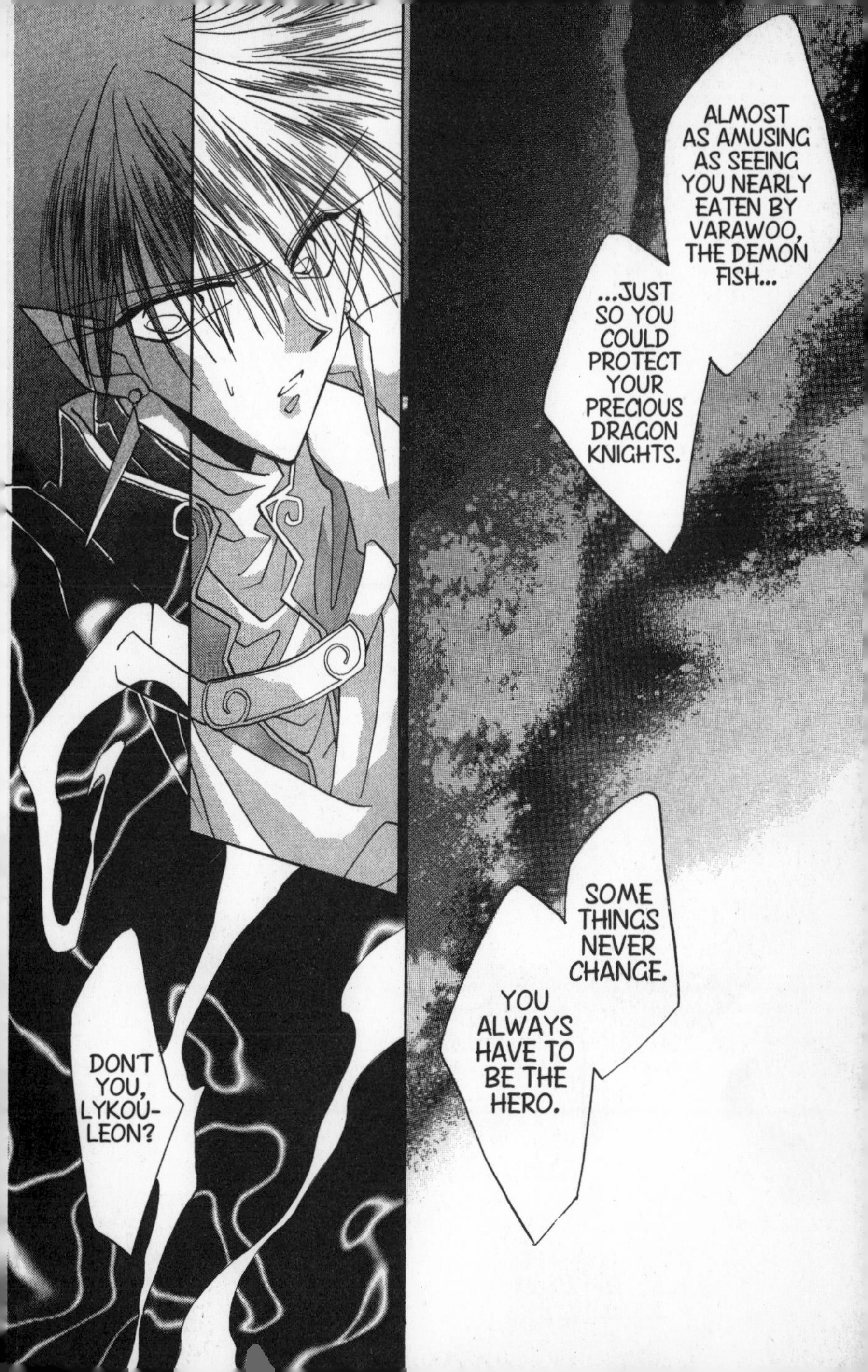
ALMOST AS AMUSING AS SEEING YOU NEARLY EATEN BY VARAWOO, THE DEMON FISH...
...JUST SO YOU COULD PROTECT YOUR PRECIOUS DRAGON KNIGHTS.
SOME THINGS NEVER CHANGE.
YOU ALWAYS HAVE TO BE THE HERO.
DON'T YOU, LYKOU-LEON?

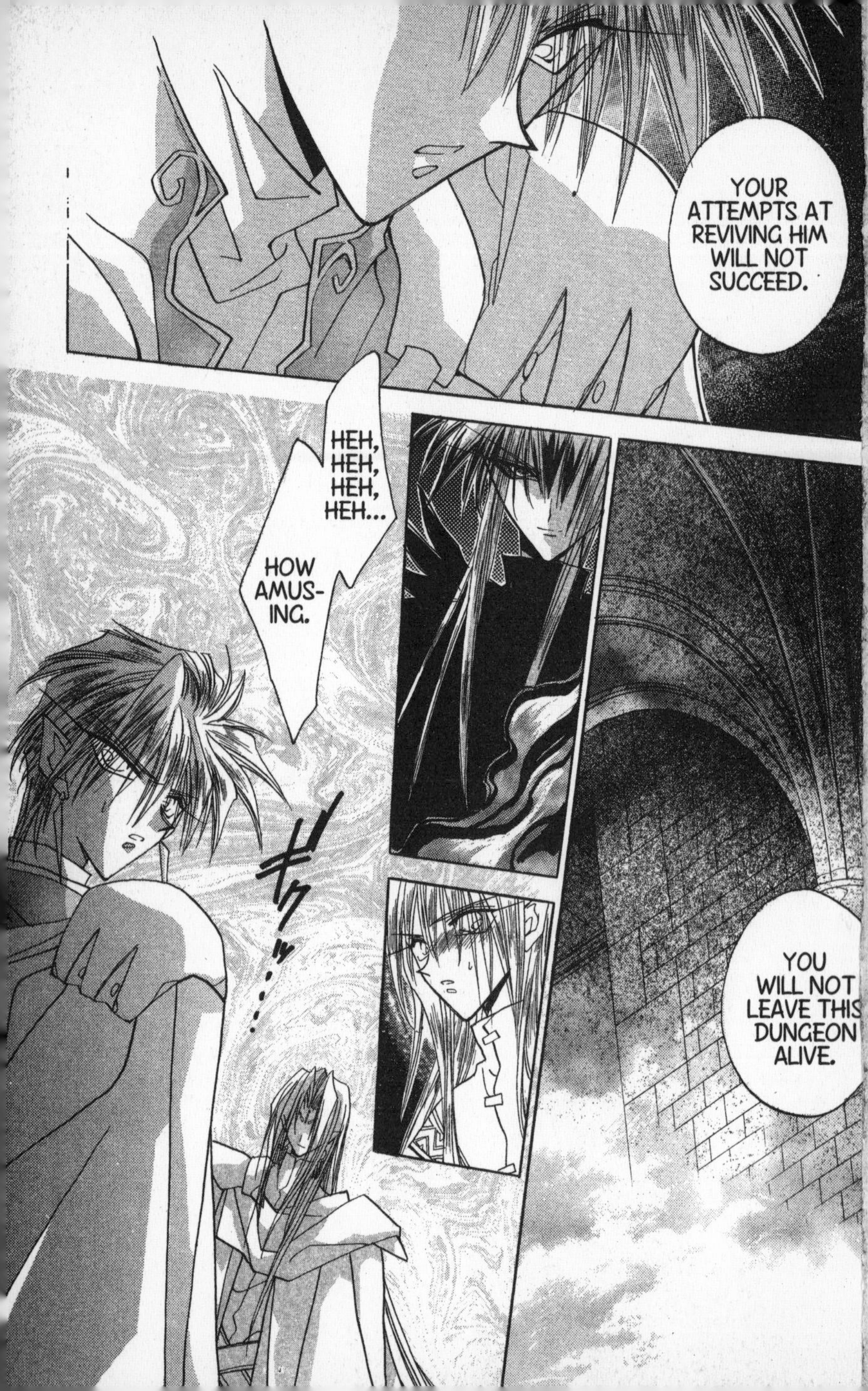
YOUR ATTEMPTS AT REVIVING HIM WILL NOT SUCCEED.
HEH, HEH, HEH, HEH...
HOW AMUS-ING.
YOU WILL NOT LEAVE THIS DUNGEON ALIVE.

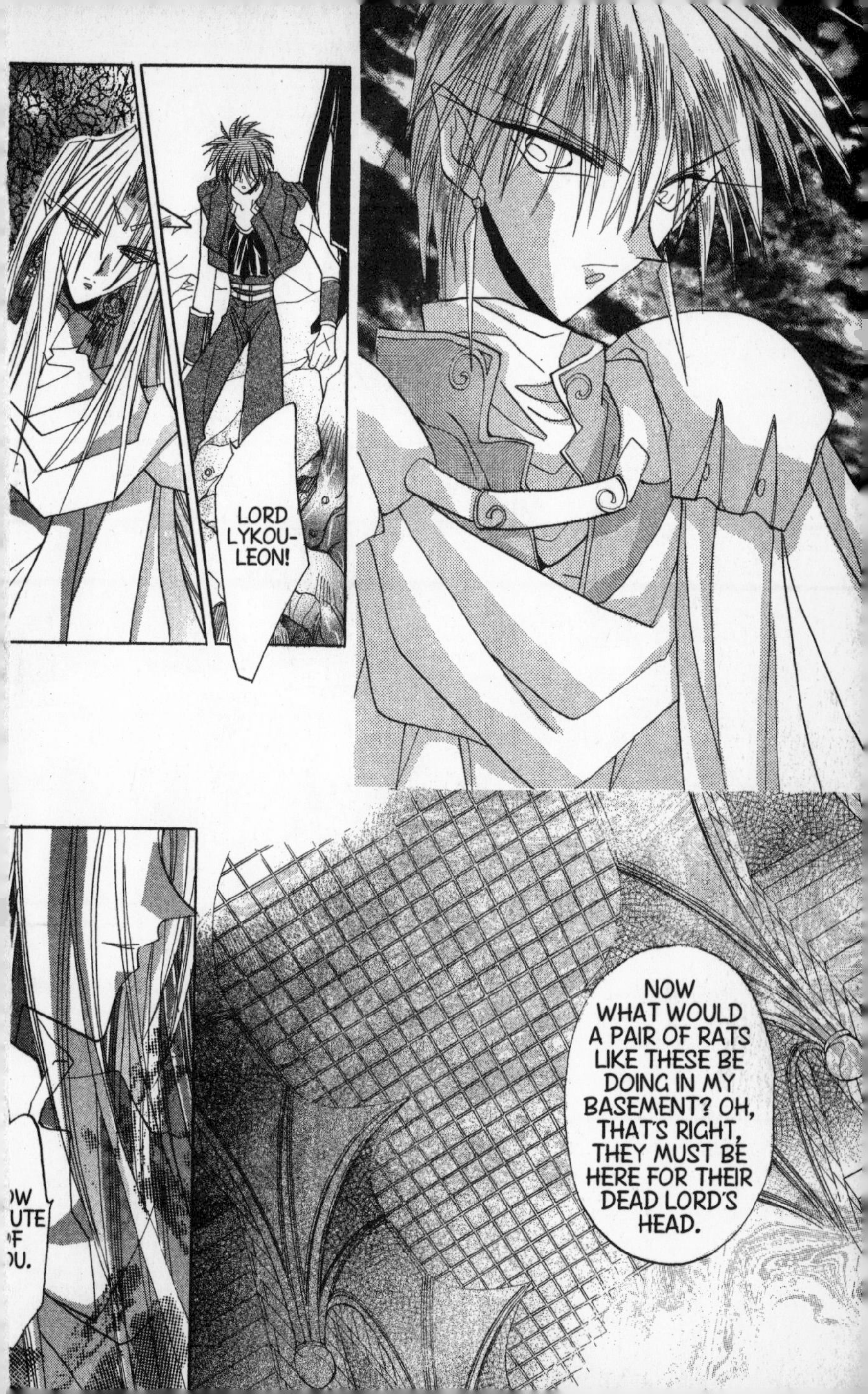
LORD LYKOU-LEON!
NOW WHAT WOULD A PAIR OF RATS LIKE THESE BE DOING IN MY BASEMENT? OH, THAT'S RIGHT, THEY MUST BE HERE FOR THEIR DEAD LORD'S HEAD.

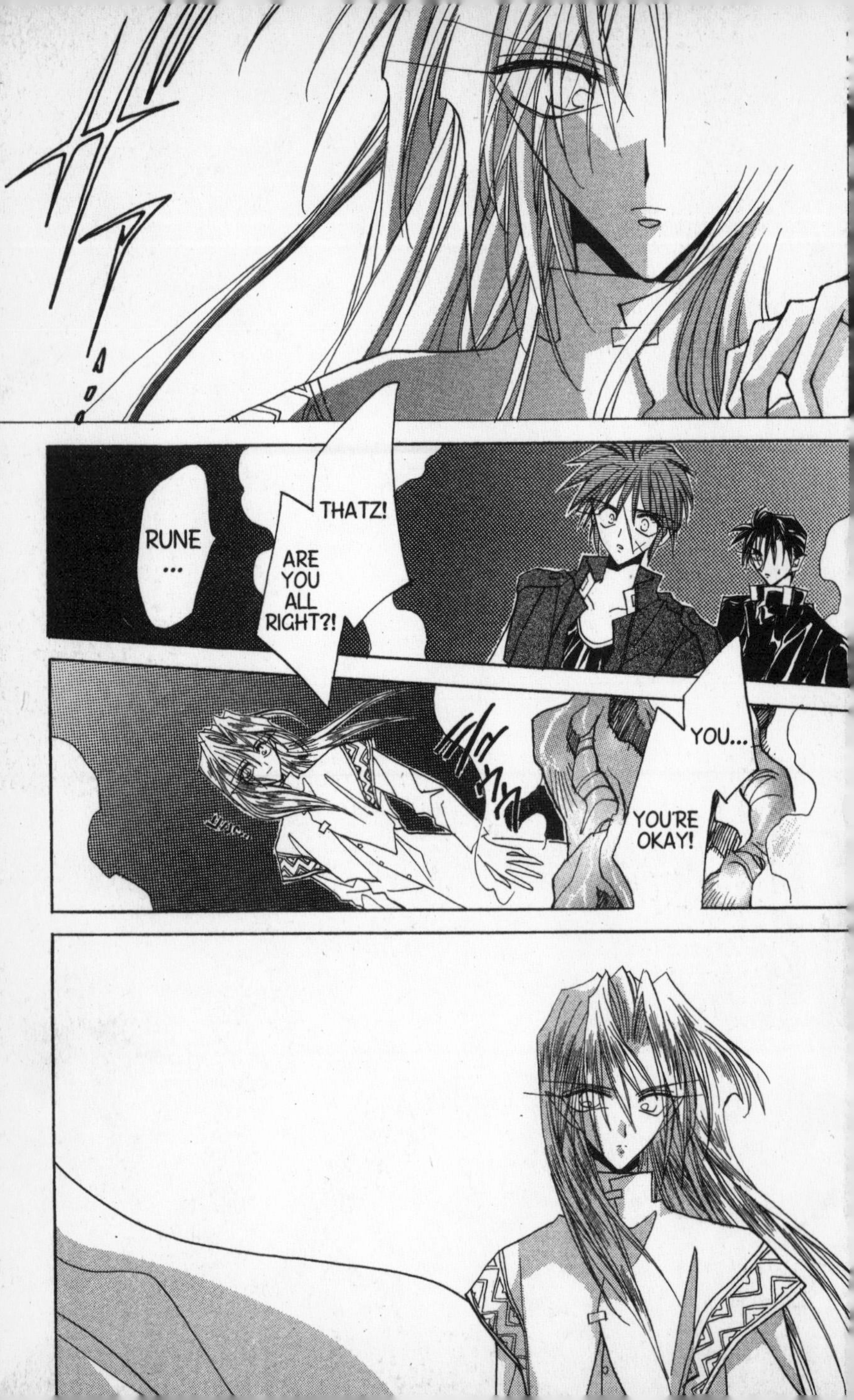
THATZ!
ARE YOU ALL RIGHT?!
RUNE ...
YOU...
YOU'RE OKAY!

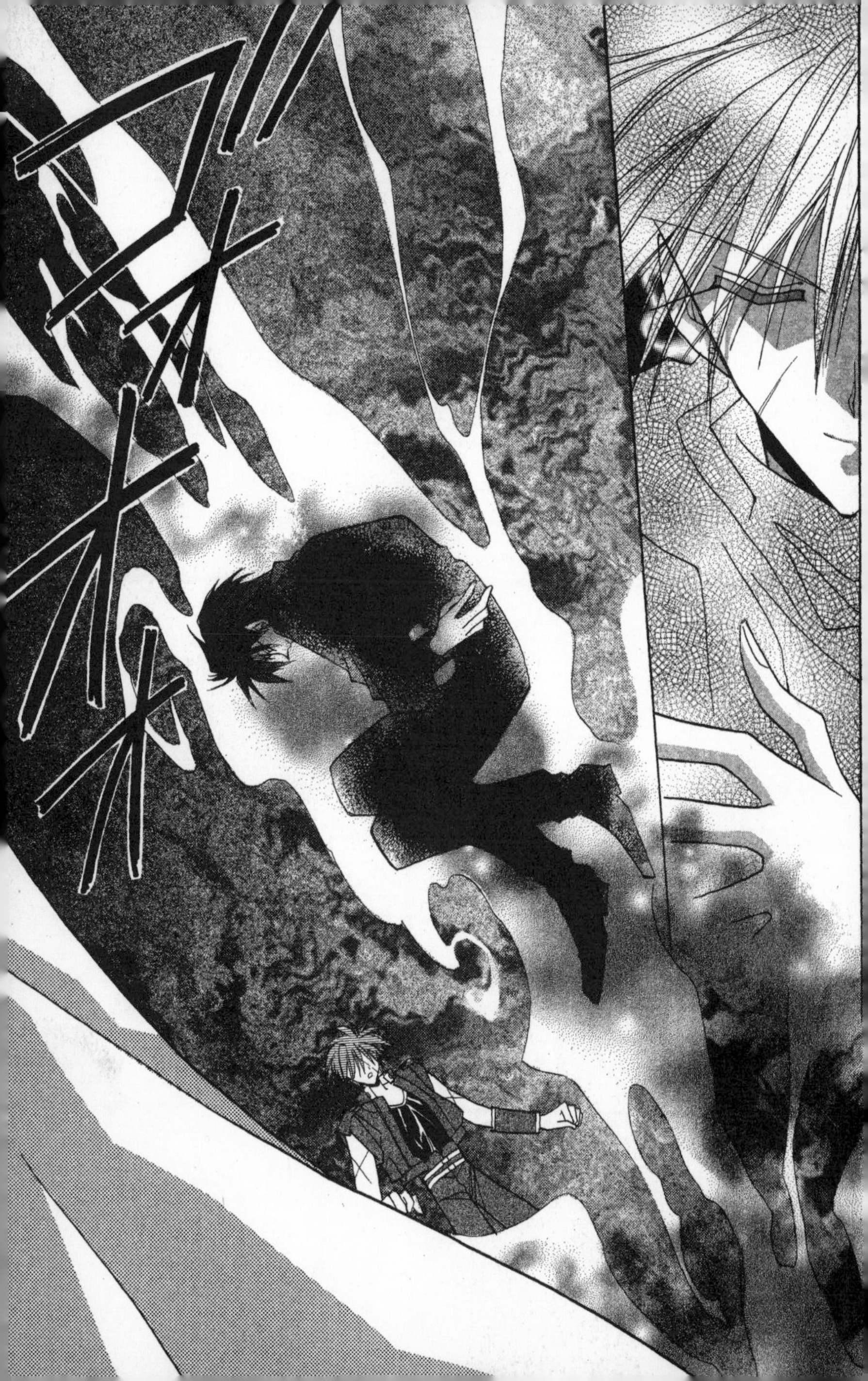

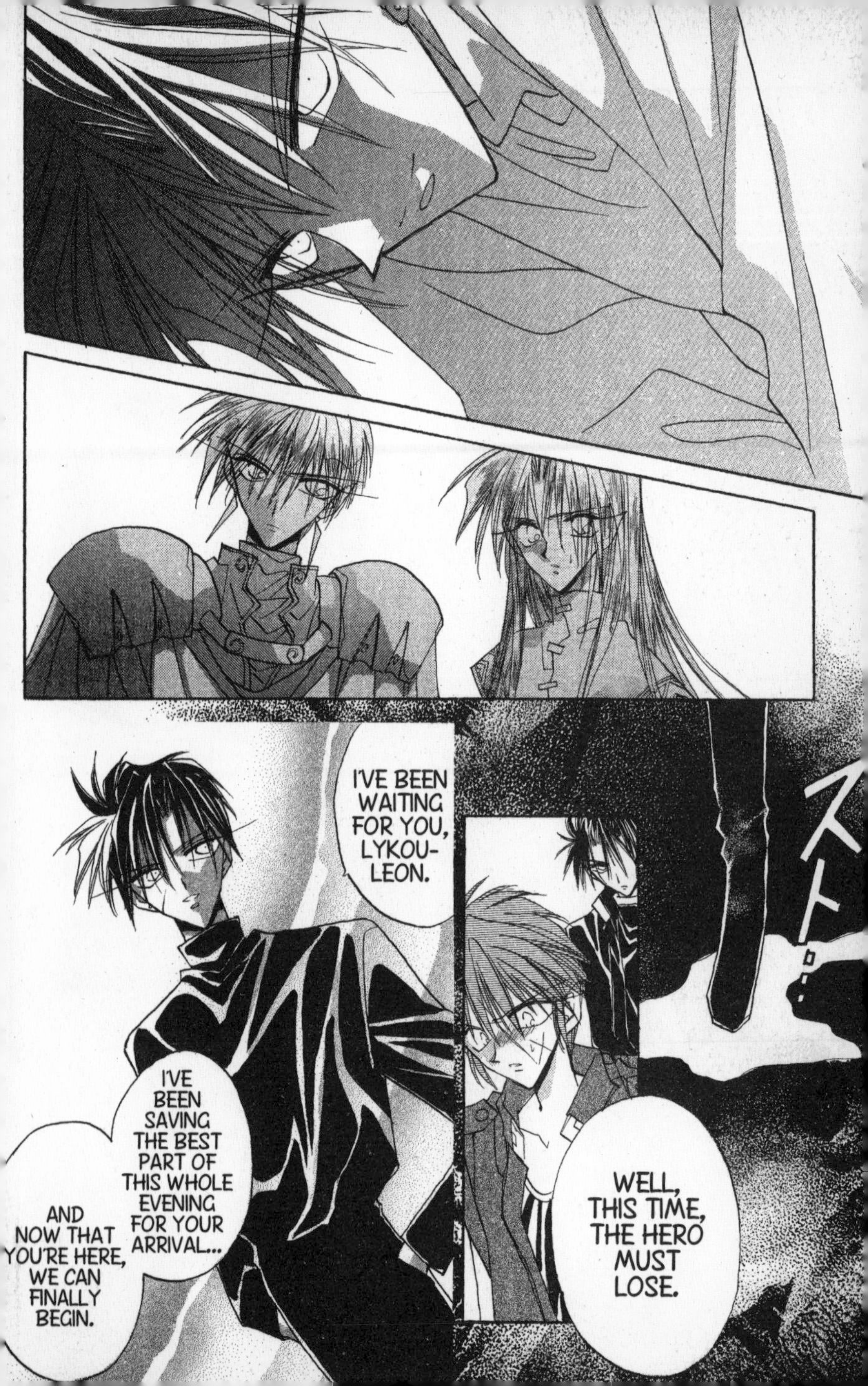
ストト…
WELL, THIS TIME, THE HERO MUST LOSE.
I'VE BEEN WAITING FOR YOU, LYKOU-LEON.
I'VE BEEN SAVING THE BEST PART OF THIS WHOLE EVENING FOR YOUR ARRIVAL...
AND NOW THAT YOU'RE HERE, WE CAN FINALLY BEGIN.

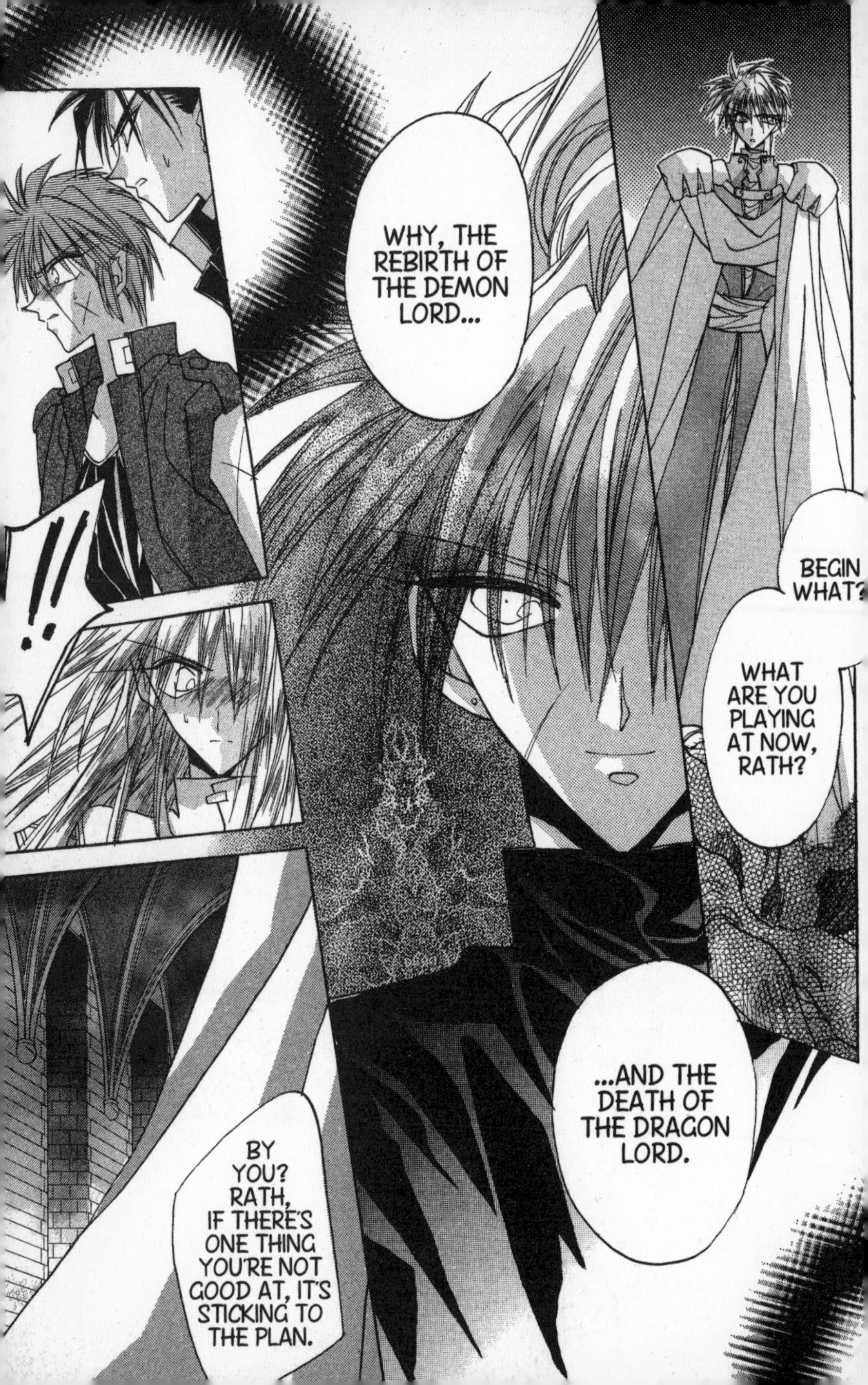
BEGIN WHAT?
WHAT ARE YOU PLAYING AT NOW, RATH?
WHY, THE REBIRTH OF THE DEMON LORD...
...AND THE DEATH OF THE DRAGON LORD.
!!
BY YOU? RATH, IF THERE'S ONE THING YOU'RE NOT GOOD AT, IT'S STICKING TO THE PLAN.

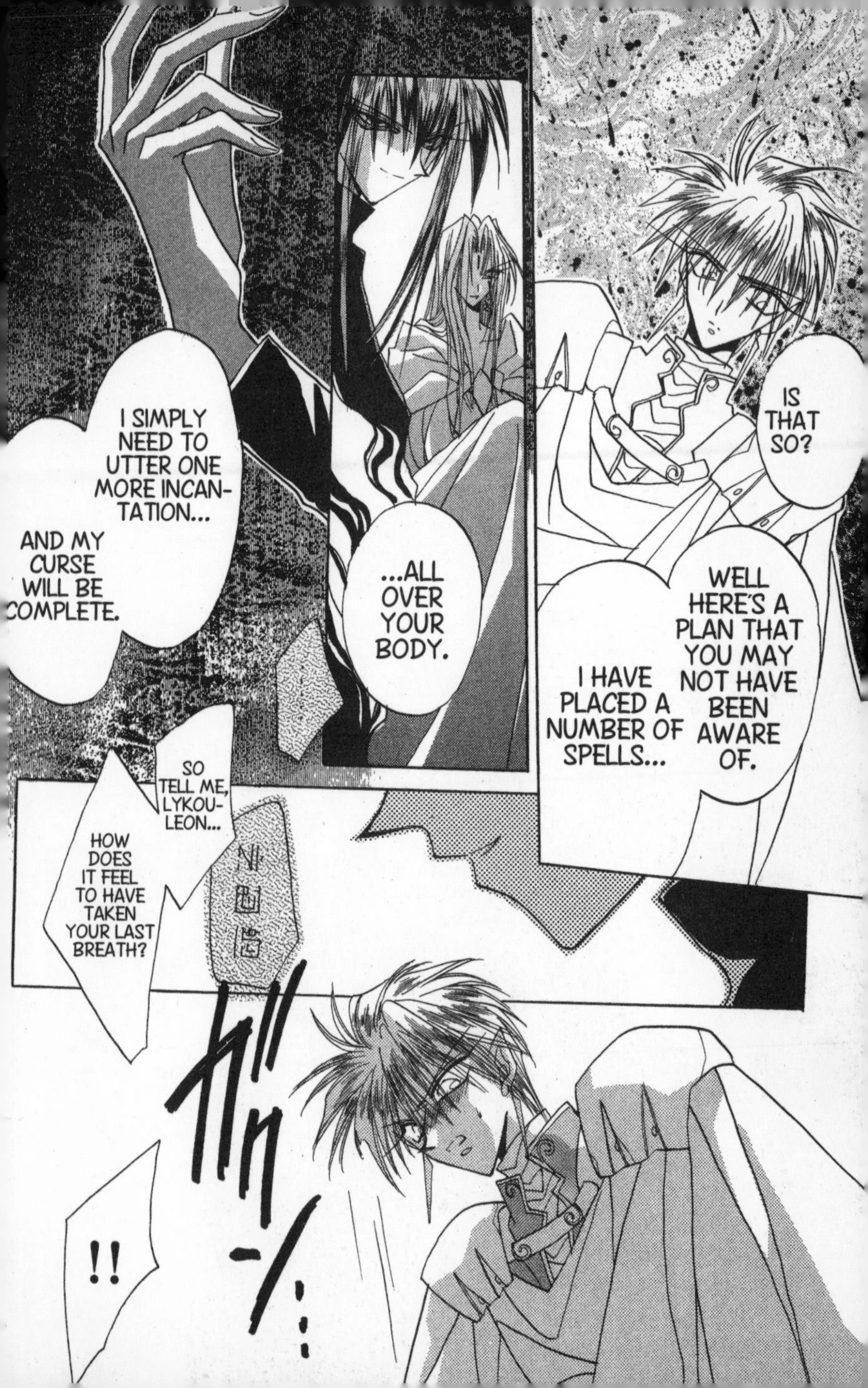
IS THAT SO?
WELL HERE'S A PLAN THAT YOU MAY NOT HAVE BEEN AWARE OF.
I HAVE PLACED A NUMBER OF SPELLS...
...ALL OVER YOUR BODY.
I SIMPLY NEED TO UTTER ONE MORE INCANTATION...
AND MY CURSE WILL BE COMPLETE.
SO TELL ME, LYKOULEON...
HOW DOES IT FEEL TO HAVE TAKEN YOUR LAST BREATH?
!!

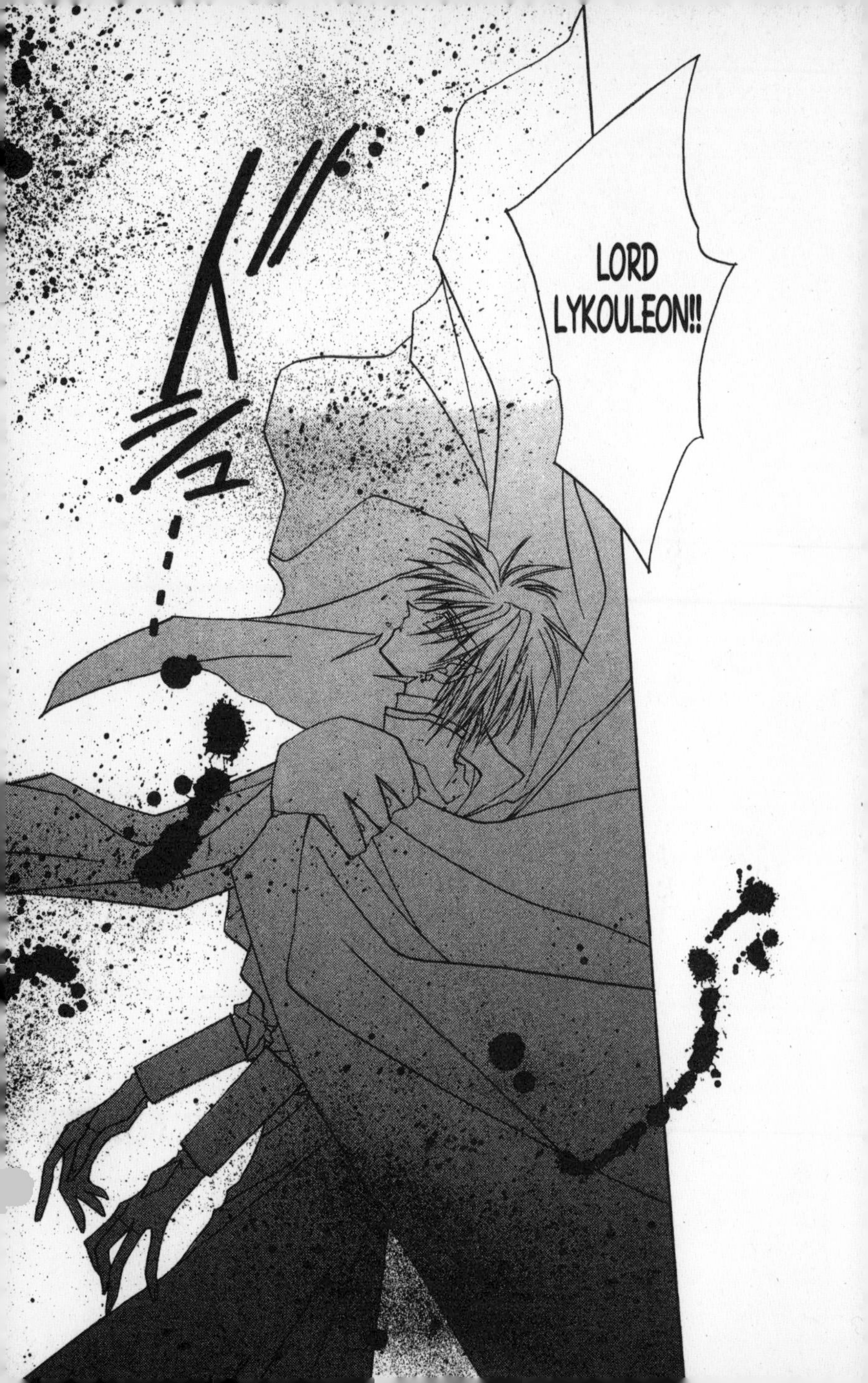
LORD LYKOULEON!!

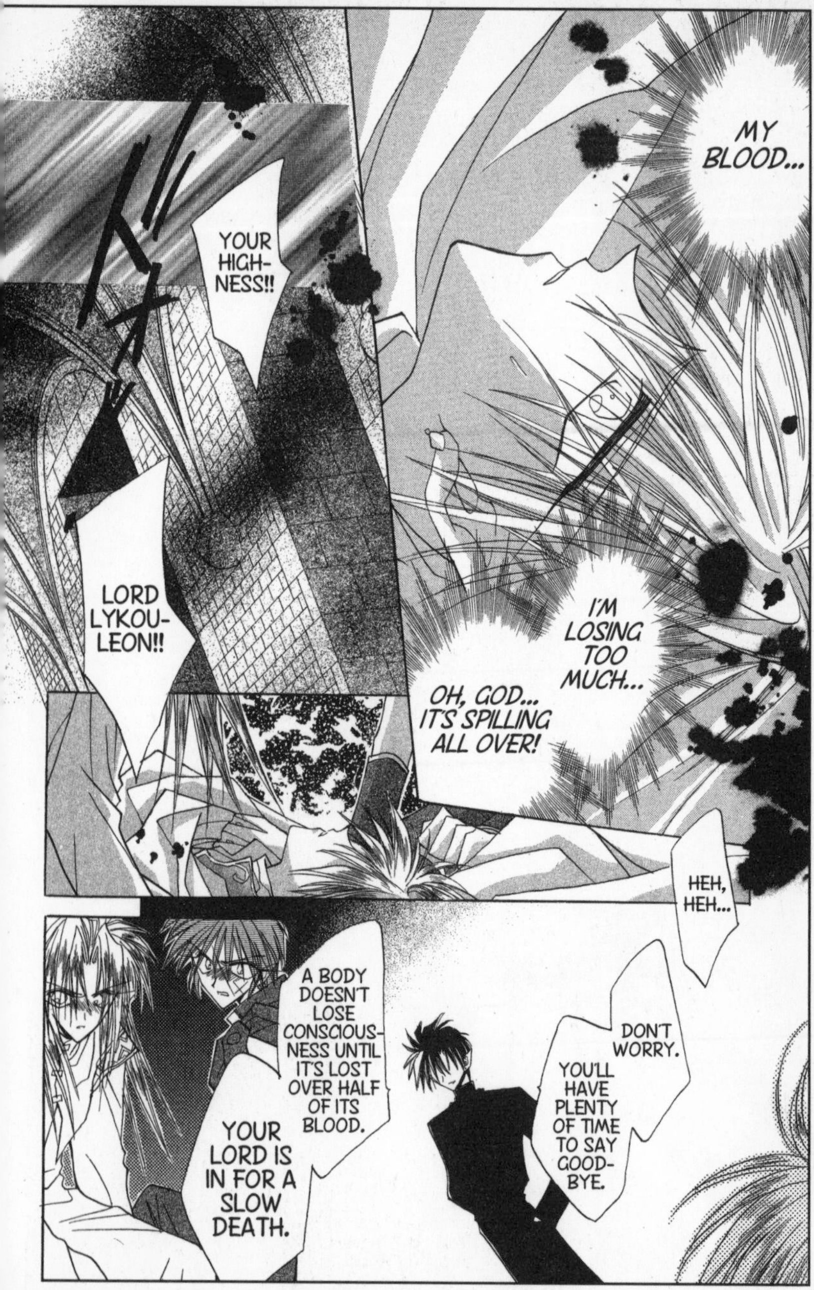
MY BLOOD...
I'M LOSING TOO MUCH...
OH, GOD... IT'S SPILLING ALL OVER!
YOUR HIGH-NESS!!
LORD LYKOU-LEON!!
HEH, HEH...
DON'T WORRY.
YOU'LL HAVE PLENTY OF TIME TO SAY GOOD-BYE.
A BODY DOESN'T LOSE CONSCIOUS-NESS UNTIL IT'S LOST OVER HALF OF ITS BLOOD.
YOUR LORD IS IN FOR A SLOW DEATH.

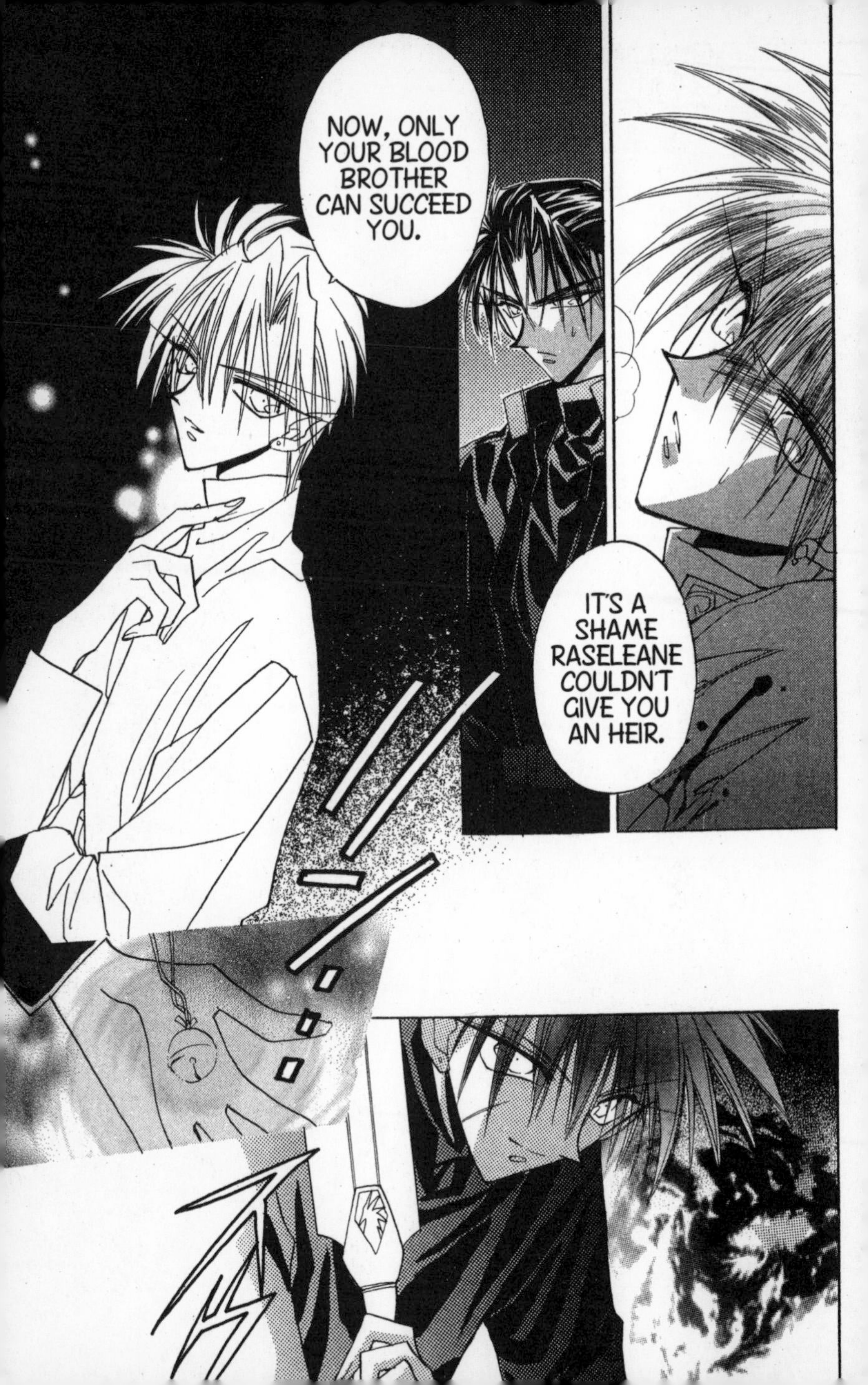
IT'S A SHAME RASELEANE COULDN'T GIVE YOU AN HEIR.
NOW, ONLY YOUR BLOOD BROTHER CAN SUCCEED YOU.

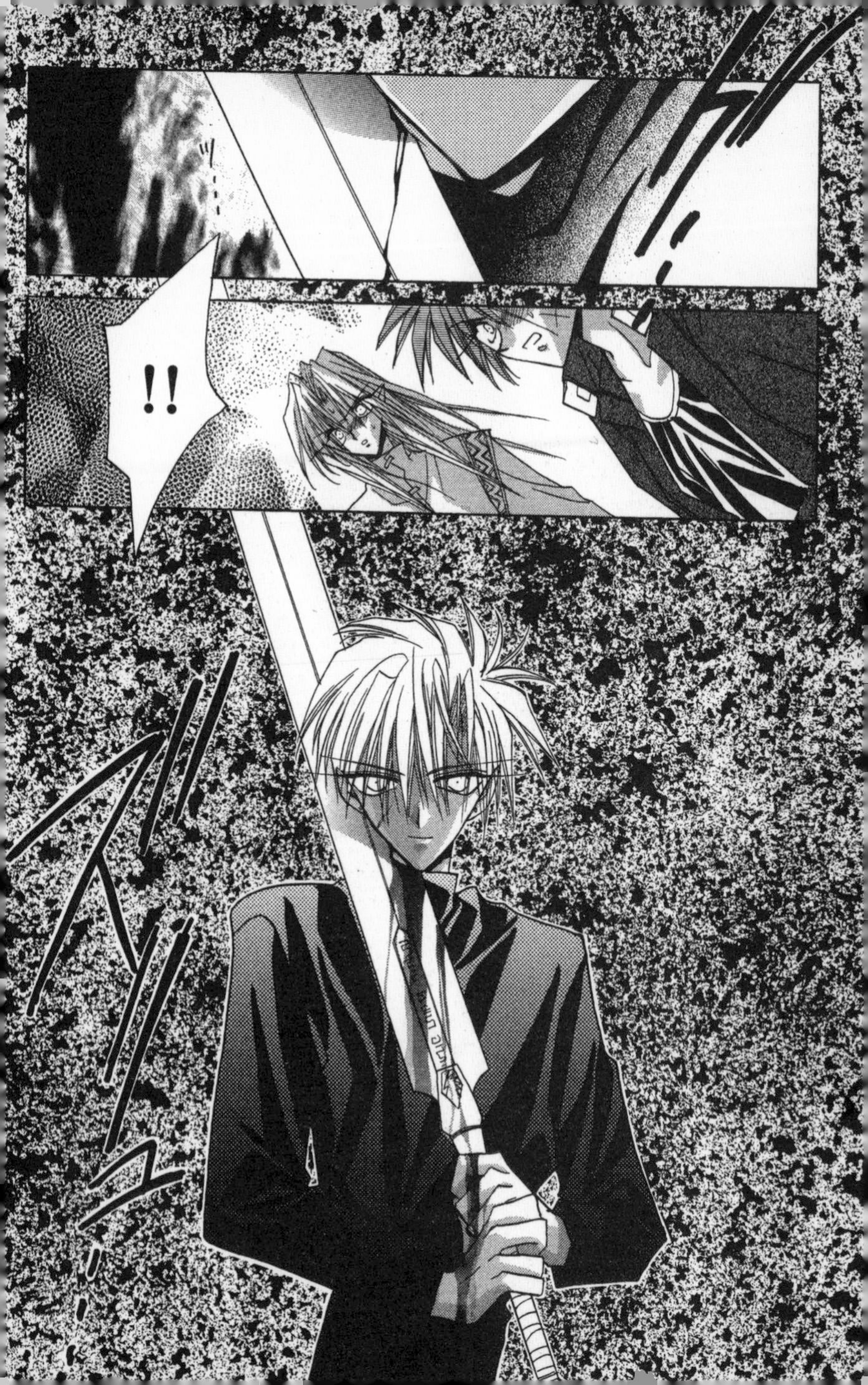
!!

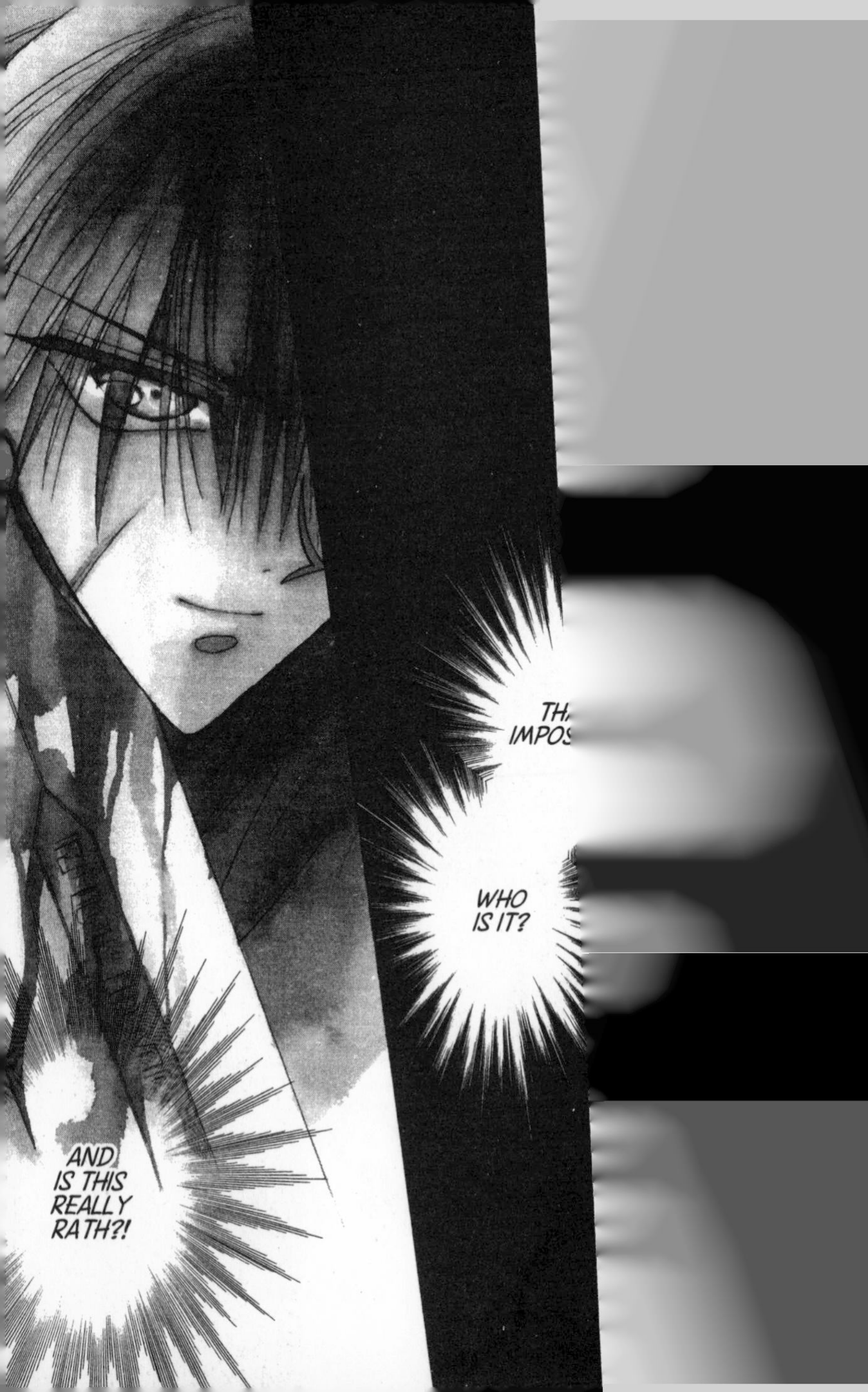
THA
IMPOS
WHO IS IT?
AND IS THIS REALLY RATH?!

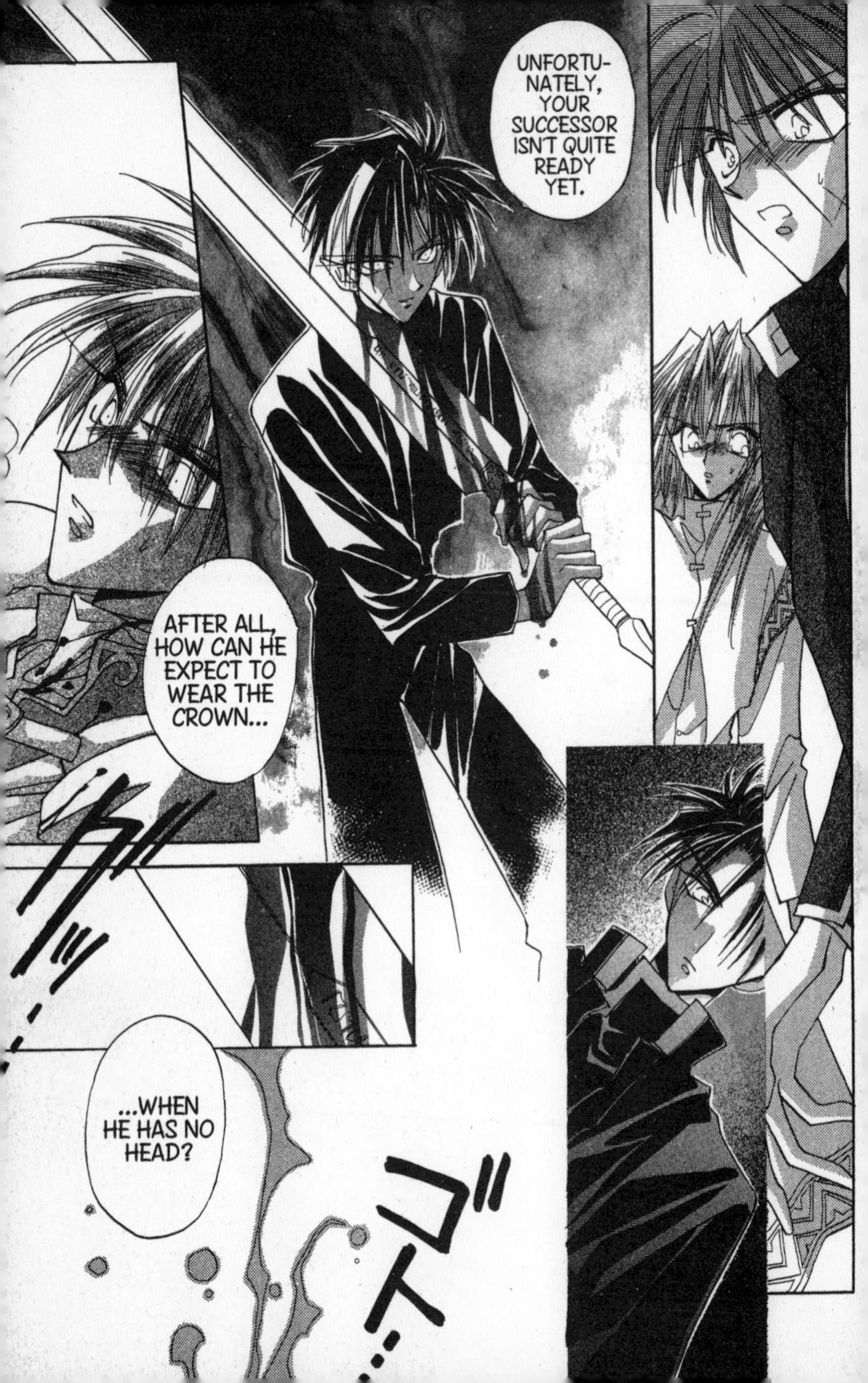
UNFORTU-NATELY, YOUR SUCCESSOR ISN'T QUITE READY YET.
AFTER ALL, HOW CAN HE EXPECT TO WEAR THE CROWN...
...WHEN HE HAS NO HEAD?
ゴト…

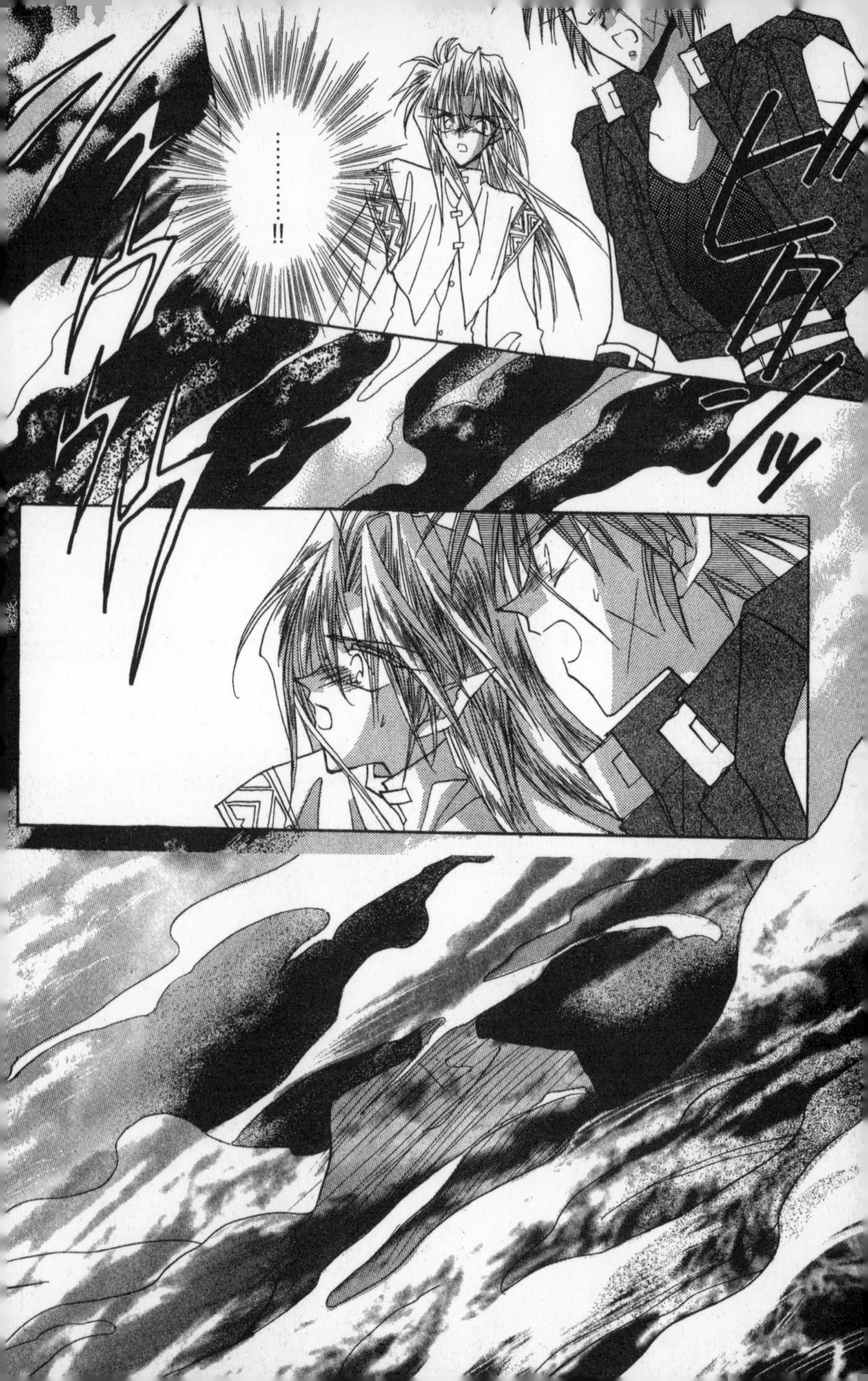
ビクッ
……!!

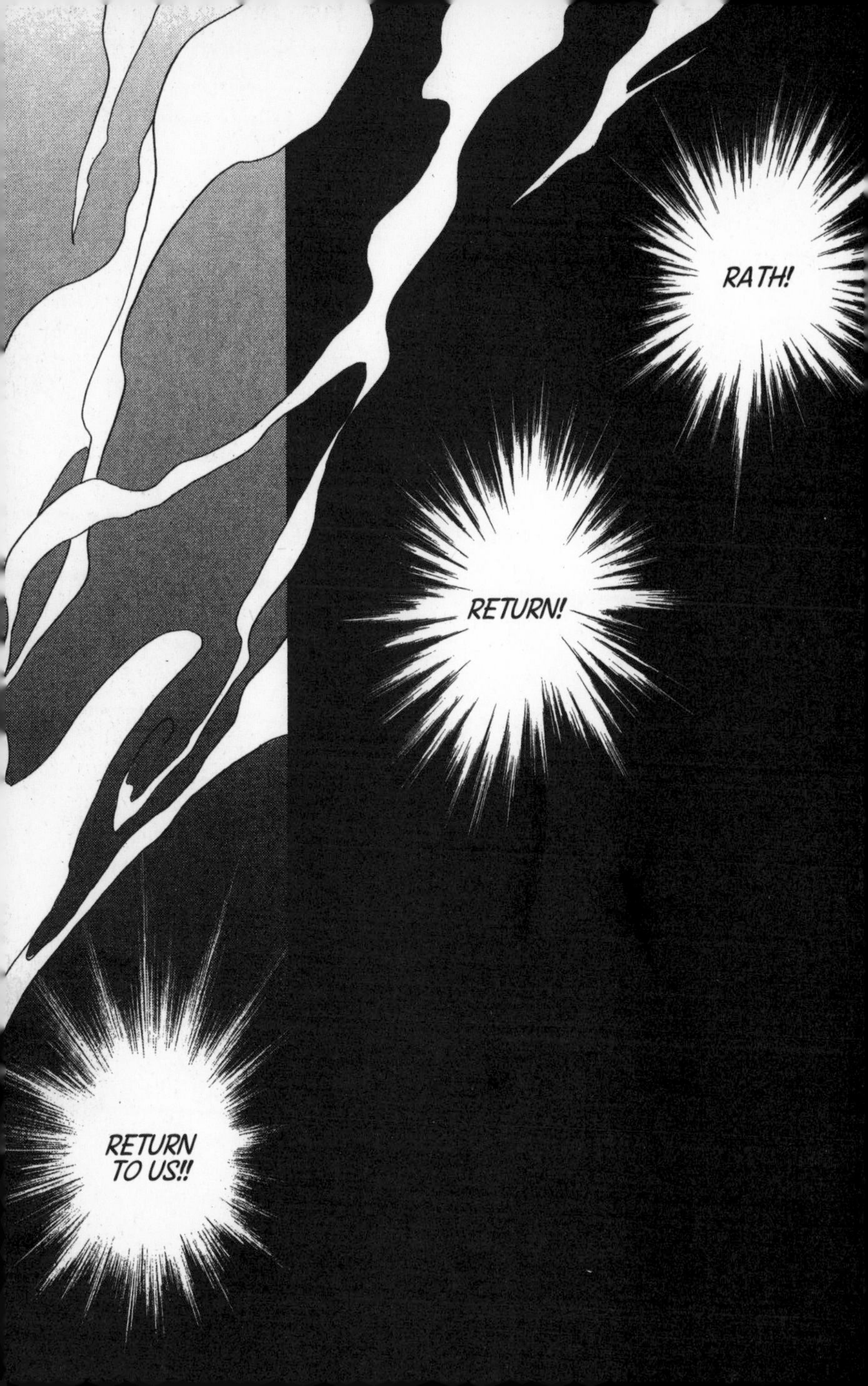
RATH!
RETURN!
RETURN TO US!!

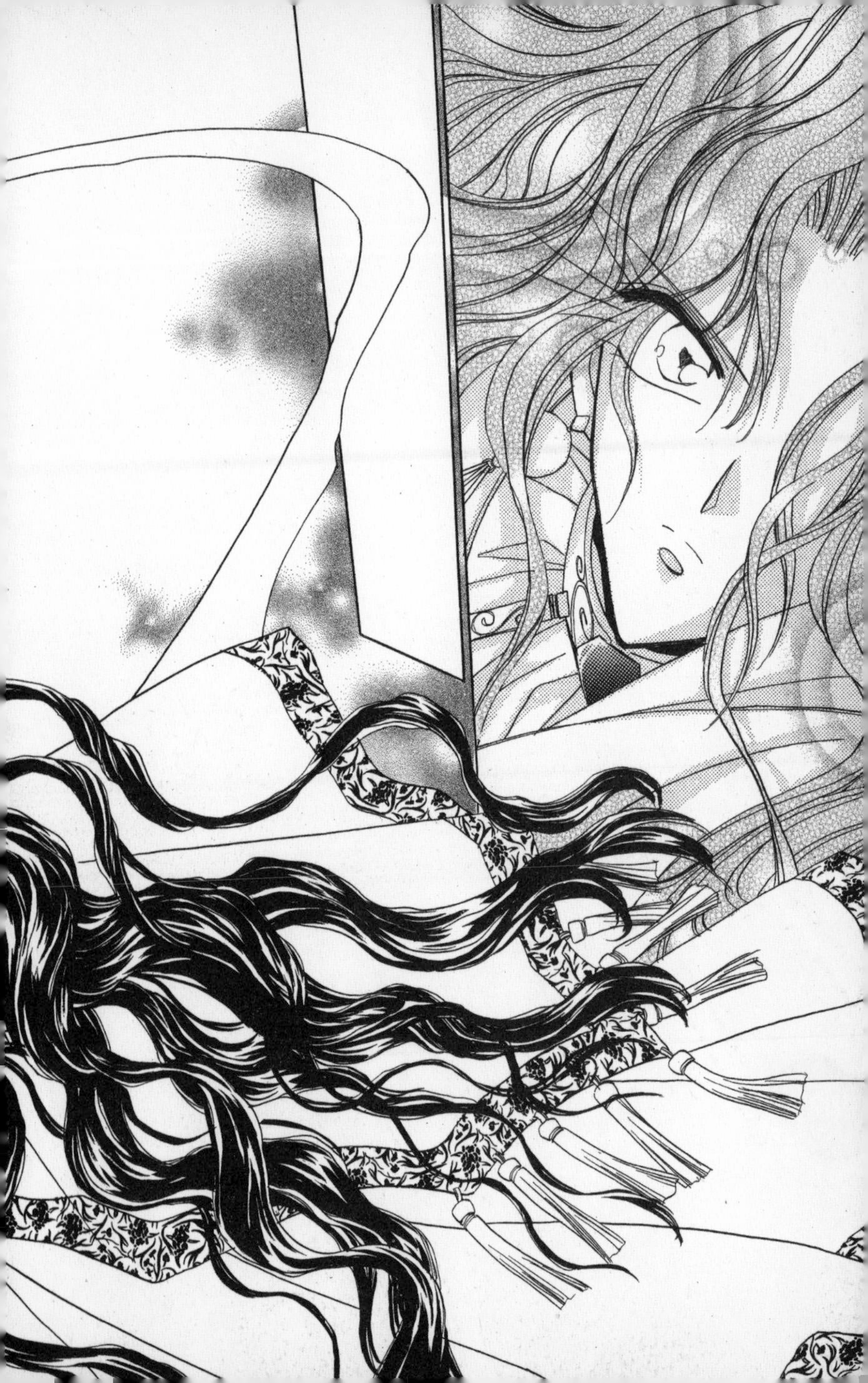

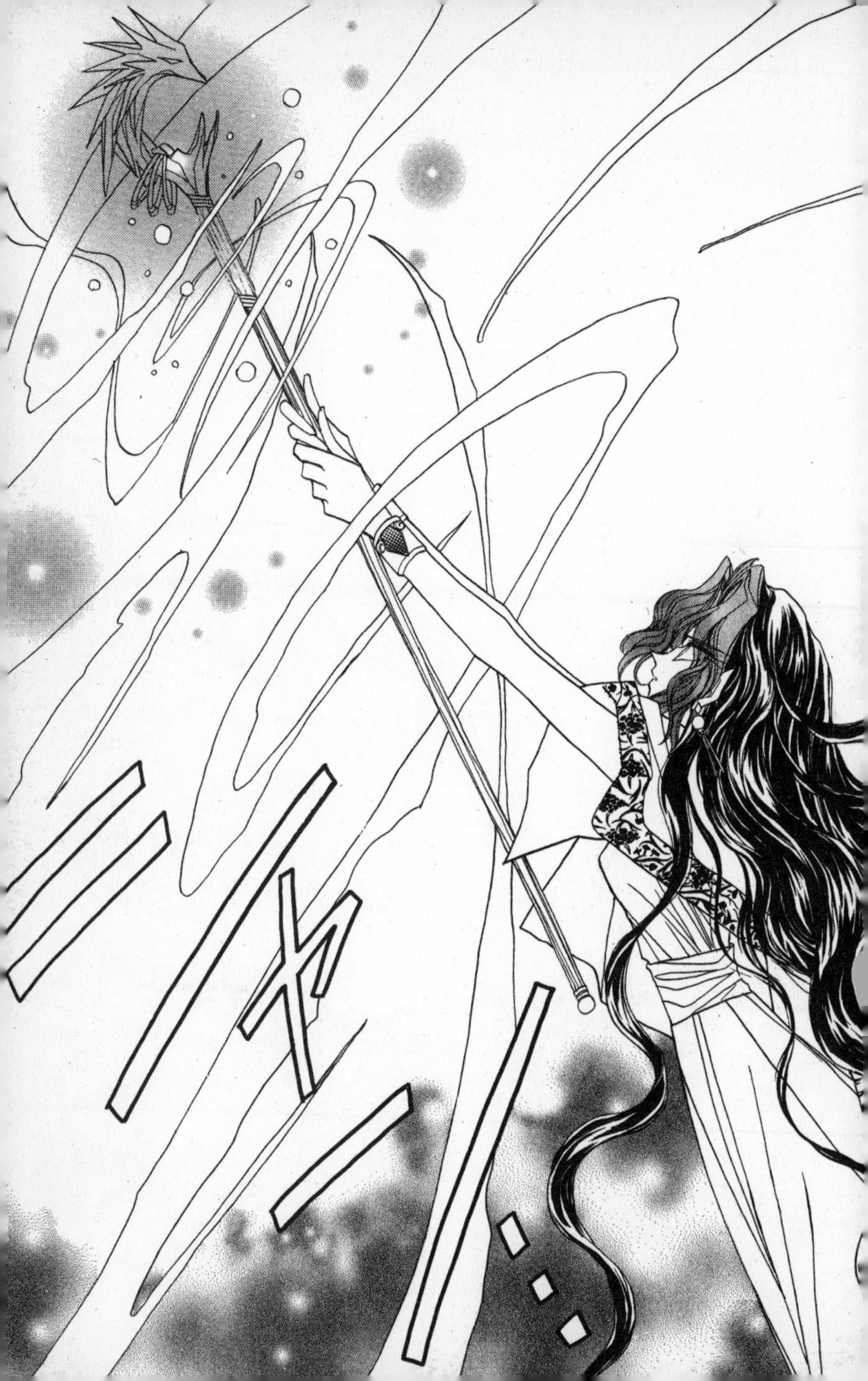

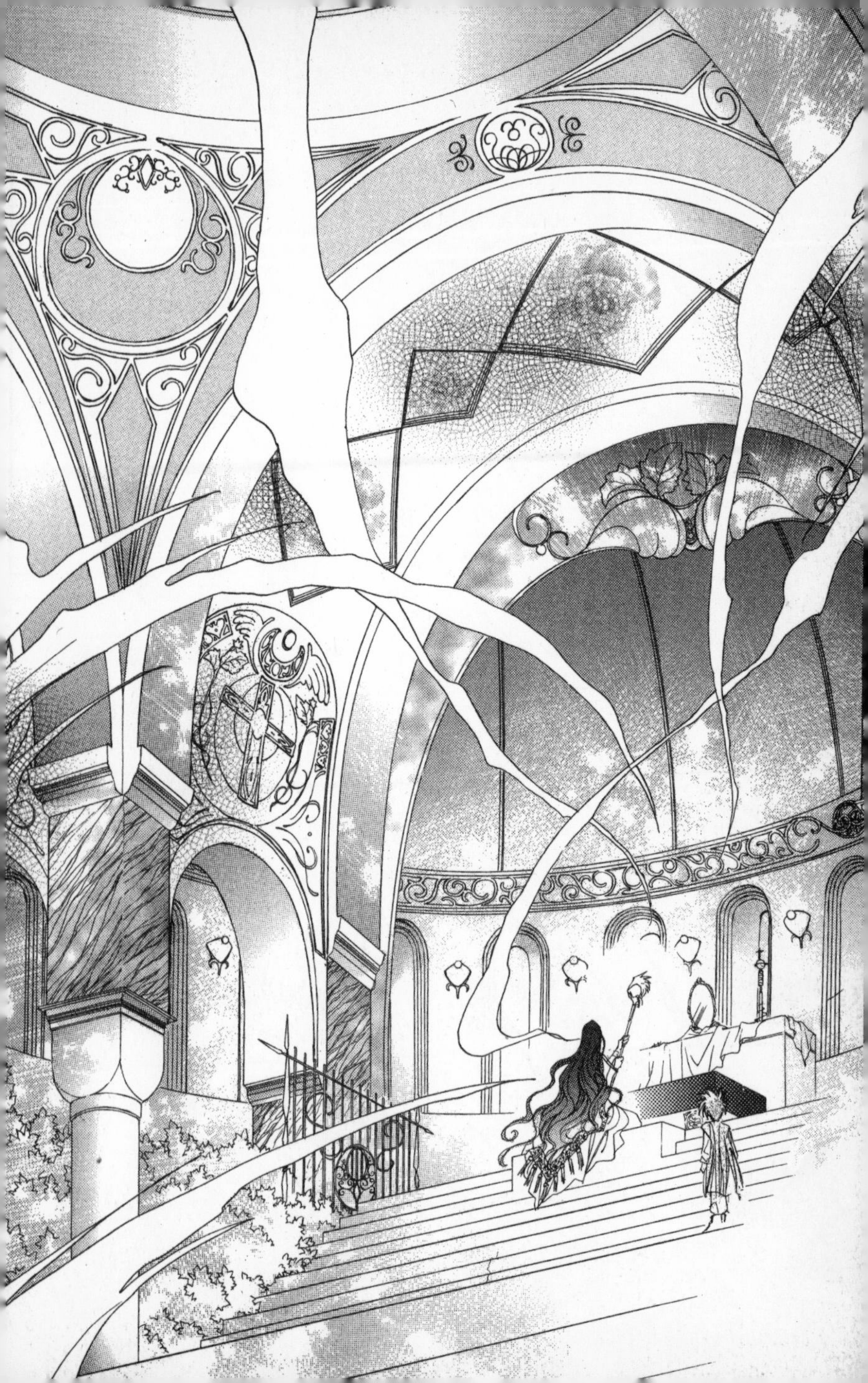

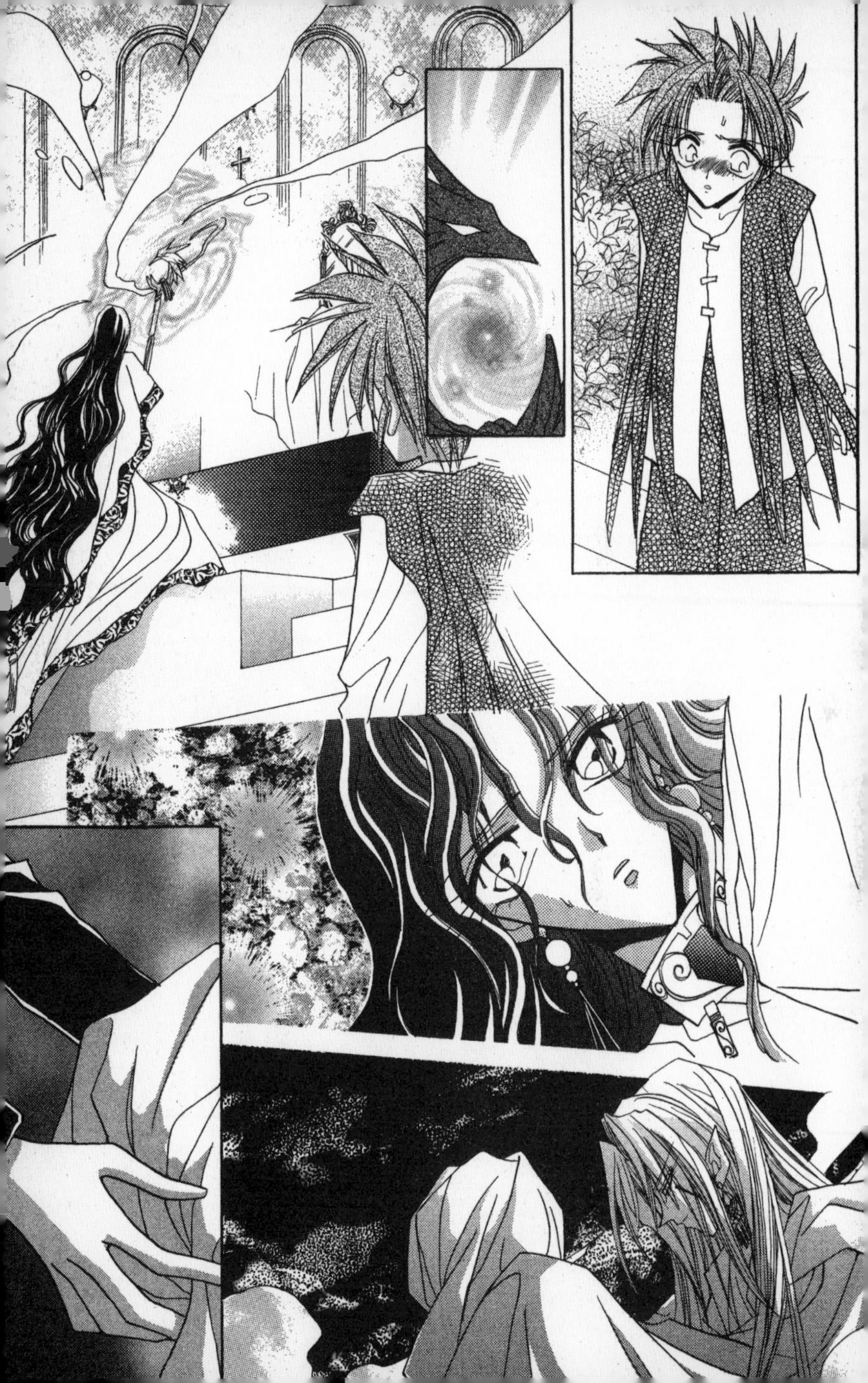

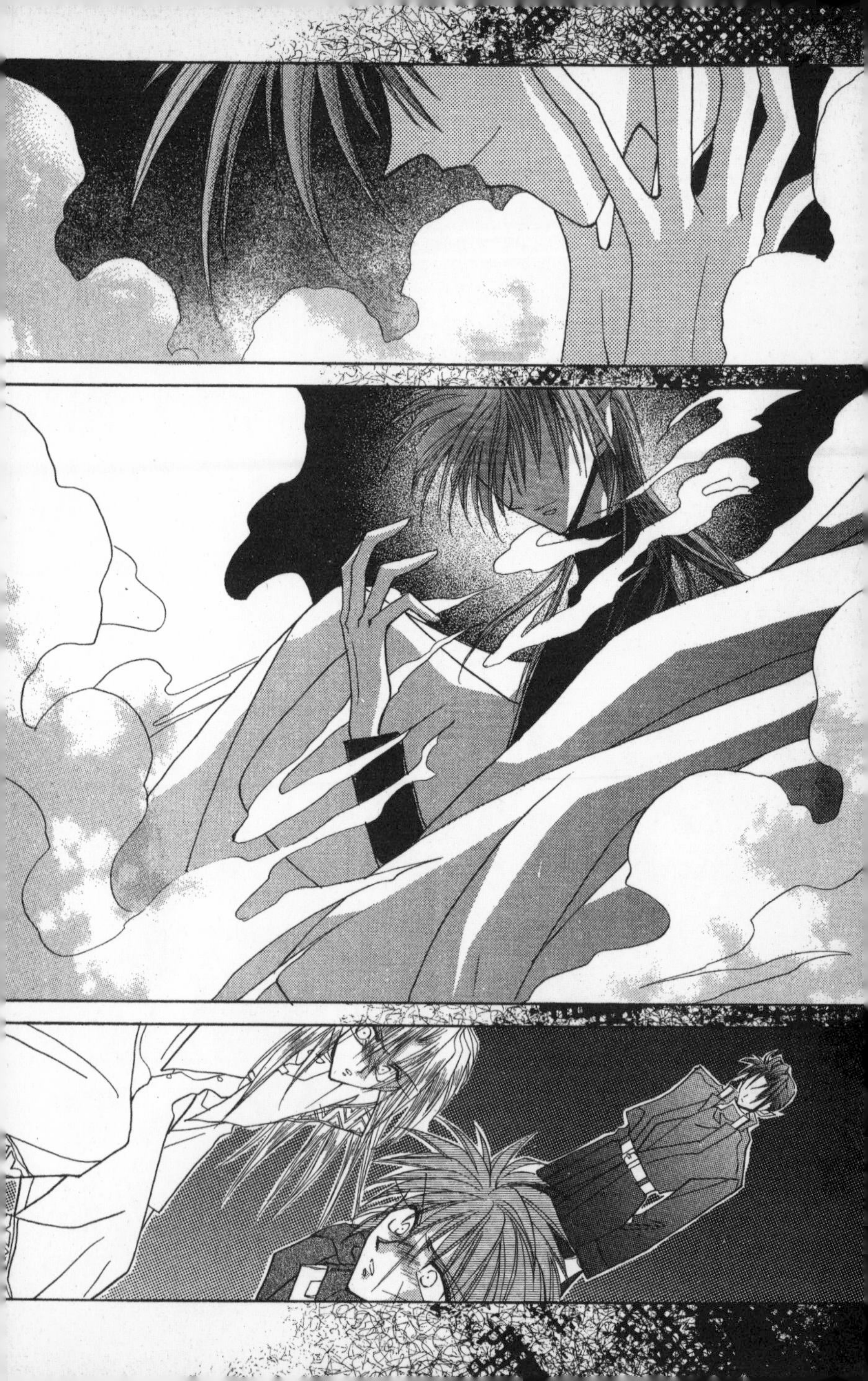

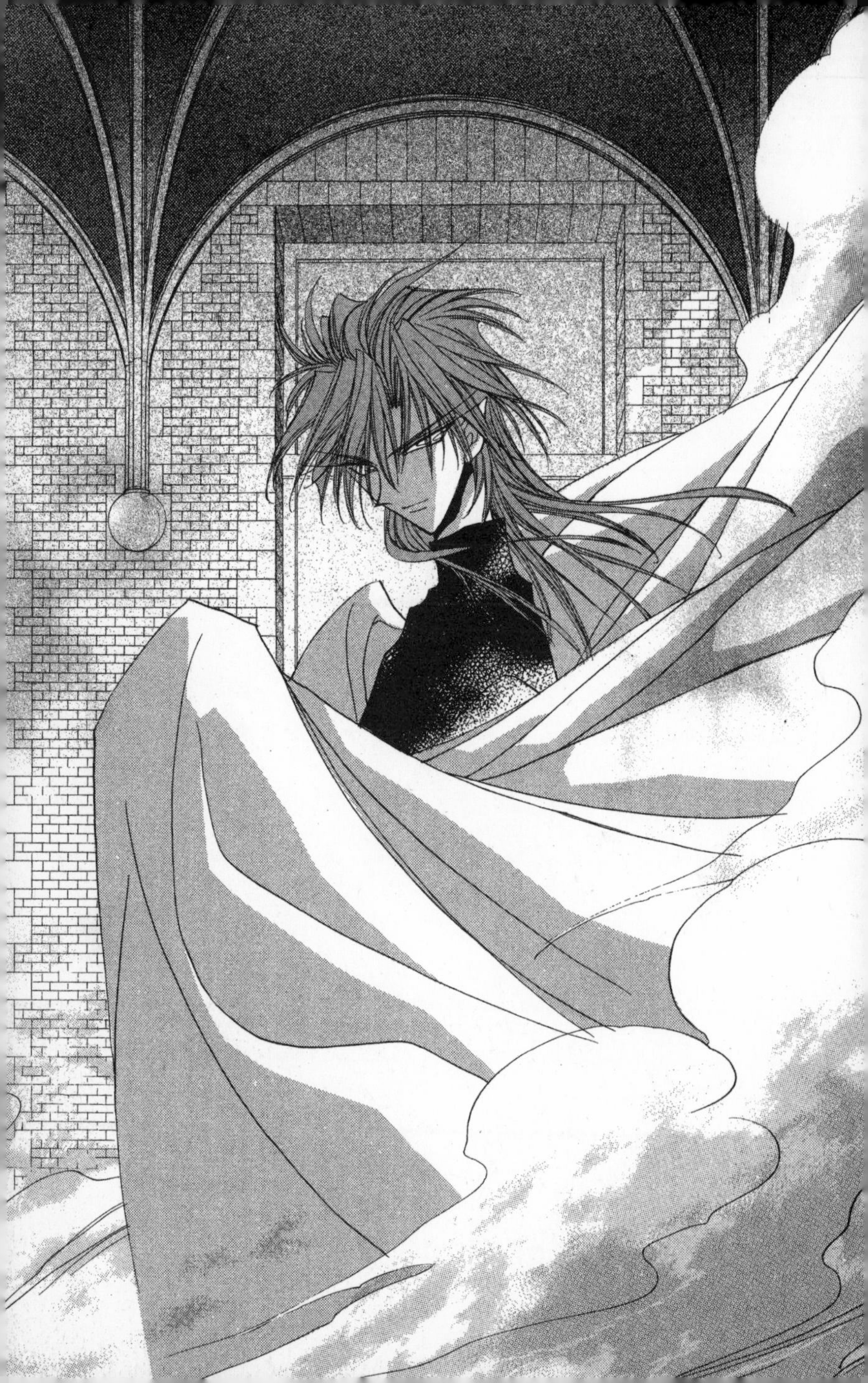

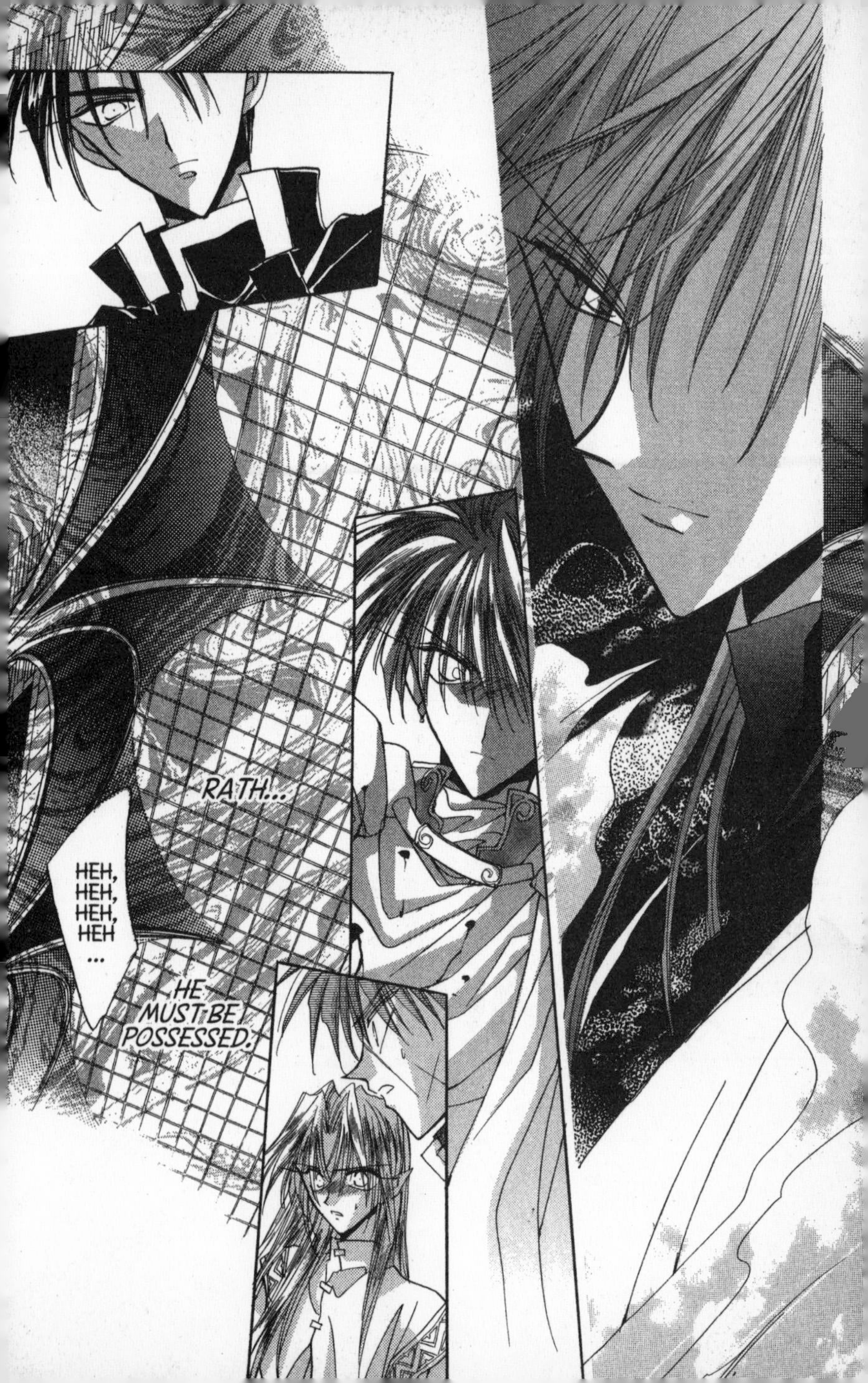
RATH...
HEH, HEH, HEH, HEH ...
HE MUST BE POSSESSED.

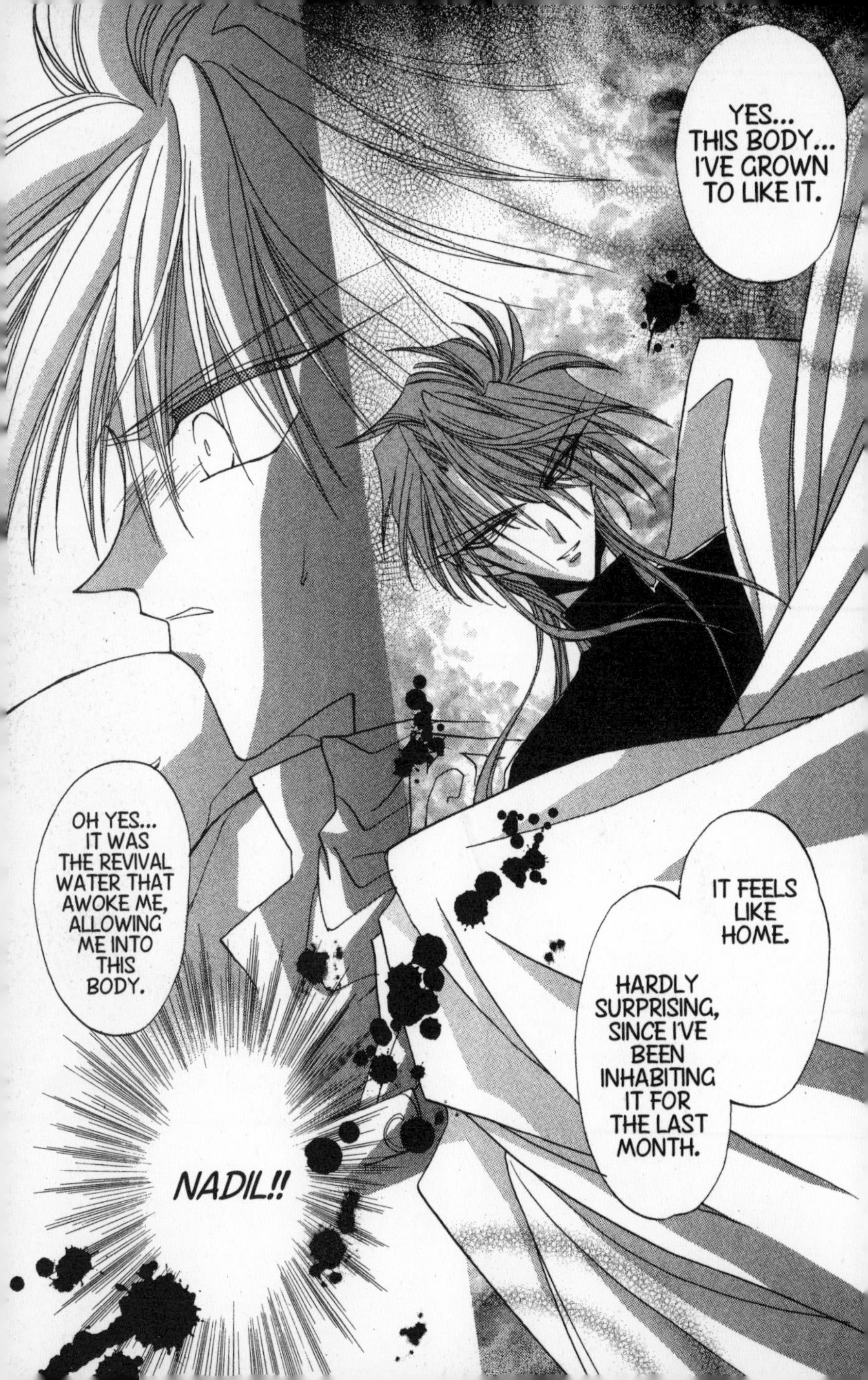
YES... THIS BODY... I'VE GROWN TO LIKE IT.
IT FEELS LIKE HOME.
HARDLY SURPRISING, SINCE I'VE BEEN INHABITING IT FOR THE LAST MONTH.
OH YES... IT WAS THE REVIVAL WATER THAT AWOKE ME, ALLOWING ME INTO THIS BODY.
NADIL!!

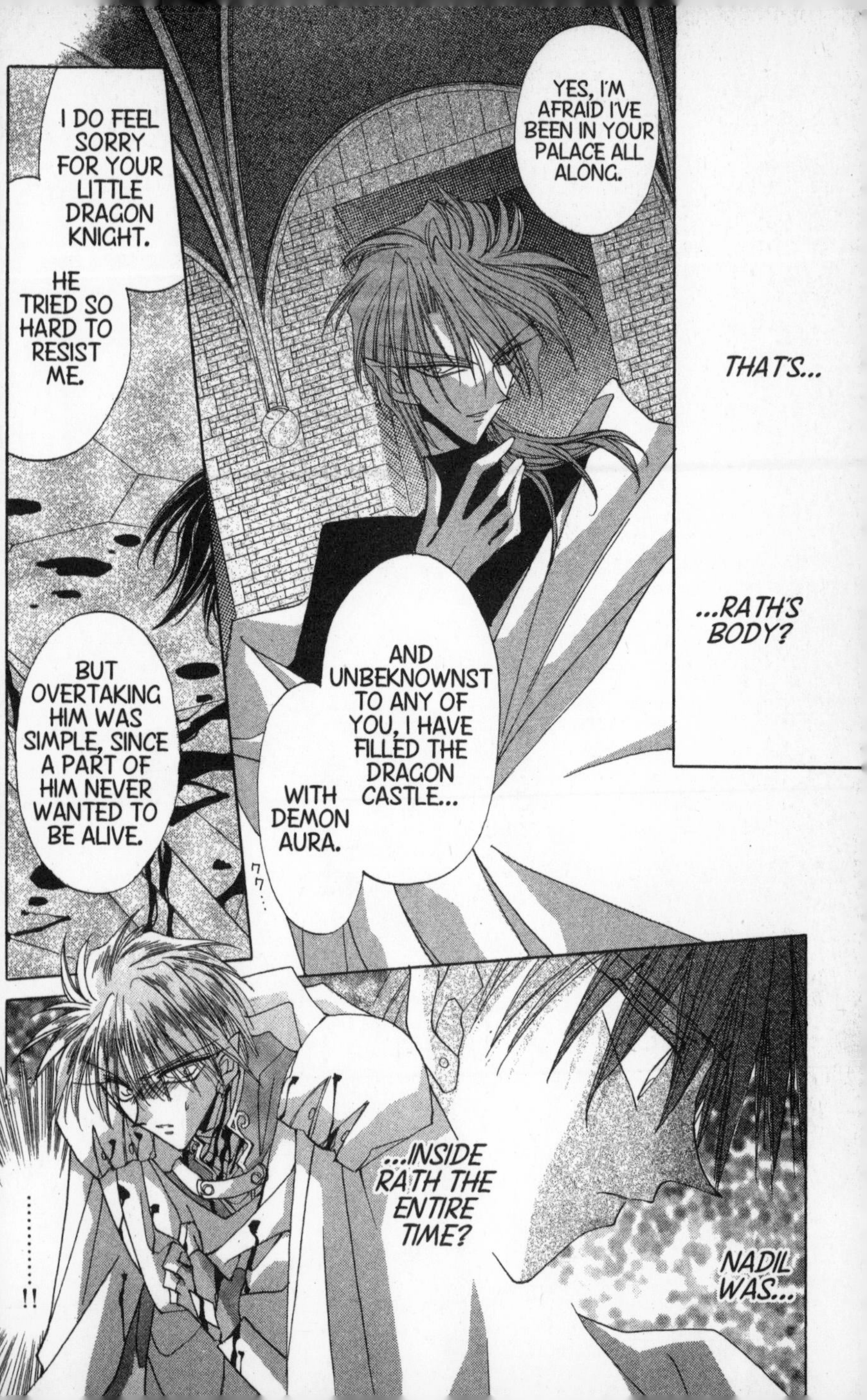
THAT'S...
...RATH'S BODY?
YES, I'M AFRAID I'VE BEEN IN YOUR PALACE ALL ALONG.
AND UNBEKNOWNST TO ANY OF YOU, I HAVE FILLED THE DRAGON CASTLE...
WITH DEMON AURA.
I DO FEEL SORRY FOR YOUR LITTLE DRAGON KNIGHT.
HE TRIED SO HARD TO RESIST ME.
BUT OVERTAKING HIM WAS SIMPLE, SINCE A PART OF HIM NEVER WANTED TO BE ALIVE.
NADIL WAS...
...INSIDE RATH THE ENTIRE TIME?
......!!

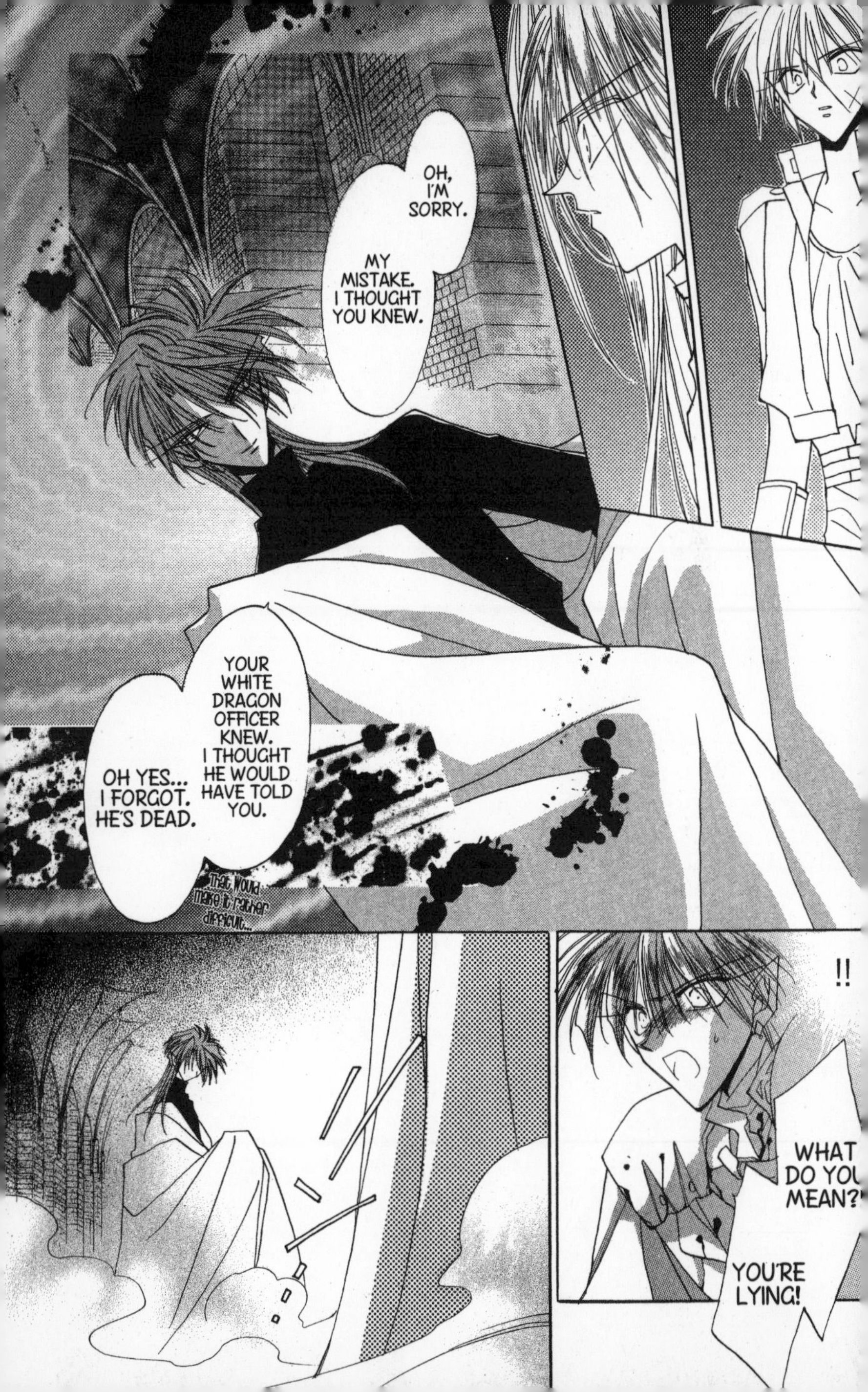
OH, I'M SORRY.
MY MISTAKE. I THOUGHT YOU KNEW.
YOUR WHITE DRAGON OFFICER KNEW. I THOUGHT HE WOULD HAVE TOLD YOU.
OH YES... I FORGOT. HE'S DEAD.
That would make it rather difficult...
!!
WHAT DO YOU MEAN?
YOU'RE LYING!

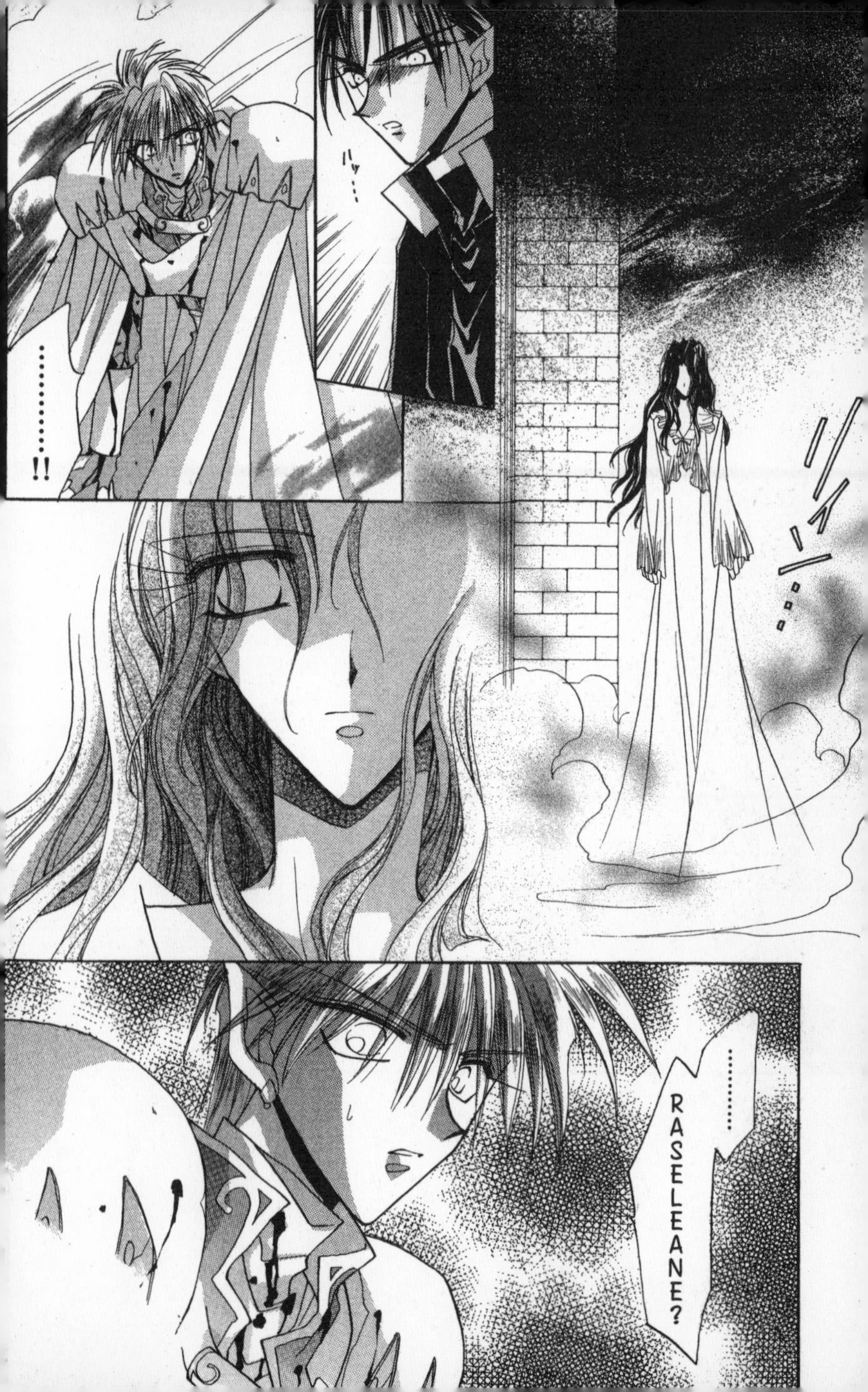

リィン...
ハッ...
......!!
......
RASELEANE?

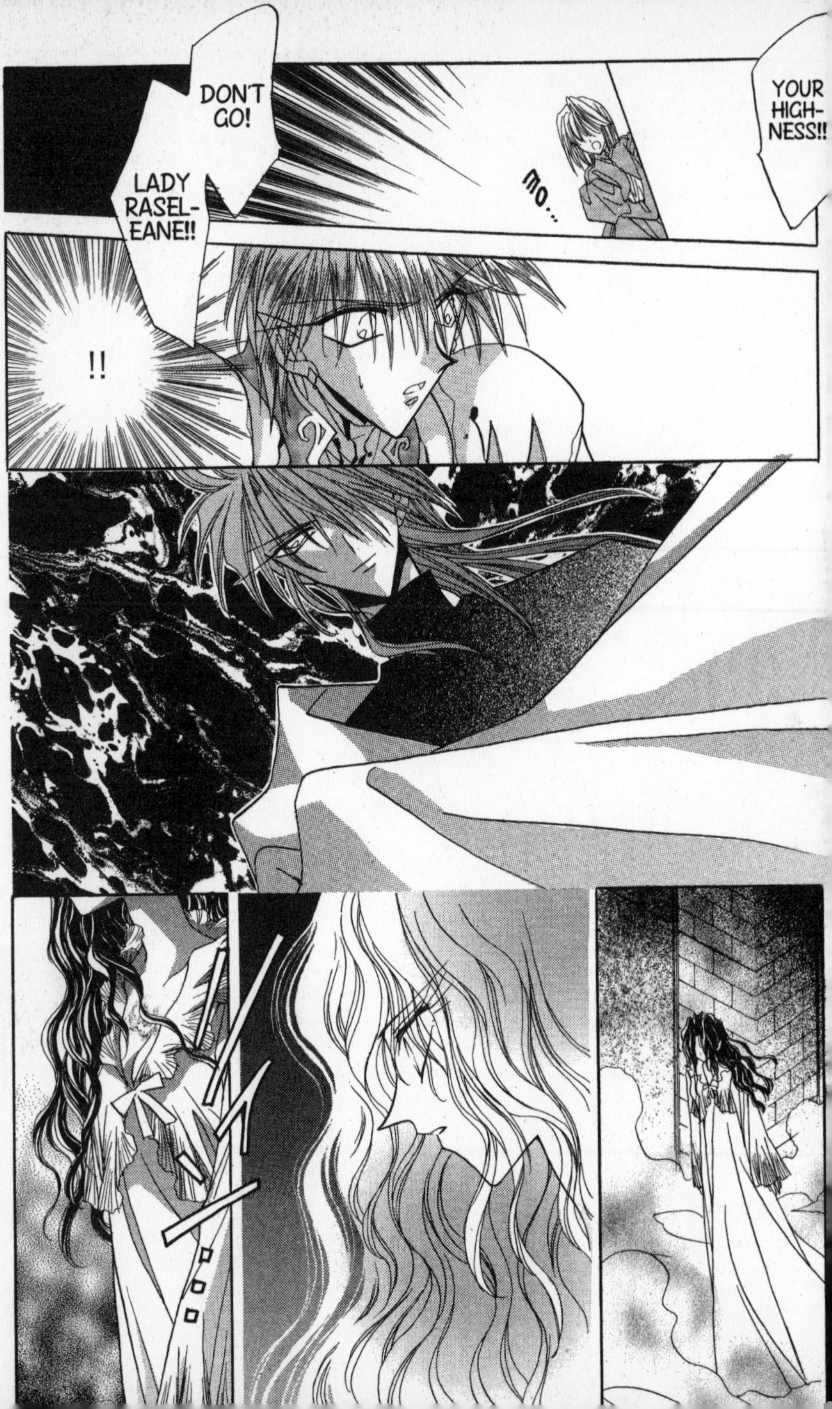
YOUR HIGH-NESS!!
mo...
DON'T GO!
LADY RASEL-EANE!!
!!

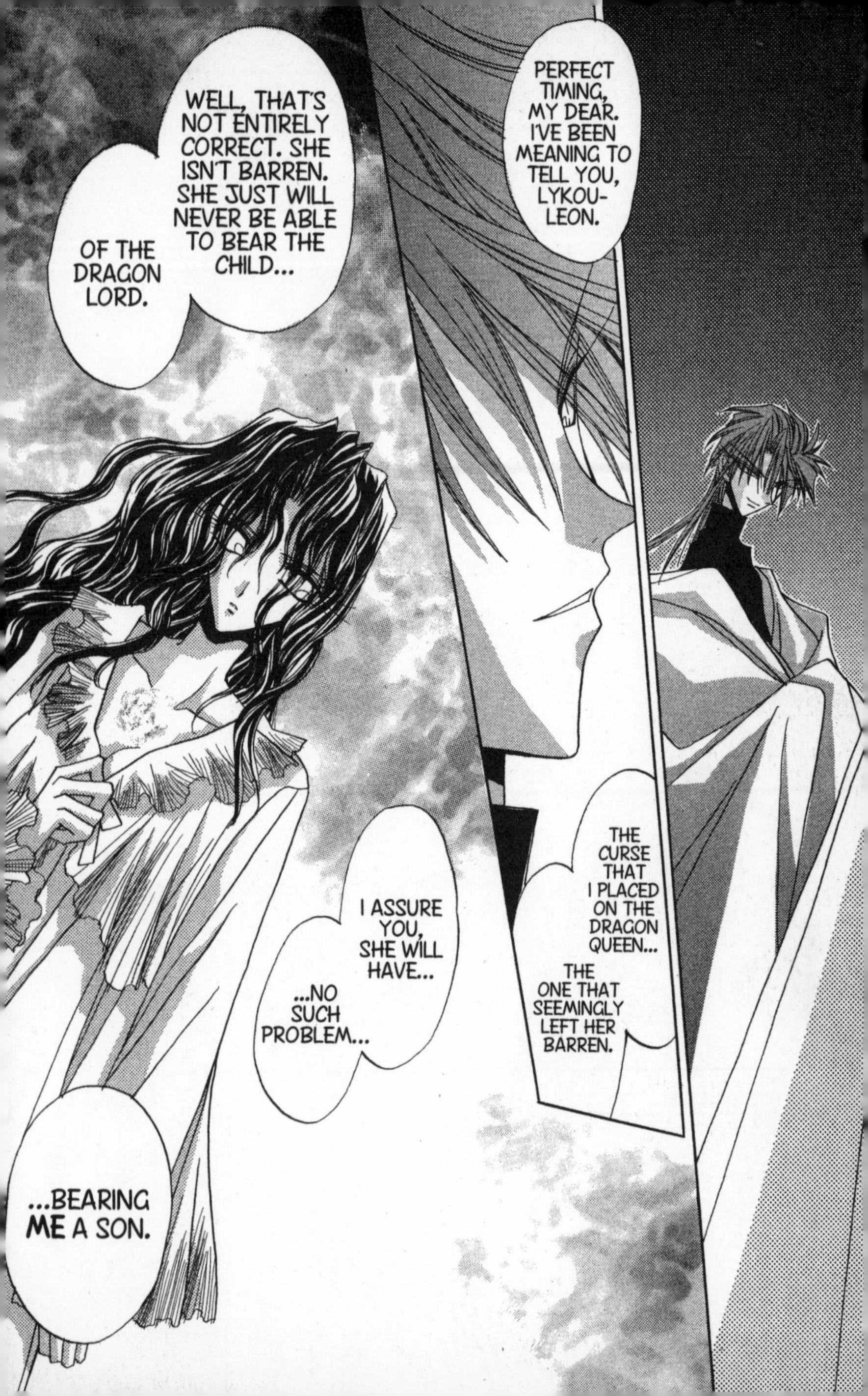
PERFECT TIMING, MY DEAR. I'VE BEEN MEANING TO TELL YOU, LYKOU-LEON.
THE CURSE THAT I PLACED ON THE DRAGON QUEEN...
THE ONE THAT SEEMINGLY LEFT HER BARREN.
WELL, THAT'S NOT ENTIRELY CORRECT. SHE ISN'T BARREN. SHE JUST WILL NEVER BE ABLE TO BEAR THE CHILD...
OF THE DRAGON LORD.
I ASSURE YOU, SHE WILL HAVE...
...NO SUCH PROBLEM...
...BEARING **ME** A SON.

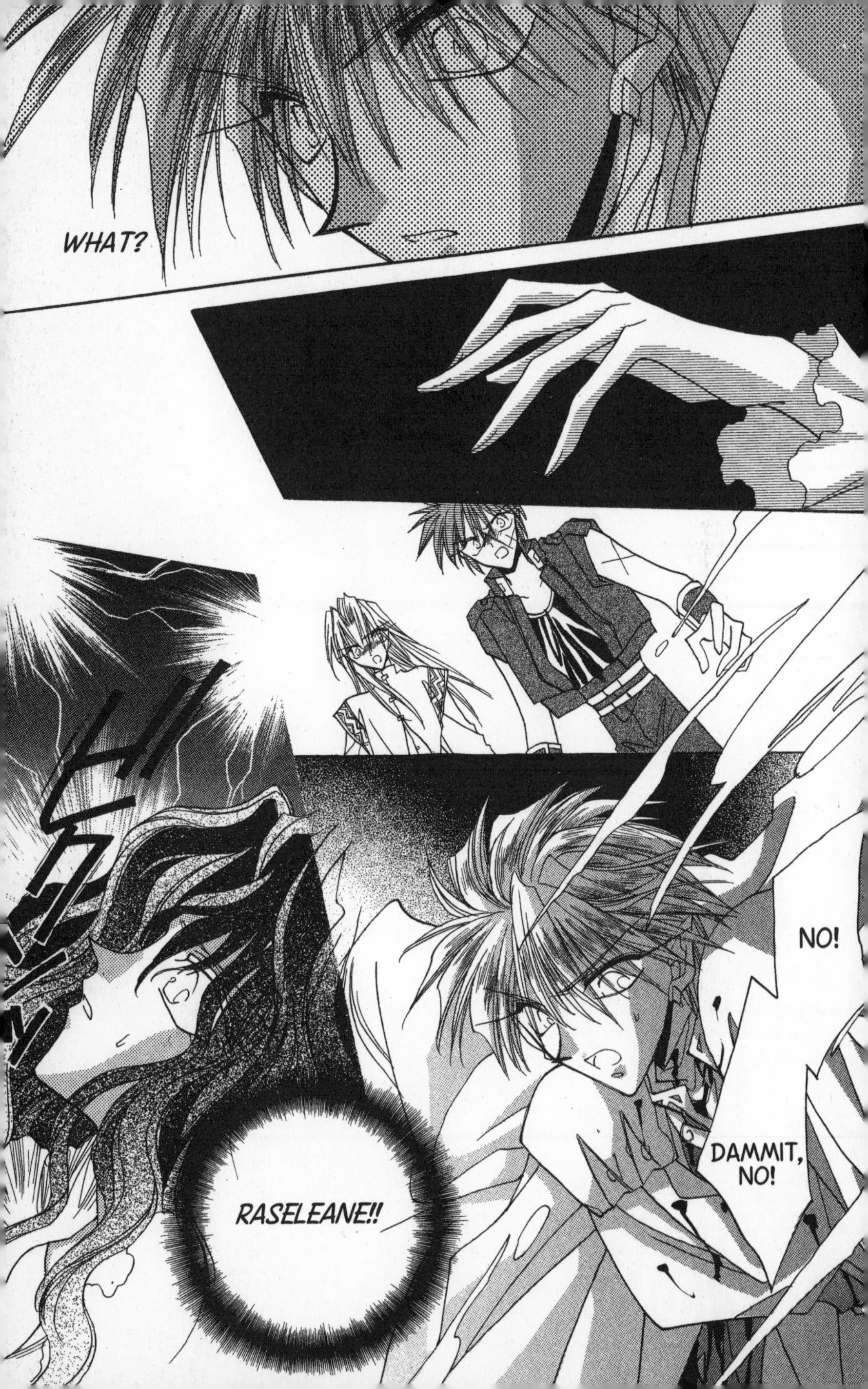
WHAT?
NO!
DAMMIT, NO!
RASELEANE!!

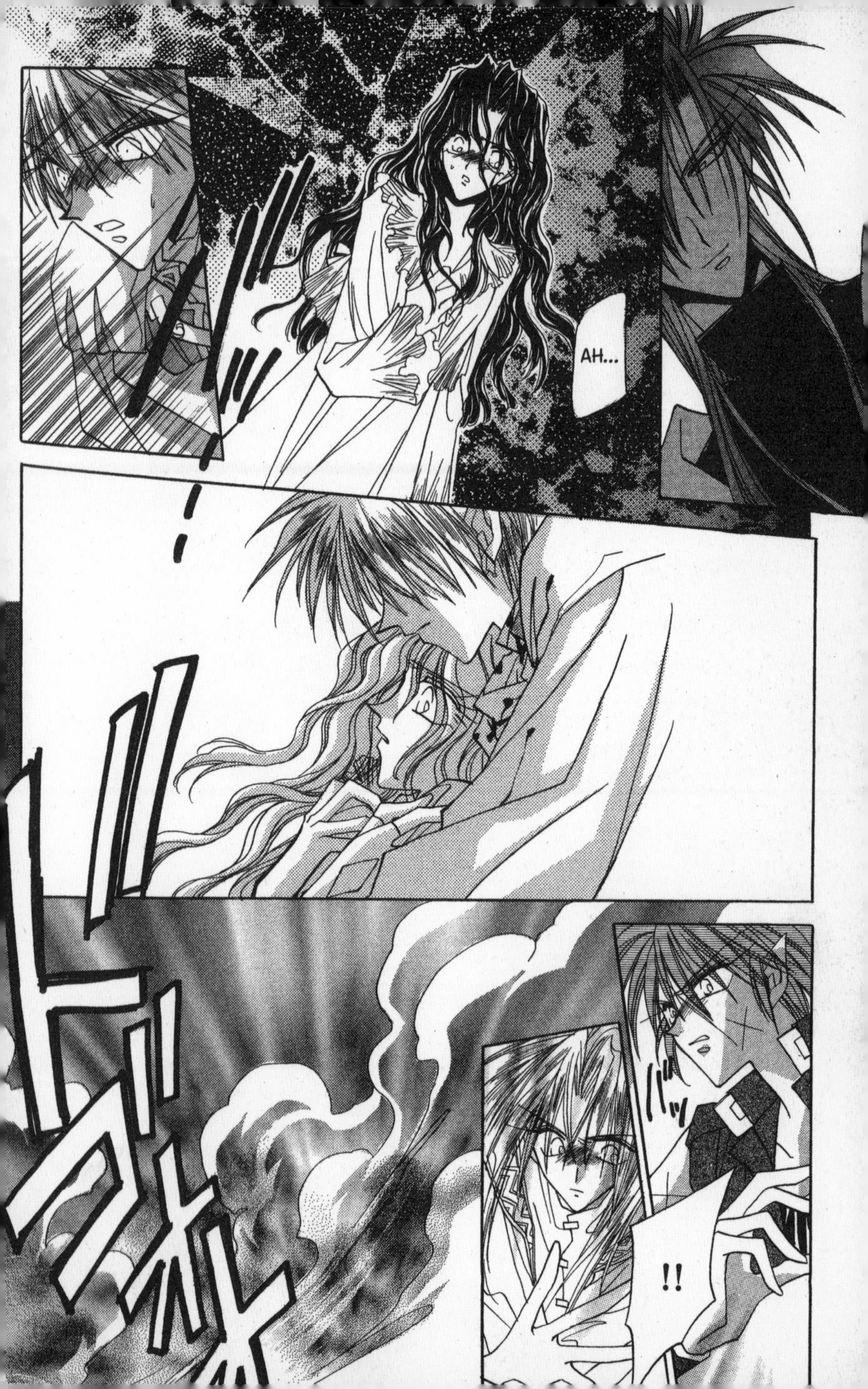
AH...
!!

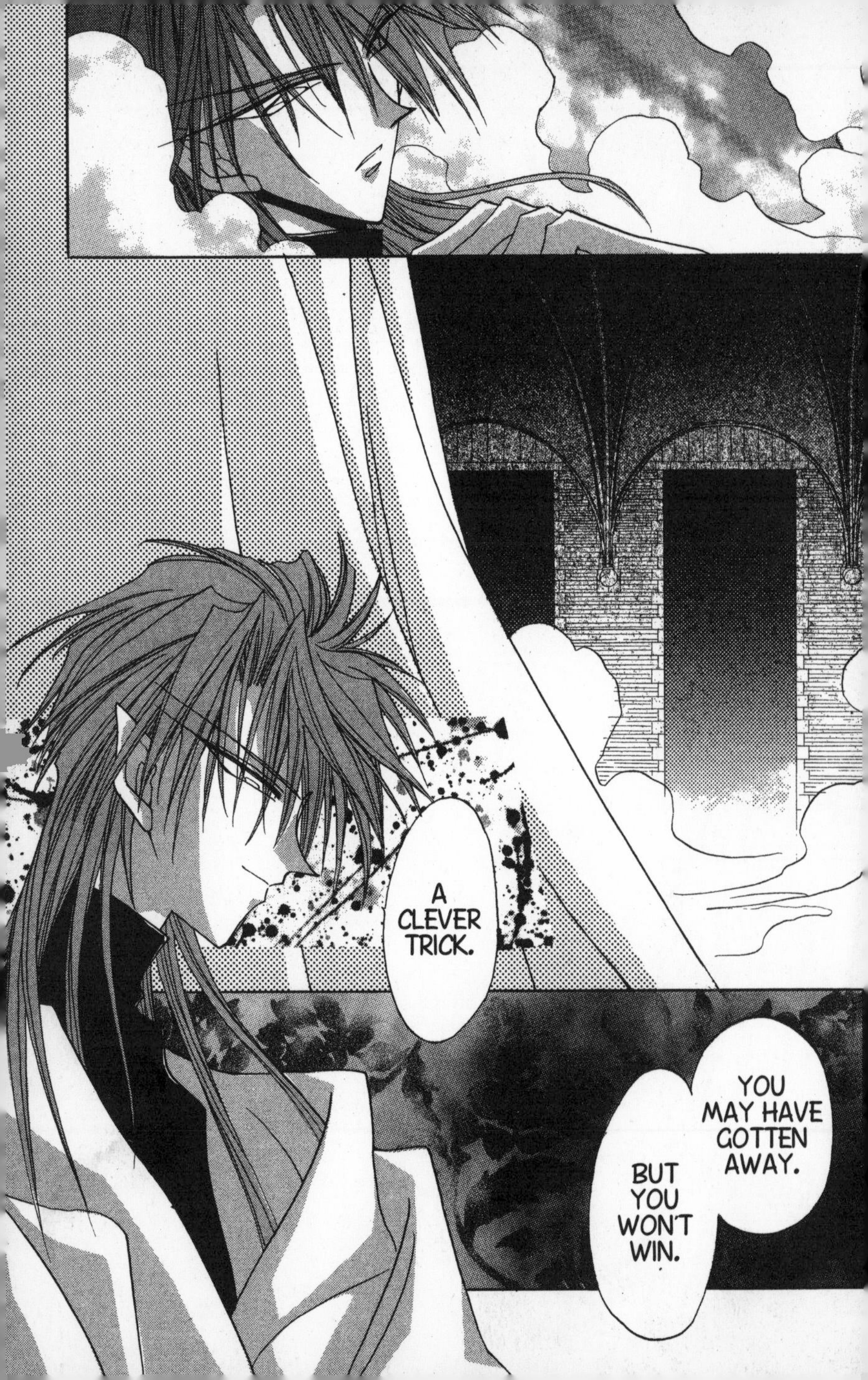
A CLEVER TRICK.
YOU MAY HAVE GOTTEN AWAY.
BUT YOU WON'T WIN.

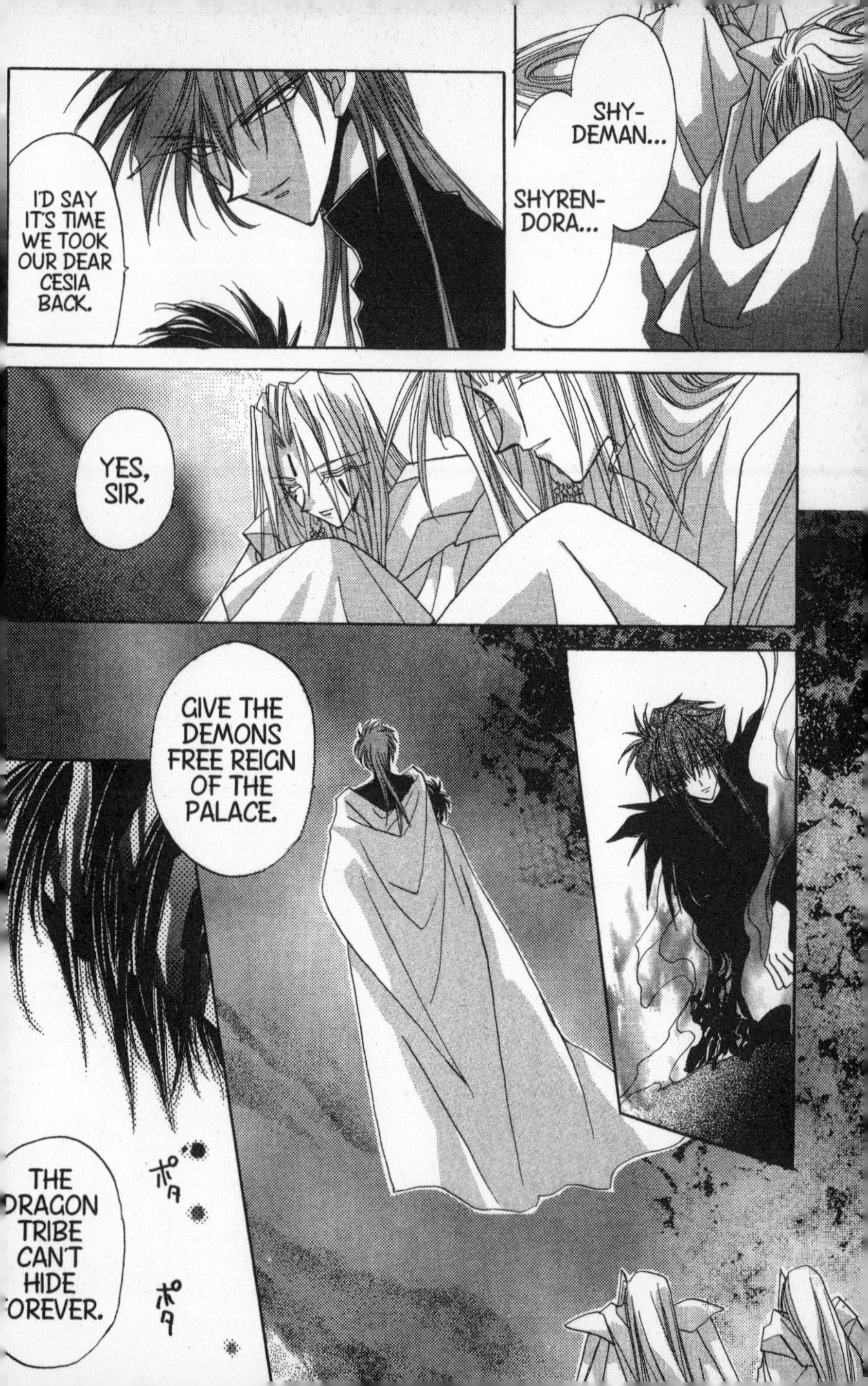
SHY-DEMAN...
SHYREN-DORA...
I'D SAY IT'S TIME WE TOOK OUR DEAR CESIA BACK.
YES, SIR.
GIVE THE DEMONS FREE REIGN OF THE PALACE.
ポタ
ポタ
THE DRAGON TRIBE CAN'T HIDE FOREVER.

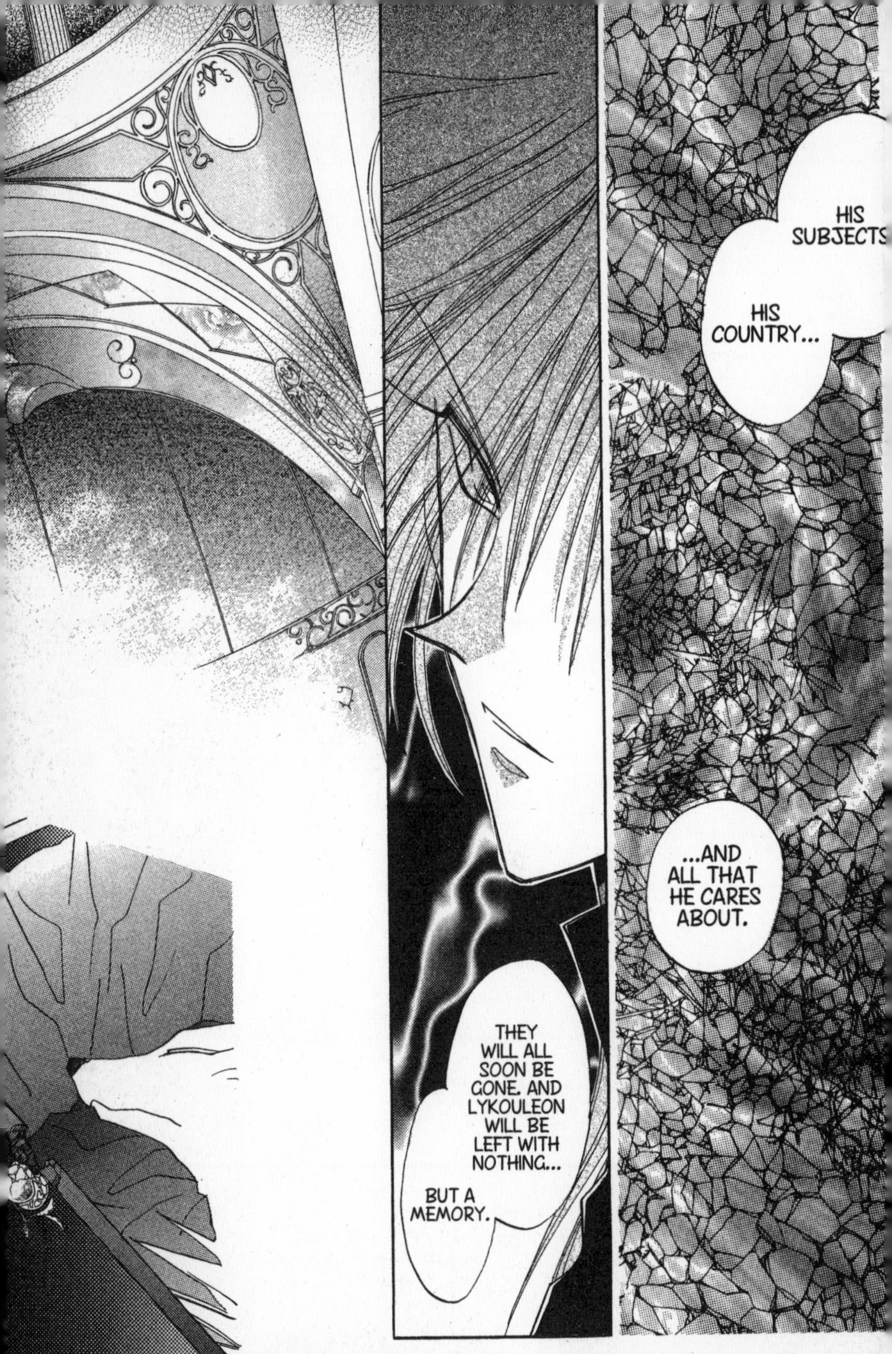
HIS SUBJECTS
HIS COUNTRY...
...AND ALL THAT HE CARES ABOUT.
THEY WILL ALL SOON BE GONE. AND LYKOULEON WILL BE LEFT WITH NOTHING...
BUT A MEMORY.

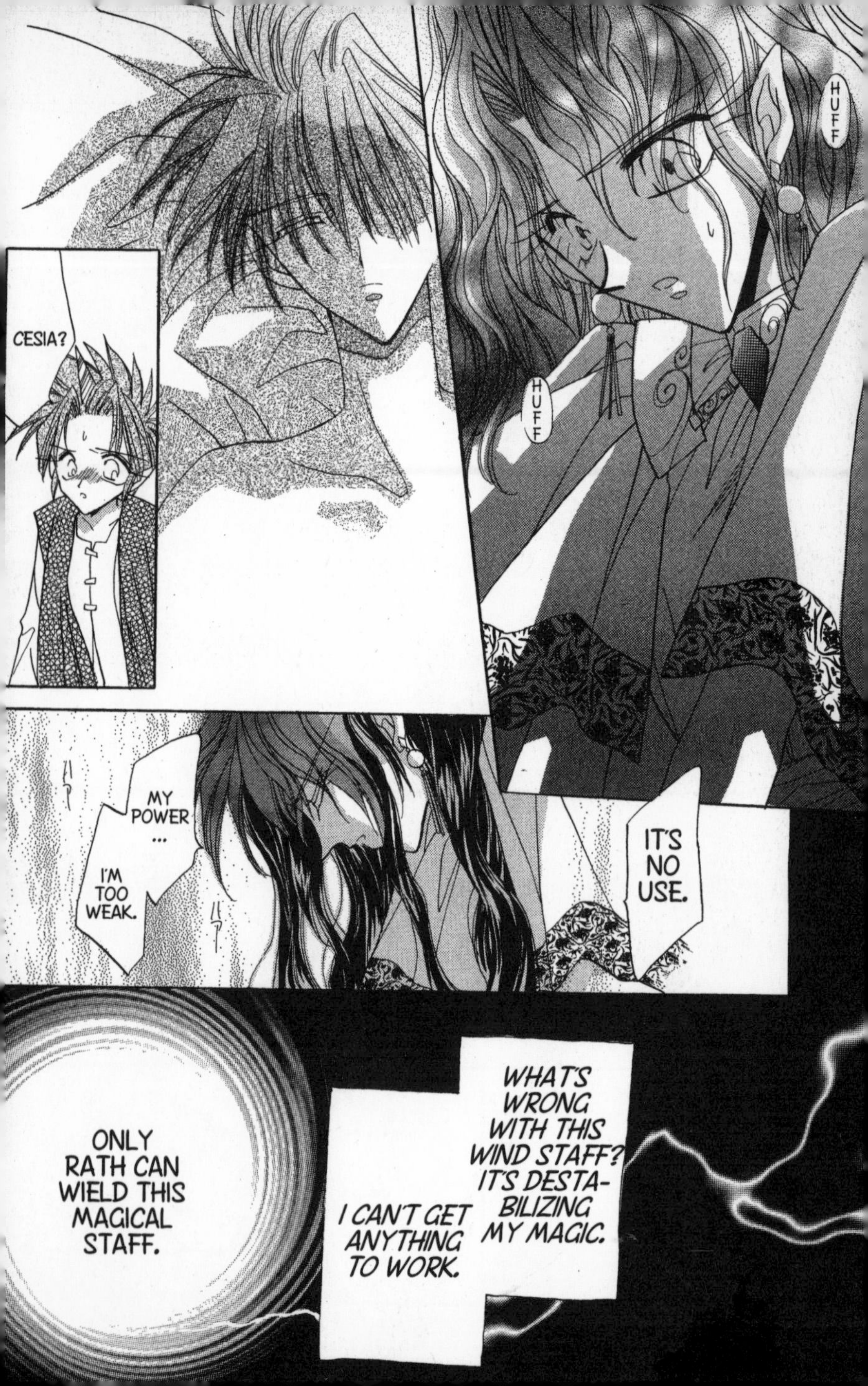
HUFF
HUFF
CESIA?
IT'S NO USE.
MY POWER...
I'M TOO WEAK.
WHAT'S WRONG WITH THIS WIND STAFF? IT'S DESTA-BILIZING MY MAGIC.
I CAN'T GET ANYTHING TO WORK.
ONLY RATH CAN WIELD THIS MAGICAL STAFF.

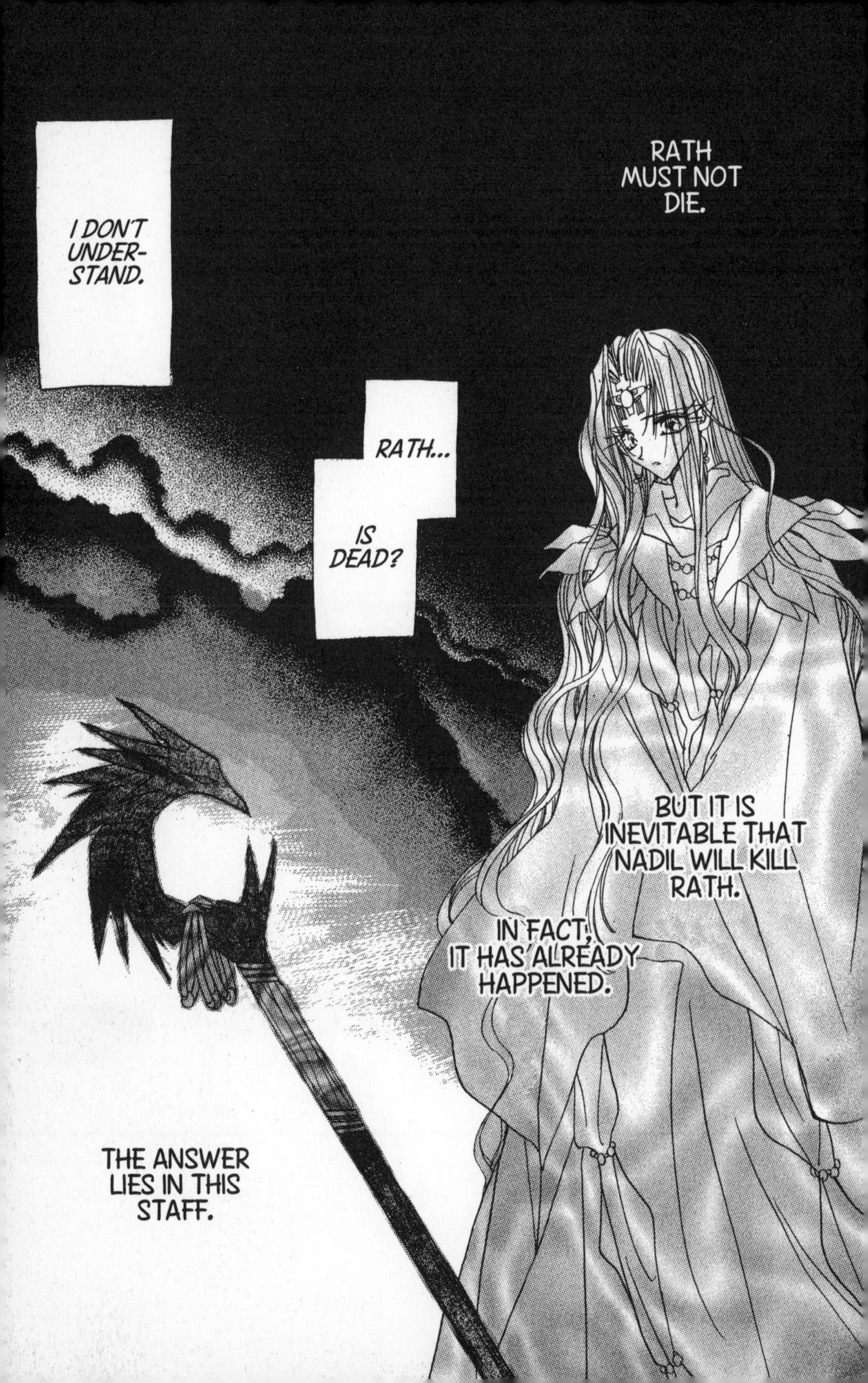
RATH MUST NOT DIE.
I DON'T UNDER-STAND.
RATH...
IS DEAD?
BUT IT IS INEVITABLE THAT NADIL WILL KILL RATH.
IN FACT, IT HAS ALREADY HAPPENED.
THE ANSWER LIES IN THIS STAFF.

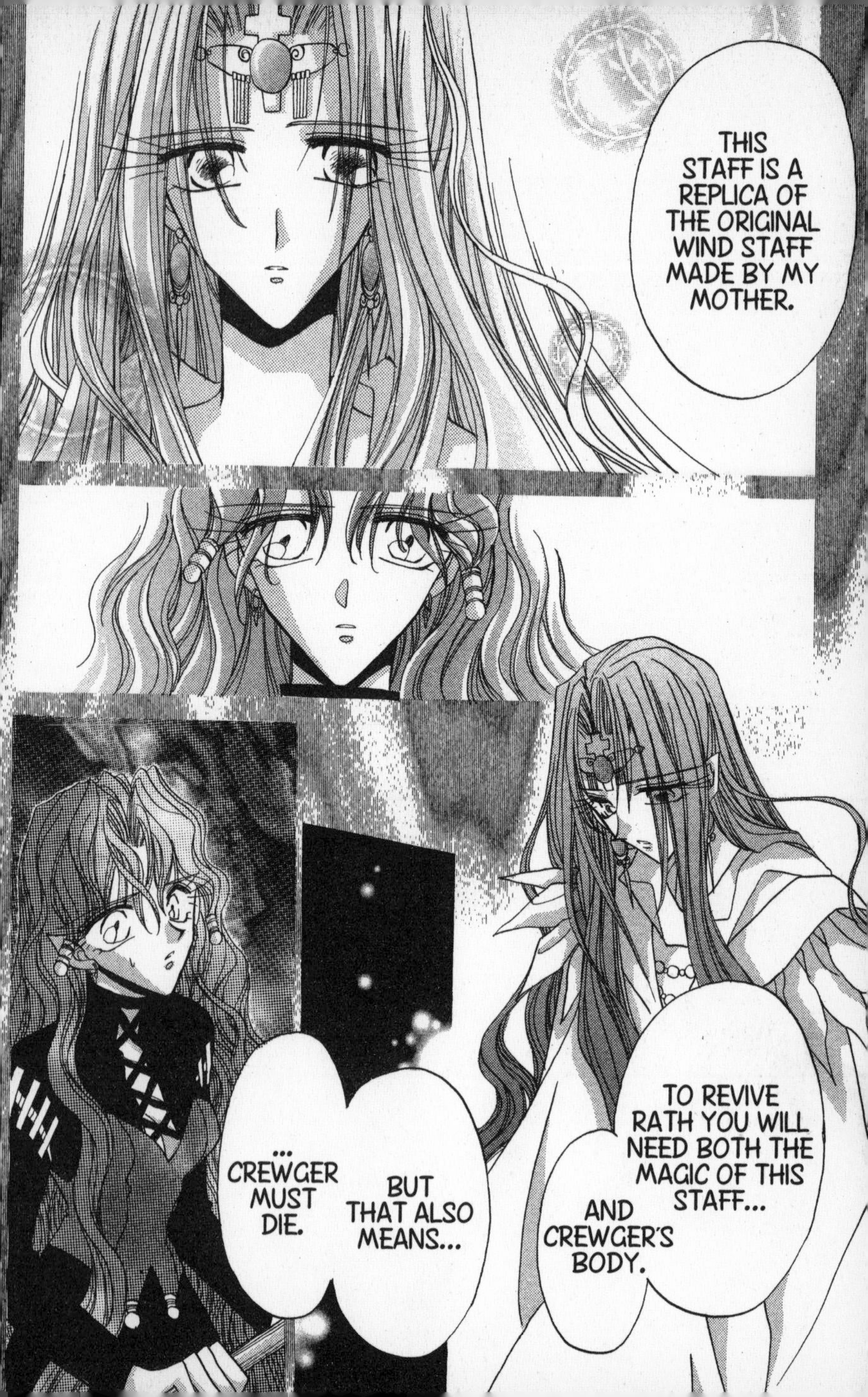
THIS STAFF IS A REPLICA OF THE ORIGINAL WIND STAFF MADE BY MY MOTHER.
TO REVIVE RATH YOU WILL NEED BOTH THE MAGIC OF THIS STAFF...
AND CREWGER'S BODY.
BUT THAT ALSO MEANS...
... CREWGER MUST DIE.

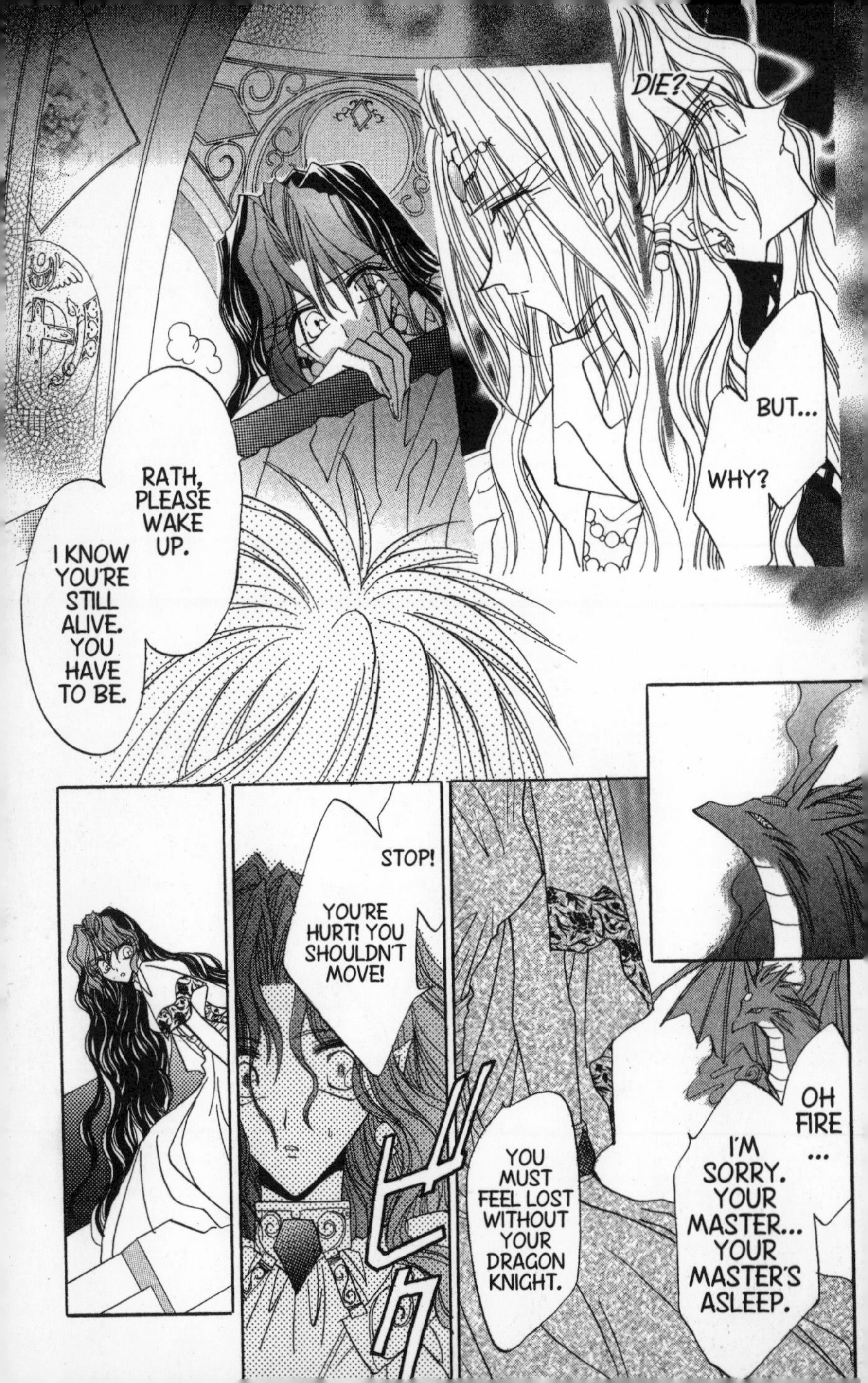
DIE?
BUT...
WHY?
RATH, PLEASE WAKE UP.
I KNOW YOU'RE STILL ALIVE. YOU HAVE TO BE.
OH FIRE...
I'M SORRY. YOUR MASTER... YOUR MASTER'S ASLEEP.
YOU MUST FEEL LOST WITHOUT YOUR DRAGON KNIGHT.
STOP!
YOU'RE HURT! YOU SHOULDN'T MOVE!

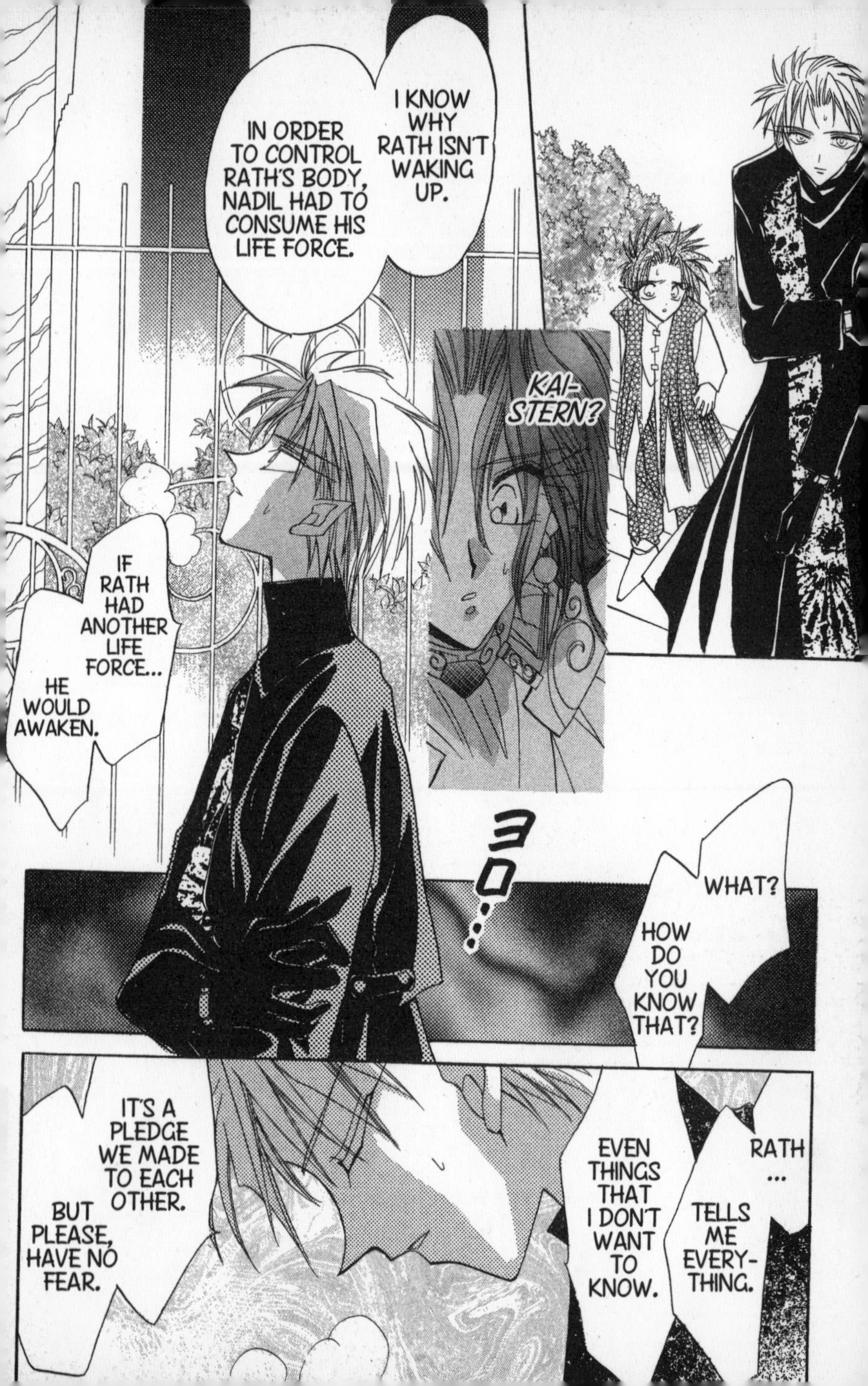
I KNOW WHY RATH ISN'T WAKING UP.
IN ORDER TO CONTROL RATH'S BODY, NADIL HAD TO CONSUME HIS LIFE FORCE.
KAI-STERN?
IF RATH HAD ANOTHER LIFE FORCE...
HE WOULD AWAKEN.
ヨロ...
WHAT?
HOW DO YOU KNOW THAT?
RATH...
TELLS ME EVERYTHING.
EVEN THINGS THAT I DON'T WANT TO KNOW.
IT'S A PLEDGE WE MADE TO EACH OTHER.
BUT PLEASE, HAVE NO FEAR.

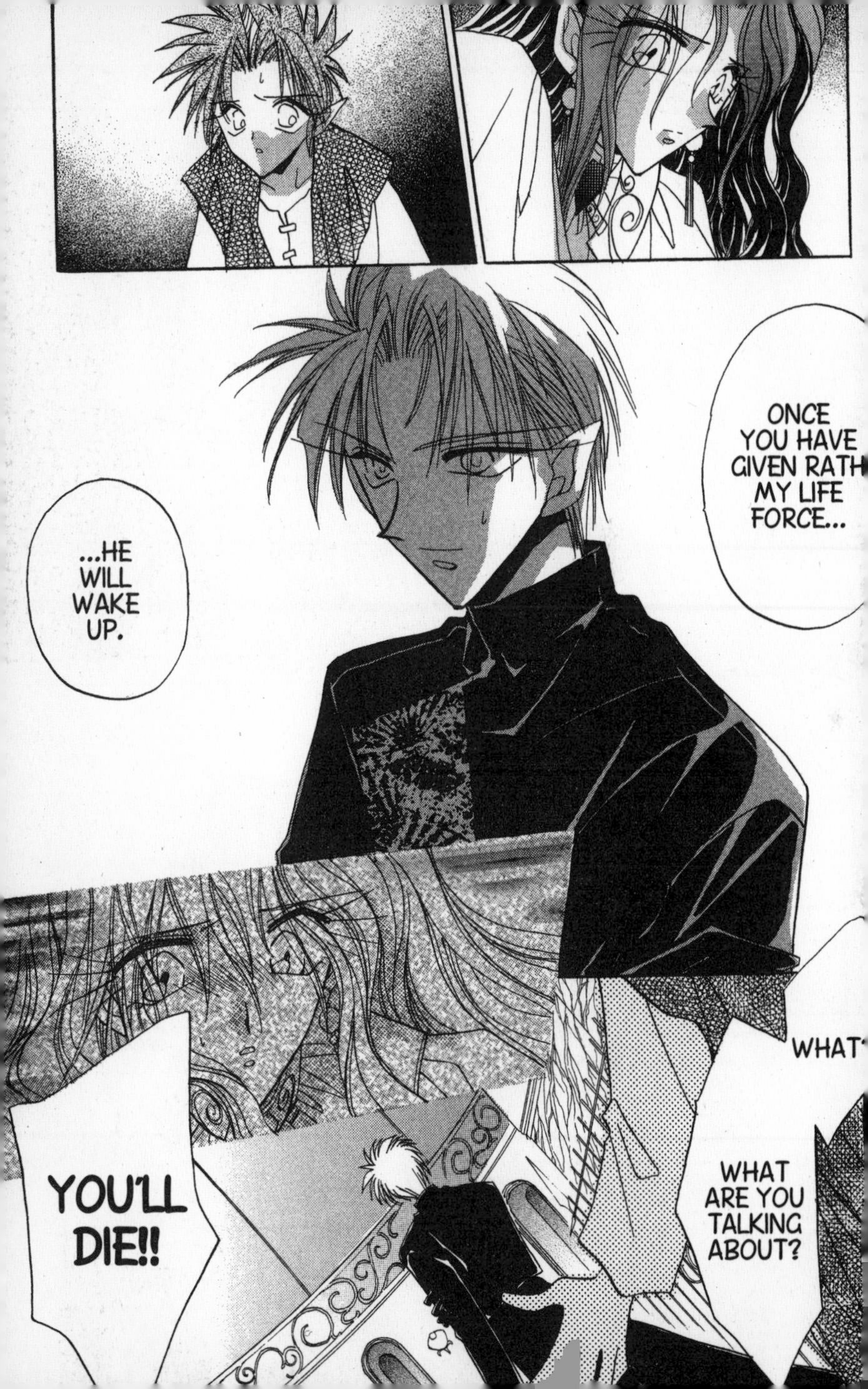
ONCE YOU HAVE GIVEN RATH MY LIFE FORCE...
...HE WILL WAKE UP.
WHAT-
WHAT ARE YOU TALKING ABOUT?
YOU'LL DIE!!

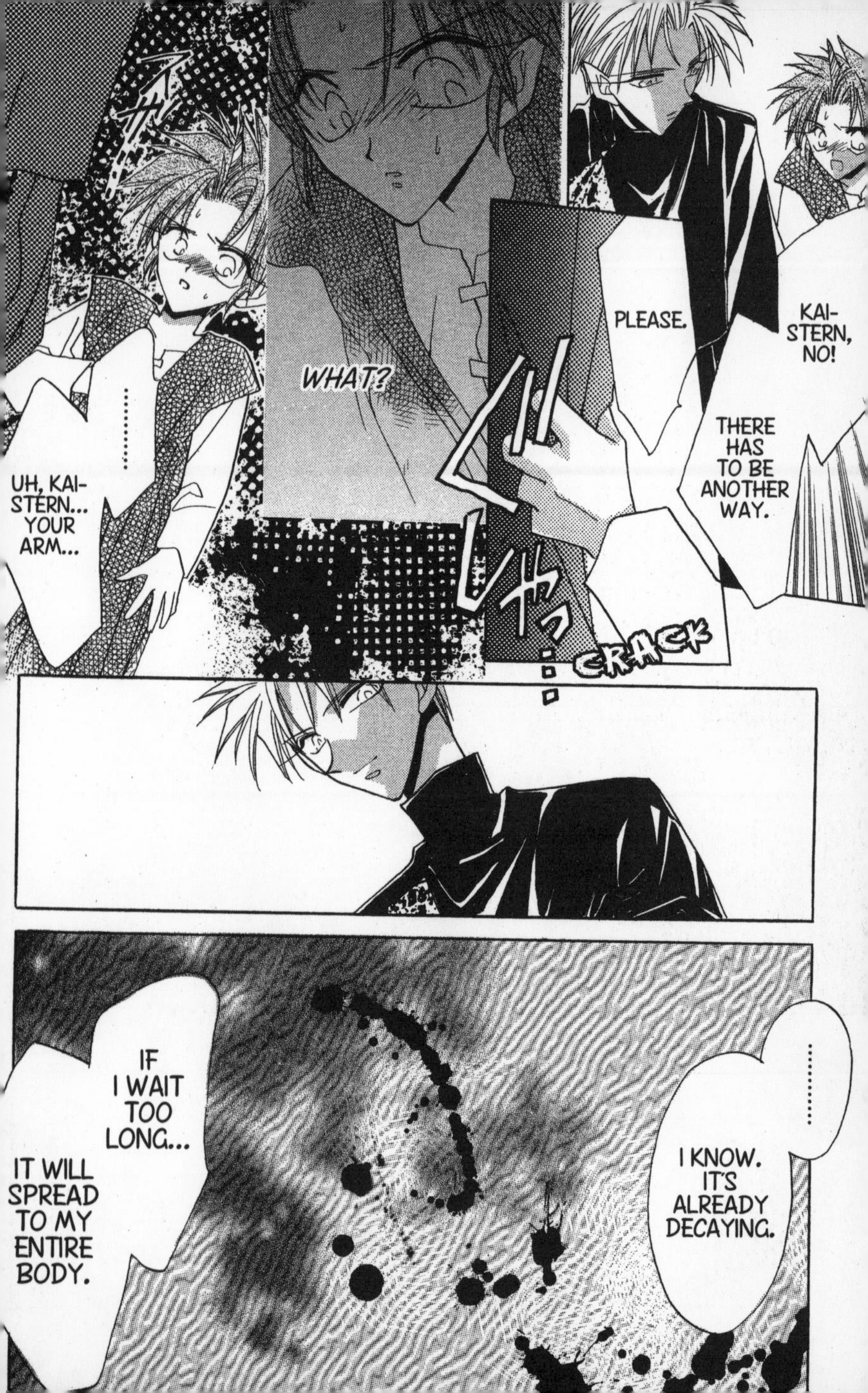
KAI-STERN, NO!
THERE HAS TO BE ANOTHER WAY.
PLEASE.
CRACK
WHAT?
......
UH, KAI-STERN... YOUR ARM...
......
I KNOW. IT'S ALREADY DECAYING.
IF I WAIT TOO LONG...
IT WILL SPREAD TO MY ENTIRE BODY.

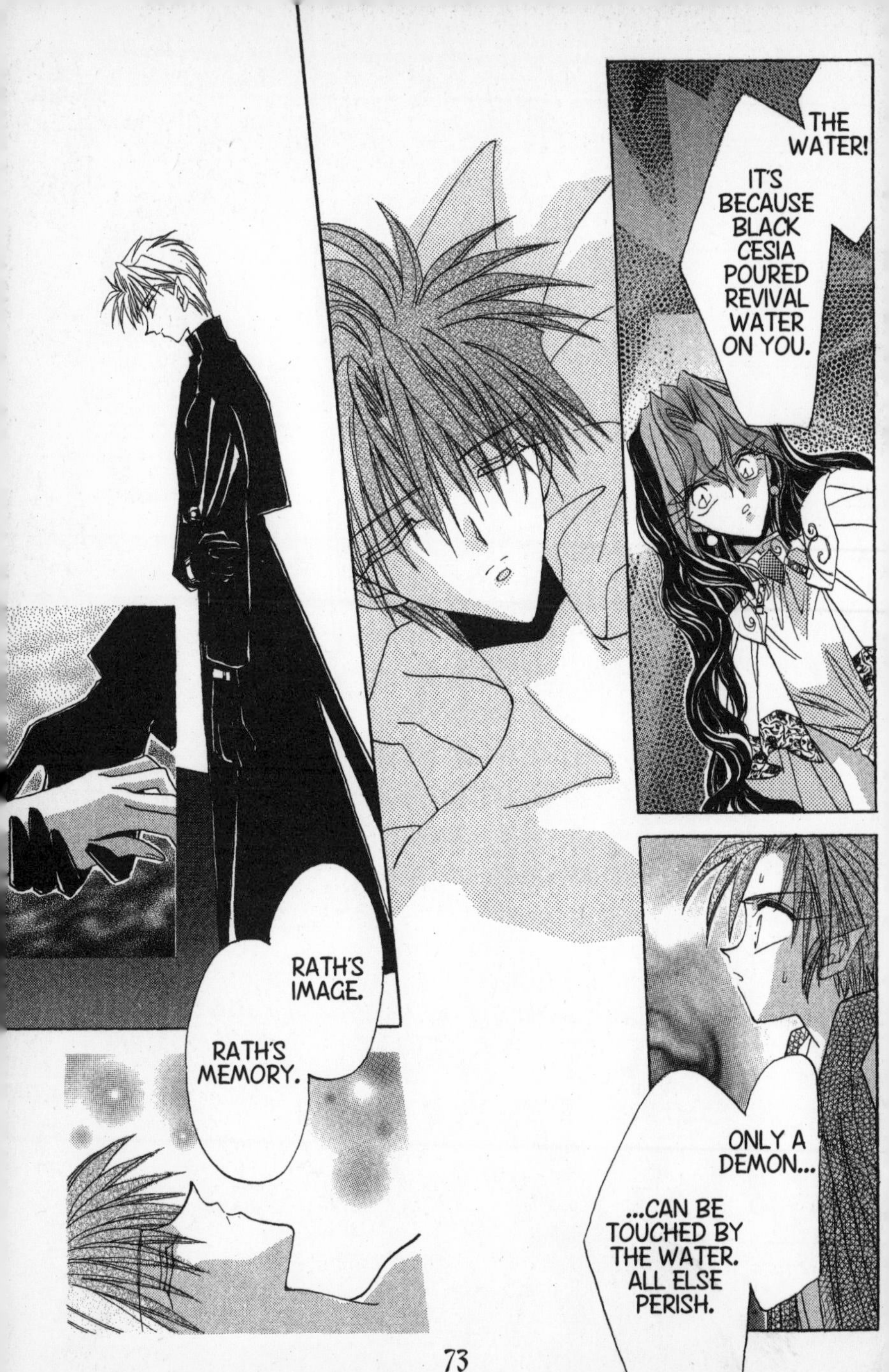
THE WATER!
IT'S BECAUSE BLACK CESIA POURED REVIVAL WATER ON YOU.
RATH'S IMAGE.
RATH'S MEMORY.
ONLY A DEMON...
...CAN BE TOUCHED BY THE WATER. ALL ELSE PERISH.

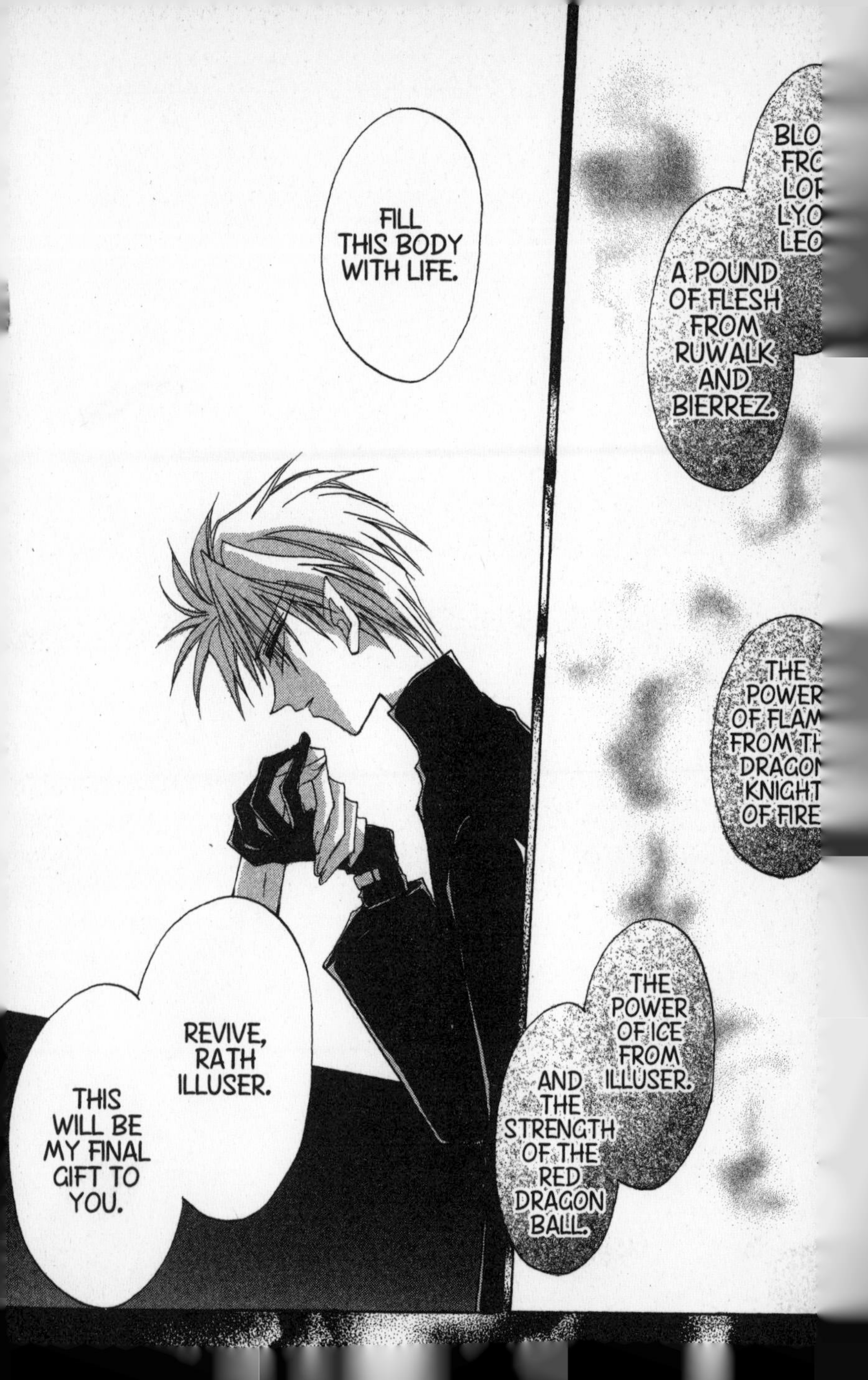
BLO FRO LOR LYO LEO
A POUND OF FLESH FROM RUWALK AND BIERREZ.
THE POWER OF FLAM FROM TH DRAGON KNIGHT OF FIRE
THE POWER OF ICE FROM ILLUSER.
AND THE STRENGTH OF THE RED DRAGON BALL.
FILL THIS BODY WITH LIFE.
REVIVE, RATH ILLUSER.
THIS WILL BE MY FINAL GIFT TO YOU.

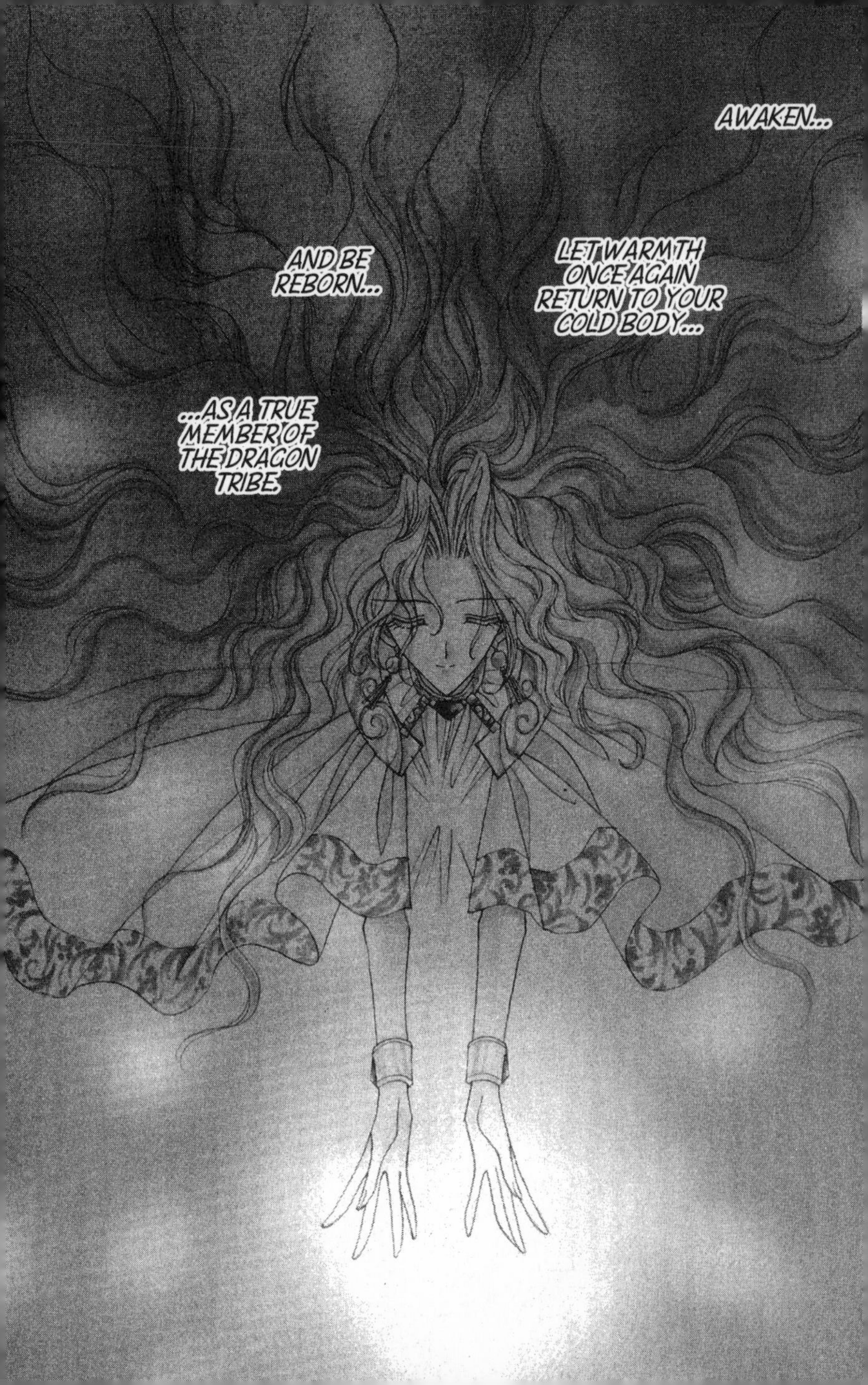
AWAKEN...
LET WARMTH ONCE AGAIN RETURN TO YOUR COLD BODY...
AND BE REBORN...
...AS A TRUE MEMBER OF THE DRAGON TRIBE.

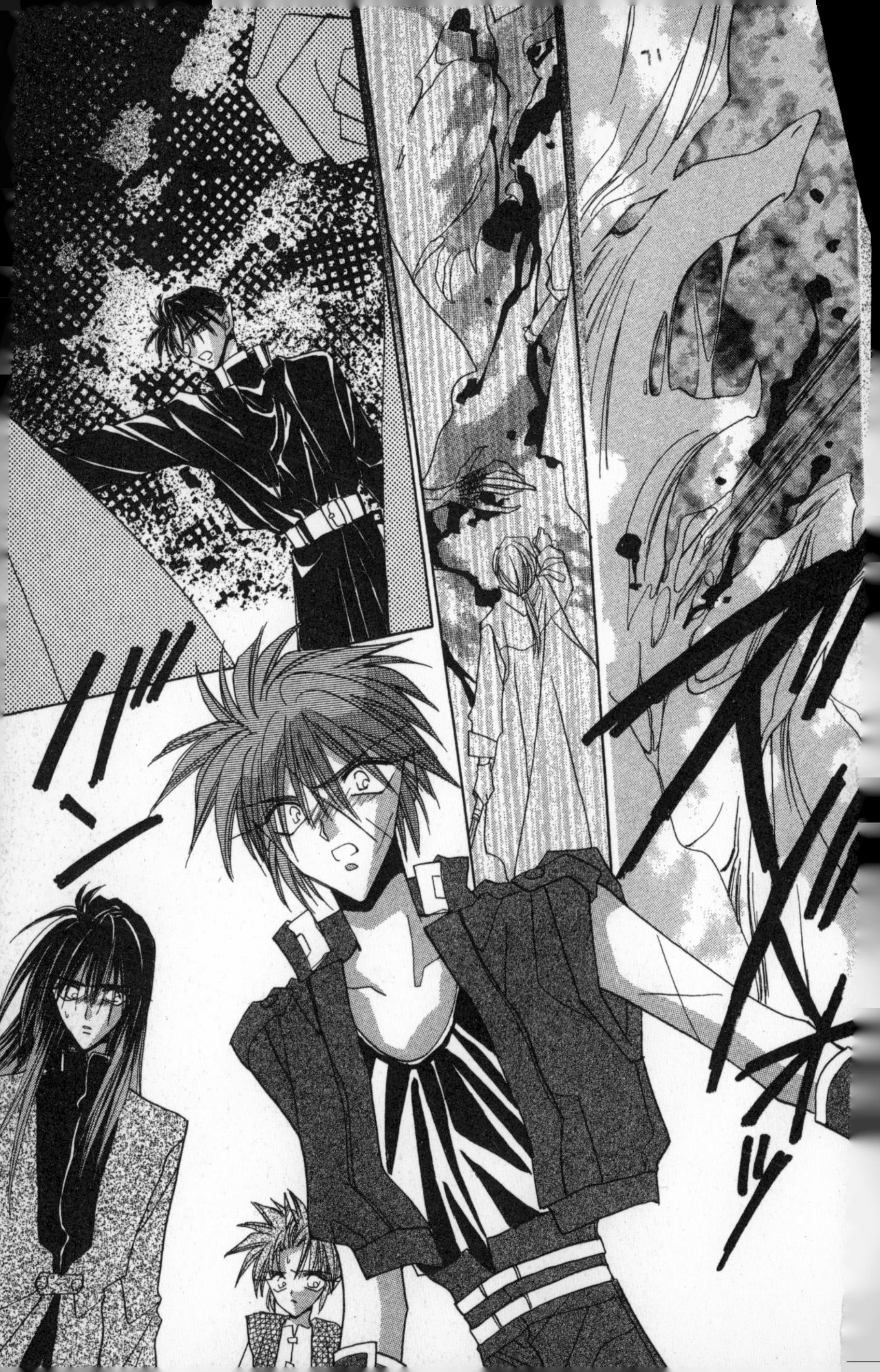

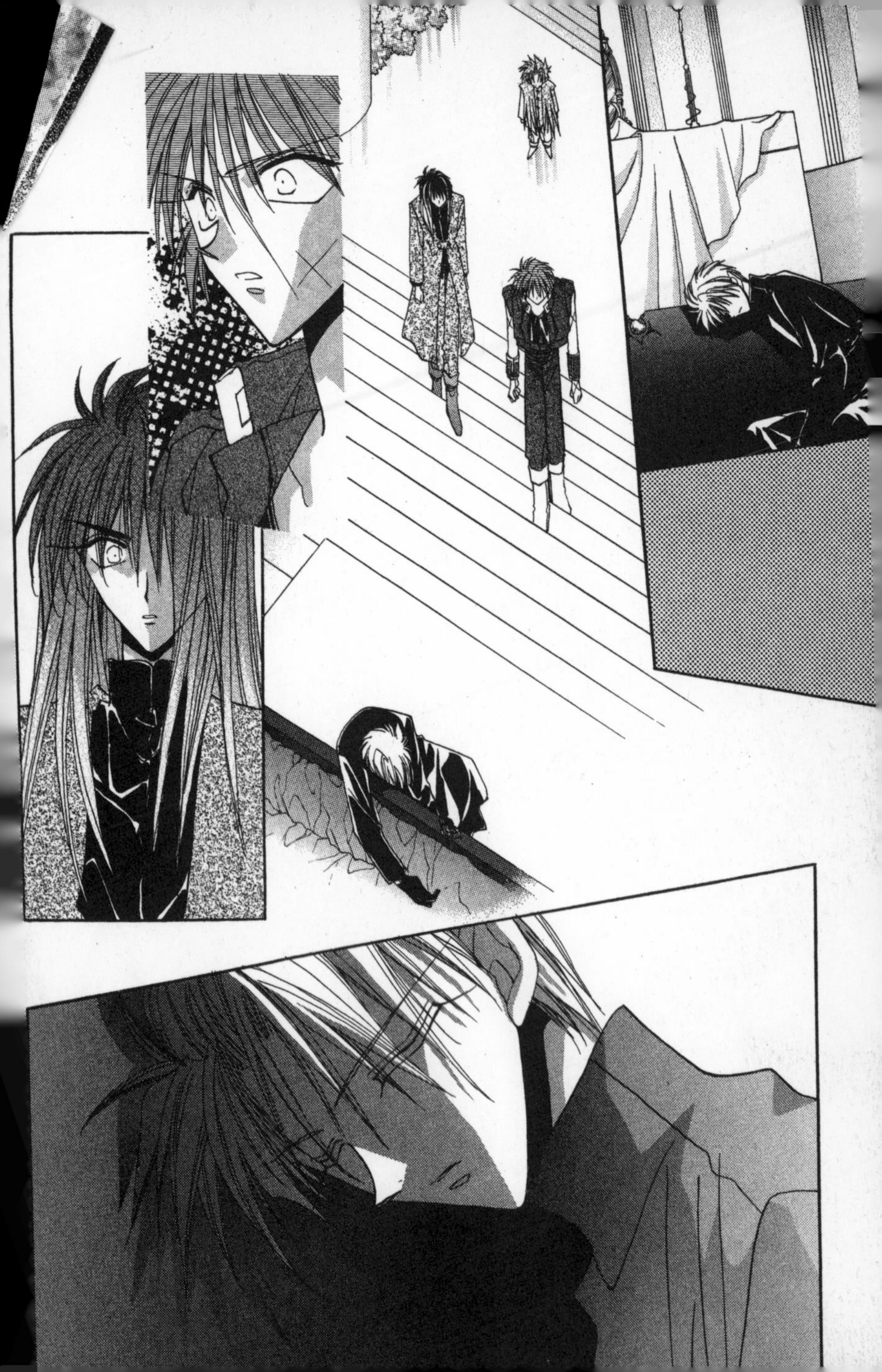

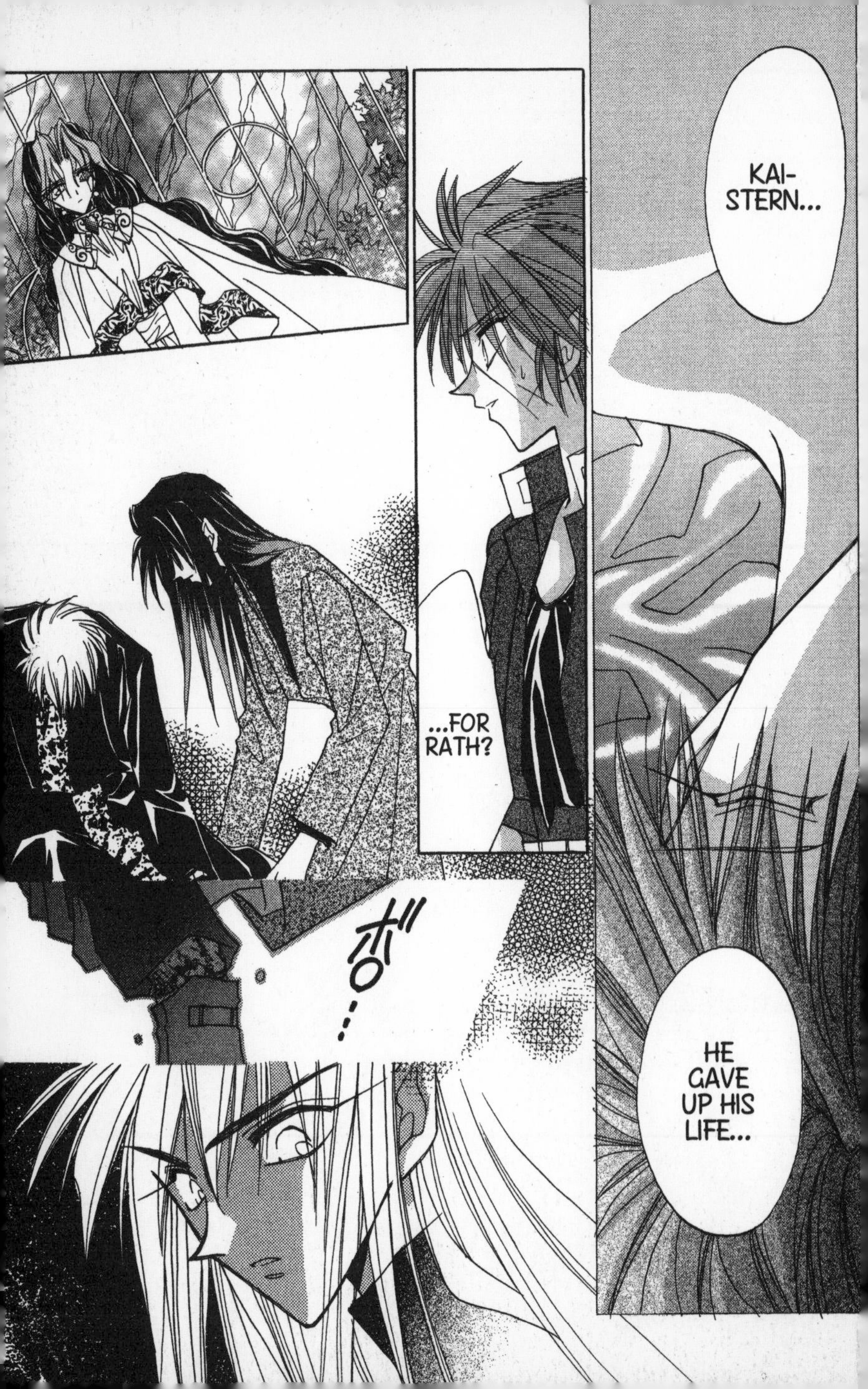
KAI-STERN...
HE GAVE UP HIS LIFE...
...FOR RATH?

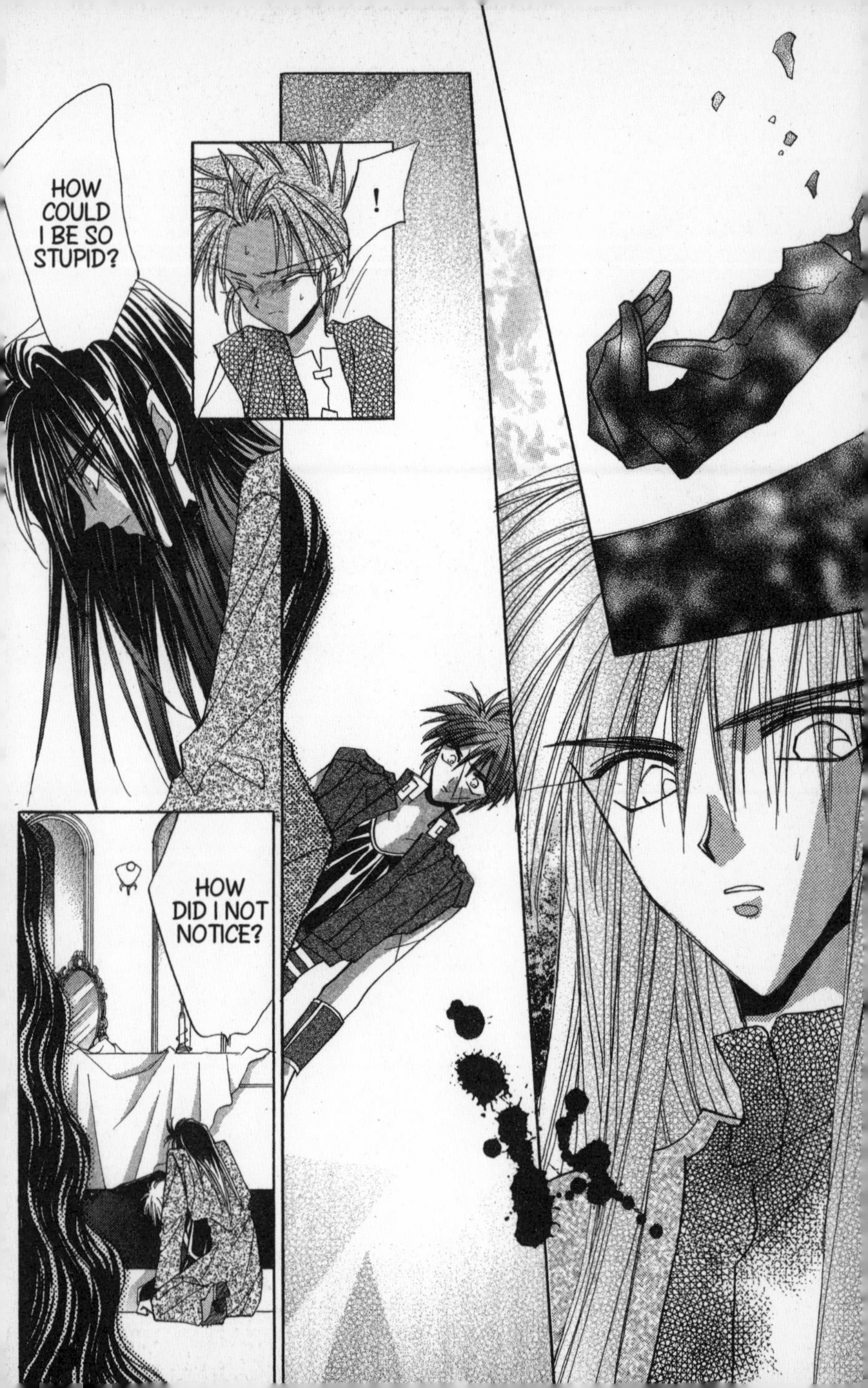
!
HOW COULD I BE SO STUPID?
HOW DID I NOT NOTICE?

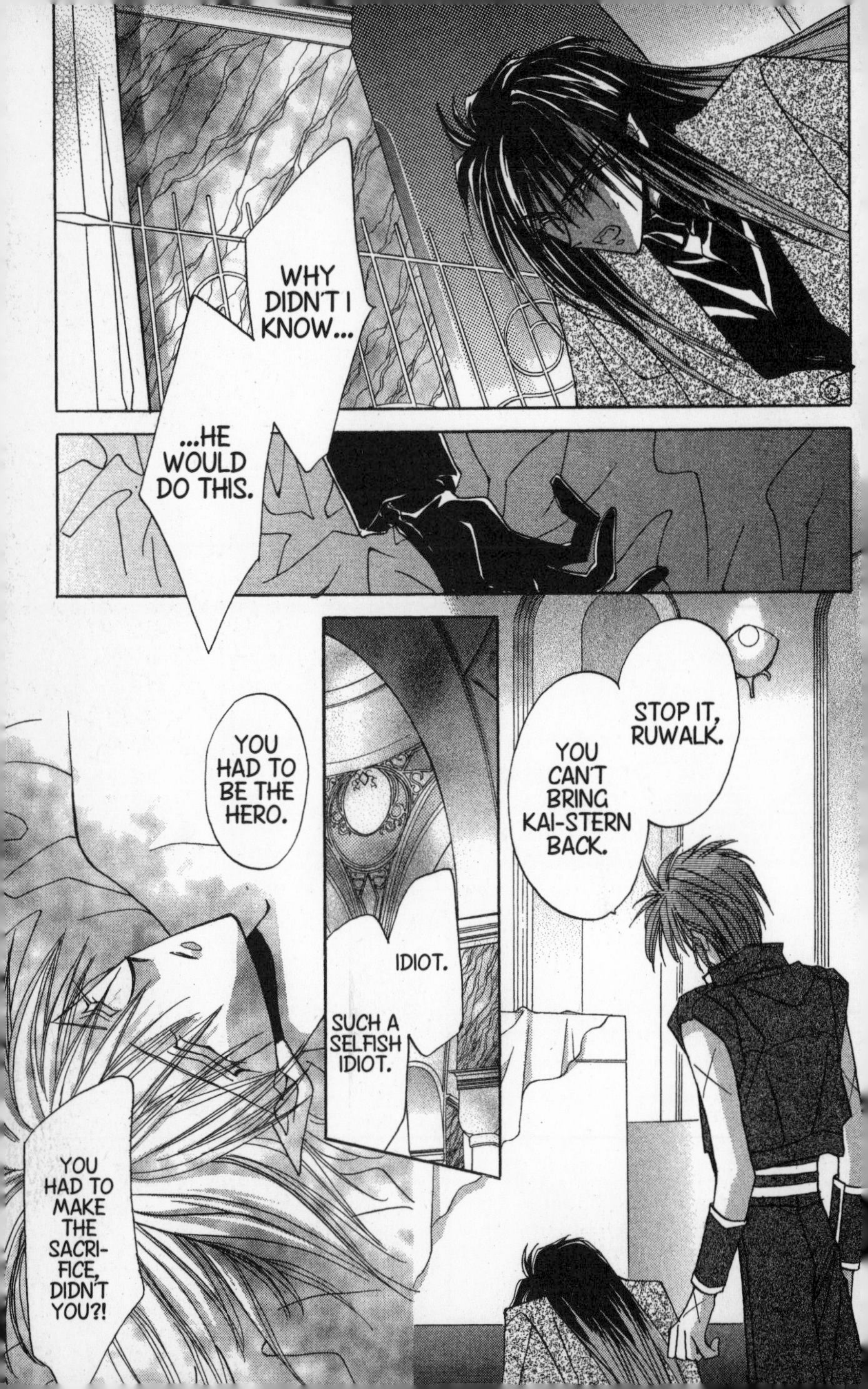
WHY DIDN'T I KNOW...
...HE WOULD DO THIS.
STOP IT, RUWALK.
YOU CAN'T BRING KAI-STERN BACK.
IDIOT.
SUCH A SELFISH IDIOT.
YOU HAD TO BE THE HERO.
YOU HAD TO MAKE THE SACRIFICE, DIDN'T YOU?!

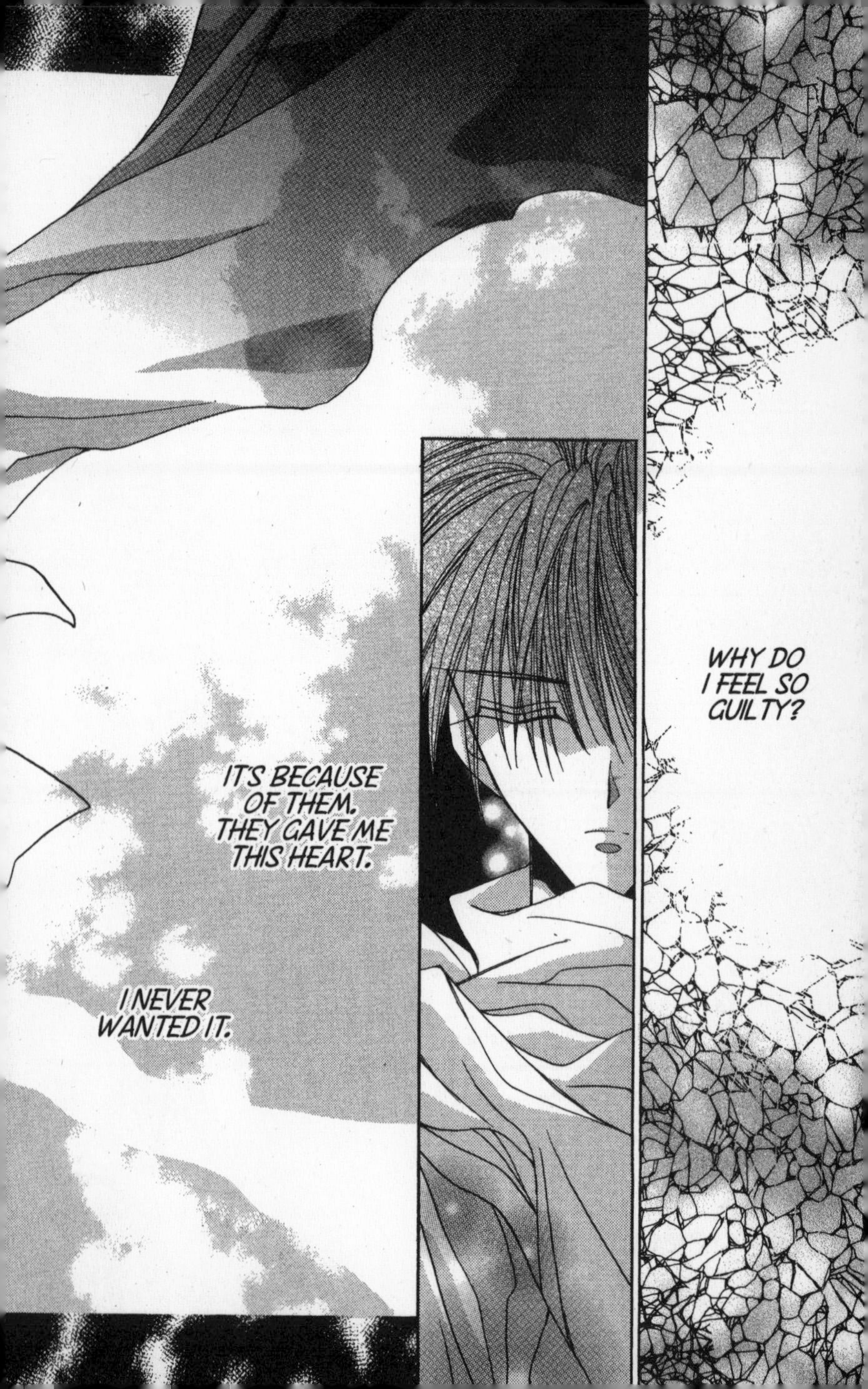
WHY DO I FEEL SO GUILTY?
IT'S BECAUSE OF THEM.
THEY GAVE ME THIS HEART.
I NEVER WANTED IT.

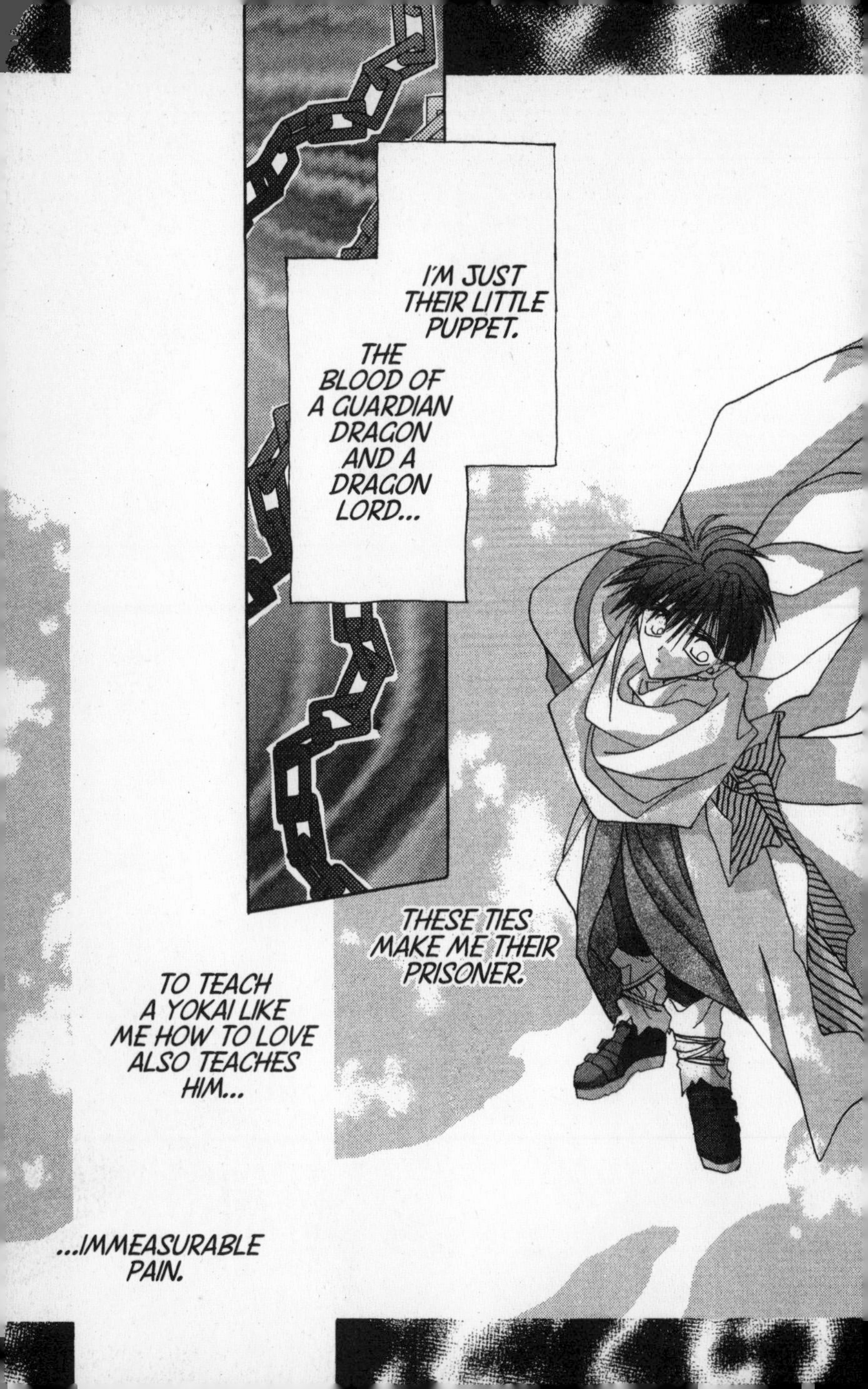
I'M JUST THEIR LITTLE PUPPET.
THE BLOOD OF A GUARDIAN DRAGON AND A DRAGON LORD...
THESE TIES MAKE ME THEIR PRISONER.
TO TEACH A YOKAI LIKE ME HOW TO LOVE ALSO TEACHES HIM...
...IMMEASURABLE PAIN.

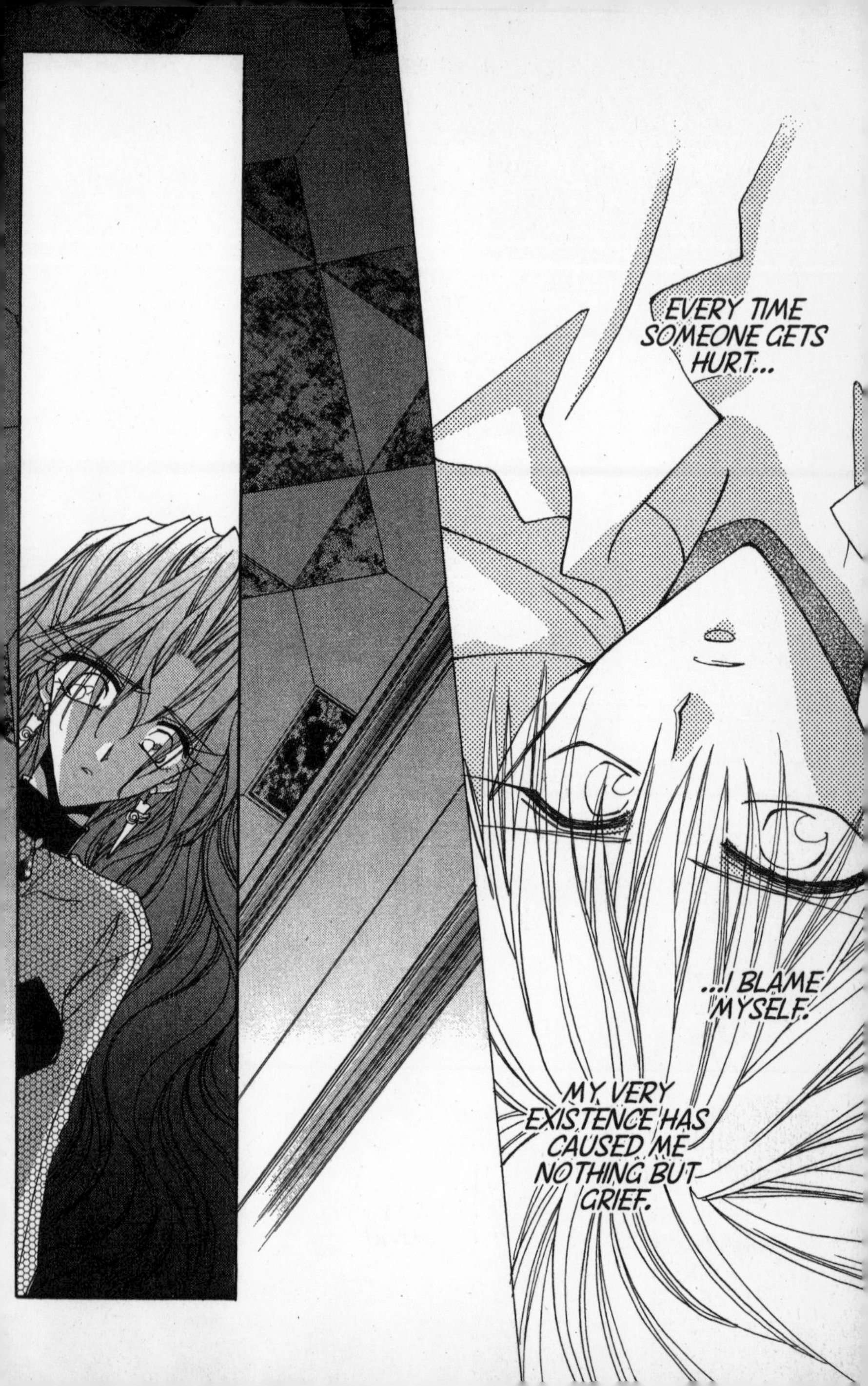
EVERY TIME SOMEONE GETS HURT...
...I BLAME MYSELF.
MY VERY EXISTENCE HAS CAUSED ME NOTHING BUT GRIEF.

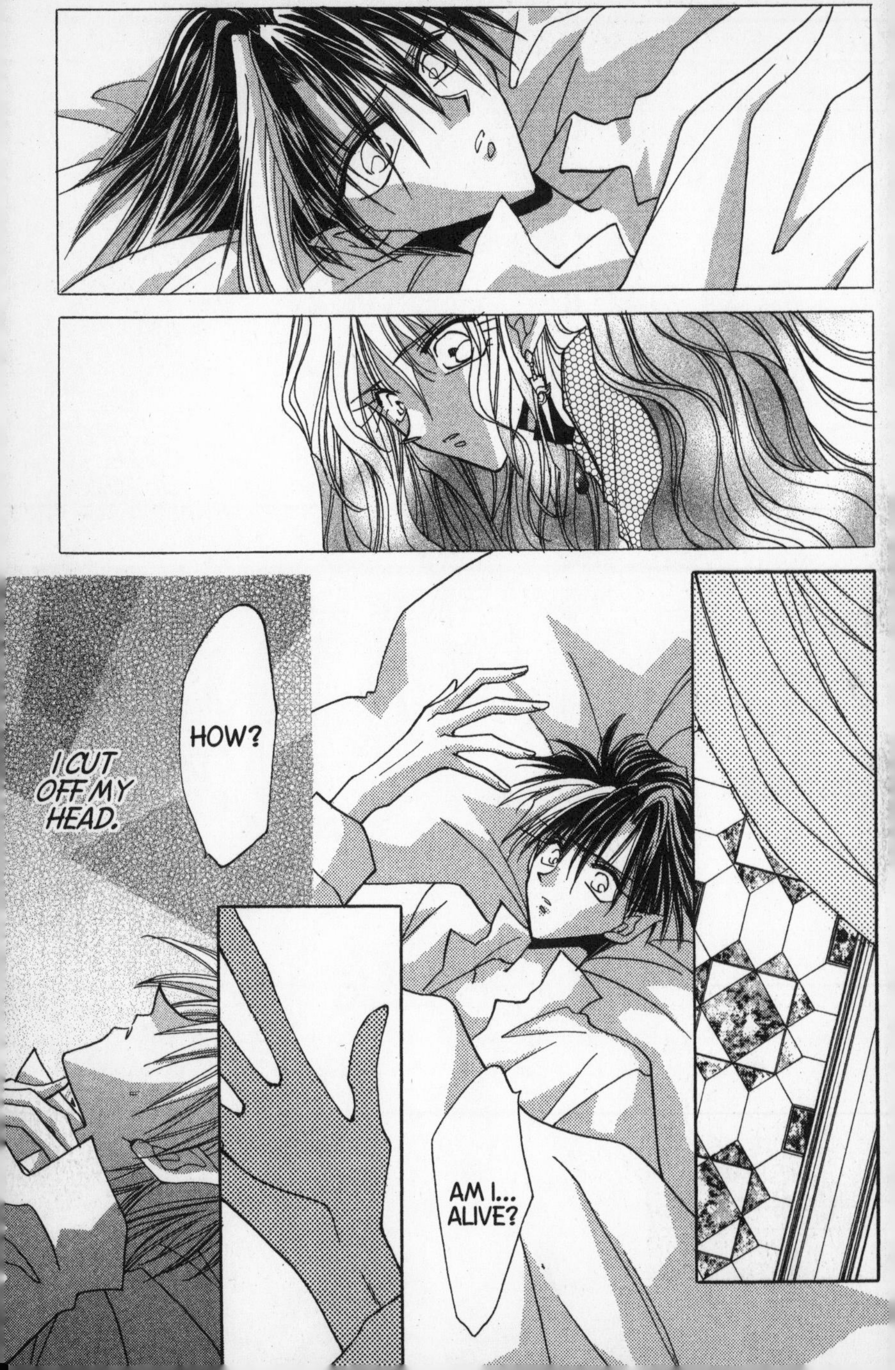
HOW?
I CUT OFF MY HEAD.
AM I... ALIVE?

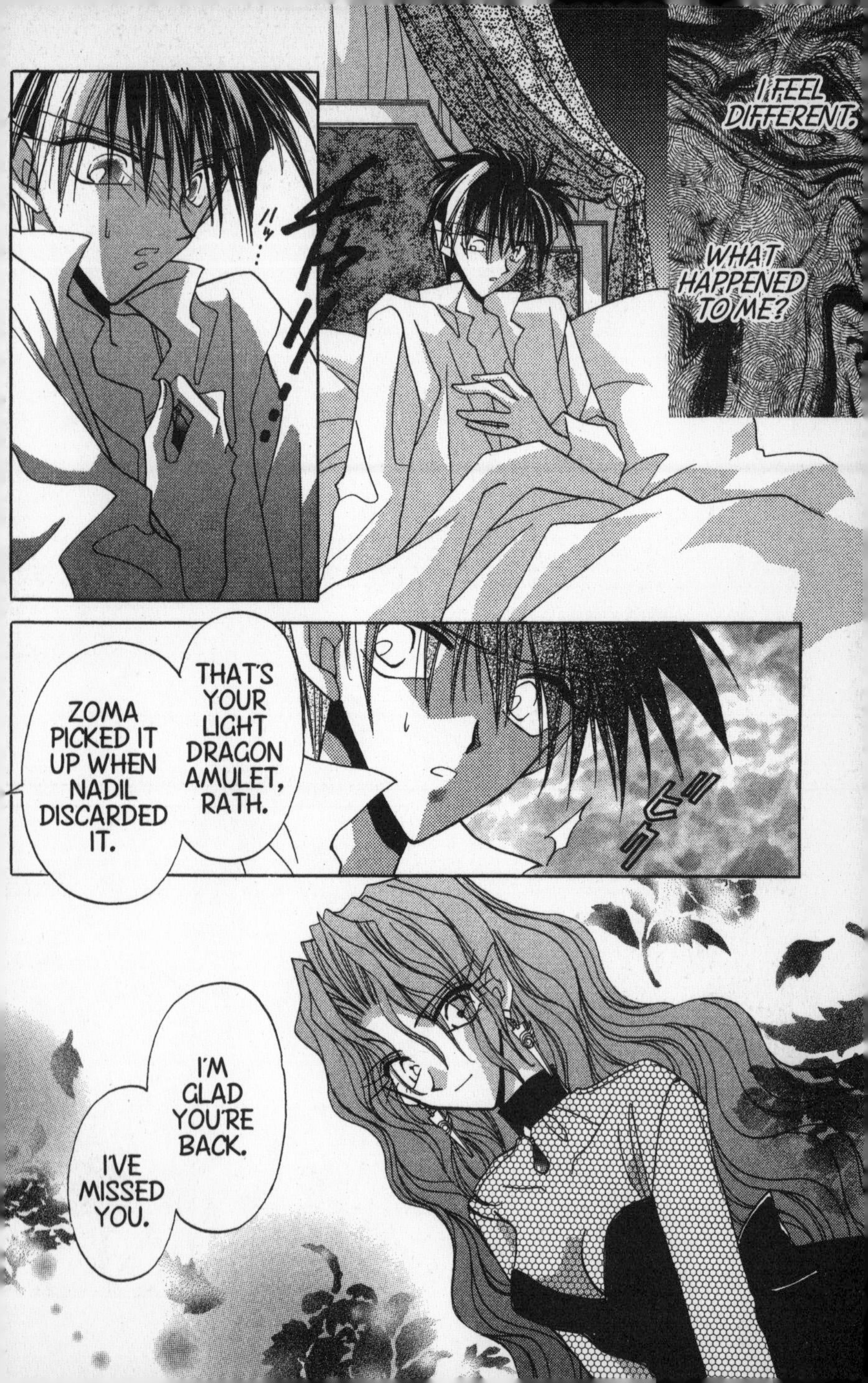
I FEEL DIFFERENT.
WHAT HAPPENED TO ME?
THAT'S YOUR LIGHT DRAGON AMULET, RATH.
ZOMA PICKED IT UP WHEN NADIL DISCARDED IT.
I'M GLAD YOU'RE BACK.
I'VE MISSED YOU.

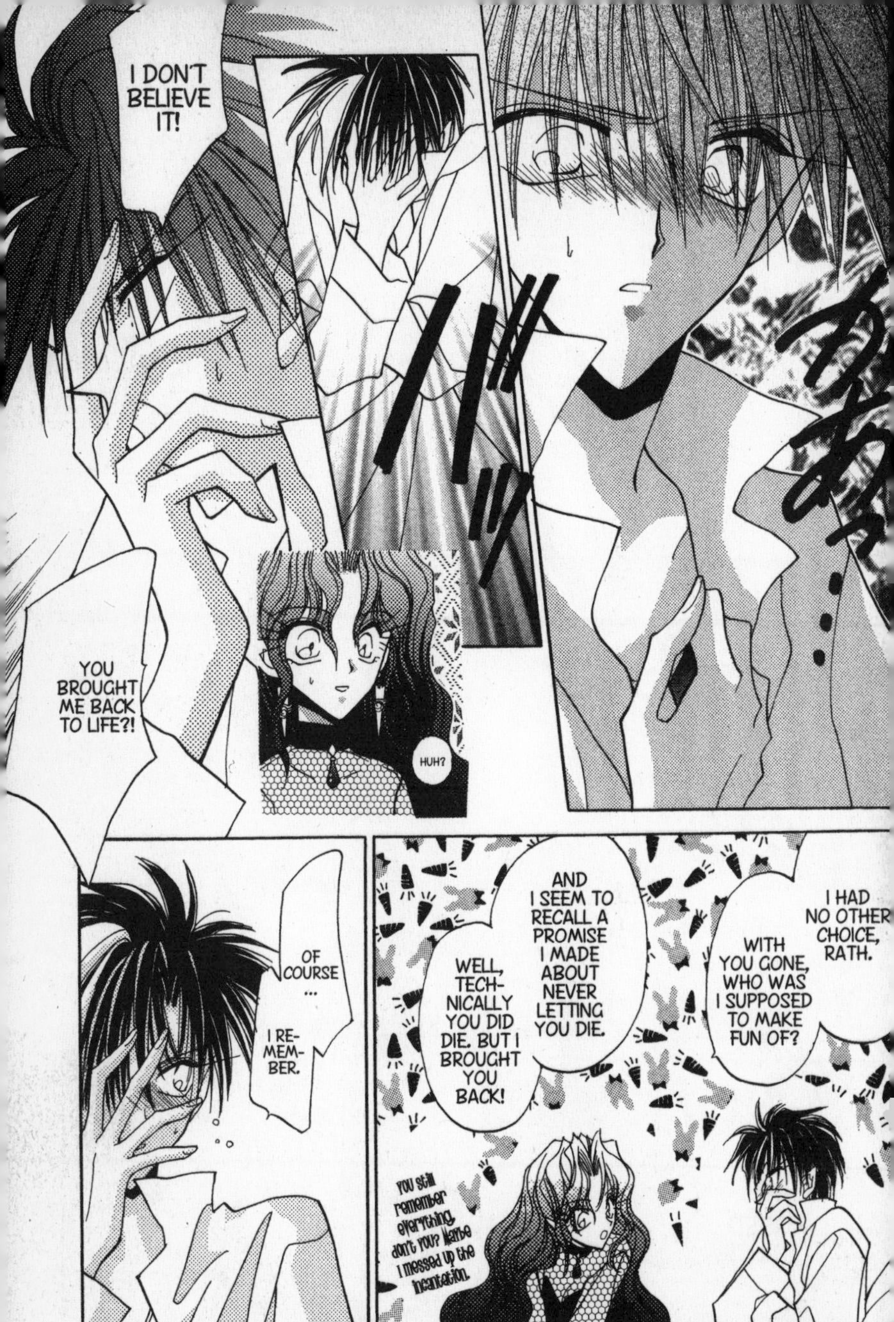
HUH?
I DON'T BELIEVE IT!
YOU BROUGHT ME BACK TO LIFE?!
I HAD NO OTHER CHOICE, RATH.
WITH YOU GONE, WHO WAS I SUPPOSED TO MAKE FUN OF?
AND I SEEM TO RECALL A PROMISE I MADE ABOUT NEVER LETTING YOU DIE.
WELL, TECHNICALLY YOU DID DIE. BUT I BROUGHT YOU BACK!
You still remember everything, don't you? Maybe I messed up the incantation.
OF COURSE ...
I REMEMBER.

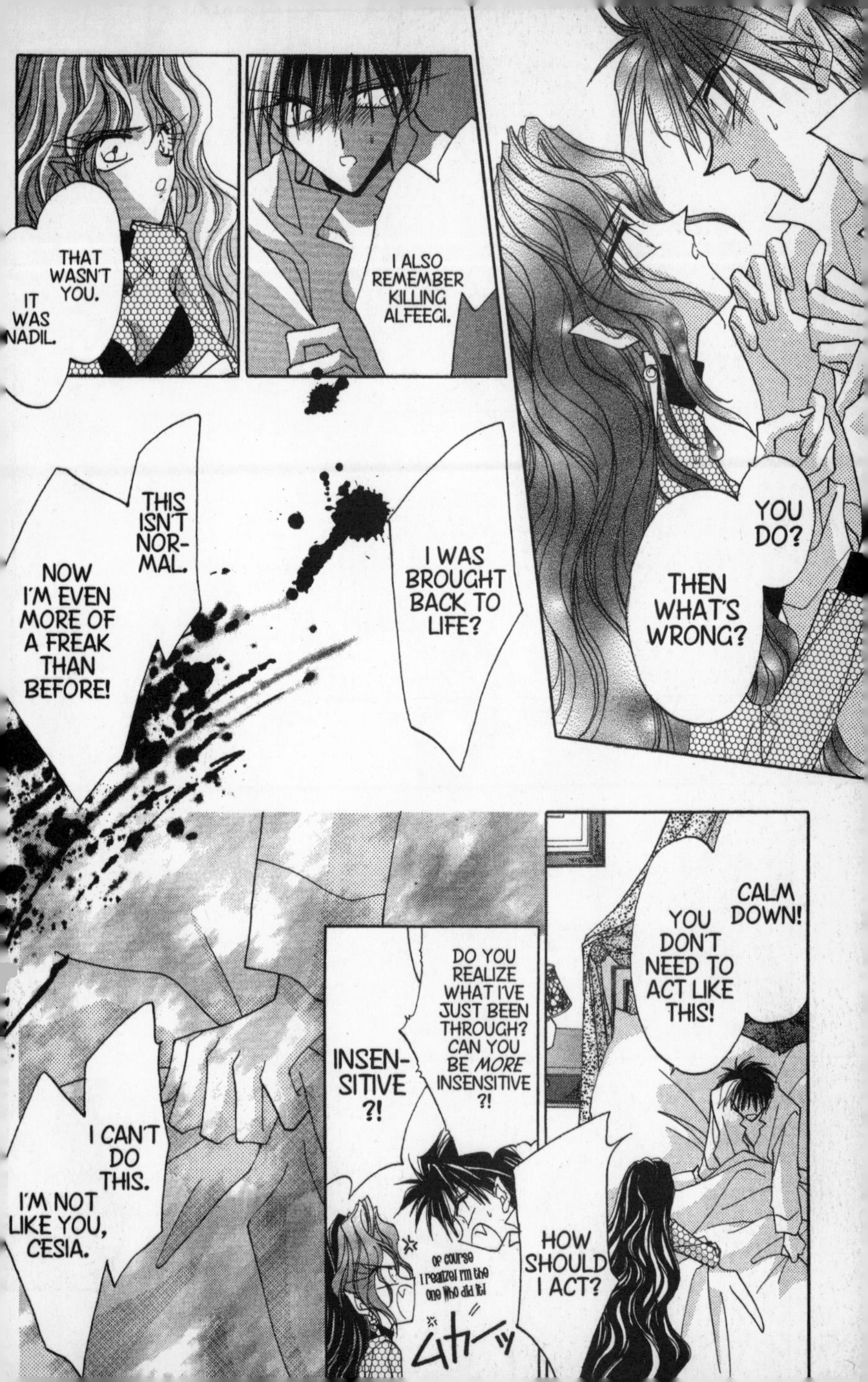
YOU DO?
THEN WHAT'S WRONG?
I ALSO REMEMBER KILLING ALFEEGI.
THAT WASN'T YOU.
IT WAS NADIL.
I WAS BROUGHT BACK TO LIFE?
THIS ISN'T NORMAL.
NOW I'M EVEN MORE OF A FREAK THAN BEFORE!
CALM DOWN!
YOU DON'T NEED TO ACT LIKE THIS!
HOW SHOULD I ACT?
DO YOU REALIZE WHAT I'VE JUST BEEN THROUGH? CAN YOU BE *MORE* INSENSITIVE?!
INSEN-SITIVE?!
Of course I realize! I'm the one who did it!
ムカーッ
I CAN'T DO THIS.
I'M NOT LIKE YOU, CESIA.

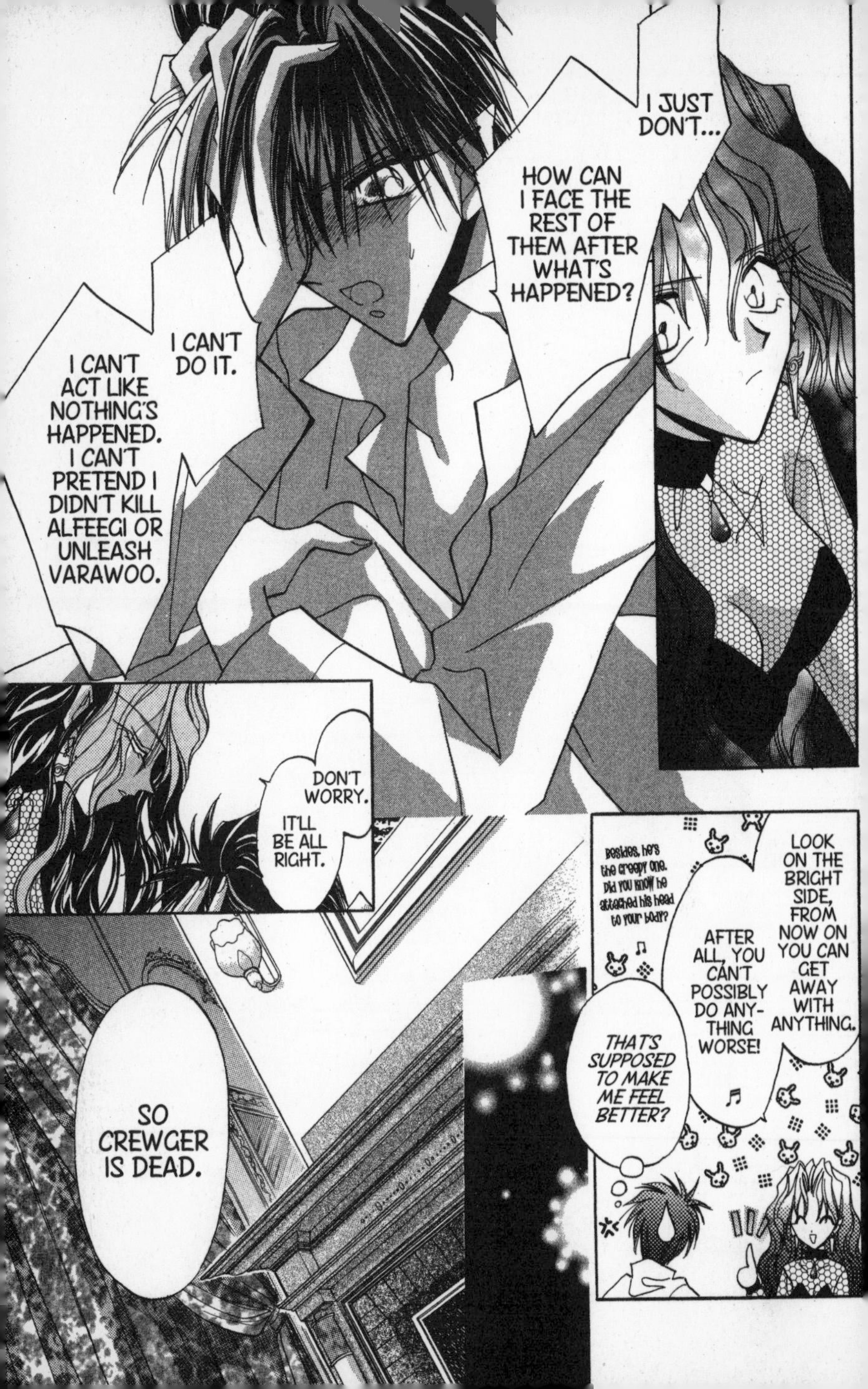
I JUST DON'T...
HOW CAN I FACE THE REST OF THEM AFTER WHAT'S HAPPENED?
I CAN'T DO IT.
I CAN'T ACT LIKE NOTHING'S HAPPENED. I CAN'T PRETEND I DIDN'T KILL ALFEEGI OR UNLEASH VARAWOO.
DON'T WORRY.
IT'LL BE ALL RIGHT.
LOOK ON THE BRIGHT SIDE, FROM NOW ON YOU CAN GET AWAY WITH ANYTHING.
AFTER ALL, YOU CAN'T POSSIBLY DO ANYTHING WORSE!
Besides, he's the creepy one. Did you know he attached his head to your body?
THAT'S SUPPOSED TO MAKE ME FEEL BETTER?
SO CREWGER IS DEAD.

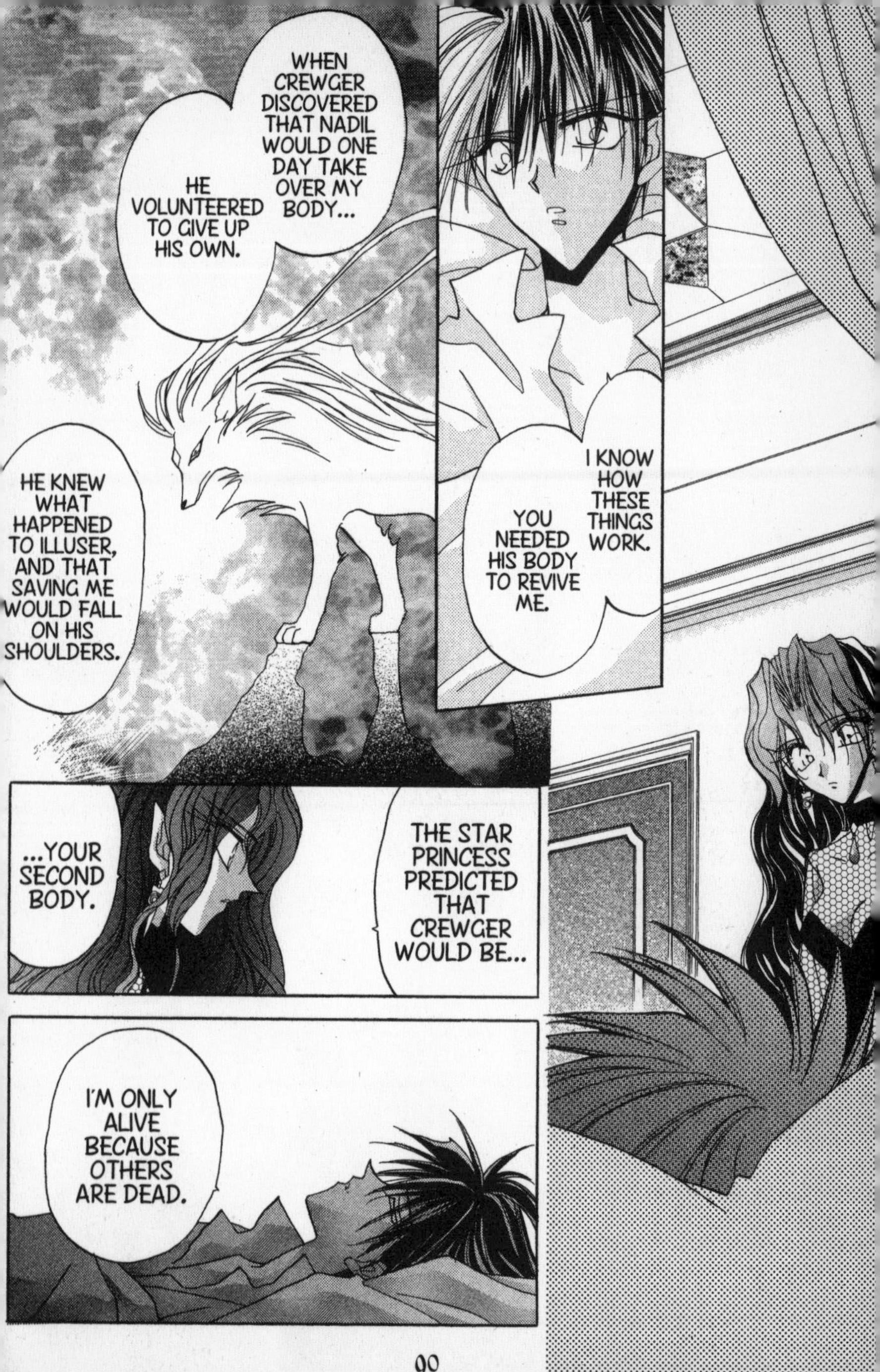
I KNOW HOW THESE THINGS WORK.
YOU NEEDED HIS BODY TO REVIVE ME.
WHEN CREWGER DISCOVERED THAT NADIL WOULD ONE DAY TAKE OVER MY BODY...
HE VOLUNTEERED TO GIVE UP HIS OWN.
HE KNEW WHAT HAPPENED TO ILLUSER, AND THAT SAVING ME WOULD FALL ON HIS SHOULDERS.
THE STAR PRINCESS PREDICTED THAT CREWGER WOULD BE...
...YOUR SECOND BODY.
I'M ONLY ALIVE BECAUSE OTHERS ARE DEAD.

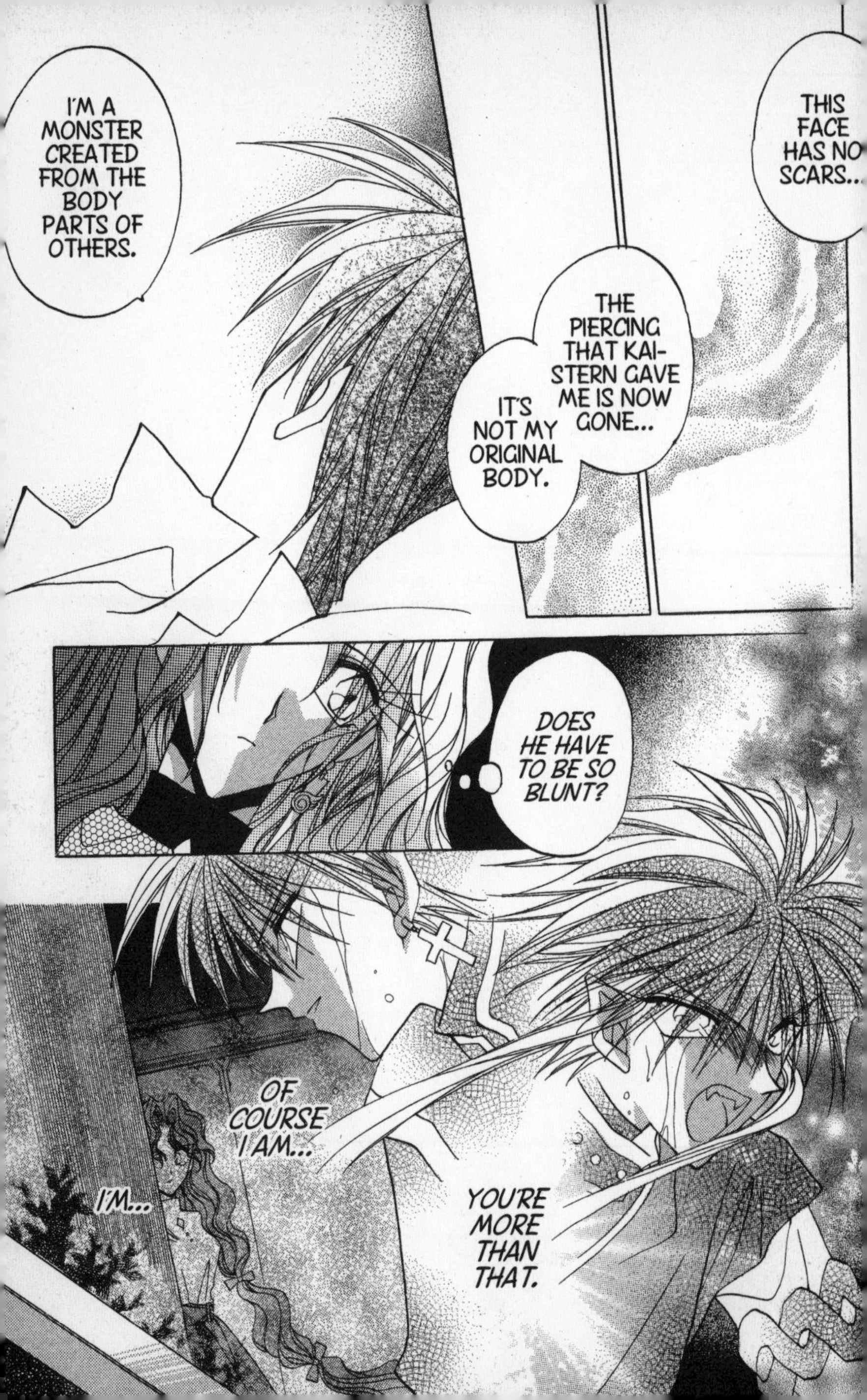
THIS FACE HAS NO SCARS...
THE PIERCING THAT KAISTERN GAVE ME IS NOW GONE...
IT'S NOT MY ORIGINAL BODY.
I'M A MONSTER CREATED FROM THE BODY PARTS OF OTHERS.
DOES HE HAVE TO BE SO BLUNT?
OF COURSE I AM...
I'M...
YOU'RE MORE THAN THAT.

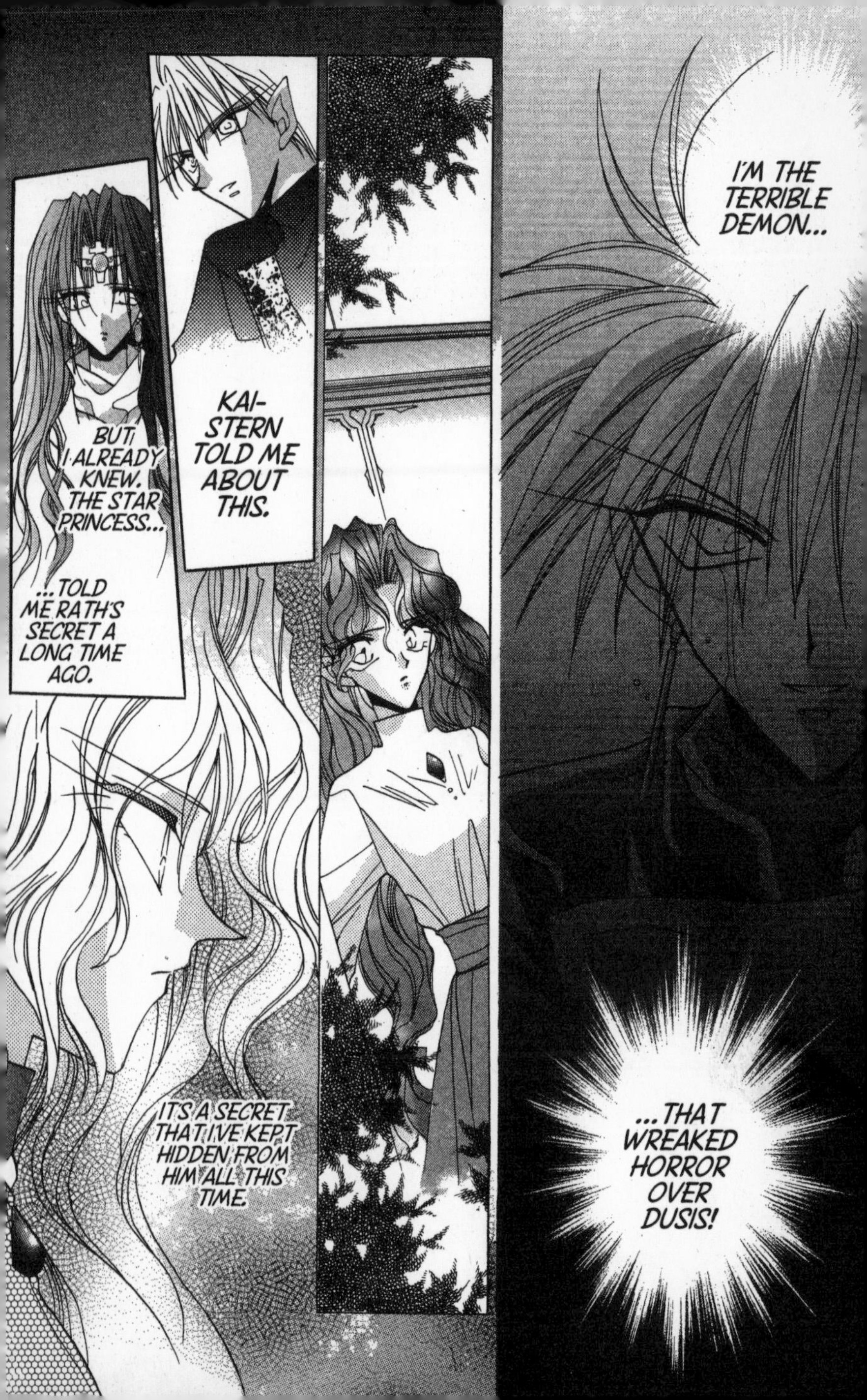
I'M THE TERRIBLE DEMON...
...THAT WREAKED HORROR OVER DUSIS!
KAI-STERN TOLD ME ABOUT THIS.
BUT I ALREADY KNEW. THE STAR PRINCESS...
...TOLD ME RATH'S SECRET A LONG TIME AGO.
IT'S A SECRET THAT I'VE KEPT HIDDEN FROM HIM ALL THIS TIME.

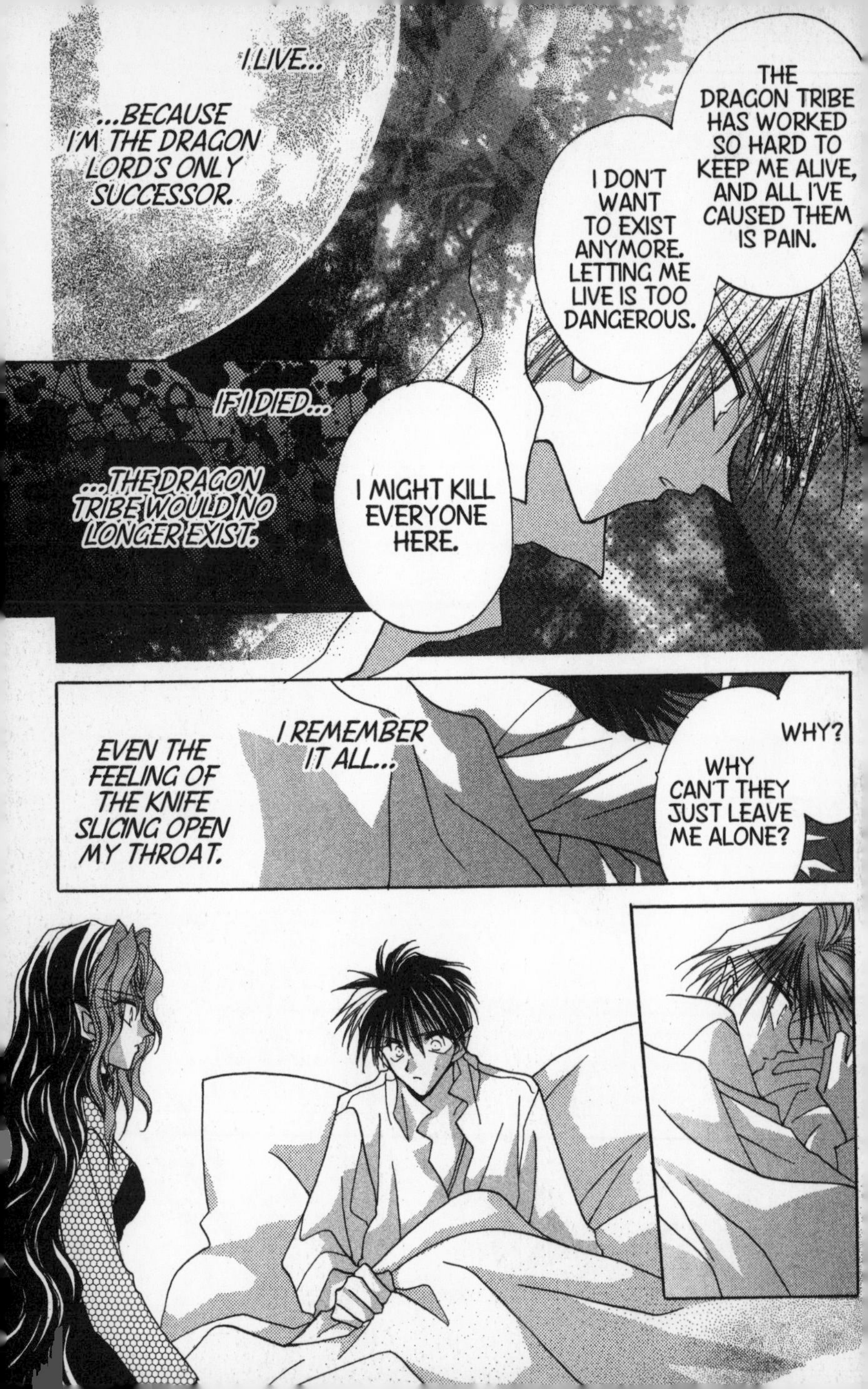
THE DRAGON TRIBE HAS WORKED SO HARD TO KEEP ME ALIVE, AND ALL I'VE CAUSED THEM IS PAIN.
I DON'T WANT TO EXIST ANYMORE. LETTING ME LIVE IS TOO DANGEROUS.
I LIVE...
...BECAUSE I'M THE DRAGON LORD'S ONLY SUCCESSOR.
I MIGHT KILL EVERYONE HERE.
IF I DIED...
...THE DRAGON TRIBE WOULD NO LONGER EXIST.
WHY?
WHY CAN'T THEY JUST LEAVE ME ALONE?
I REMEMBER IT ALL...
EVEN THE FEELING OF THE KNIFE SLICING OPEN MY THROAT.

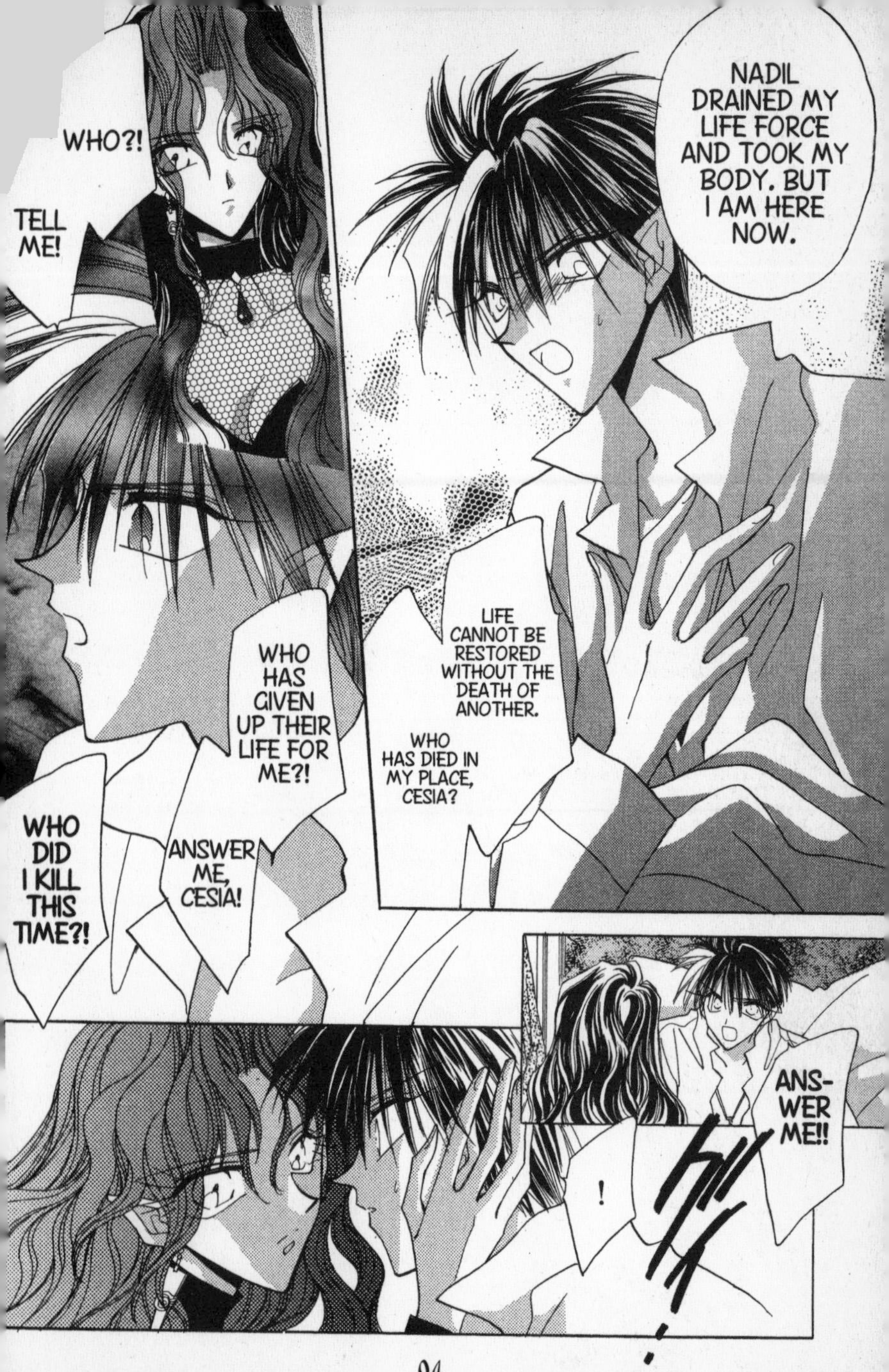
NADIL DRAINED MY LIFE FORCE AND TOOK MY BODY. BUT I AM HERE NOW.
LIFE CANNOT BE RESTORED WITHOUT THE DEATH OF ANOTHER.
WHO HAS DIED IN MY PLACE, CESIA?
WHO?!
TELL ME!
WHO HAS GIVEN UP THEIR LIFE FOR ME?!
ANSWER ME, CESIA!
WHO DID I KILL THIS TIME?!
ANS-WER ME!!
!

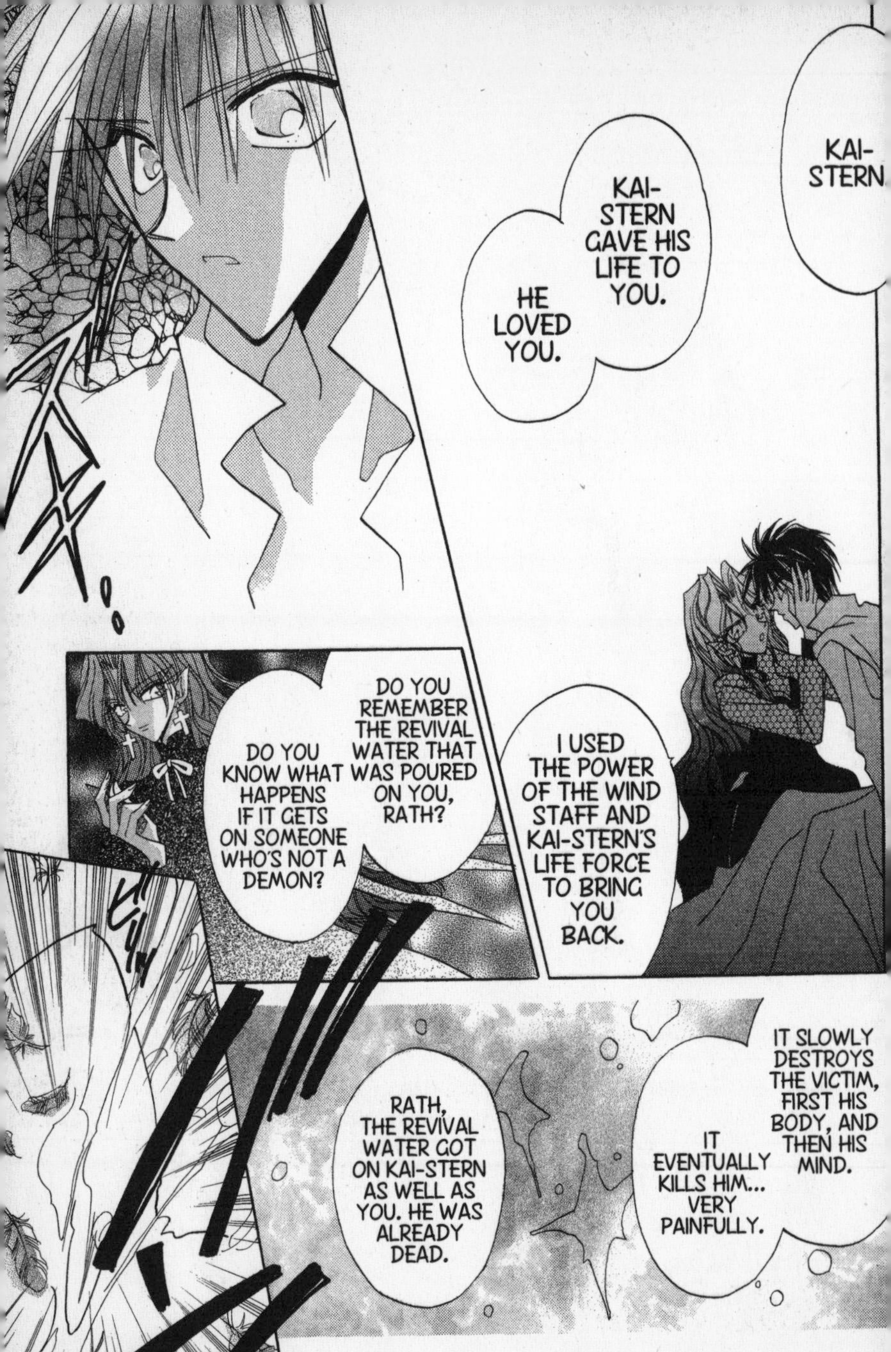
KAI-STERN.
KAI-STERN GAVE HIS LIFE TO YOU.
HE LOVED YOU.
I USED THE POWER OF THE WIND STAFF AND KAI-STERN'S LIFE FORCE TO BRING YOU BACK.
DO YOU REMEMBER THE REVIVAL WATER THAT WAS POURED ON YOU, RATH?
DO YOU KNOW WHAT HAPPENS IF IT GETS ON SOMEONE WHO'S NOT A DEMON?
IT SLOWLY DESTROYS THE VICTIM, FIRST HIS BODY, AND THEN HIS MIND.
IT EVENTUALLY KILLS HIM... VERY PAINFULLY.
RATH, THE REVIVAL WATER GOT ON KAI-STERN AS WELL AS YOU. HE WAS ALREADY DEAD.

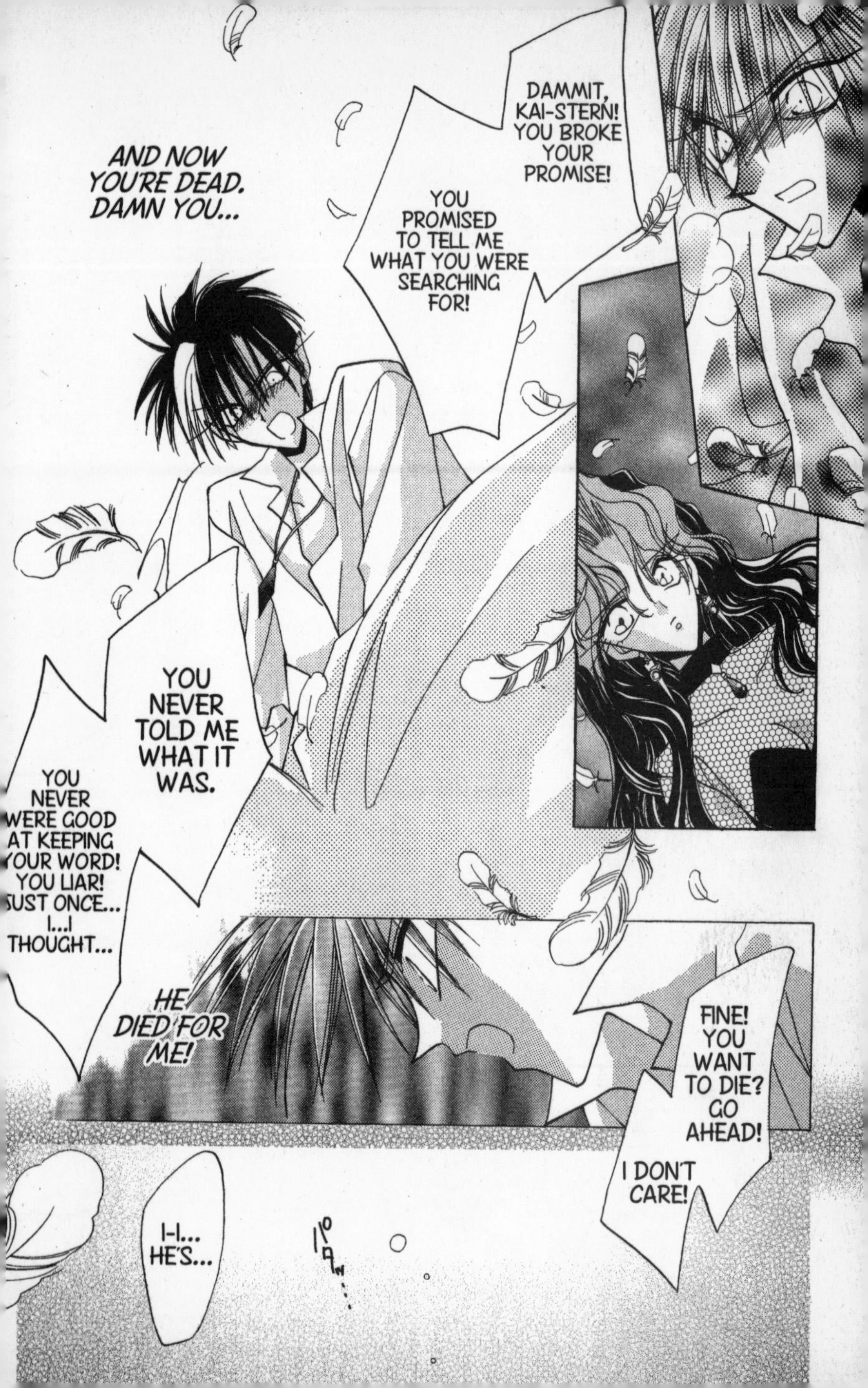
DAMMIT, KAI-STERN! YOU BROKE YOUR PROMISE!
YOU PROMISED TO TELL ME WHAT YOU WERE SEARCHING FOR!
AND NOW YOU'RE DEAD. DAMN YOU...
YOU NEVER TOLD ME WHAT IT WAS.
YOU NEVER WERE GOOD AT KEEPING YOUR WORD! YOU LIAR! JUST ONCE... I...I THOUGHT...
FINE! YOU WANT TO DIE? GO AHEAD!
I DON'T CARE!
HE DIED FOR ME!
I-I... HE'S...

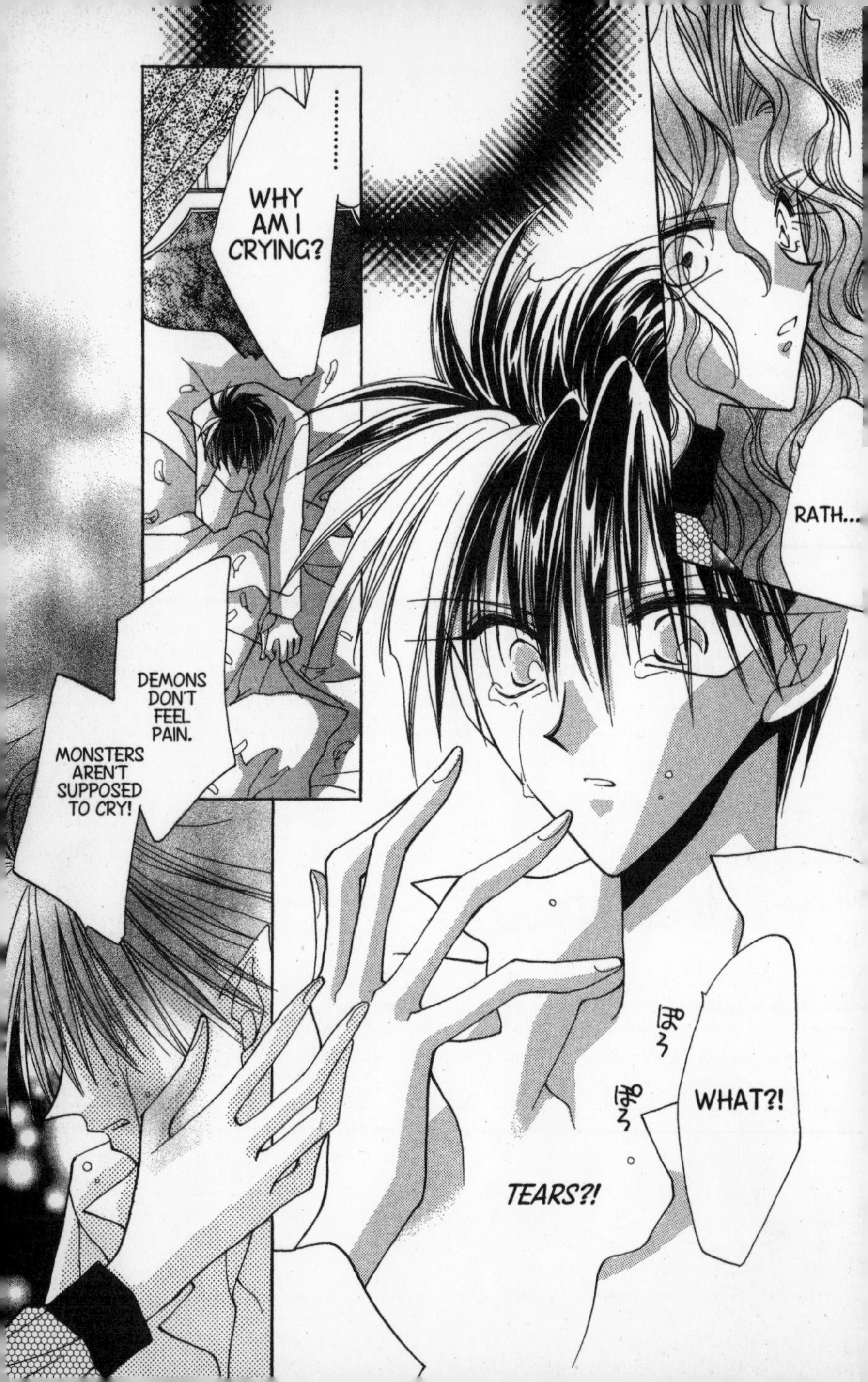
RATH...
WHAT?!
ぽろ ぽろ
TEARS?!
......
WHY AM I CRYING?
DEMONS DON'T FEEL PAIN.
MONSTERS AREN'T SUPPOSED TO CRY!

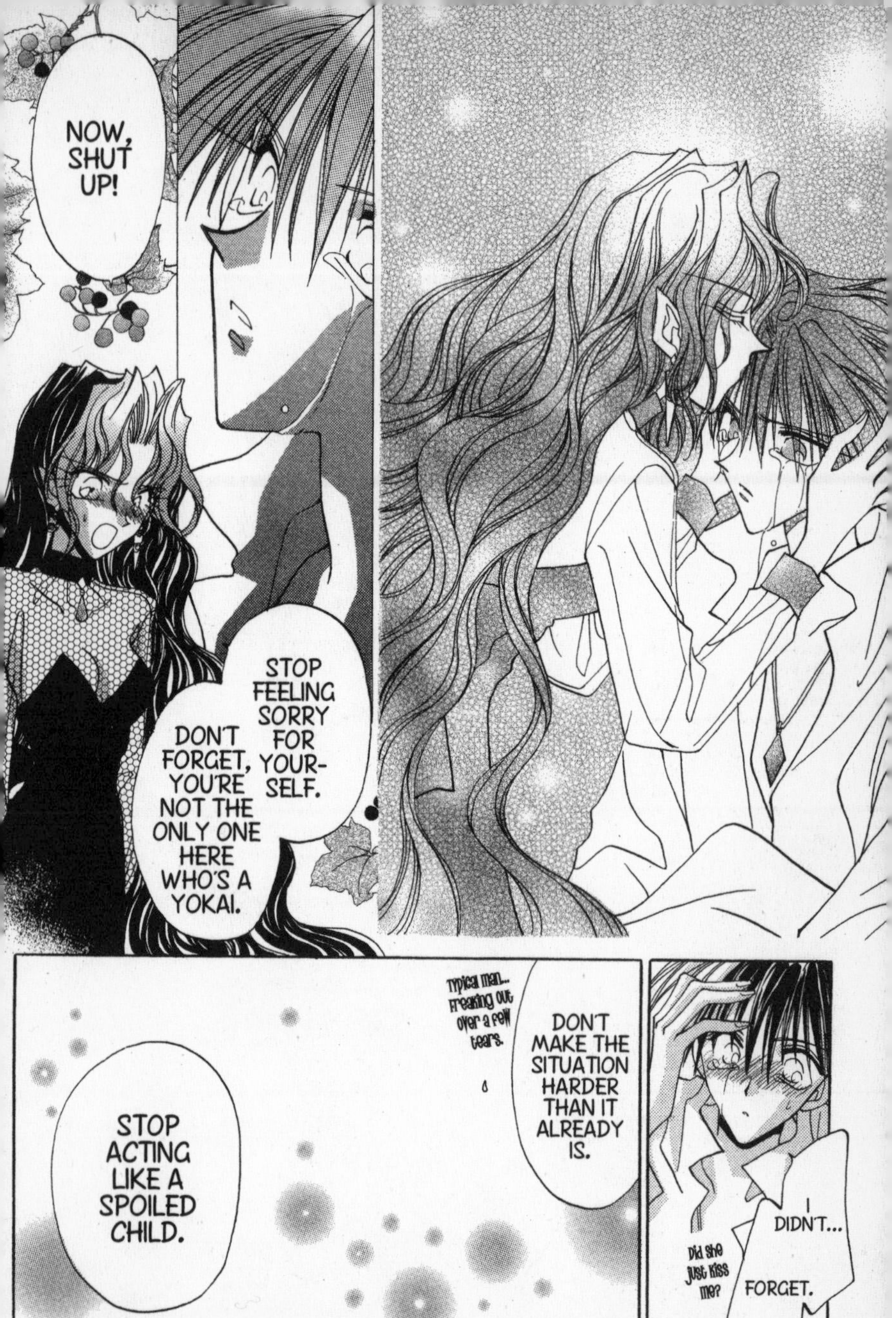
NOW, SHUT UP!
STOP FEELING SORRY FOR YOURSELF.
DON'T FORGET, YOU'RE NOT THE ONLY ONE HERE WHO'S A YOKAI.
I DIDN'T... FORGET.
Did she just kiss me?
DON'T MAKE THE SITUATION HARDER THAN IT ALREADY IS.
Typical man... Freaking out over a few tears.
STOP ACTING LIKE A SPOILED CHILD.

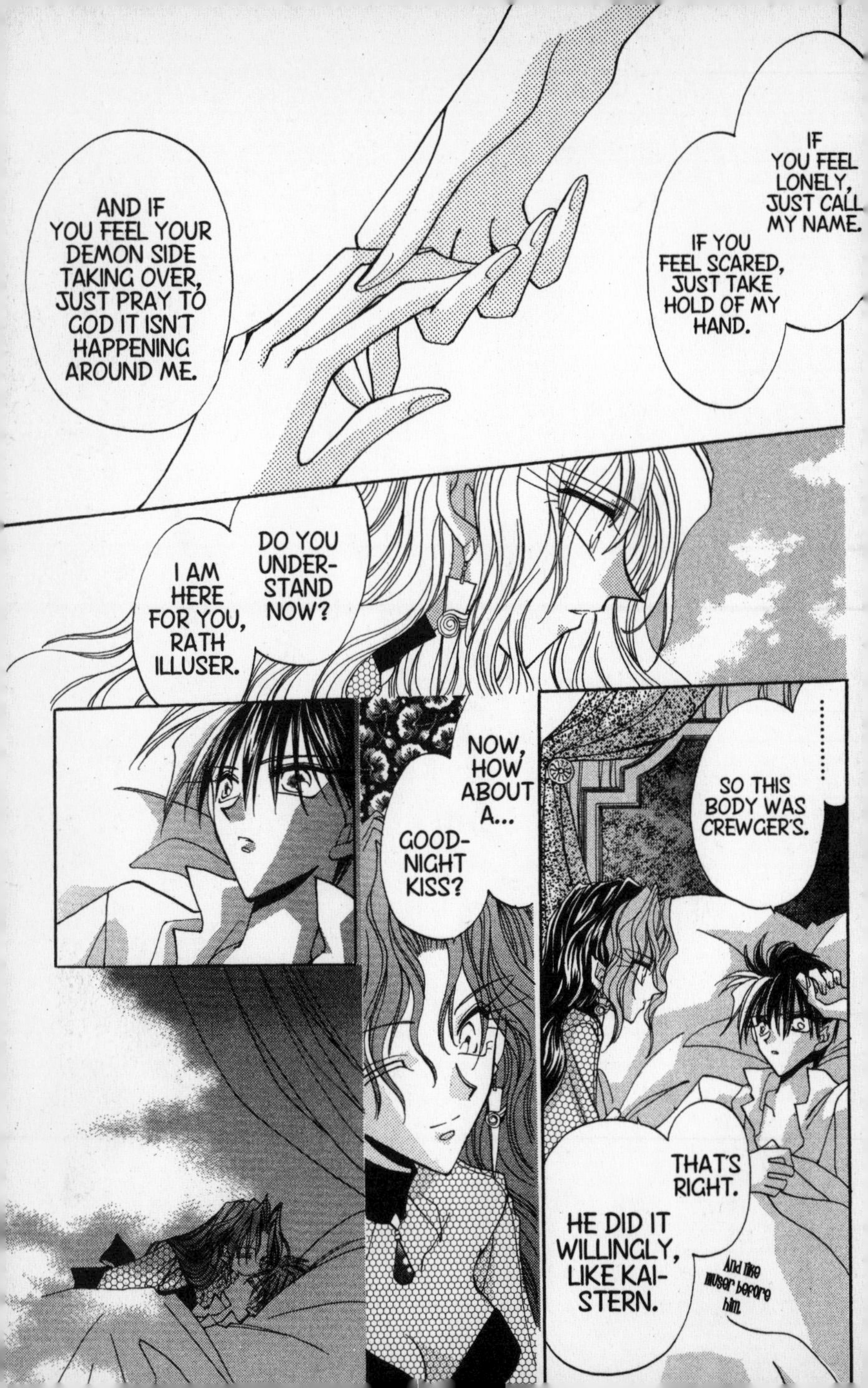
IF YOU FEEL LONELY, JUST CALL MY NAME.
IF YOU FEEL SCARED, JUST TAKE HOLD OF MY HAND.
AND IF YOU FEEL YOUR DEMON SIDE TAKING OVER, JUST PRAY TO GOD IT ISN'T HAPPENING AROUND ME.
DO YOU UNDERSTAND NOW?
I AM HERE FOR YOU, RATH ILLUSER.
......
SO THIS BODY WAS CREWGER'S.
THAT'S RIGHT.
HE DID IT WILLINGLY, LIKE KAI-STERN.
And like Illuser before him.
NOW, HOW ABOUT A...
GOOD-NIGHT KISS?

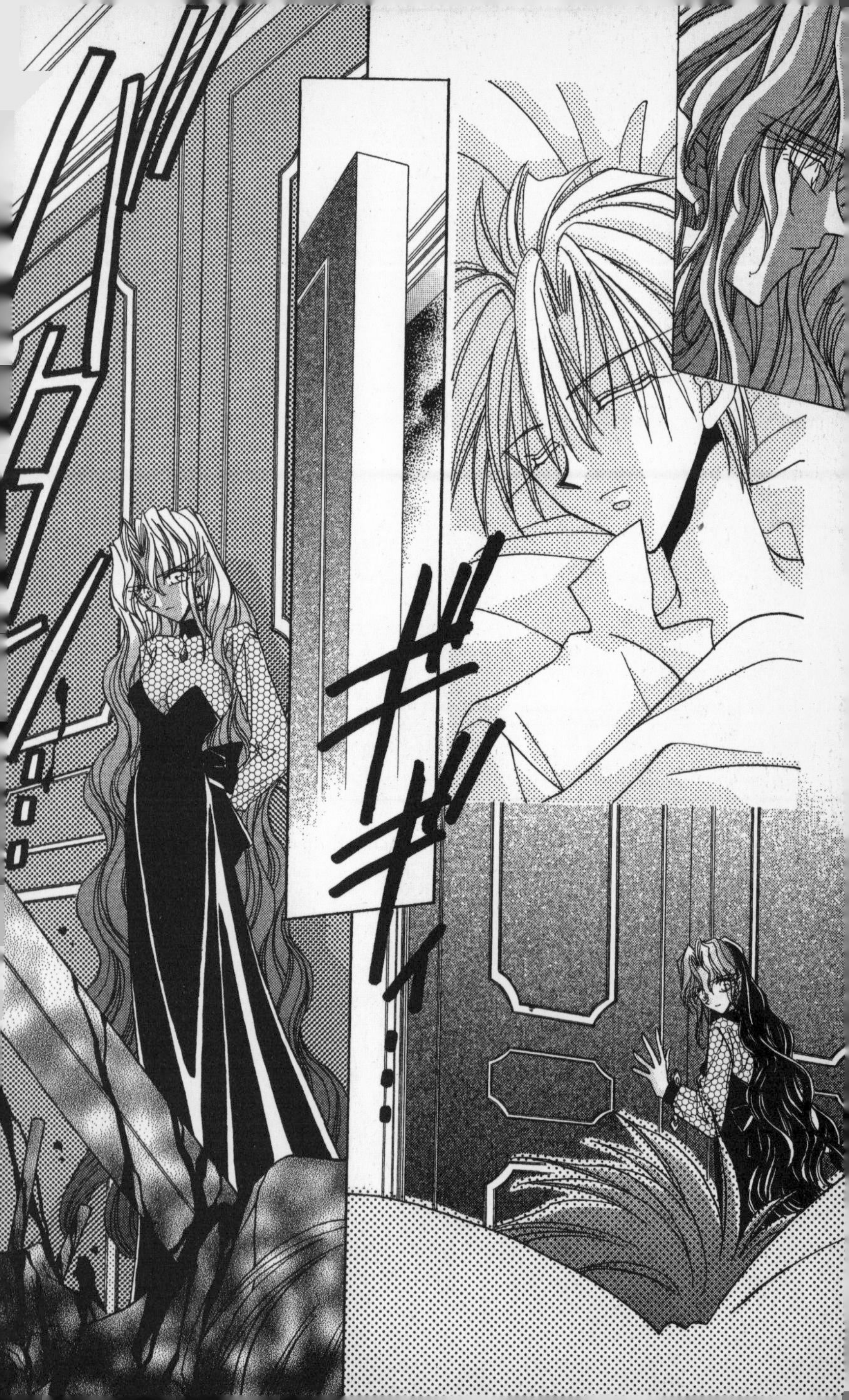
ギギィ…
バタン…

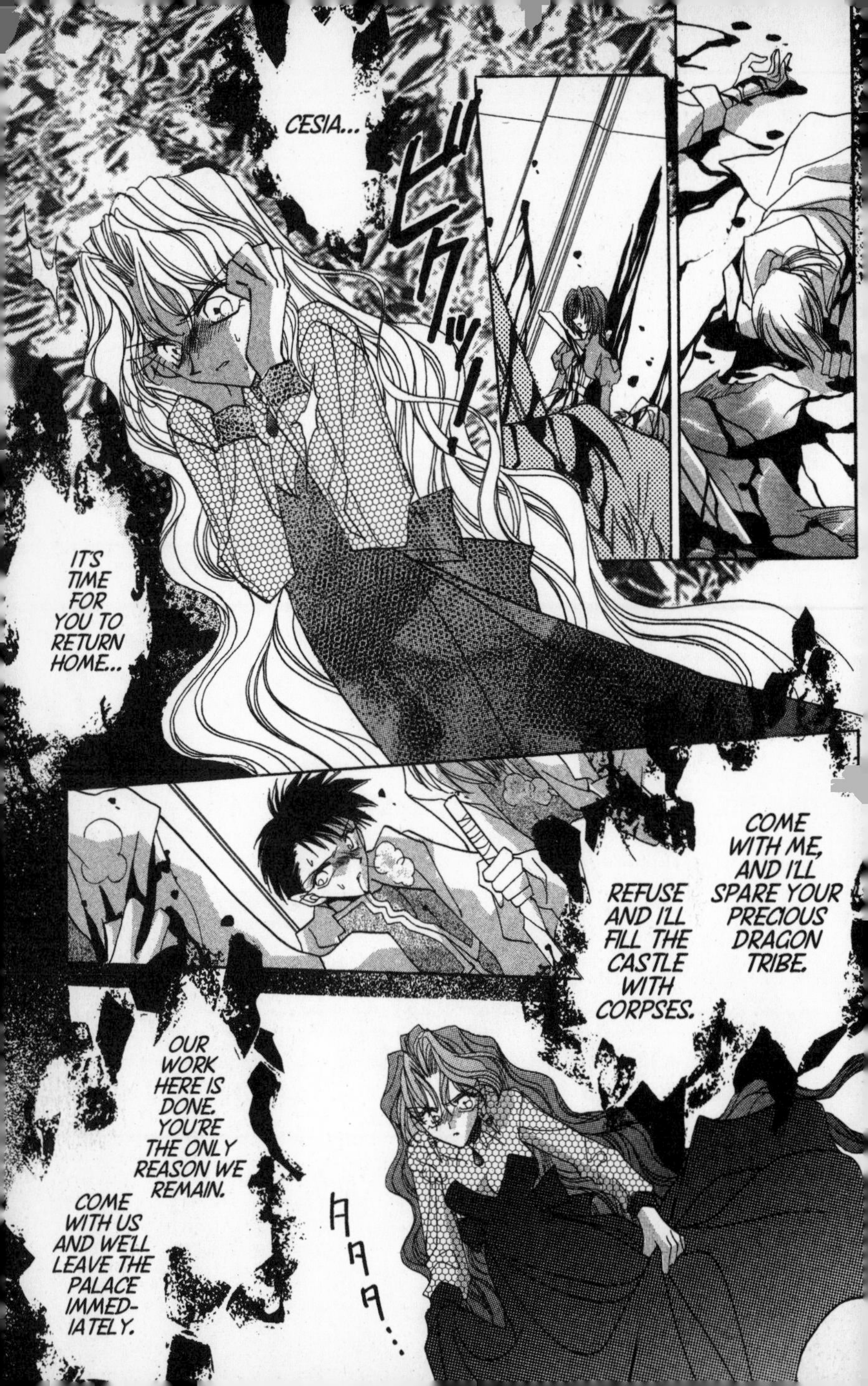
ビクッ!
CESIA...
IT'S TIME FOR YOU TO RETURN HOME...
COME WITH ME, AND I'LL SPARE YOUR PRECIOUS DRAGON TRIBE.
REFUSE AND I'LL FILL THE CASTLE WITH CORPSES.
OUR WORK HERE IS DONE. YOU'RE THE ONLY REASON WE REMAIN.
COME WITH US AND WE'LL LEAVE THE PALACE IMMED-IATELY.
アアア...

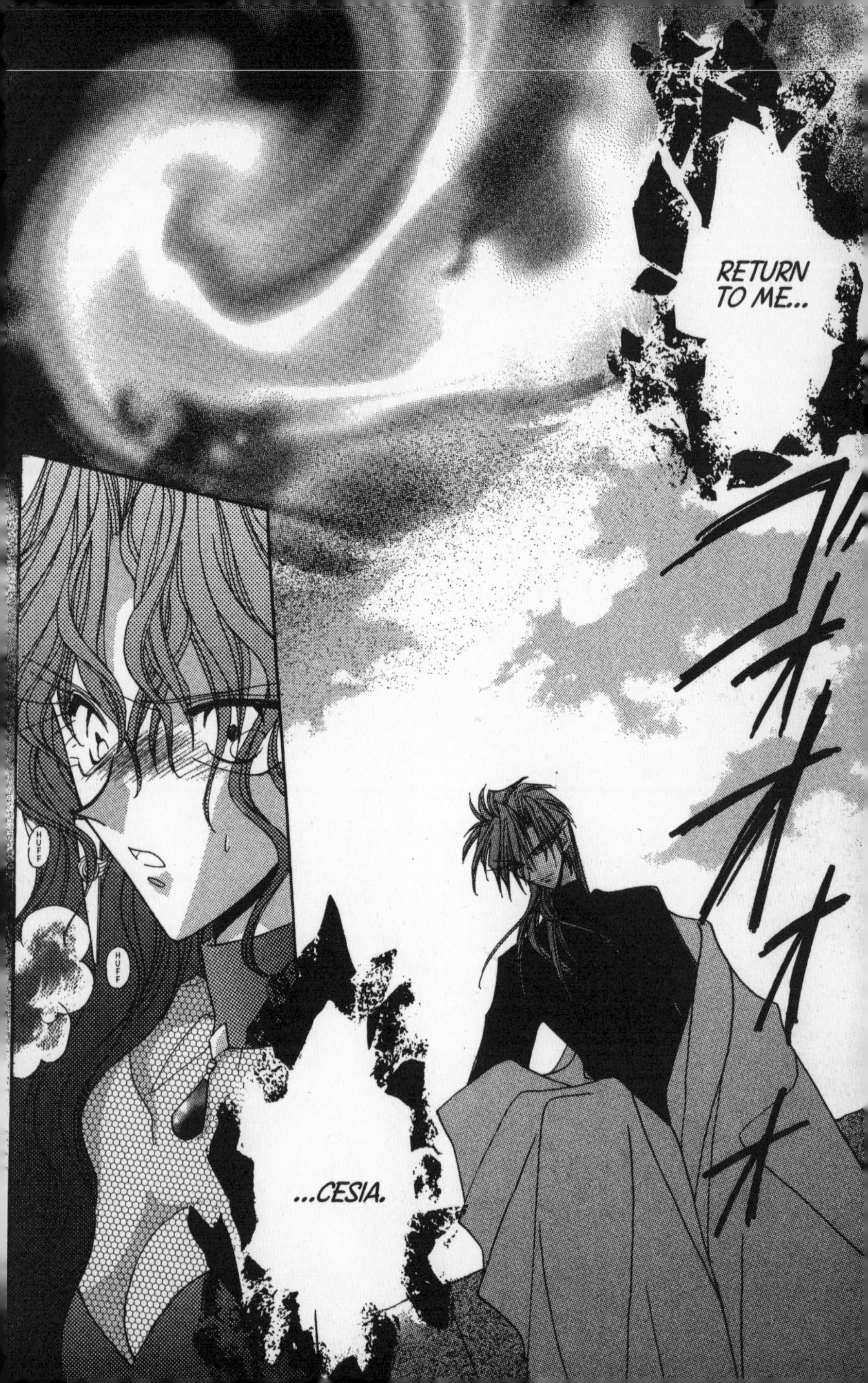
RETURN TO ME...
HUFF
HUFF
...CESIA.

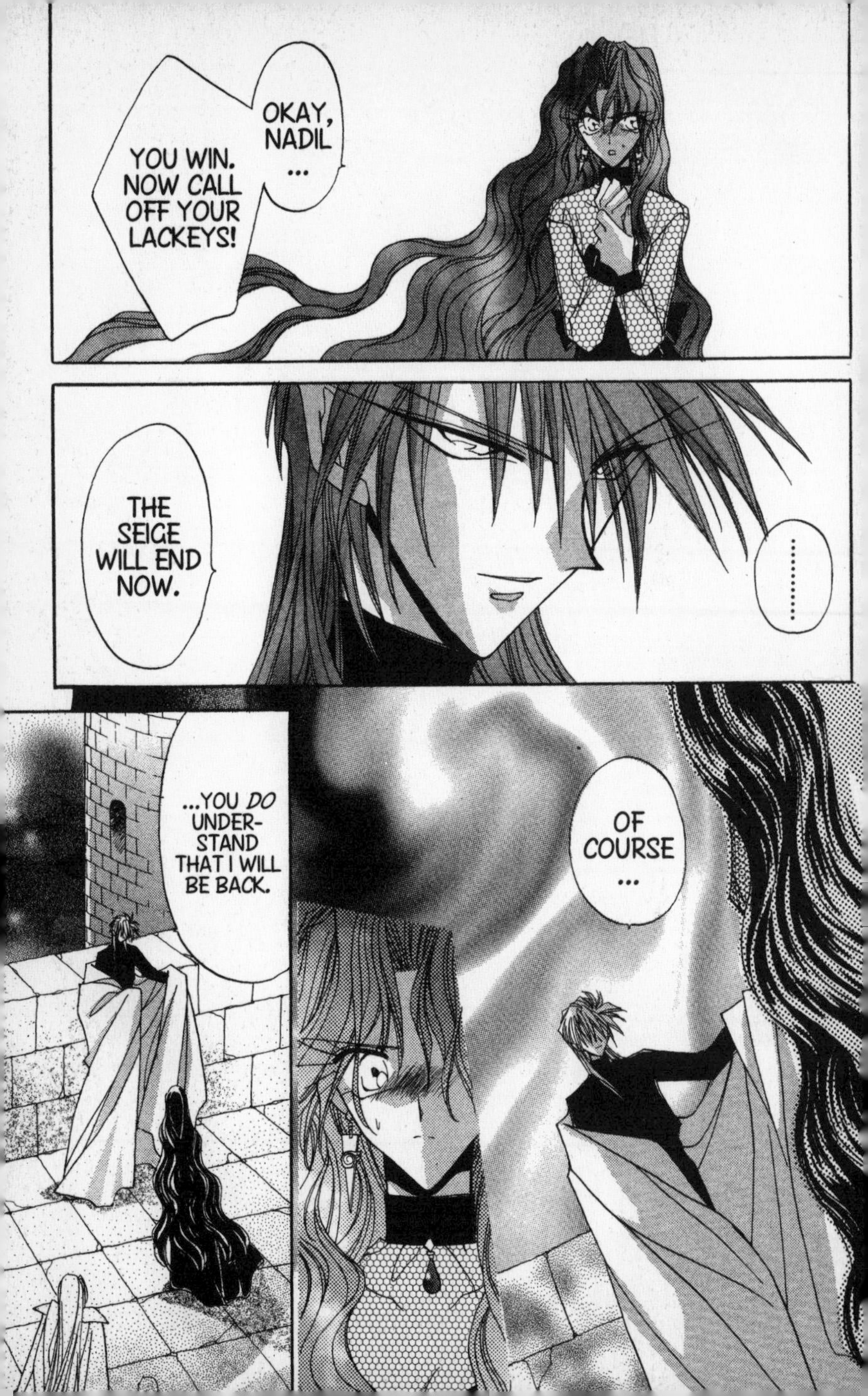
OKAY, NADIL ...
YOU WIN. NOW CALL OFF YOUR LACKEYS!
......
THE SEIGE WILL END NOW.
OF COURSE ...
...YOU *DO* UNDER-STAND THAT I WILL BE BACK.

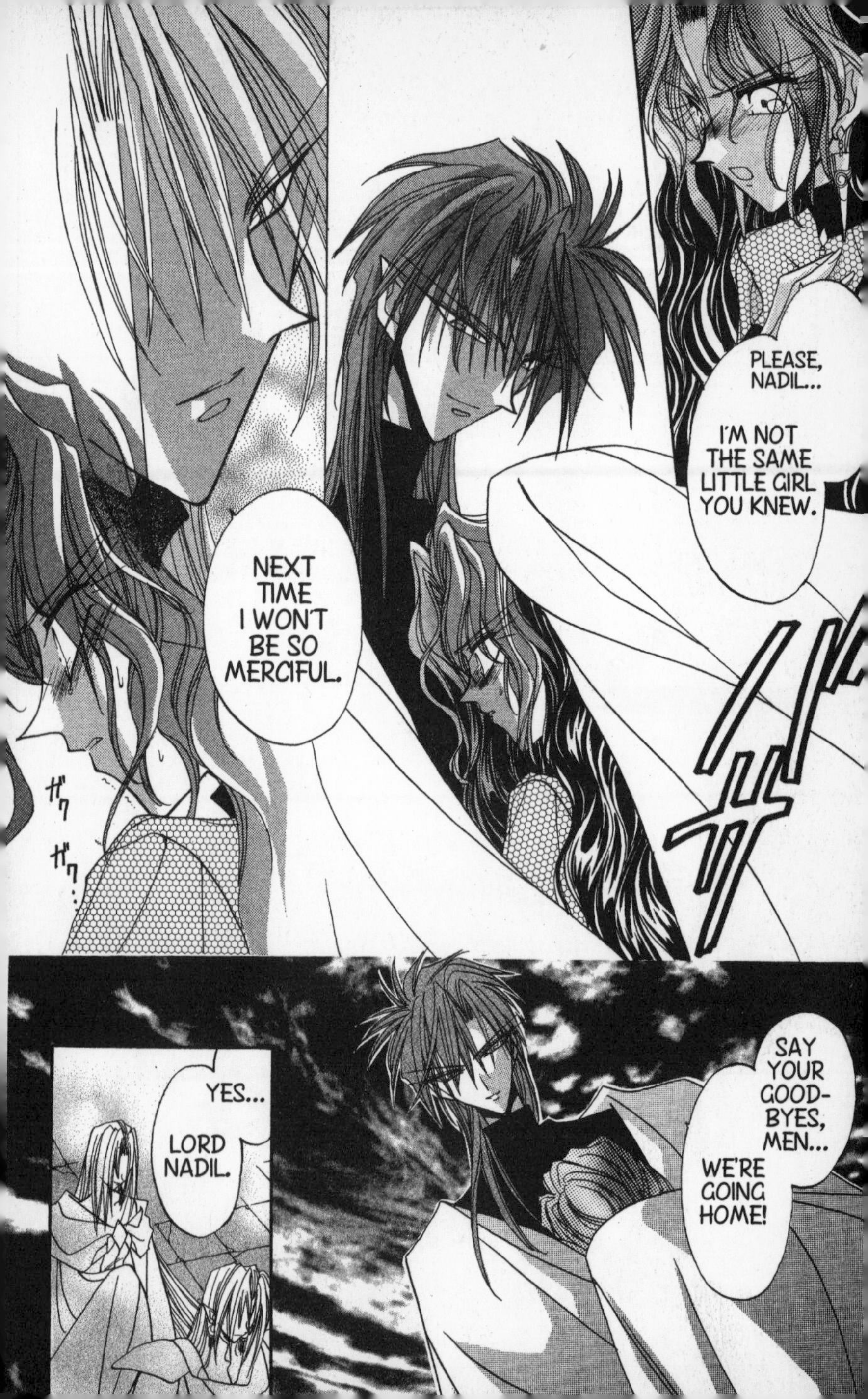
PLEASE, NADIL...
I'M NOT THE SAME LITTLE GIRL YOU KNEW.
NEXT TIME I WON'T BE SO MERCIFUL.
ガク
ガク…
SAY YOUR GOOD-BYES, MEN...
WE'RE GOING HOME!
YES...
LORD NADIL.

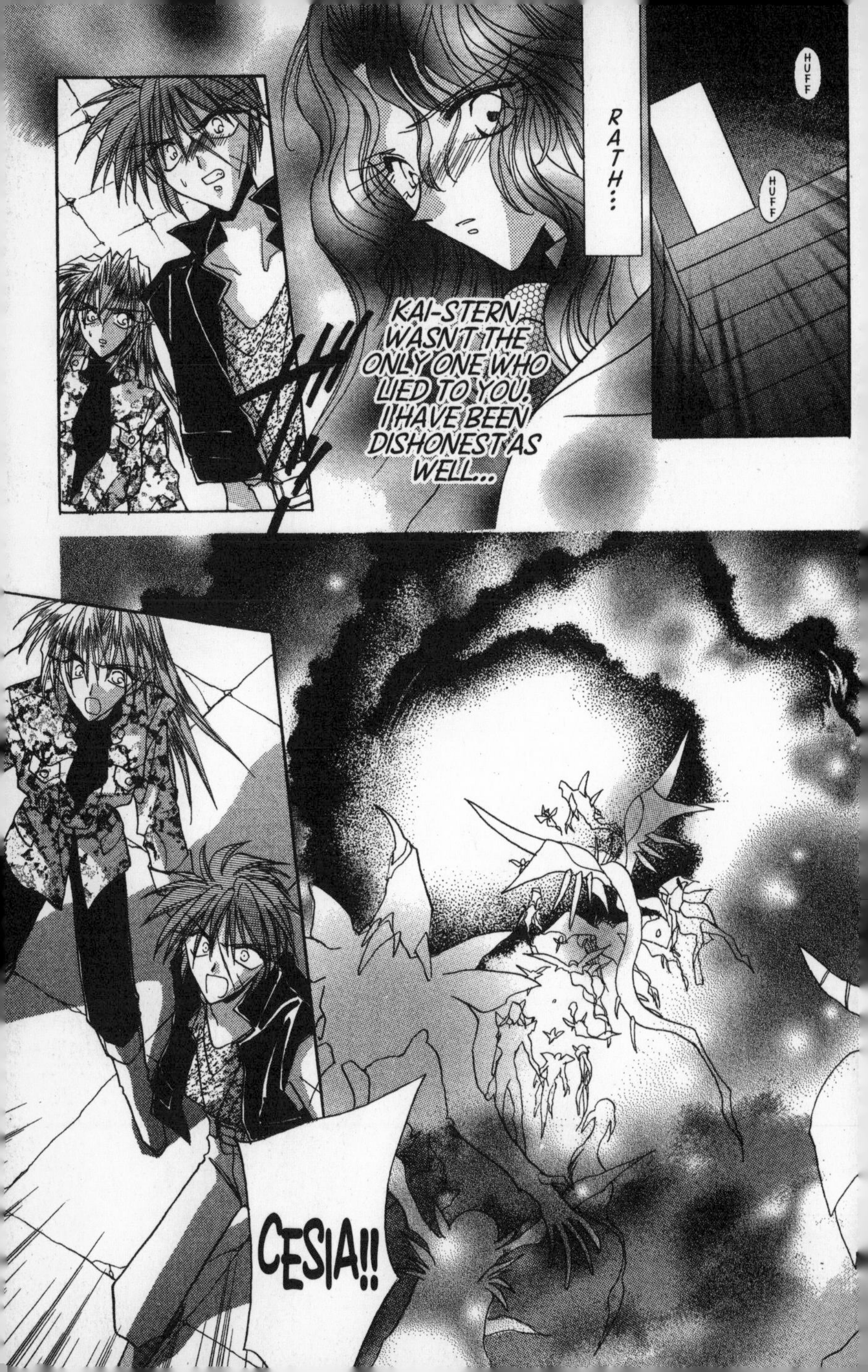
HUFF
HUFF
RATH...
KAI-STERN WASN'T THE ONLY ONE WHO LIED TO YOU. I HAVE BEEN DISHONEST AS WELL...
CESIA!!

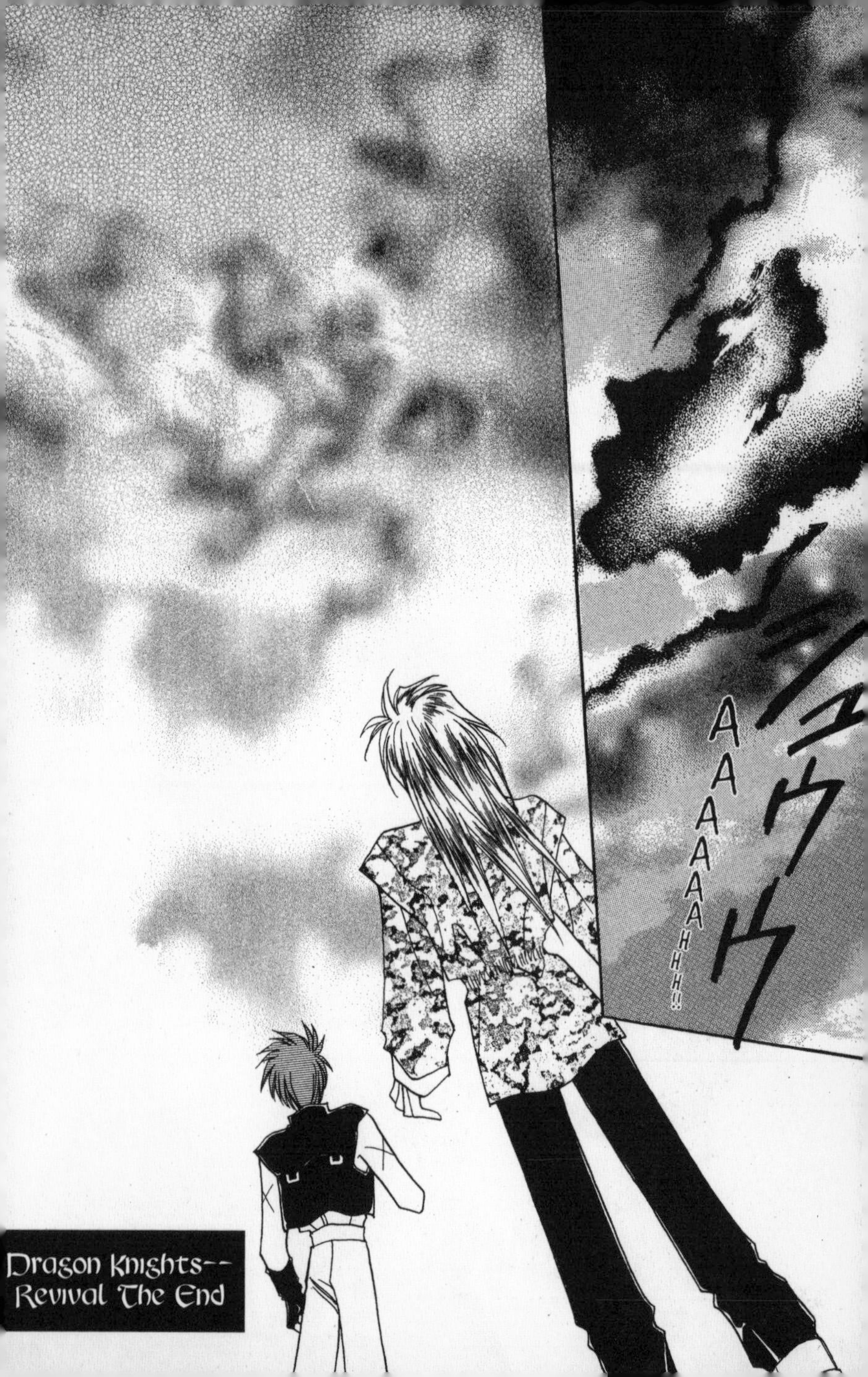
AAAAAAHHH!!
Dragon Knights--
Revival The End

The Villains of Dragon Knights

Nadil

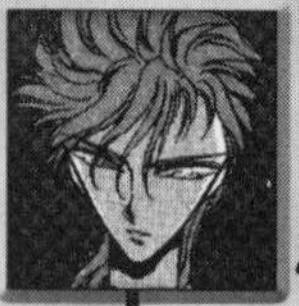

Leader of the Demon Forces who was decapitated by Lykouleon. His army is trying to retrieve his head and resurrect him.

Shydeman

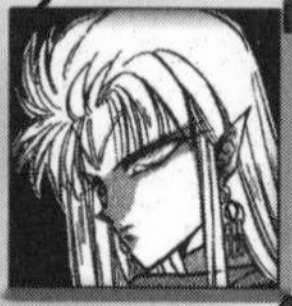

Shyrendora

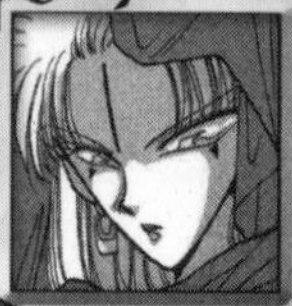

Current leaders of Nadil's army. They are fortunetellers with the express goal of reviving Nadil and destroying the Dragon Tribe.

Bierrez

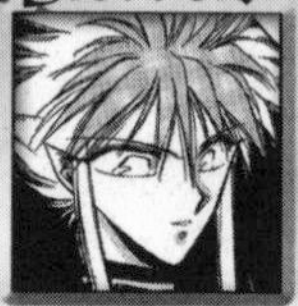

The only Yokai who can penetrate the shield of the Dragon Castle. Though a demon, he isn't a loyal follower of Nadil.

Lady Medicinea

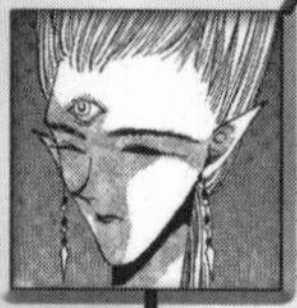

A demon leader in Nadil's army responsible for the Black Smoke in Dusis. Has a competitive relationship with Fedelta.

Jilge

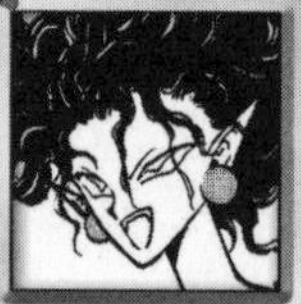

A witch who worked for Nadil's forces until her untimely death at the hands of the Dragon Knights.

Fedelta

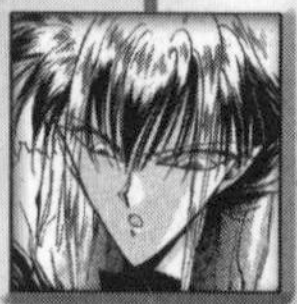

One of the leaders in Nadil's army. Answers to Shydeman and is competitive with Medicinea.

Kharl

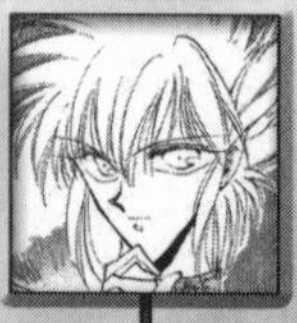

Kharl is an Alchemist and a Renkin Wizard who can create demons. He longs to control Dusis himself but sometimes assists Nadil's army. Garfakcy is sneaky, vicious and serves Kharl, but harbors a desire to be a demon himself.

Garfakcy

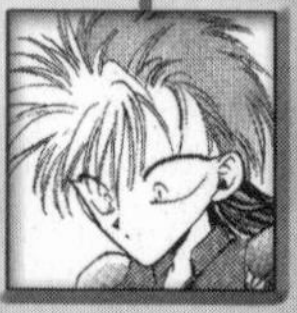

Kirukulus

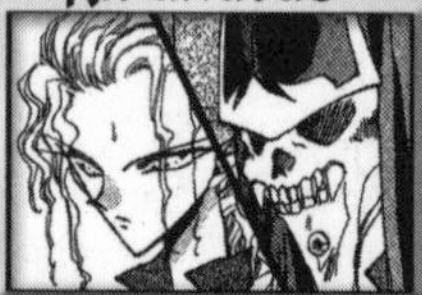

An evil sorcerer intent on capturing Cesia and using her to make him stronger. Was defeated by Rath but still lives and is determined to control Dusis.

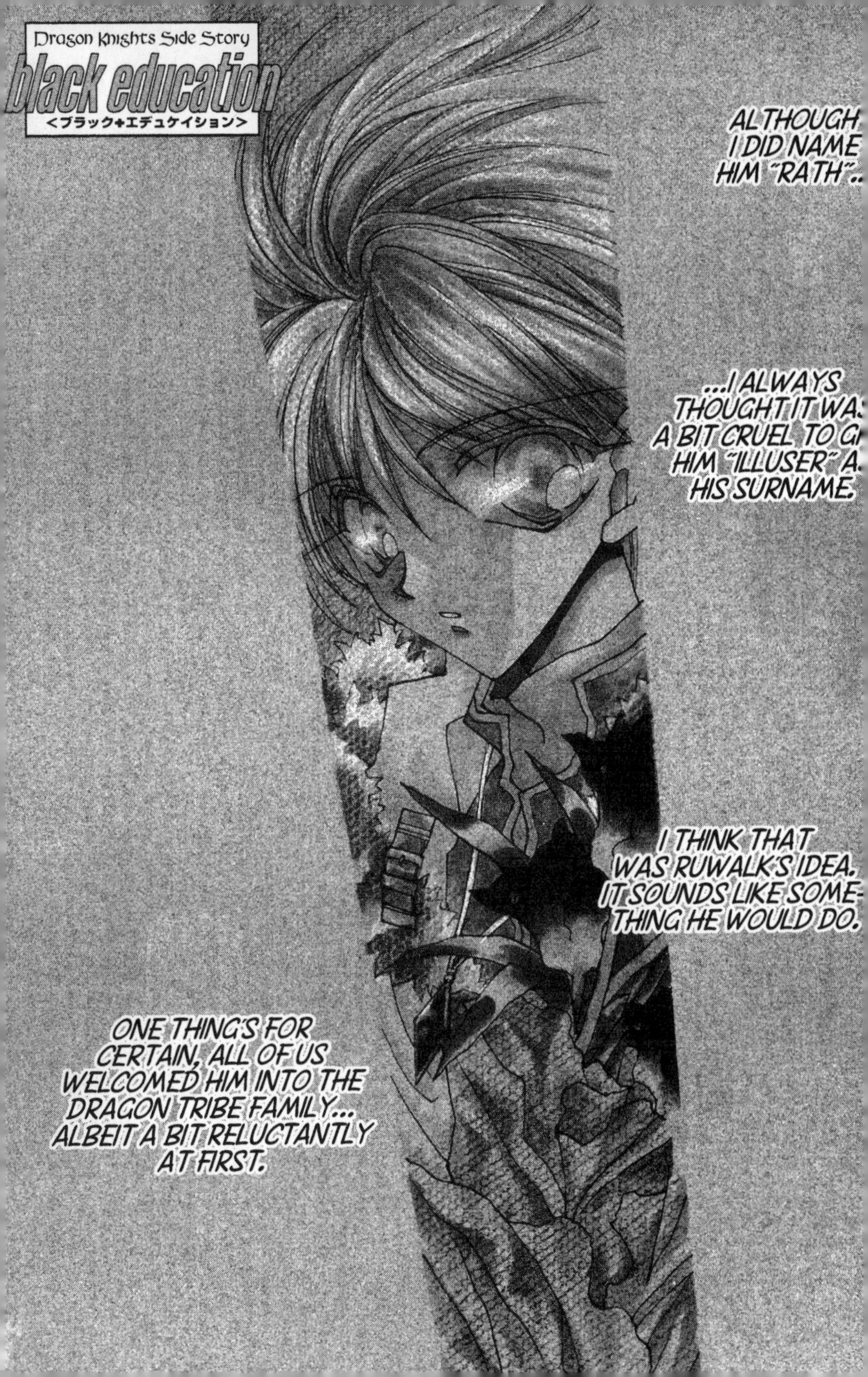
Dragon Knights Side Story
black education
<ブラック+エデュケイション>
ALTHOUGH I DID NAME HIM "RATH"...
...I ALWAYS THOUGHT IT WAS A BIT CRUEL TO GI HIM "ILLUSER" A HIS SURNAME.
I THINK THAT WAS RUWALK'S IDEA. IT SOUNDS LIKE SOME-THING HE WOULD DO.
ONE THING'S FOR CERTAIN, ALL OF US WELCOMED HIM INTO THE DRAGON TRIBE FAMILY... ALBEIT A BIT RELUCTANTLY AT FIRST.

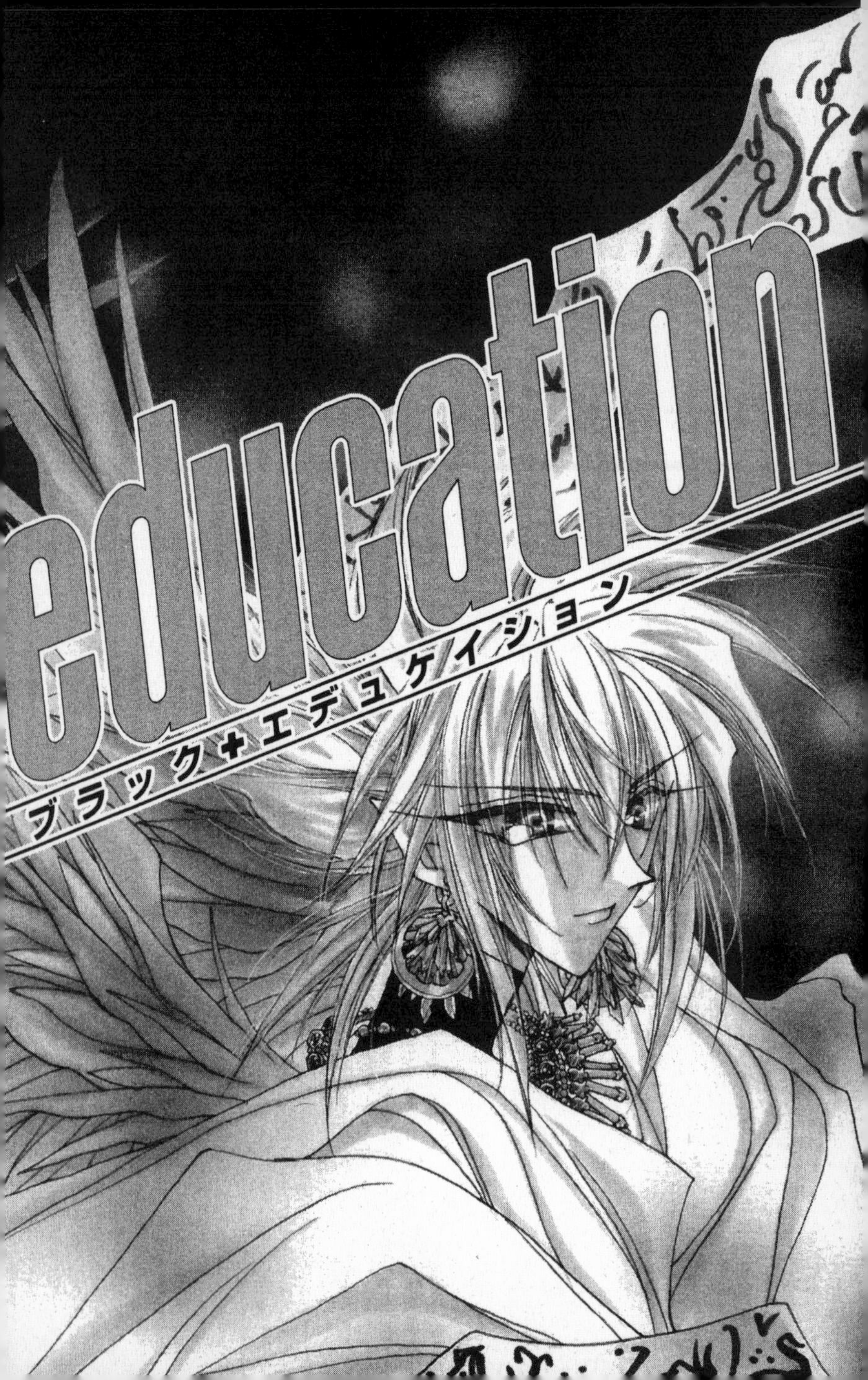
education
ブラック✚エデュケイション

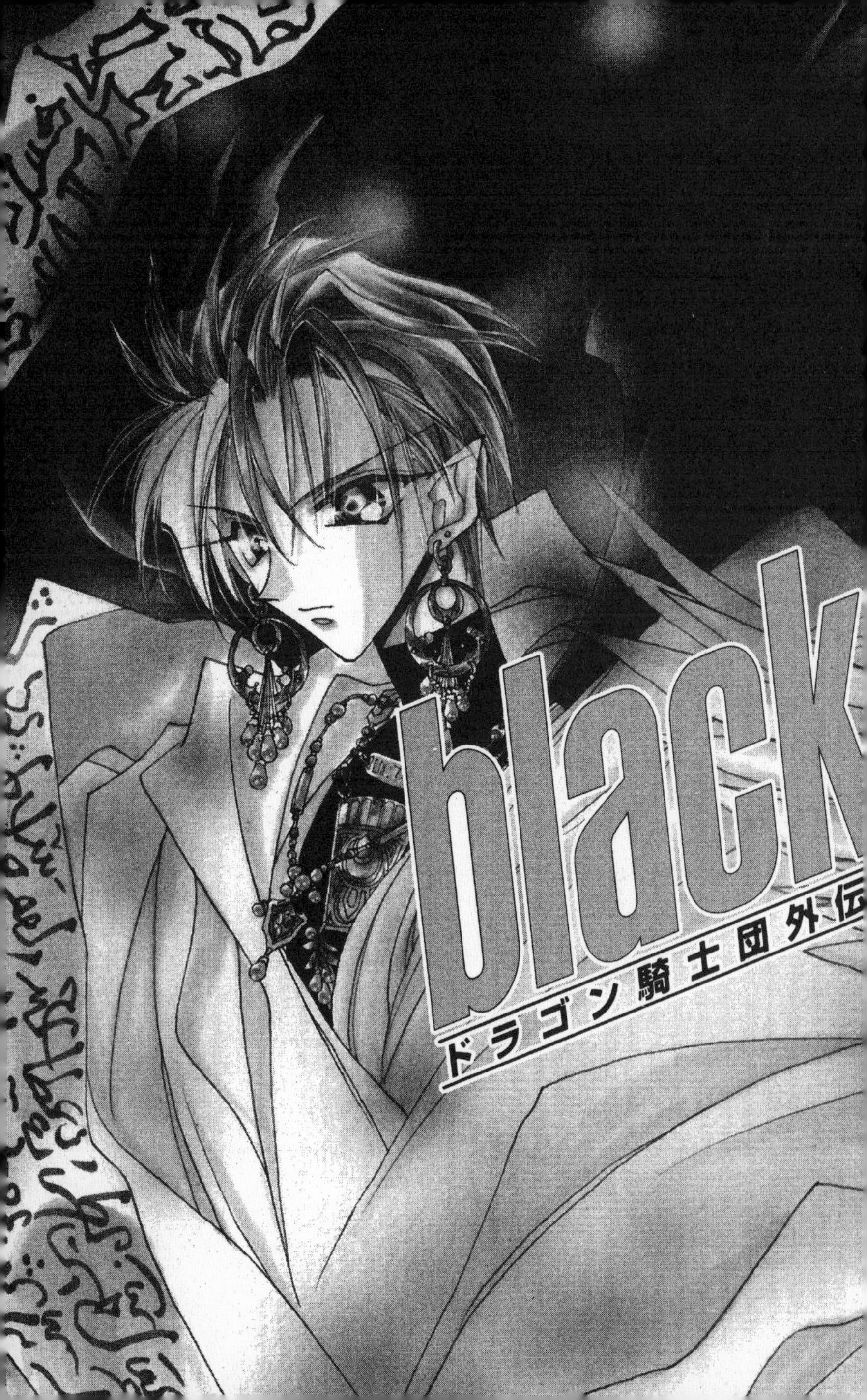
black
ドラゴン騎士団外伝

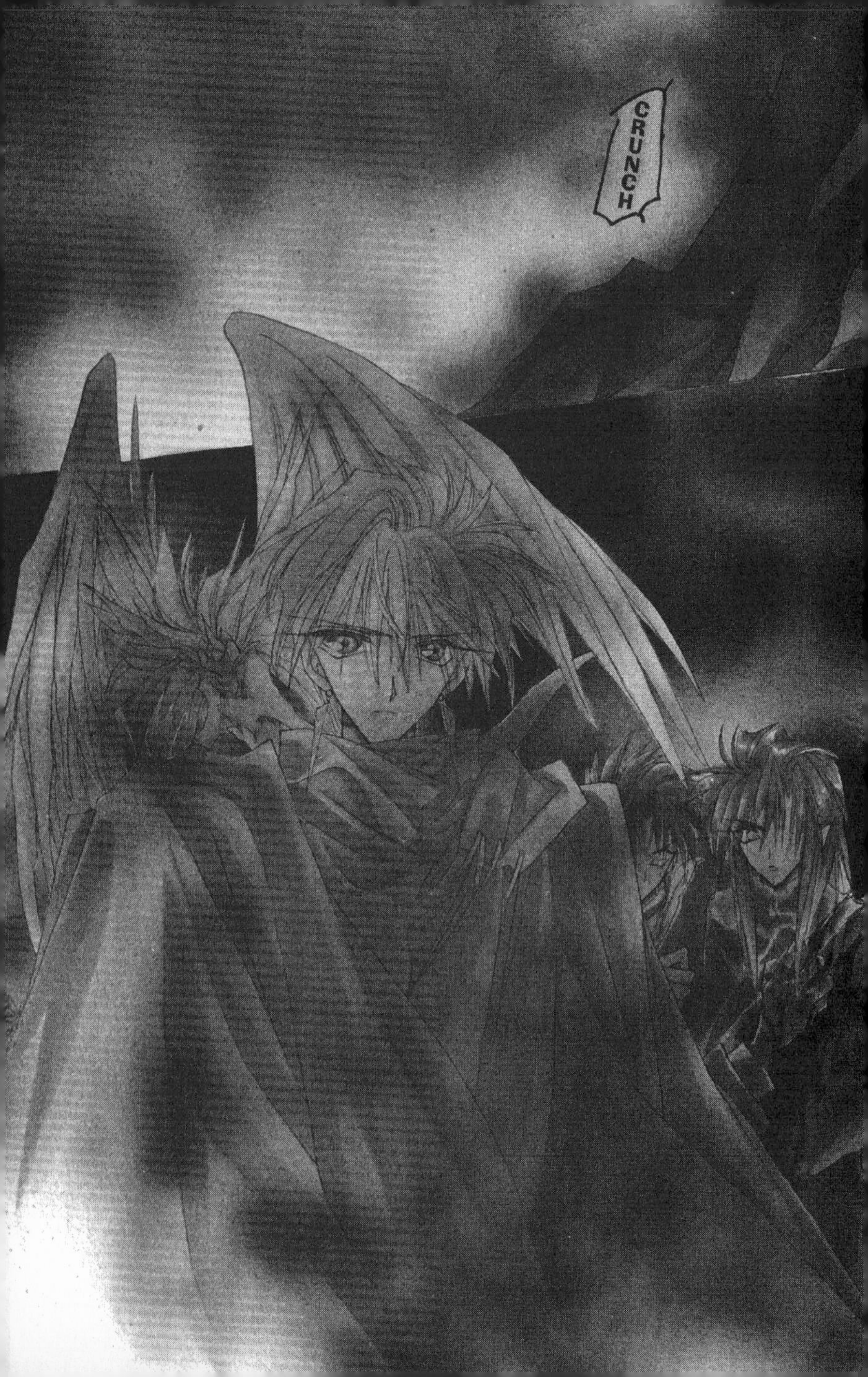
CRUNCH

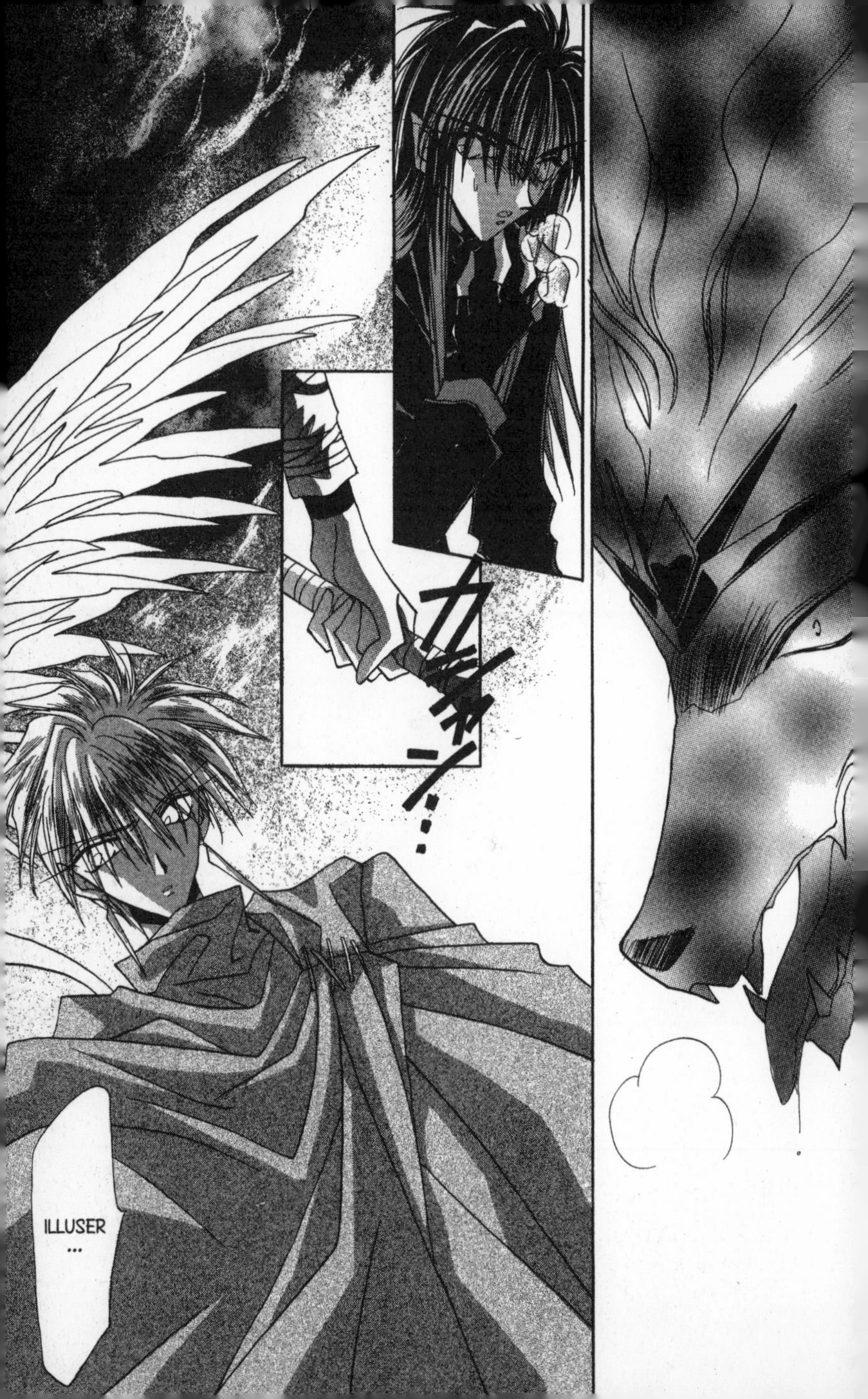
ILLUSER
...

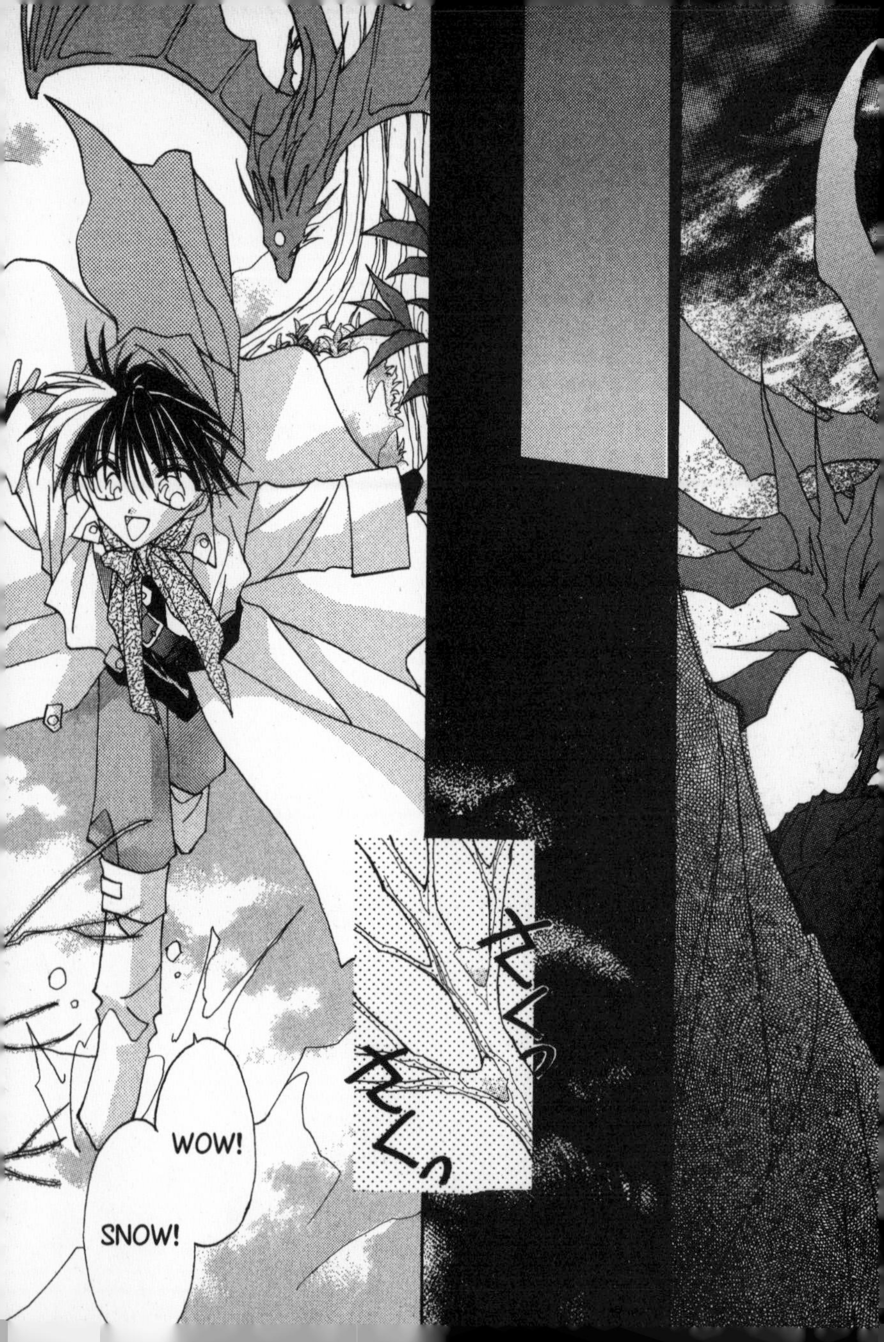
さくっ さくっ
WOW!
SNOW!

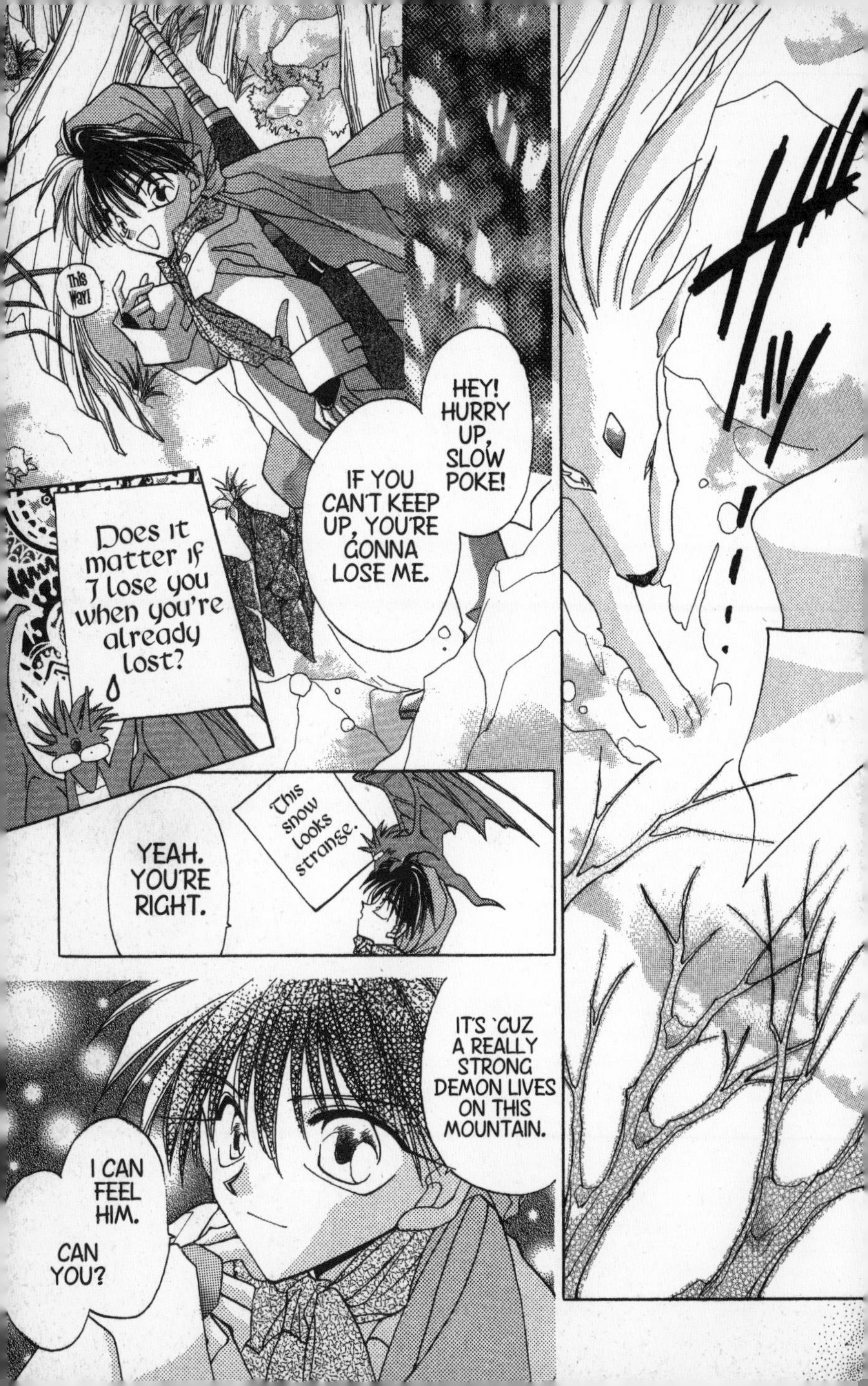
This Way!
HEY! HURRY UP, SLOW POKE!
IF YOU CAN'T KEEP UP, YOU'RE GONNA LOSE ME.
Does it matter if I lose you when you're already lost?
This snow looks strange.
YEAH. YOU'RE RIGHT.
IT'S 'CUZ A REALLY STRONG DEMON LIVES ON THIS MOUNTAIN.
I CAN FEEL HIM.
CAN YOU?

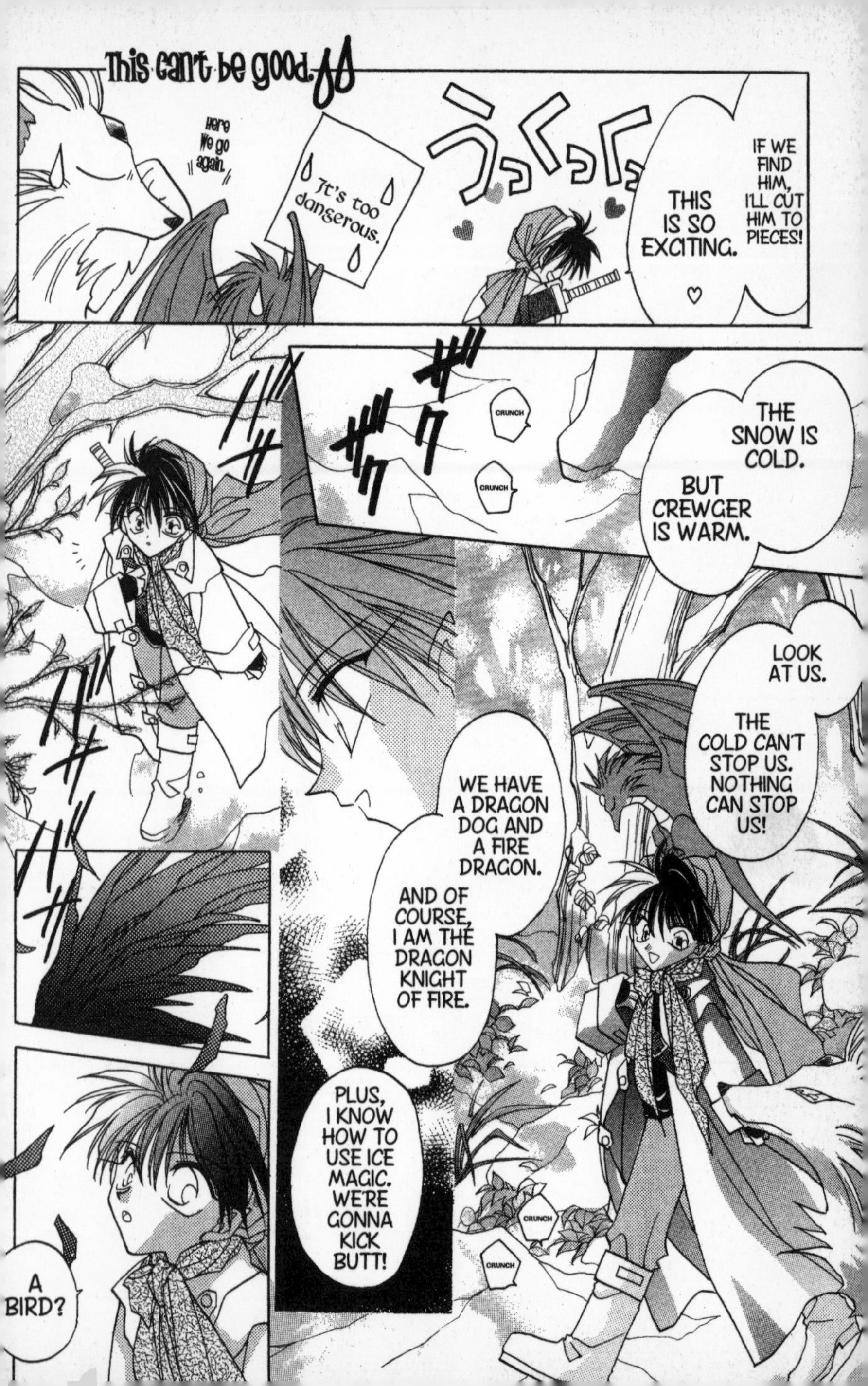
This can't be good.
IF WE FIND HIM, I'LL CUT HIM TO PIECES!
THIS IS SO EXCITING. ♡
うっくっくっ
It's too dangerous.
Here we go again.
ザク
ザク
CRUNCH
CRUNCH
THE SNOW IS COLD.
BUT CREWGER IS WARM.
LOOK AT US.
THE COLD CAN'T STOP US. NOTHING CAN STOP US!
WE HAVE A DRAGON DOG AND A FIRE DRAGON.
AND OF COURSE, I AM THE DRAGON KNIGHT OF FIRE.
PLUS, I KNOW HOW TO USE ICE MAGIC. WE'RE GONNA KICK BUTT!
CRUNCH
CRUNCH
A BIRD?

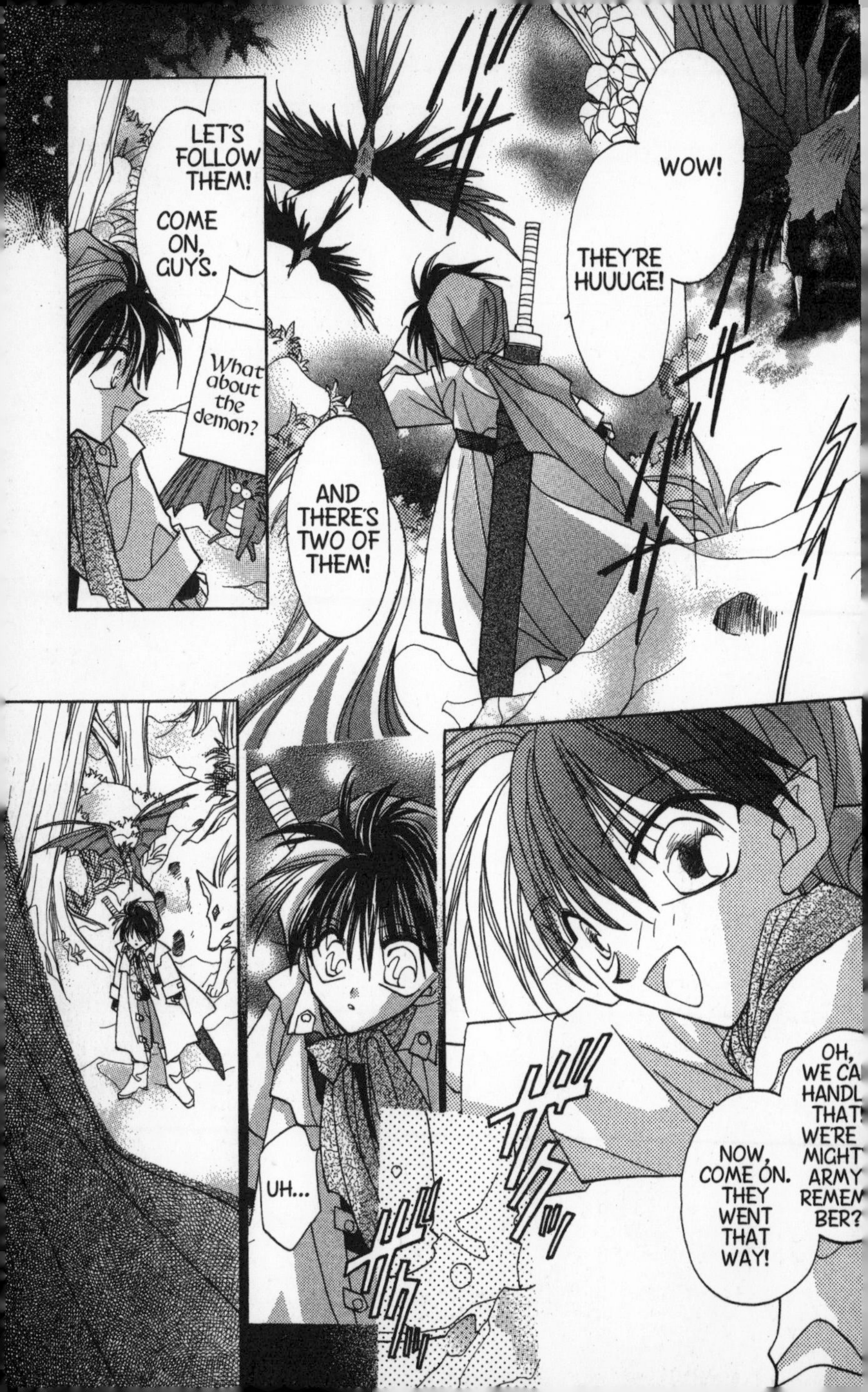
WOW!
THEY'RE HUUUGE!
AND THERE'S TWO OF THEM!
LET'S FOLLOW THEM!
COME ON, GUYS.
What about the demon?
OH, WE CA HANDL THAT WE'RE MIGHT ARMY REMEM BER?
NOW, COME ON. THEY WENT THAT WAY!
UH...

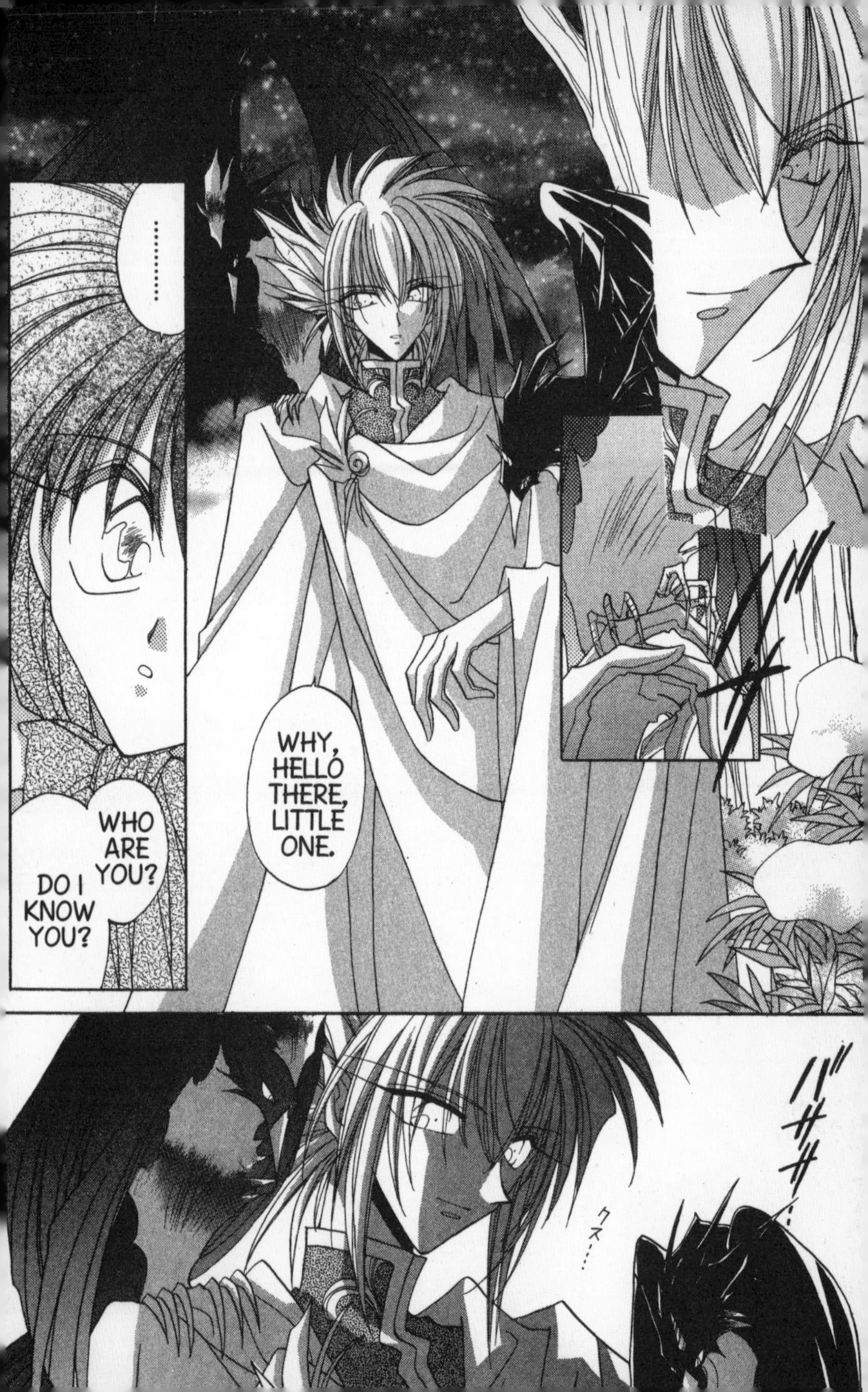
WHY, HELLO THERE, LITTLE ONE.
......
WHO ARE YOU? DO I KNOW YOU?
バササ…
クス…

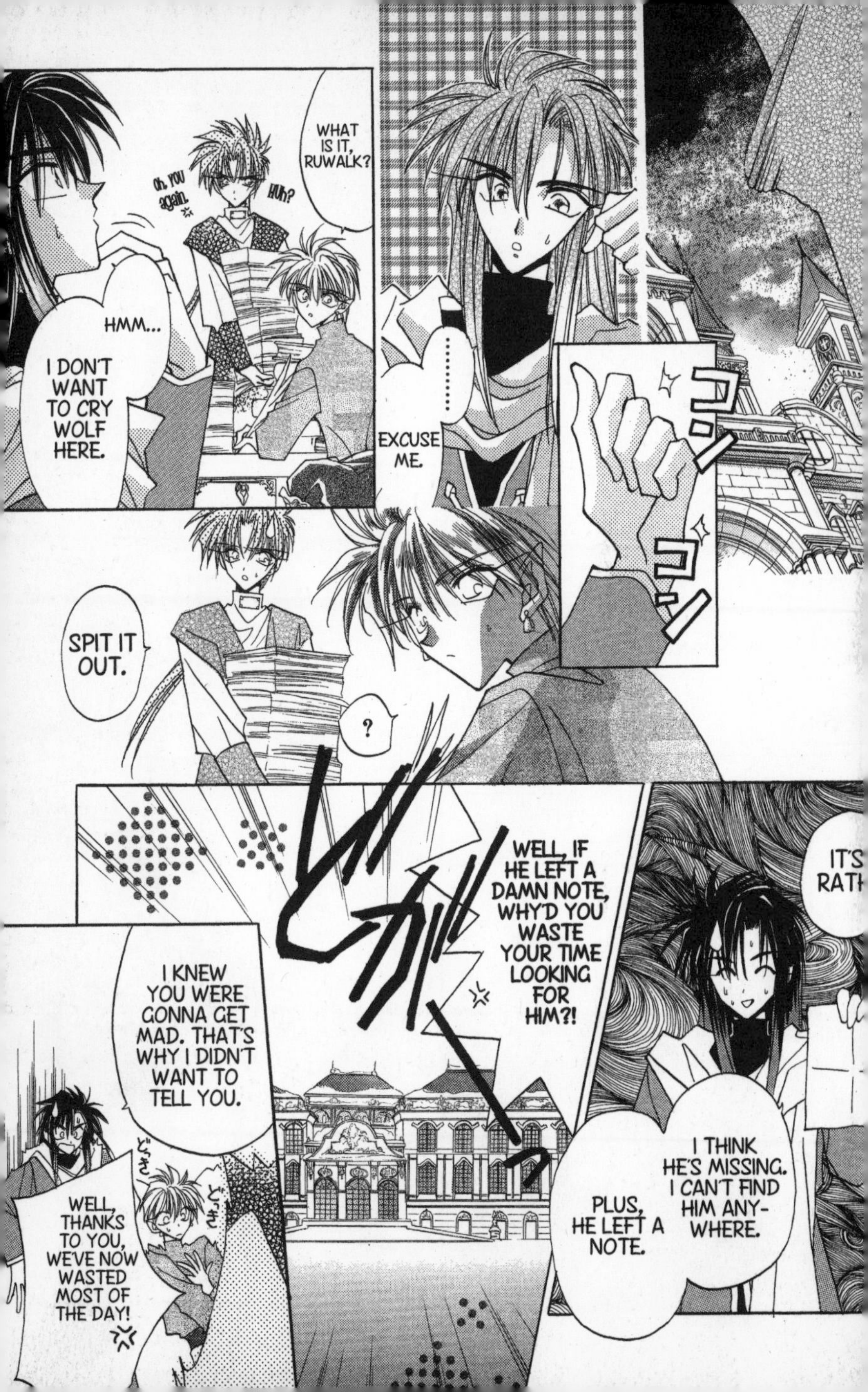
コン
コン
......
EXCUSE ME.
WHAT IS IT, RUWALK?
Oh, you again.
Huh?
HMM...
I DON'T WANT TO CRY WOLF HERE.
SPIT IT OUT.
?
IT'S RATH
I THINK HE'S MISSING. I CAN'T FIND HIM ANY-WHERE.
PLUS, HE LEFT A NOTE.
WELL, IF HE LEFT A DAMN NOTE, WHY'D YOU WASTE YOUR TIME LOOKING FOR HIM?!
I KNEW YOU WERE GONNA GET MAD. THAT'S WHY I DIDN'T WANT TO TELL YOU.
どき
どき
WELL, THANKS TO YOU, WE'VE NOW WASTED MOST OF THE DAY!

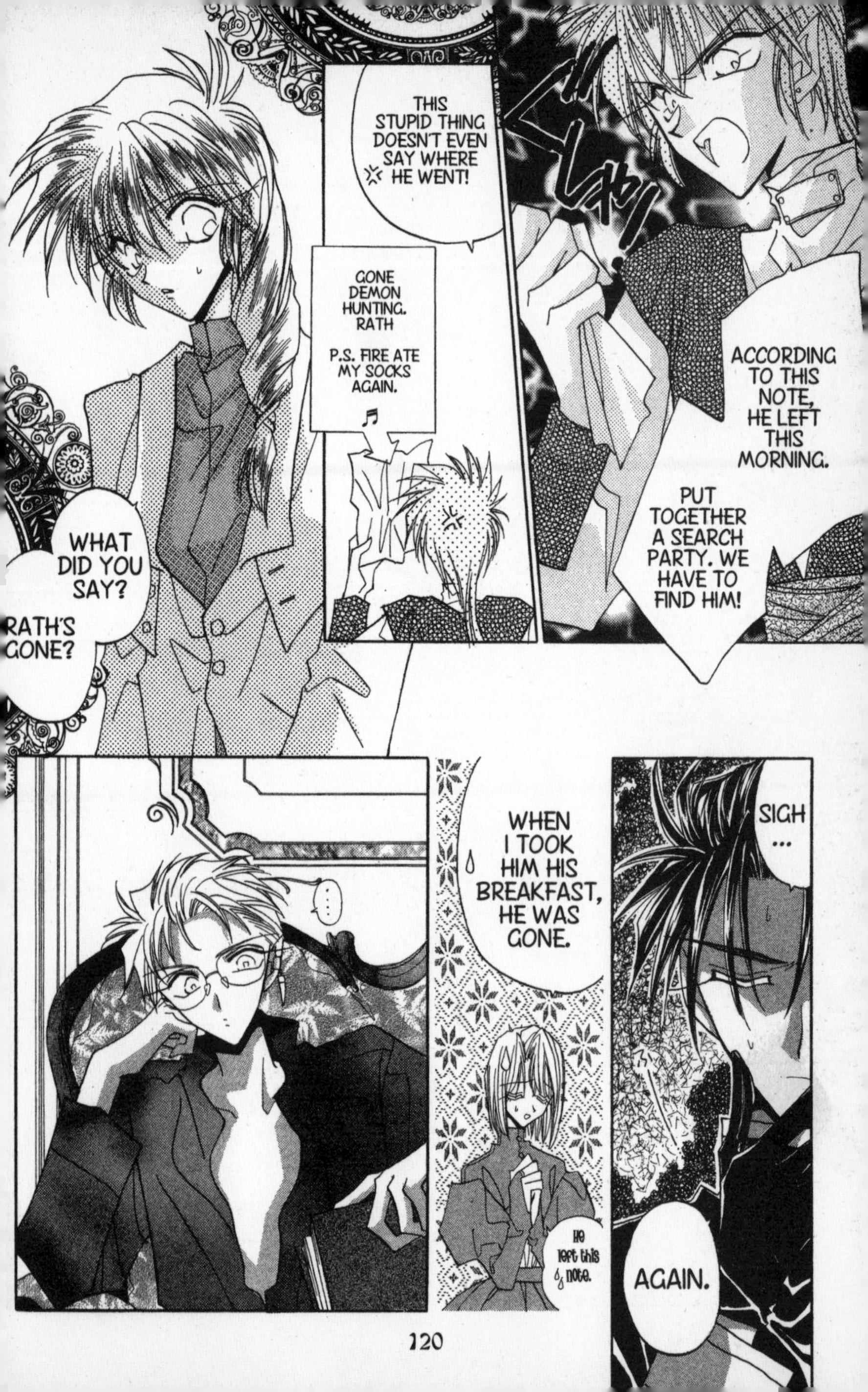
ACCORDING TO THIS NOTE, HE LEFT THIS MORNING.
PUT TOGETHER A SEARCH PARTY. WE HAVE TO FIND HIM!
THIS STUPID THING DOESN'T EVEN SAY WHERE HE WENT!
GONE DEMON HUNTING. RATH
P.S. FIRE ATE MY SOCKS AGAIN.
WHAT DID YOU SAY?
RATH'S GONE?
SIGH...
AGAIN.
WHEN I TOOK HIM HIS BREAKFAST, HE WAS GONE.
He left this note.
...

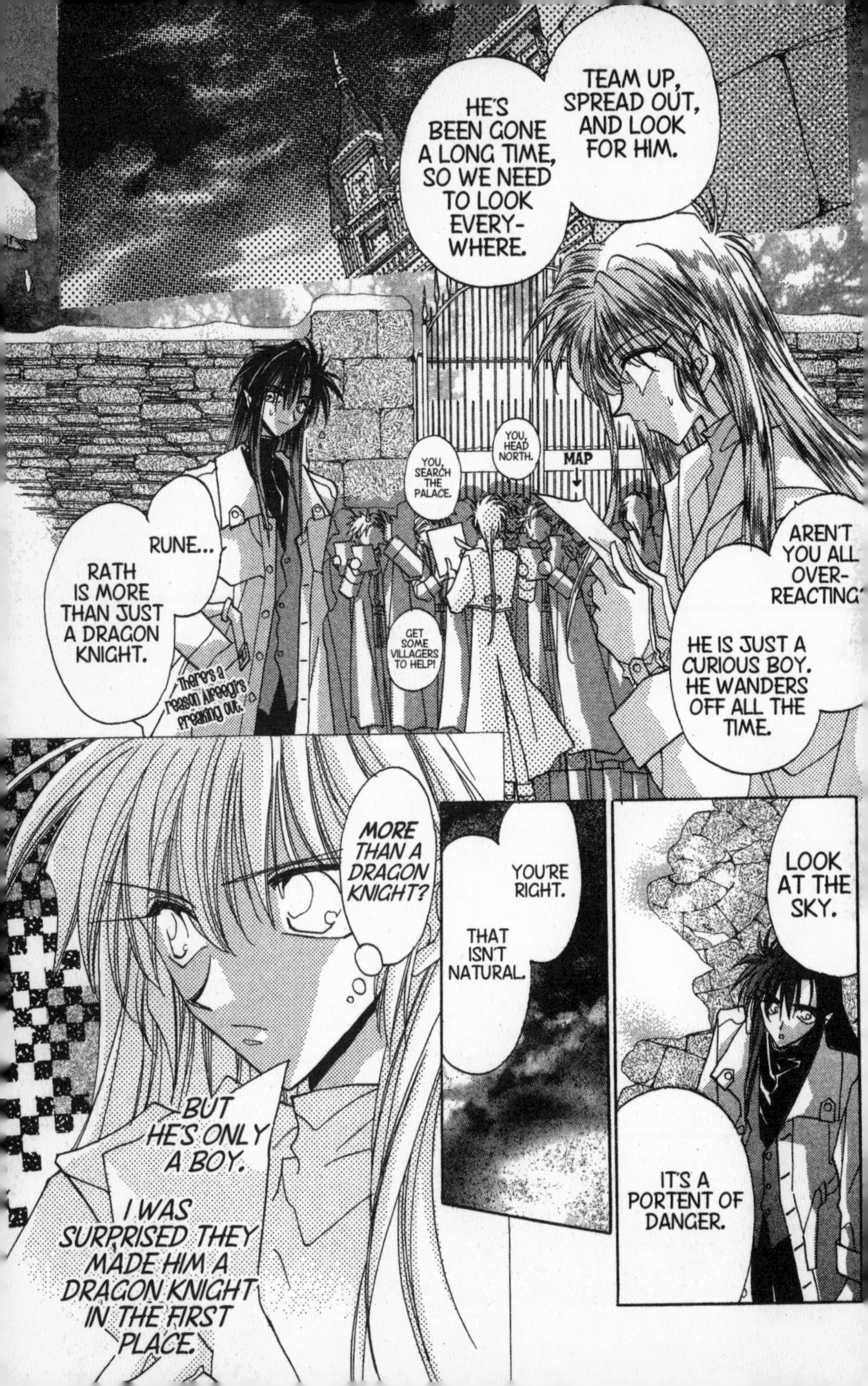
TEAM UP, SPREAD OUT, AND LOOK FOR HIM.
HE'S BEEN GONE A LONG TIME, SO WE NEED TO LOOK EVERY-WHERE.
YOU, HEAD NORTH.
YOU, SEARCH THE PALACE.
MAP
GET SOME VILLAGERS TO HELP!
AREN'T YOU ALL OVER-REACTING?
HE IS JUST A CURIOUS BOY. HE WANDERS OFF ALL THE TIME.
RUNE...
RATH IS MORE THAN JUST A DRAGON KNIGHT.
There's a reason Alfeegi's freaking out.
LOOK AT THE SKY.
IT'S A PORTENT OF DANGER.
YOU'RE RIGHT.
THAT ISN'T NATURAL.
MORE THAN A DRAGON KNIGHT?
BUT HE'S ONLY A BOY.
I WAS SURPRISED THEY MADE HIM A DRAGON KNIGHT IN THE FIRST PLACE.

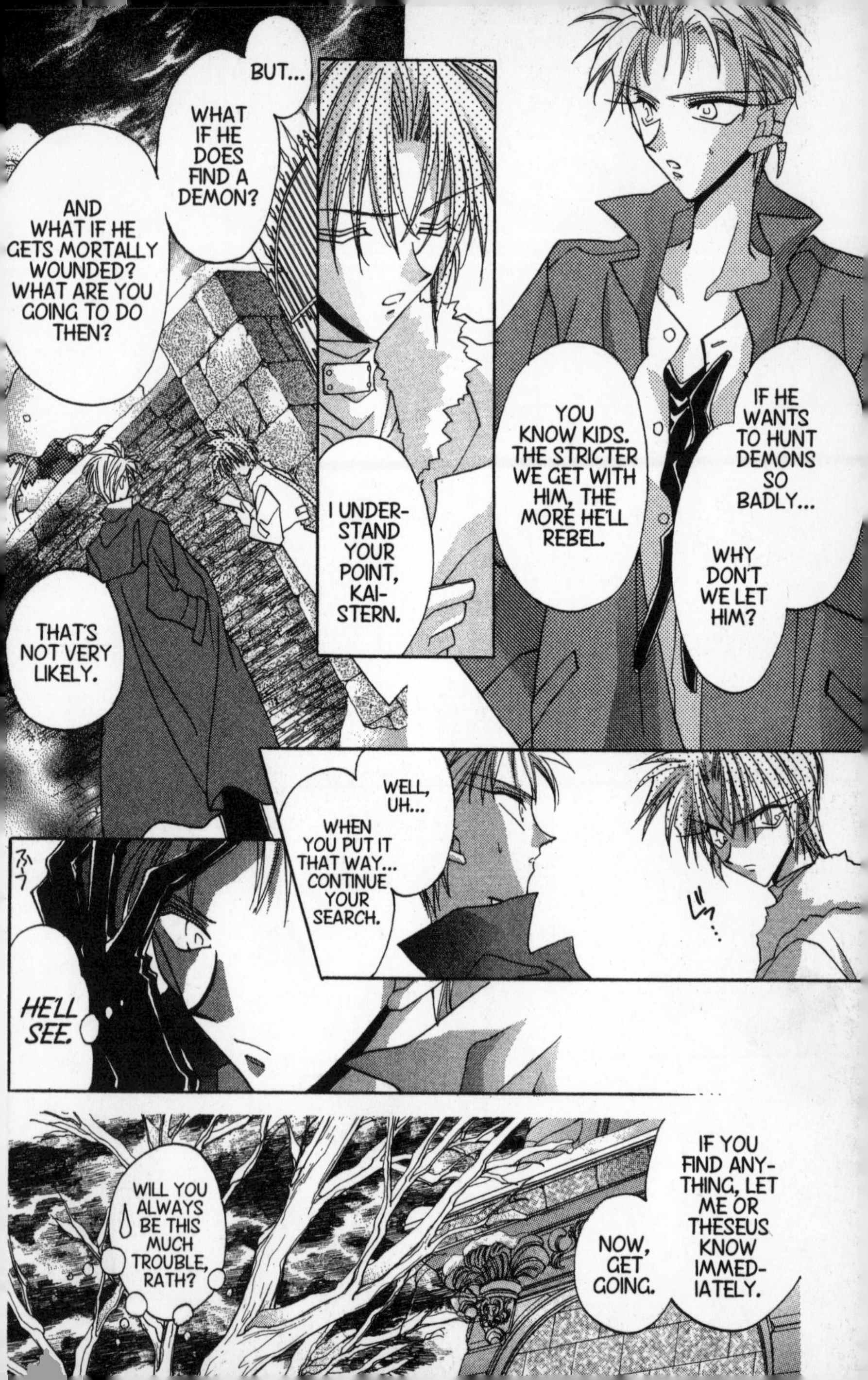

IF HE WANTS TO HUNT DEMONS SO BADLY...
WHY DON'T WE LET HIM?
YOU KNOW KIDS. THE STRICTER WE GET WITH HIM, THE MORE HE'LL REBEL.
I UNDER-STAND YOUR POINT, KAI-STERN.
BUT...
WHAT IF HE DOES FIND A DEMON?
AND WHAT IF HE GETS MORTALLY WOUNDED? WHAT ARE YOU GOING TO DO THEN?
THAT'S NOT VERY LIKELY.
WELL, UH...
WHEN YOU PUT IT THAT WAY... CONTINUE YOUR SEARCH.
HE'LL SEE.
IF YOU FIND ANY-THING, LET ME OR THESEUS KNOW IMMED-IATELY.
NOW, GET GOING.
WILL YOU ALWAYS BE THIS MUCH TROUBLE, RATH?

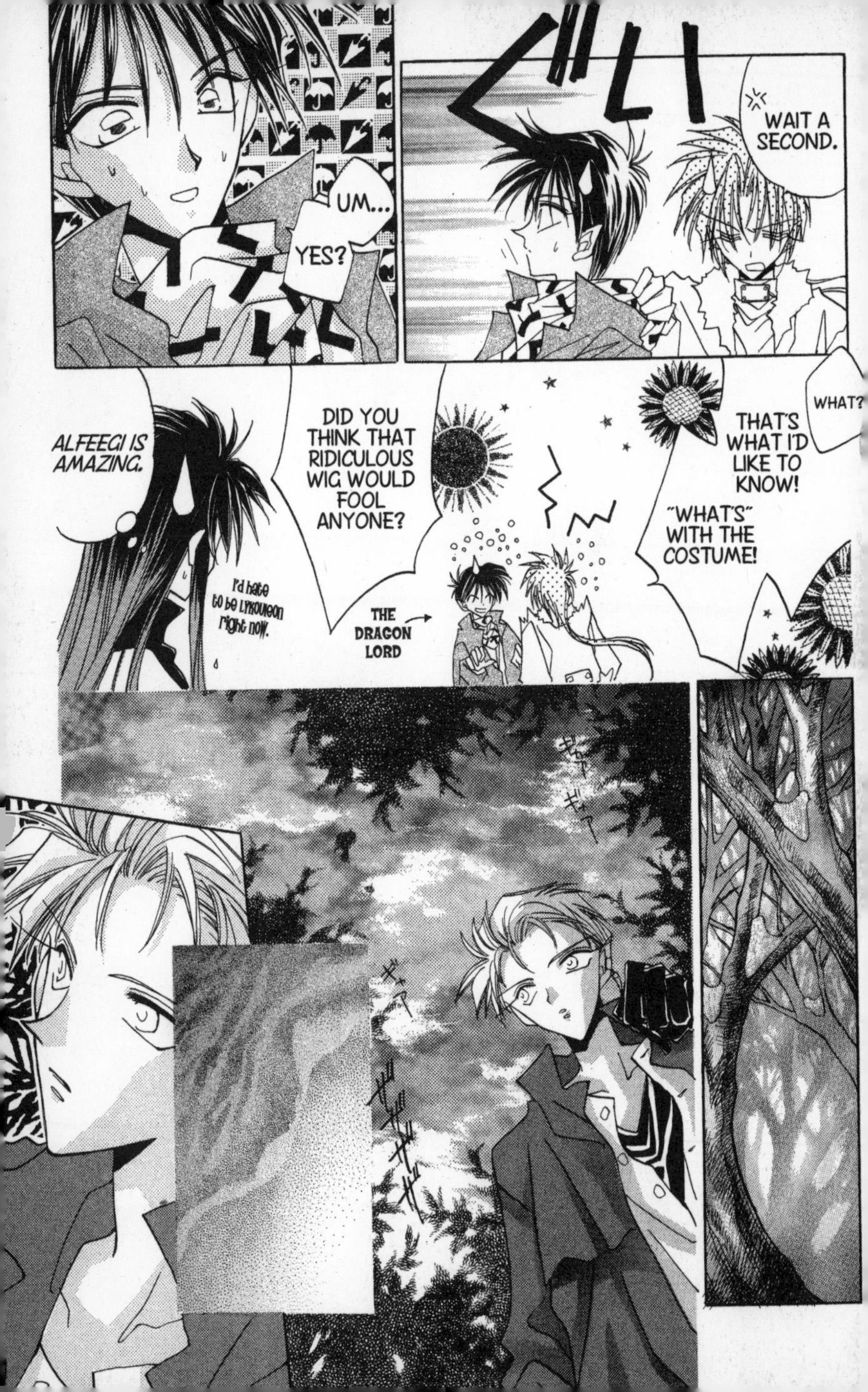
WAIT A SECOND.
UM...
YES?
WHAT?
THAT'S WHAT I'D LIKE TO KNOW!
"WHAT'S" WITH THE COSTUME!
DID YOU THINK THAT RIDICULOUS WIG WOULD FOOL ANYONE?
THE DRAGON LORD
ALFEEGI IS AMAZING.
I'd hate to be Lykouleon right now.

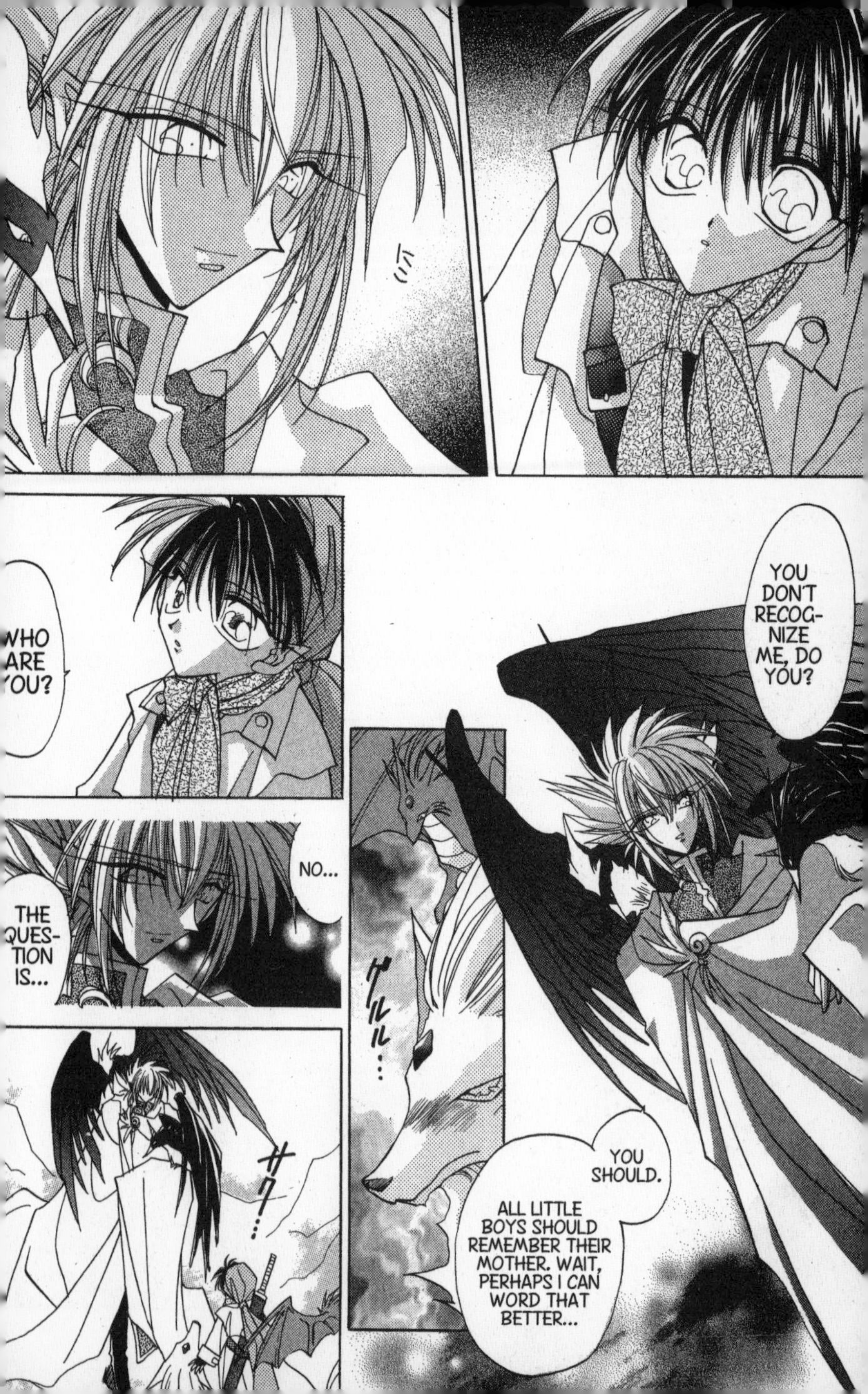
にこ
YOU DON'T RECOGNIZE ME, DO YOU?
YOU SHOULD.
ALL LITTLE BOYS SHOULD REMEMBER THEIR MOTHER. WAIT, PERHAPS I CAN WORD THAT BETTER...
グルル…
WHO ARE YOU?
NO...
THE QUESTION IS...
サク…

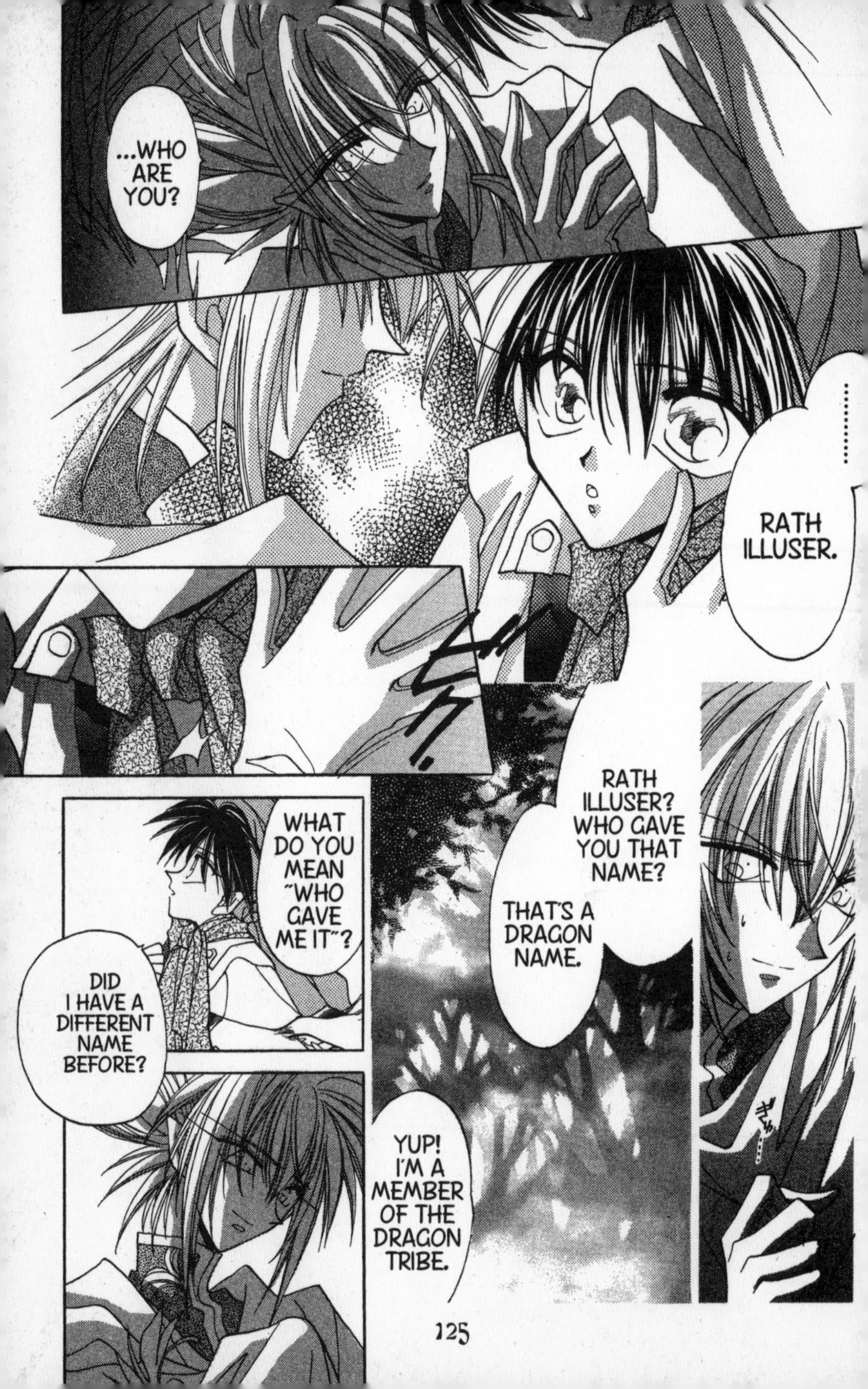
...WHO ARE YOU?
......
RATH ILLUSER.
RATH ILLUSER? WHO GAVE YOU THAT NAME?
THAT'S A DRAGON NAME.
WHAT DO YOU MEAN "WHO GAVE ME IT"?
DID I HAVE A DIFFERENT NAME BEFORE?
YUP! I'M A MEMBER OF THE DRAGON TRIBE.

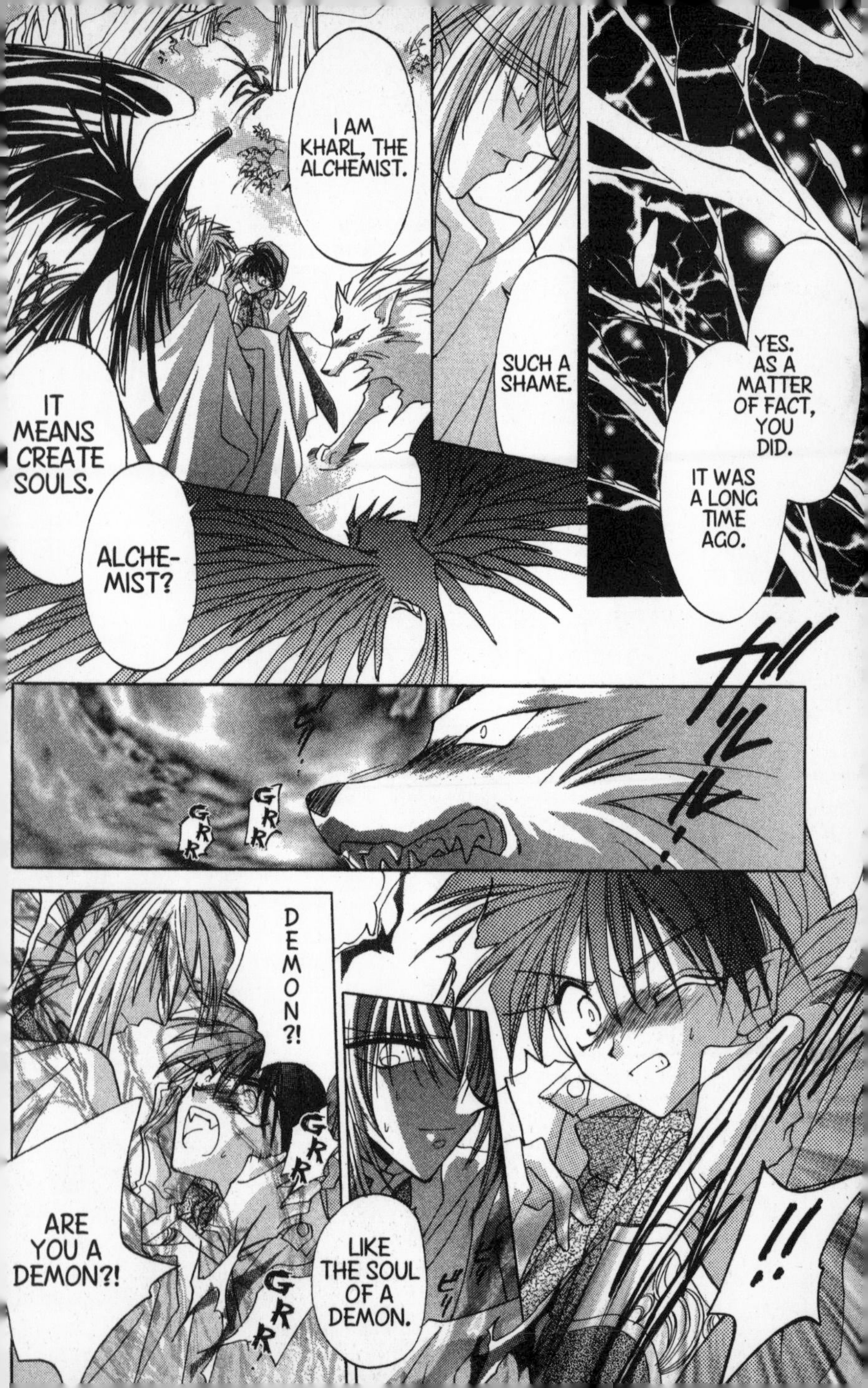
YES. AS A MATTER OF FACT, YOU DID.
IT WAS A LONG TIME AGO.
SUCH A SHAME.
I AM KHARL, THE ALCHEMIST.
ALCHE-MIST?
IT MEANS CREATE SOULS.
ガルル!!
GRR
GRR
!!
LIKE THE SOUL OF A DEMON.
DEMON?!
ARE YOU A DEMON?!
GRR
GRR

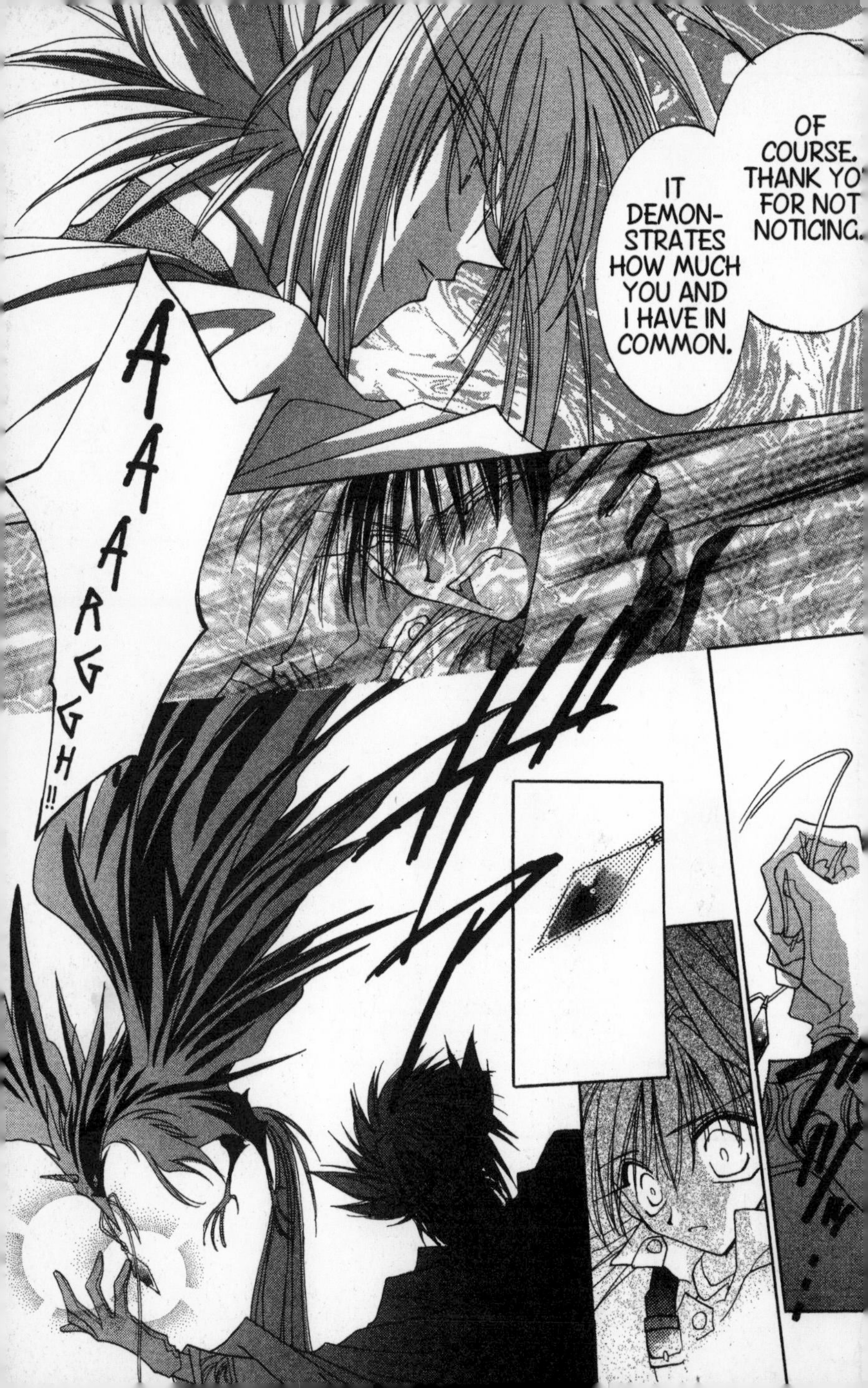
OF COURSE. THANK YO FOR NOT NOTICING.
IT DEMON-STRATES HOW MUCH YOU AND I HAVE IN COMMON.
AAAARGGH!!

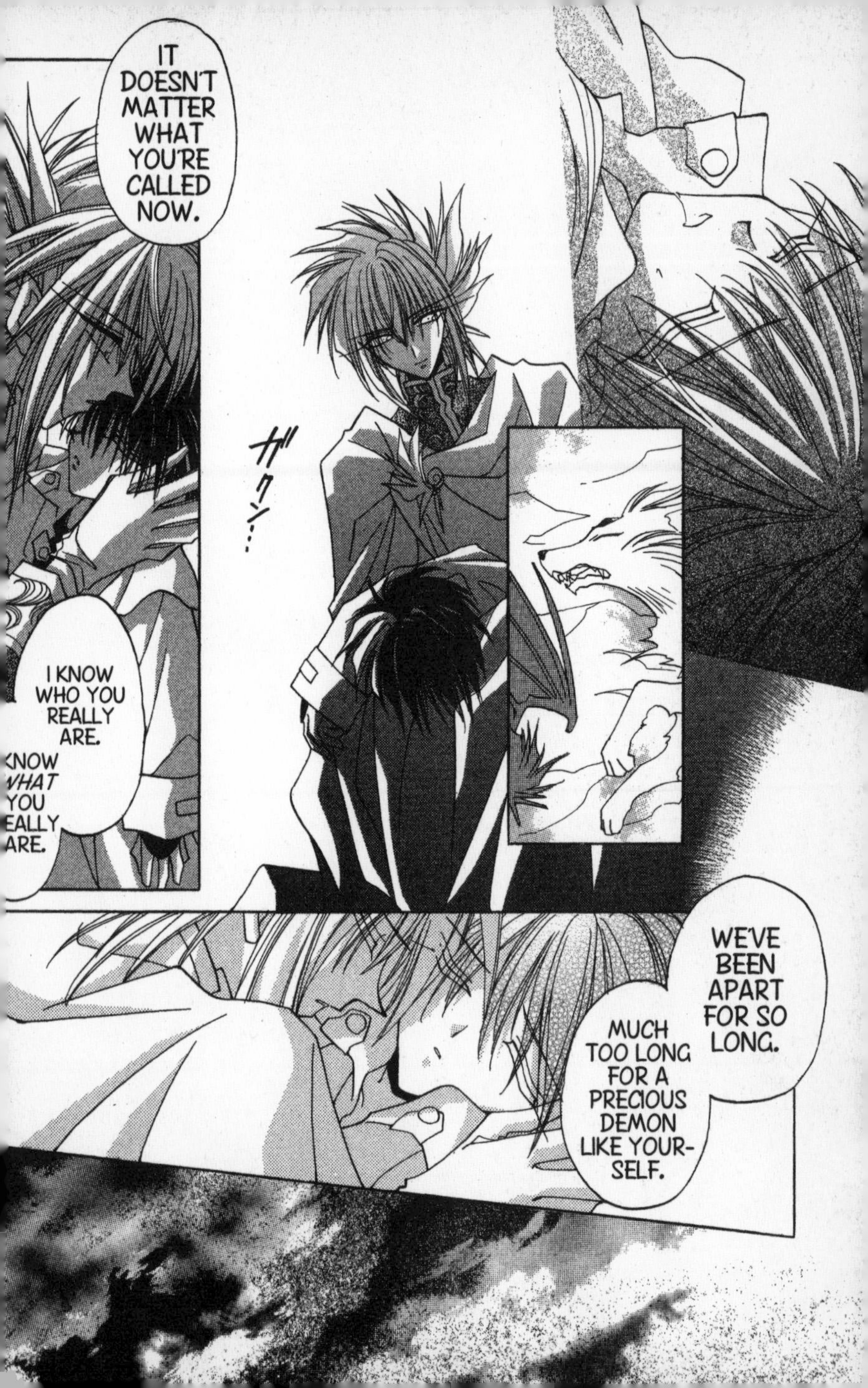
IT DOESN'T MATTER WHAT YOU'RE CALLED NOW.
ガクン…
I KNOW WHO YOU REALLY ARE.
KNOW WHAT YOU EALLY ARE.
WE'VE BEEN APART FOR SO LONG.
MUCH TOO LONG FOR A PRECIOUS DEMON LIKE YOUR-SELF.

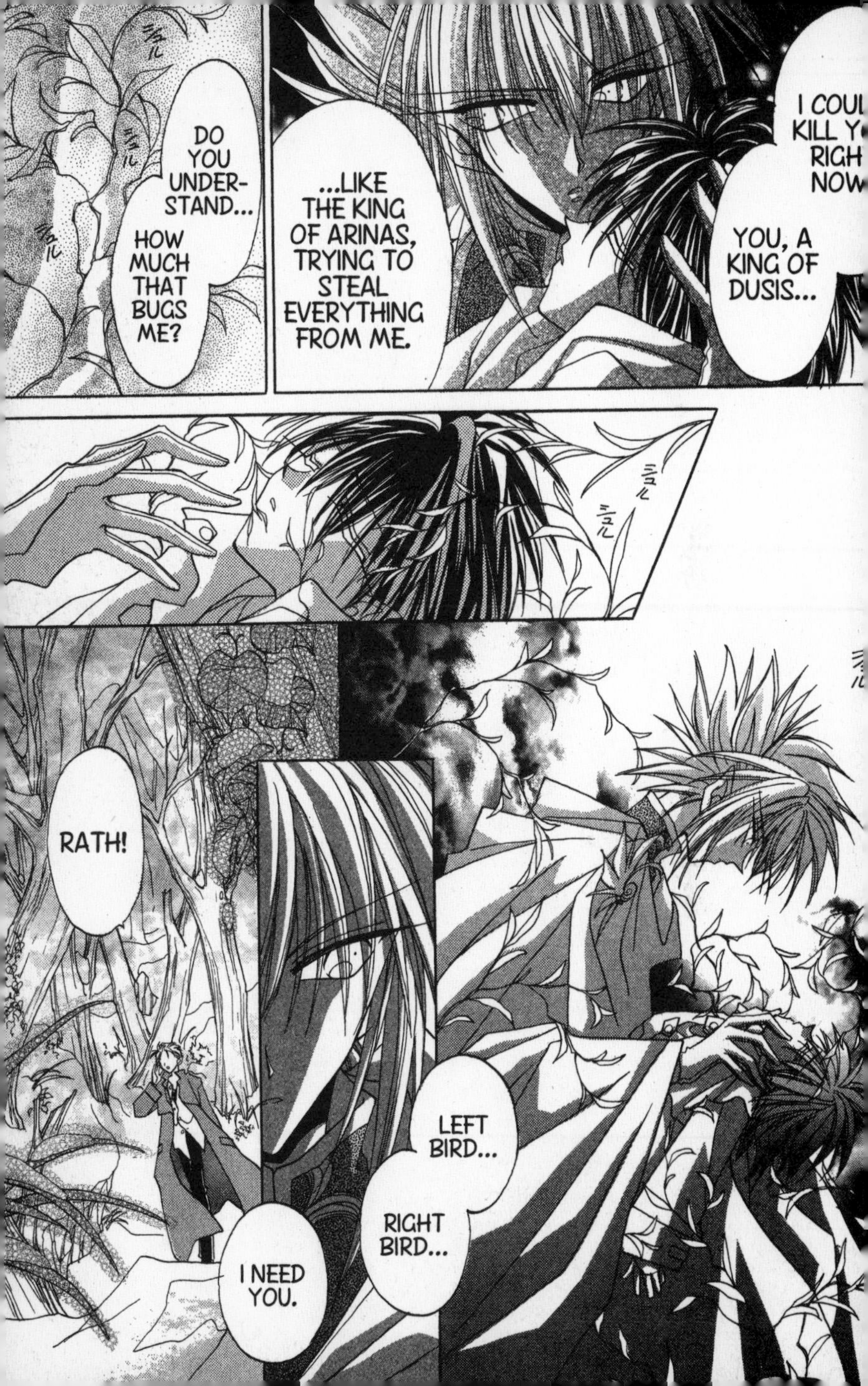
I COUL
KILL Y
RIGH
NOW
YOU, A KING OF DUSIS...
...LIKE THE KING OF ARINAS, TRYING TO STEAL EVERYTHING FROM ME.
DO YOU UNDER-STAND...
HOW MUCH THAT BUGS ME?
LEFT BIRD...
RIGHT BIRD...
I NEED YOU.
RATH!

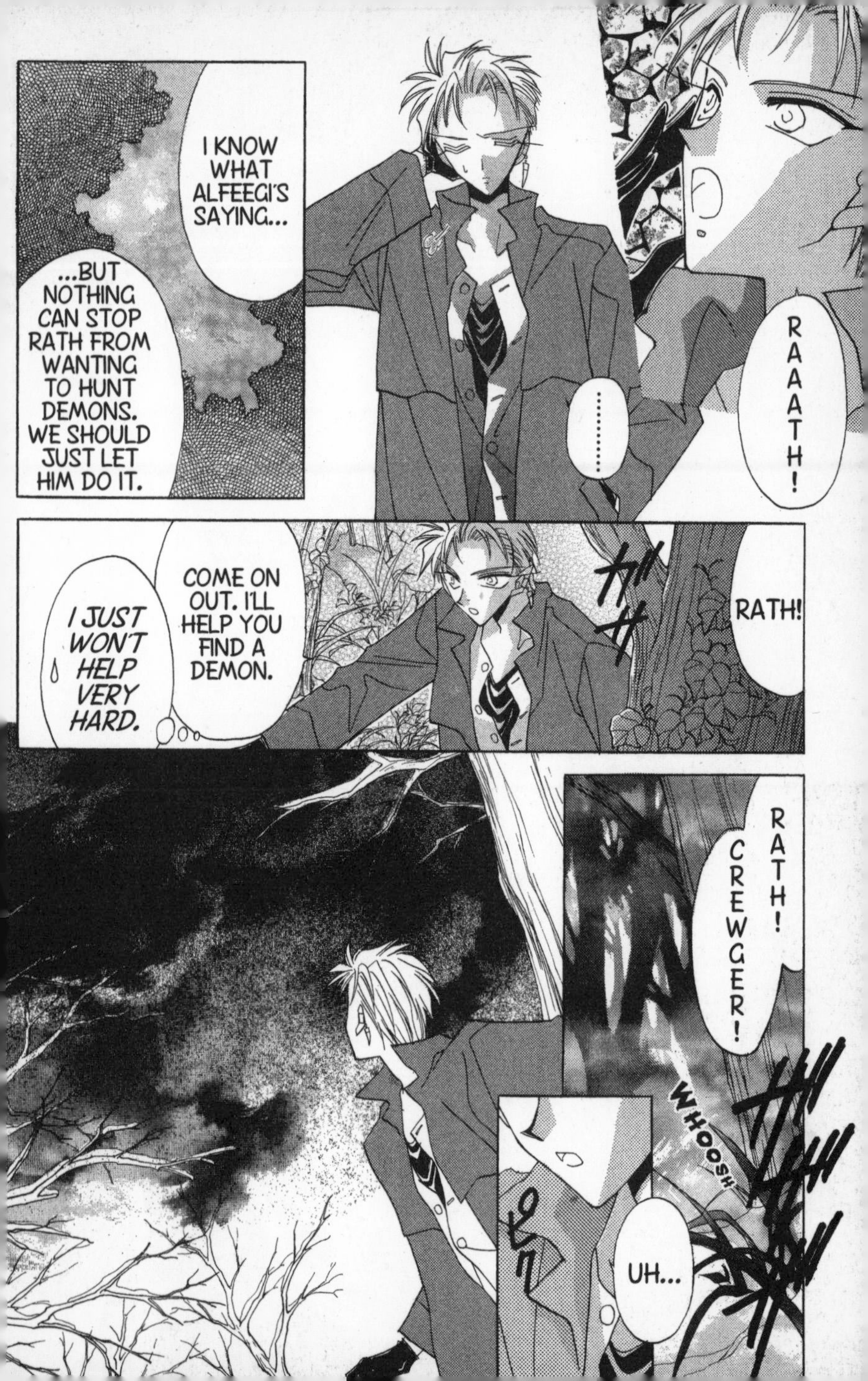
RAAATH!
I KNOW WHAT ALFEEGI'S SAYING...
...BUT NOTHING CAN STOP RATH FROM WANTING TO HUNT DEMONS. WE SHOULD JUST LET HIM DO IT.
......
RATH!
COME ON OUT. I'LL HELP YOU FIND A DEMON.
I JUST WON'T HELP VERY HARD.
RATH! CREWGER!
WHOOSH
UH...

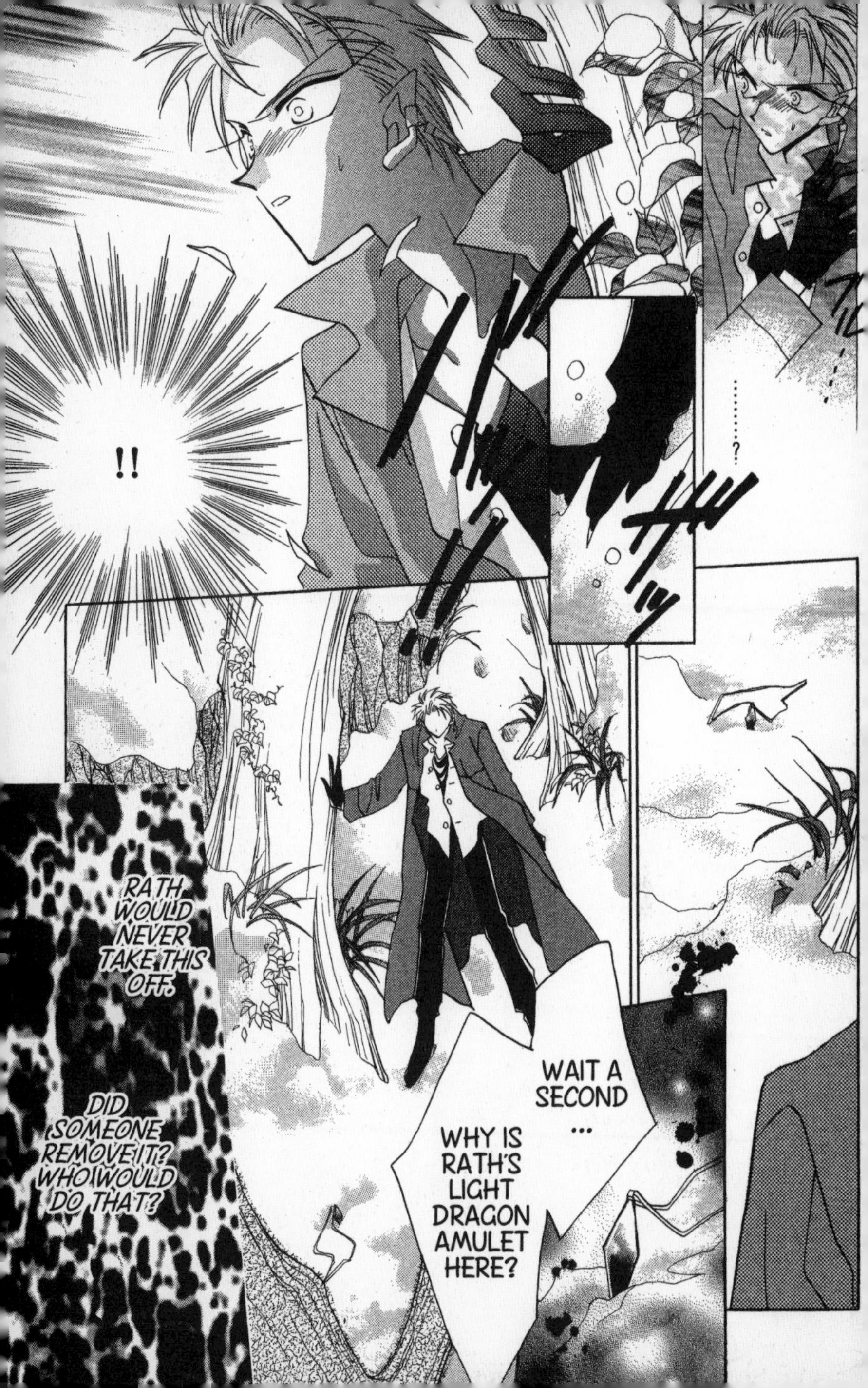
......?
!!
WAIT A SECOND ...
WHY IS RATH'S LIGHT DRAGON AMULET HERE?
RATH WOULD NEVER TAKE THIS OFF.
DID SOMEONE REMOVE IT? WHO WOULD DO THAT?

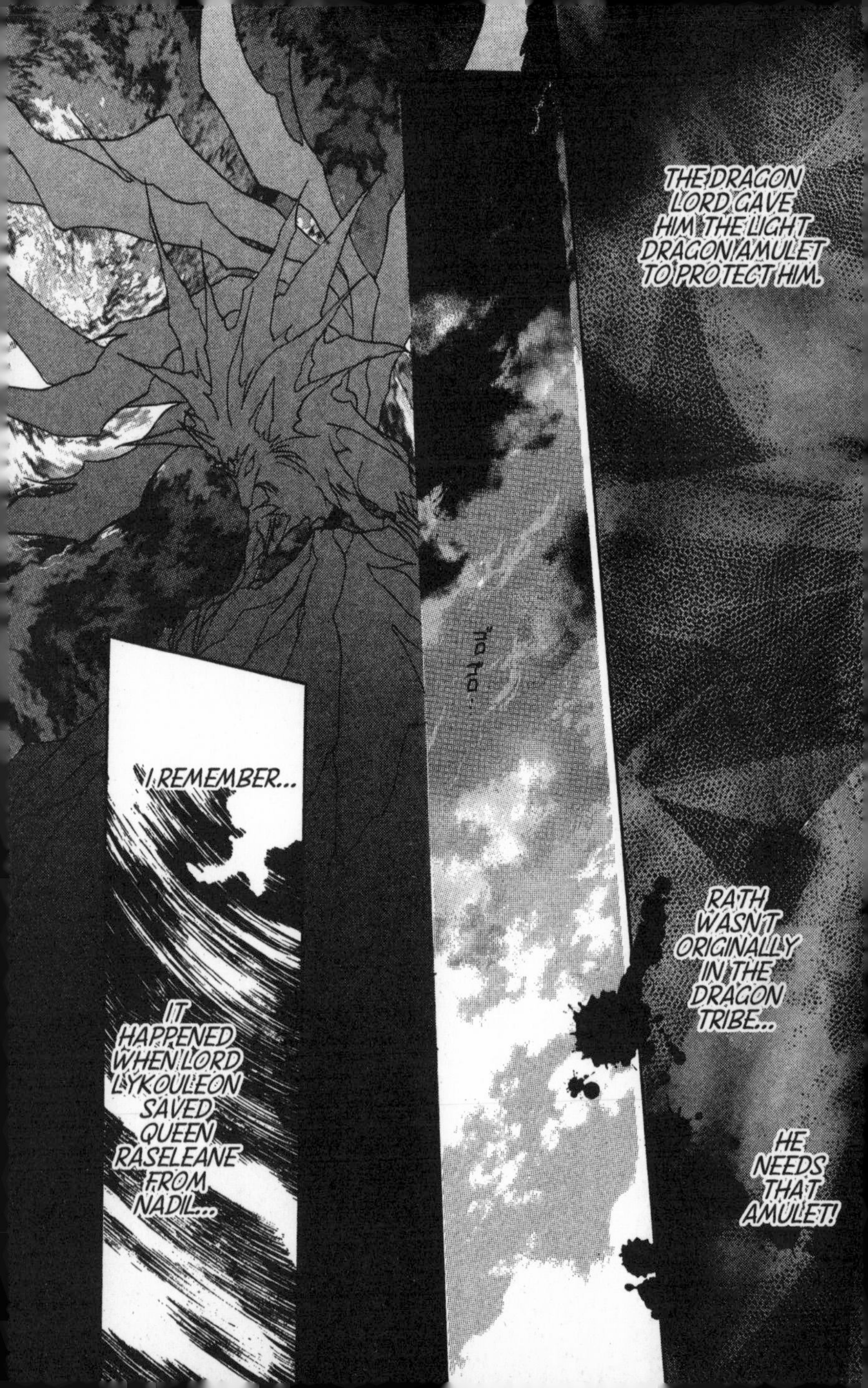
THE DRAGON LORD GAVE HIM THE LIGHT DRAGON AMULET TO PROTECT HIM.
RATH WASN'T ORIGINALLY IN THE DRAGON TRIBE...
HE NEEDS THAT AMULET!
ha ha...
I REMEMBER...
IT HAPPENED WHEN LORD LYKOULEON SAVED QUEEN RASELEANE FROM NADIL...

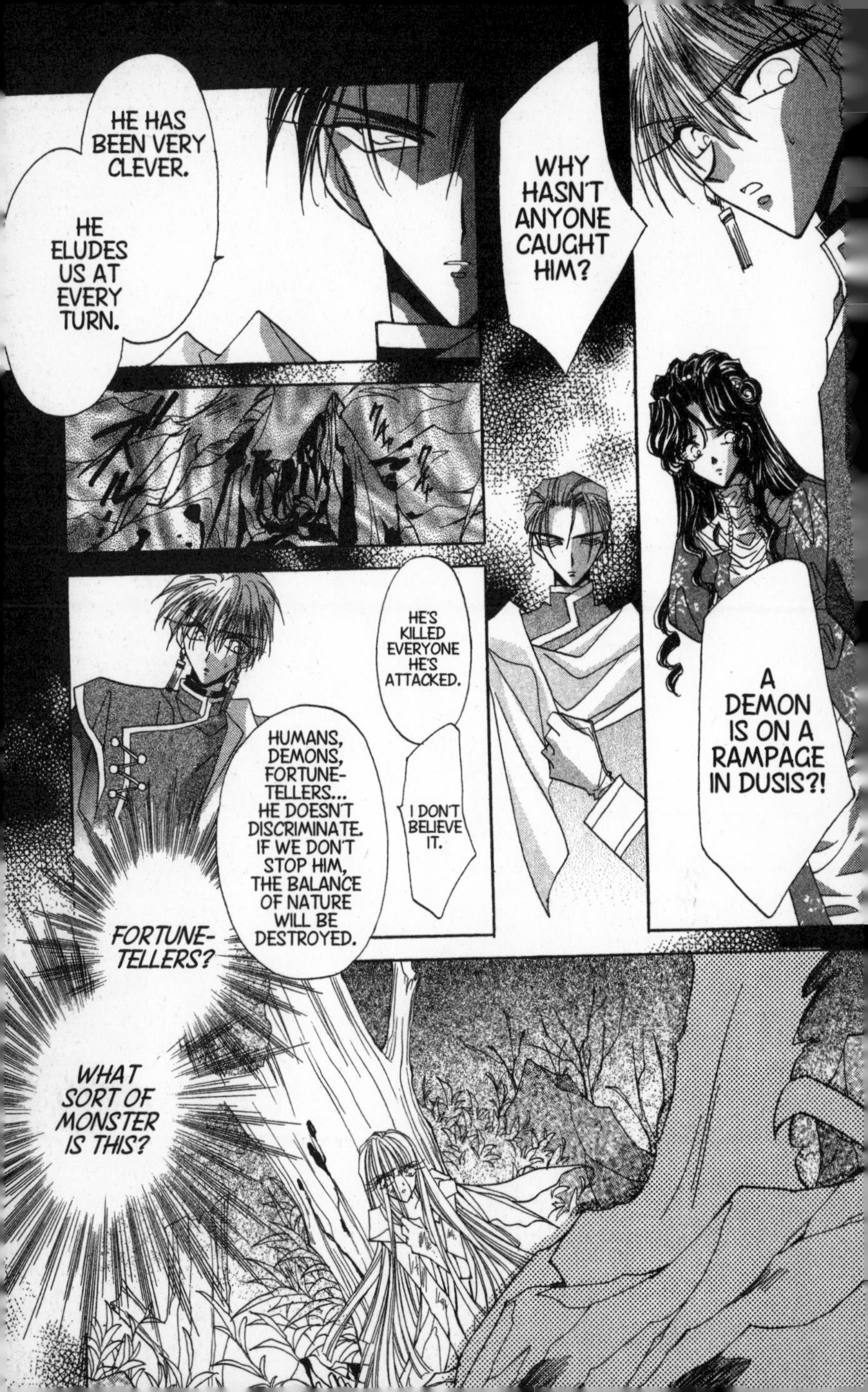
WHY HASN'T ANYONE CAUGHT HIM?
HE HAS BEEN VERY CLEVER.
HE ELUDES US AT EVERY TURN.
A DEMON IS ON A RAMPAGE IN DUSIS?!
HE'S KILLED EVERYONE HE'S ATTACKED.
I DON'T BELIEVE IT.
HUMANS, DEMONS, FORTUNE-TELLERS... HE DOESN'T DISCRIMINATE. IF WE DON'T STOP HIM, THE BALANCE OF NATURE WILL BE DESTROYED.
FORTUNE-TELLERS?
WHAT SORT OF MONSTER IS THIS?

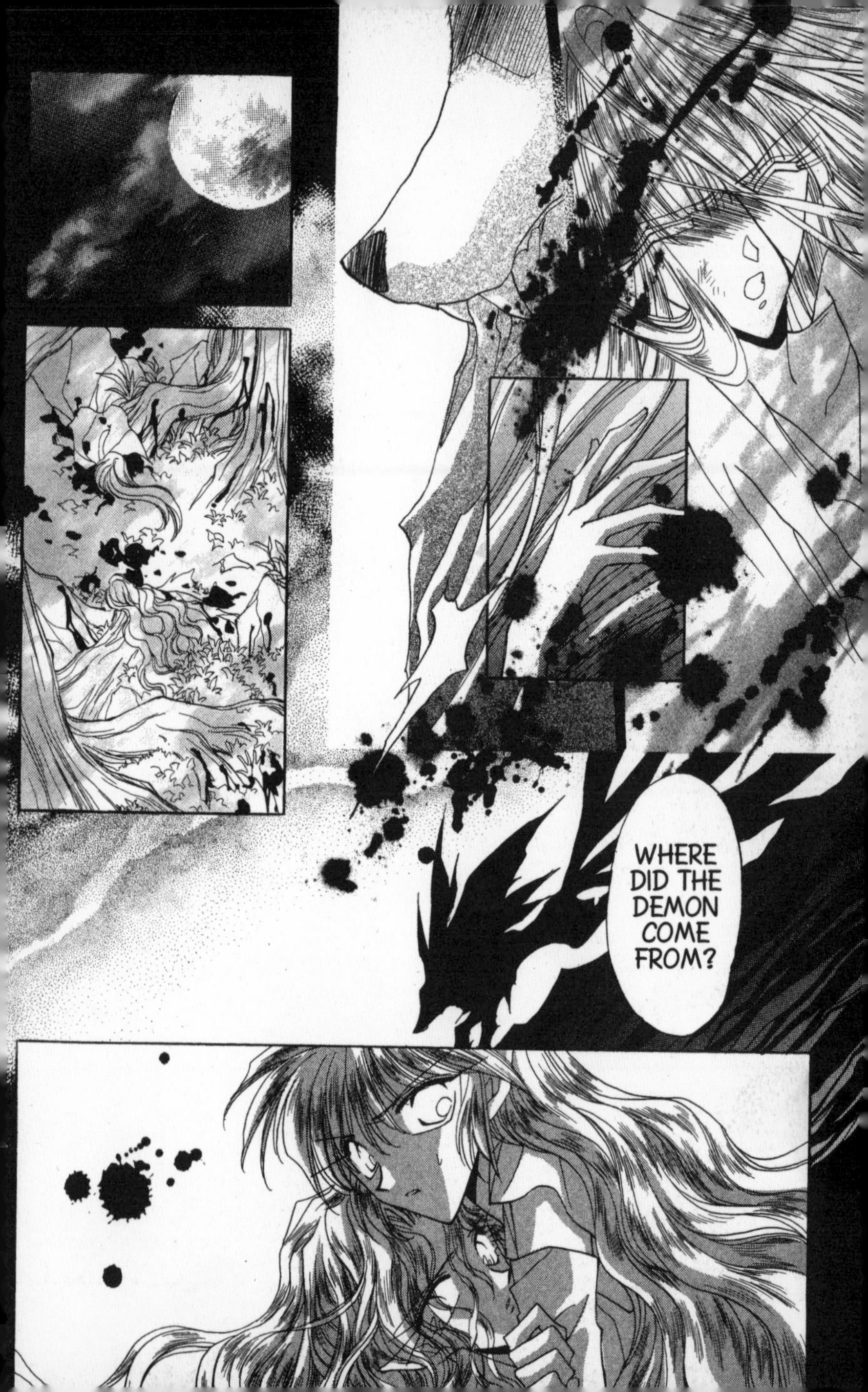
WHERE DID THE DEMON COME FROM?

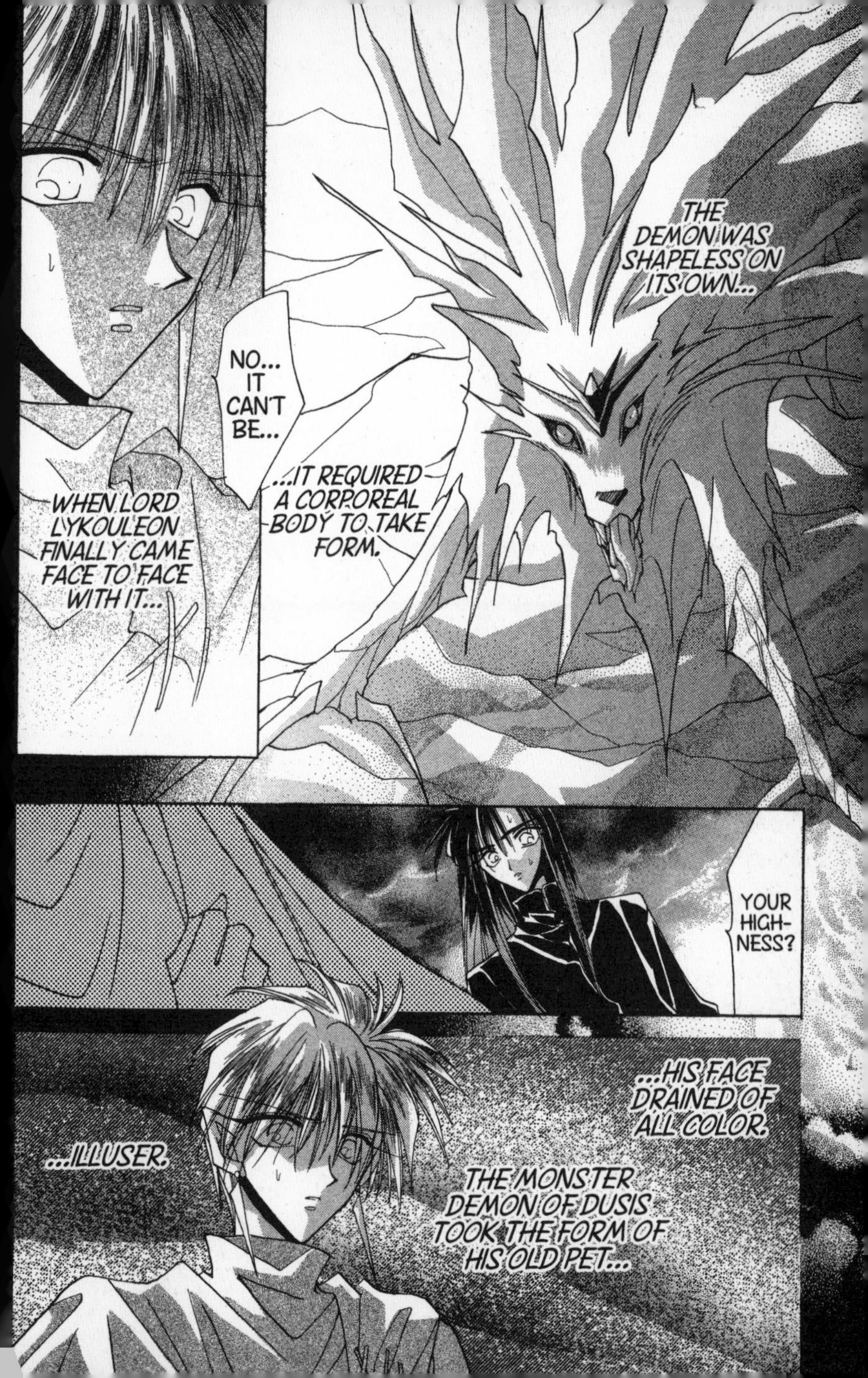
THE DEMON WAS SHAPELESS ON ITS OWN...
...IT REQUIRED A CORPOREAL BODY TO TAKE FORM.
NO... IT CAN'T BE...
WHEN LORD LYKOULEON FINALLY CAME FACE TO FACE WITH IT...
YOUR HIGH-NESS?
...HIS FACE DRAINED OF ALL COLOR.
THE MONSTER DEMON OF DUSIS TOOK THE FORM OF HIS OLD PET...
...ILLUSER.

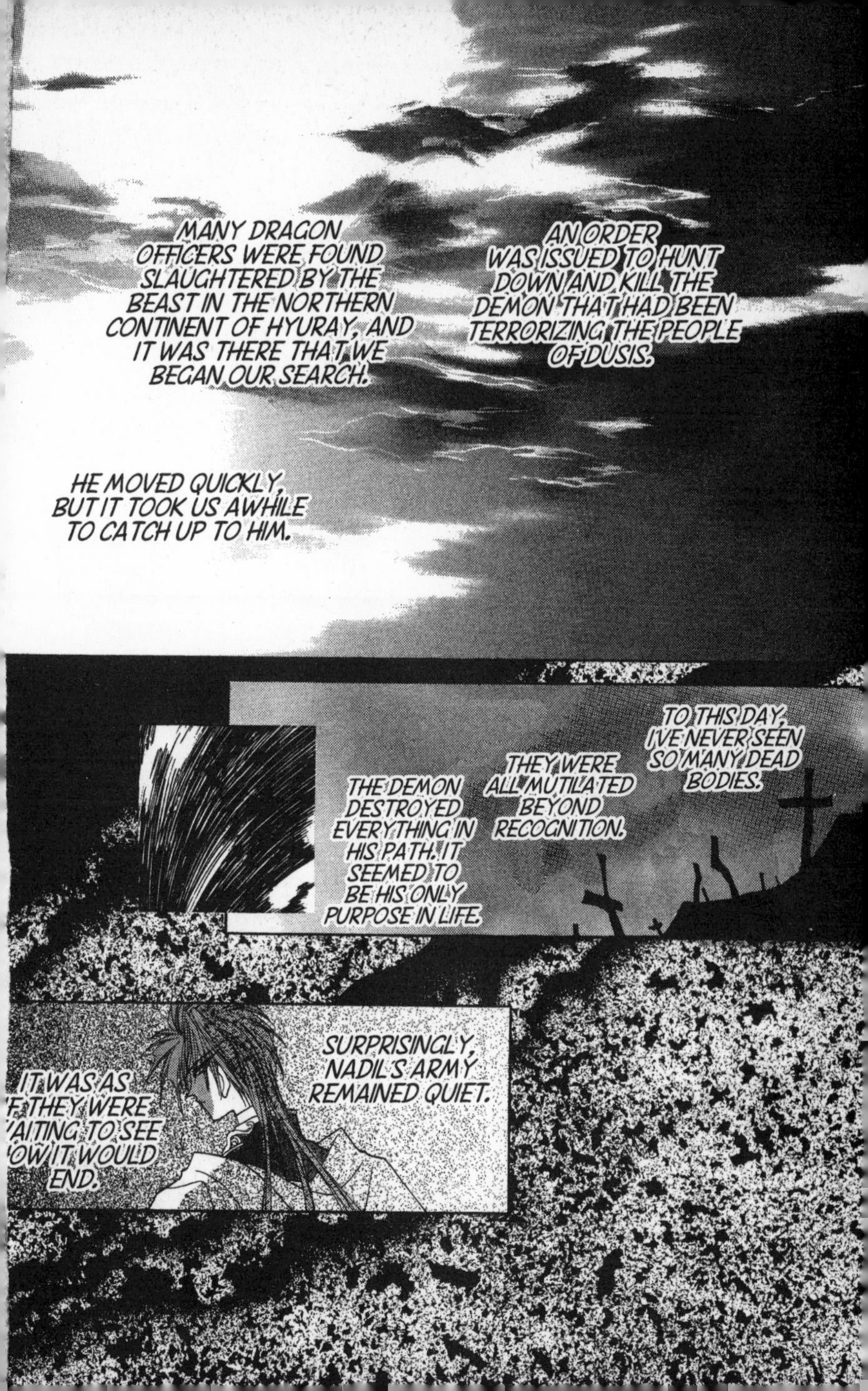
AN ORDER WAS ISSUED TO HUNT DOWN AND KILL THE DEMON THAT HAD BEEN TERRORIZING THE PEOPLE OF DUSIS.
MANY DRAGON OFFICERS WERE FOUND SLAUGHTERED BY THE BEAST IN THE NORTHERN CONTINENT OF HYURAY, AND IT WAS THERE THAT WE BEGAN OUR SEARCH.
HE MOVED QUICKLY, BUT IT TOOK US AWHILE TO CATCH UP TO HIM.
TO THIS DAY, I'VE NEVER SEEN SO MANY DEAD BODIES.
THEY WERE ALL MUTILATED BEYOND RECOGNITION.
THE DEMON DESTROYED EVERYTHING IN HIS PATH. IT SEEMED TO BE HIS ONLY PURPOSE IN LIFE.
SURPRISINGLY, NADIL'S ARMY REMAINED QUIET.
IT WAS AS F THEY WERE AITING TO SEE OW IT WOULD END.

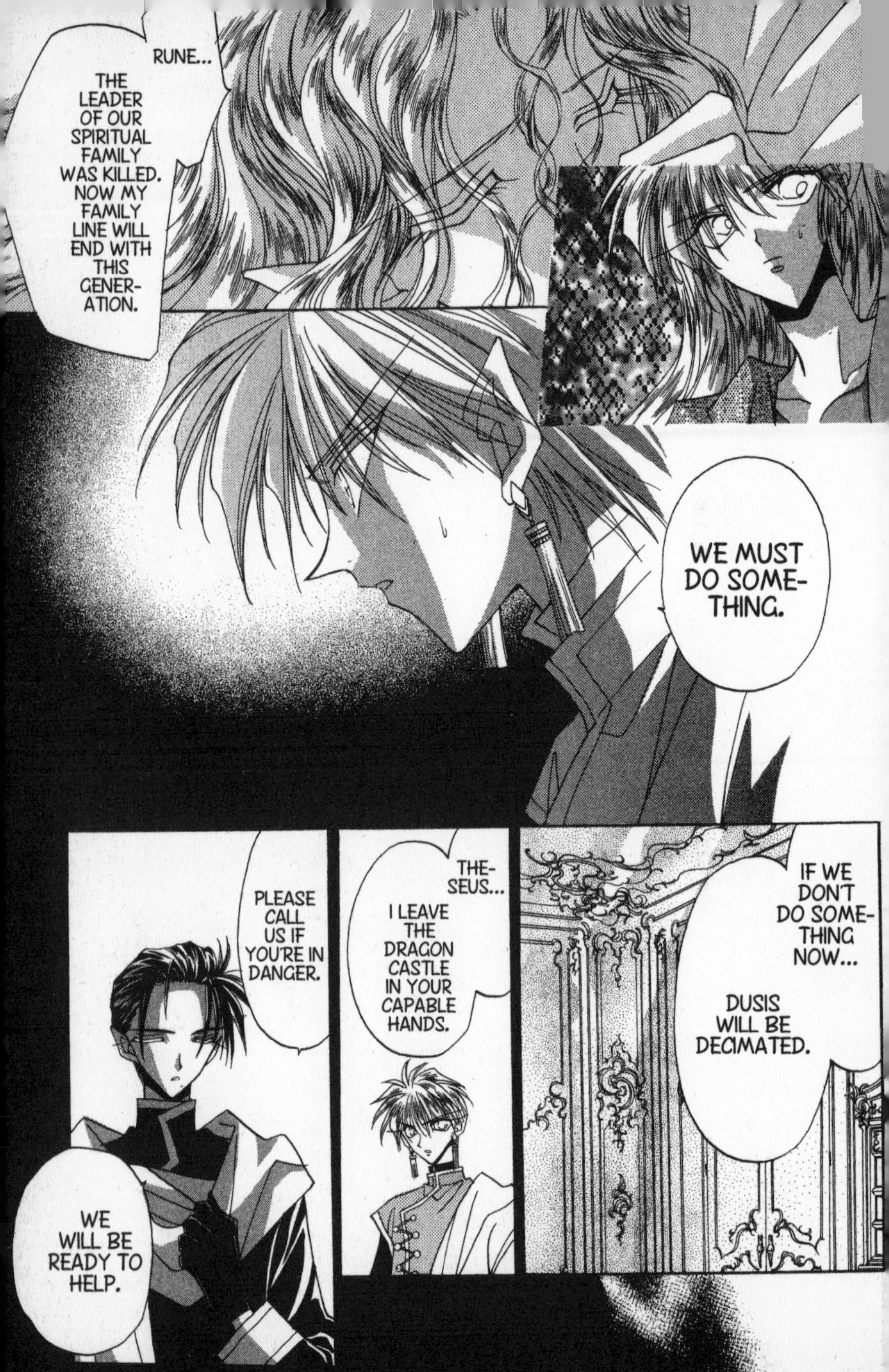
RUNE... THE LEADER OF OUR SPIRITUAL FAMILY WAS KILLED. NOW MY FAMILY LINE WILL END WITH THIS GENERATION.
WE MUST DO SOMETHING.
IF WE DON'T DO SOMETHING NOW...
DUSIS WILL BE DECIMATED.
THESEUS...
I LEAVE THE DRAGON CASTLE IN YOUR CAPABLE HANDS.
PLEASE CALL US IF YOU'RE IN DANGER.
WE WILL BE READY TO HELP.

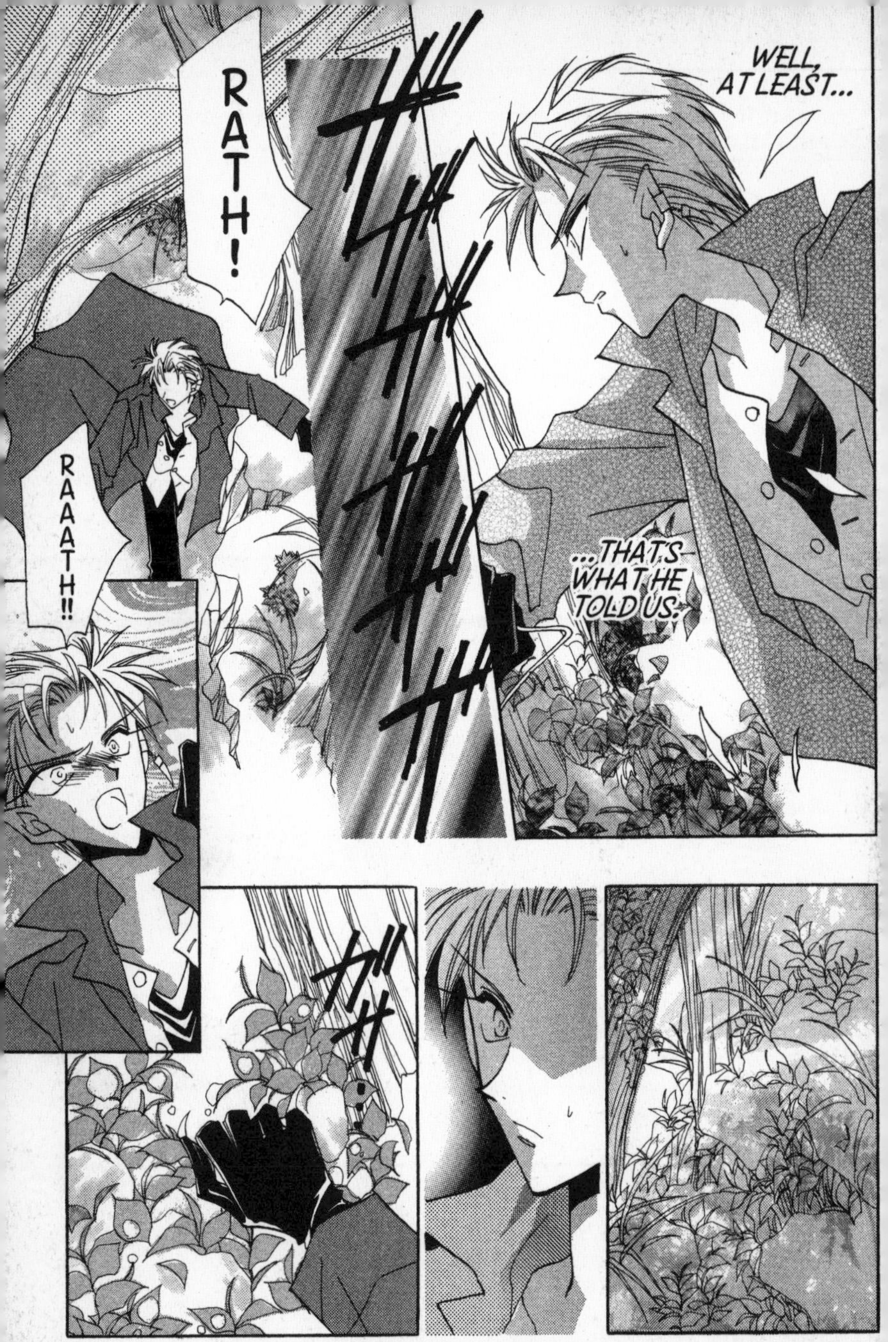
WELL, AT LEAST...
...THAT'S WHAT HE TOLD US.
RATH!
RAAAATH!!

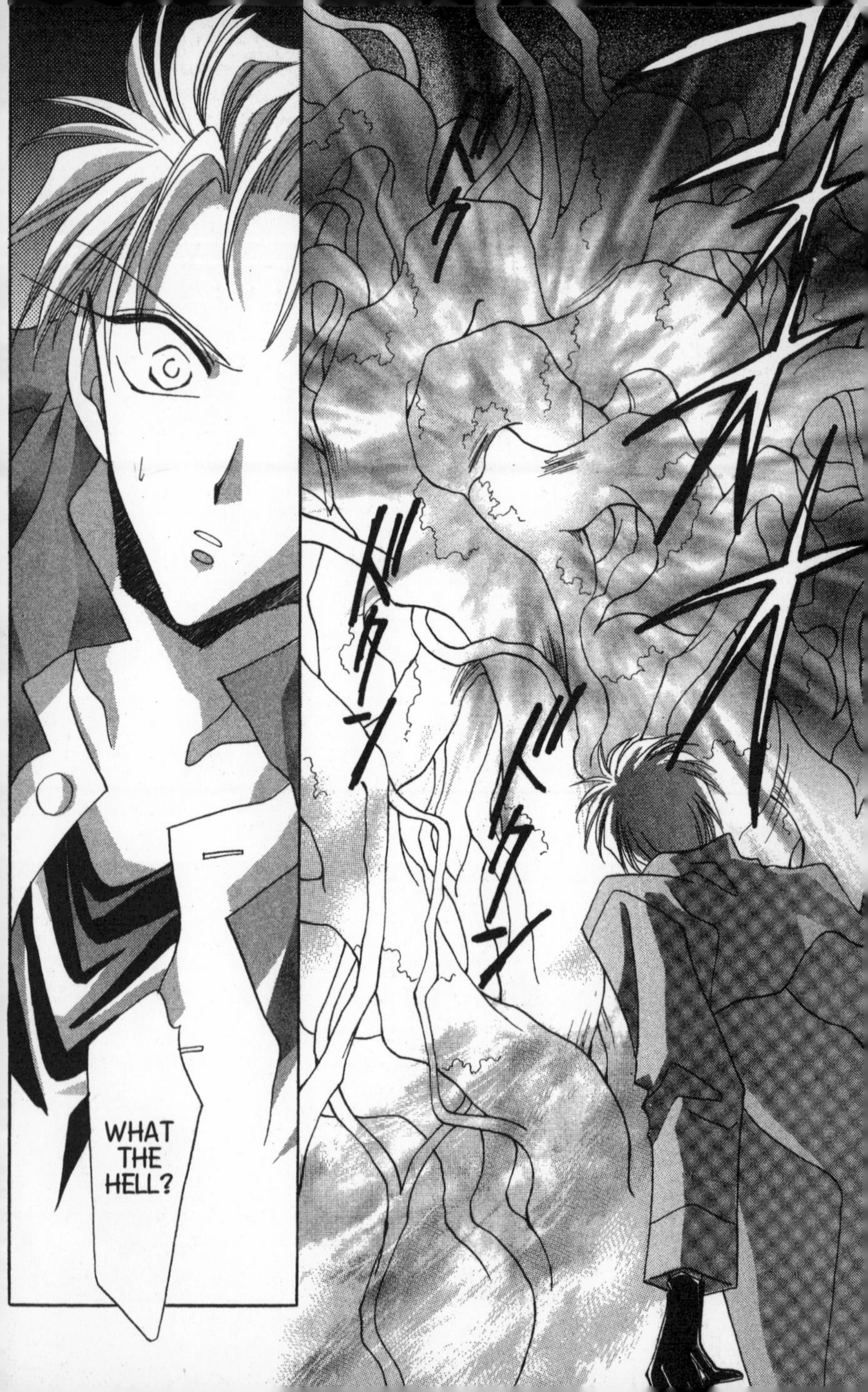
WHAT THE HELL?

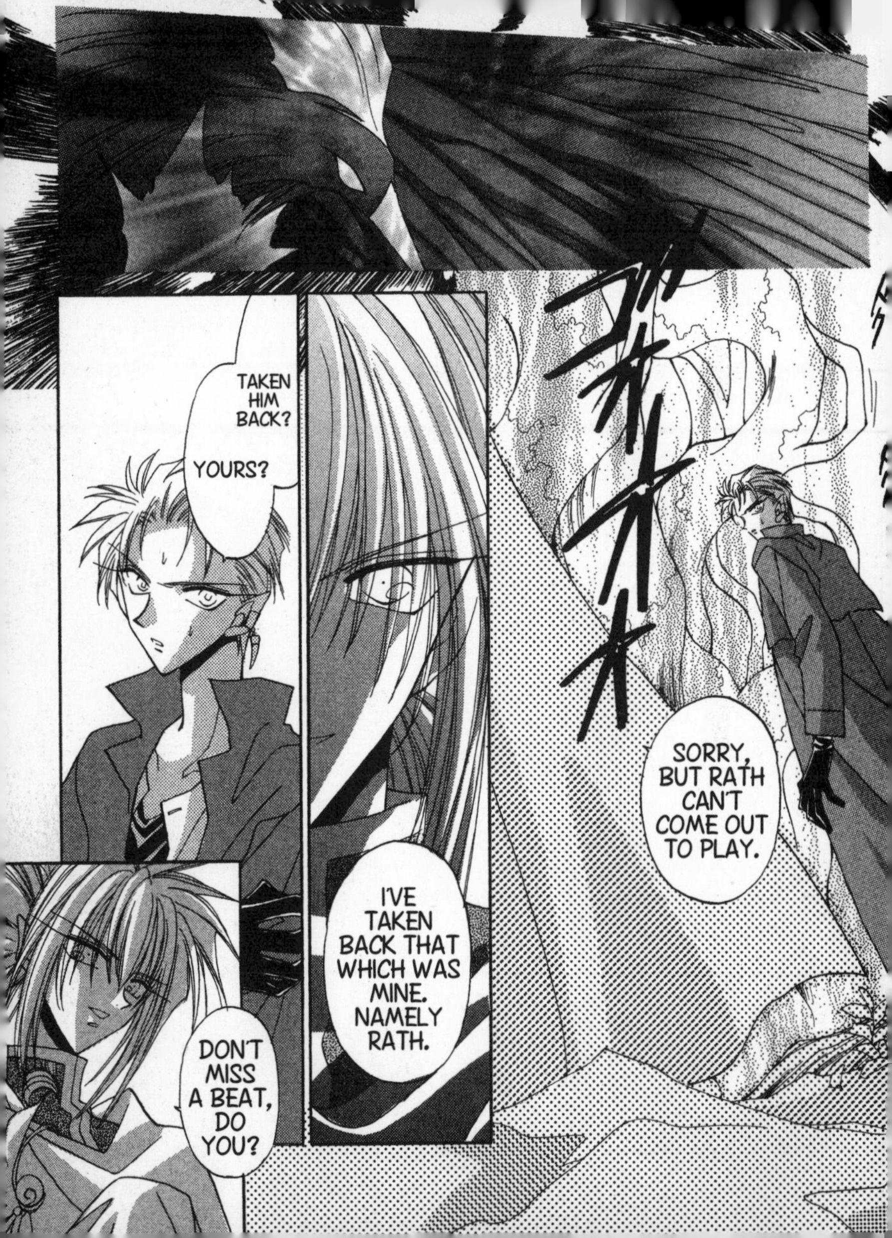
SORRY, BUT RATH CAN'T COME OUT TO PLAY.
I'VE TAKEN BACK THAT WHICH WAS MINE. NAMELY RATH.
TAKEN HIM BACK?
YOURS?
DON'T MISS A BEAT, DO YOU?

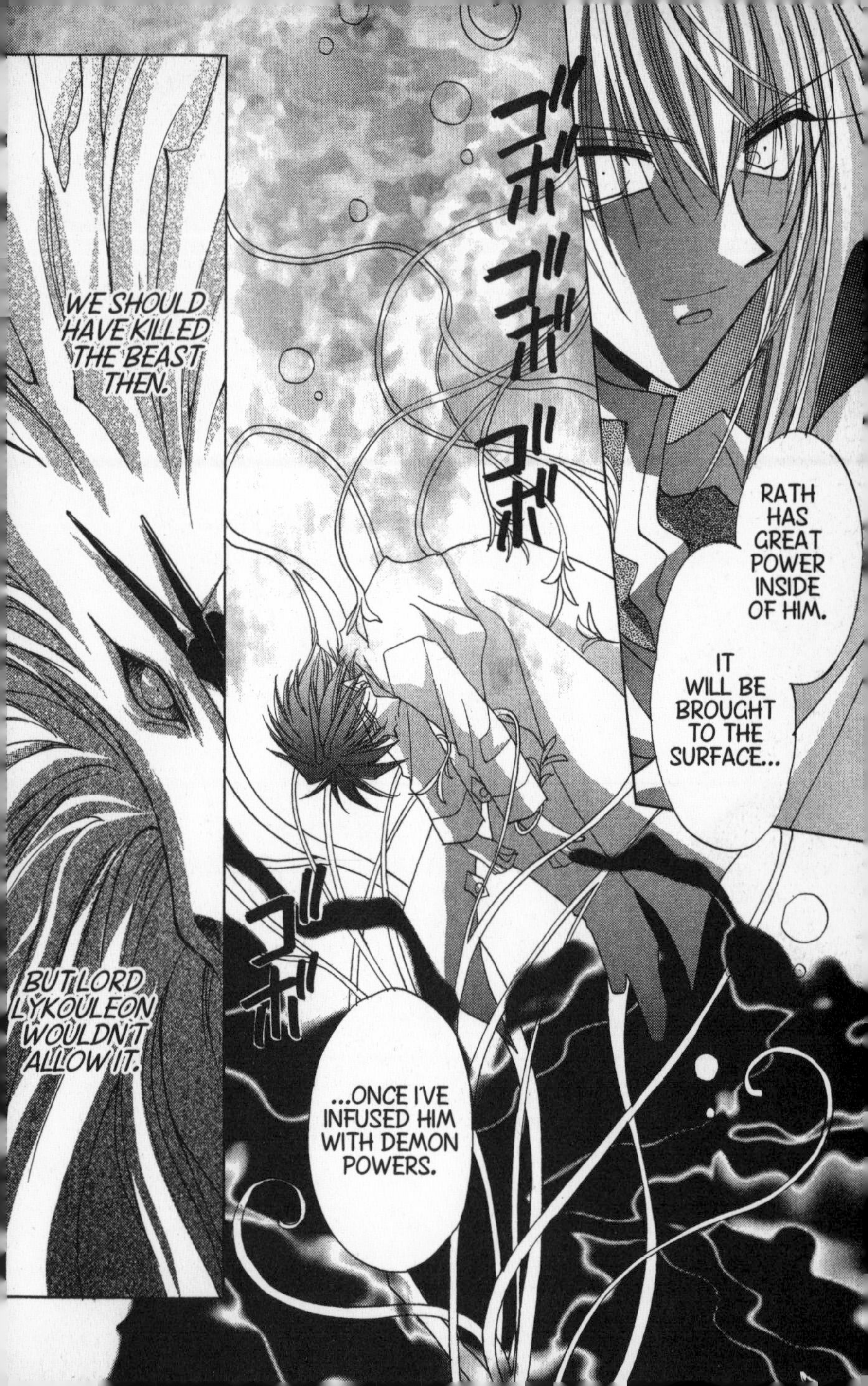
ゴボゴボゴボ
RATH HAS GREAT POWER INSIDE OF HIM.
IT WILL BE BROUGHT TO THE SURFACE...
ゴボ
...ONCE I'VE INFUSED HIM WITH DEMON POWERS.
WE SHOULD HAVE KILLED THE BEAST THEN.
BUT LORD LYKOULEON WOULDN'T ALLOW IT.

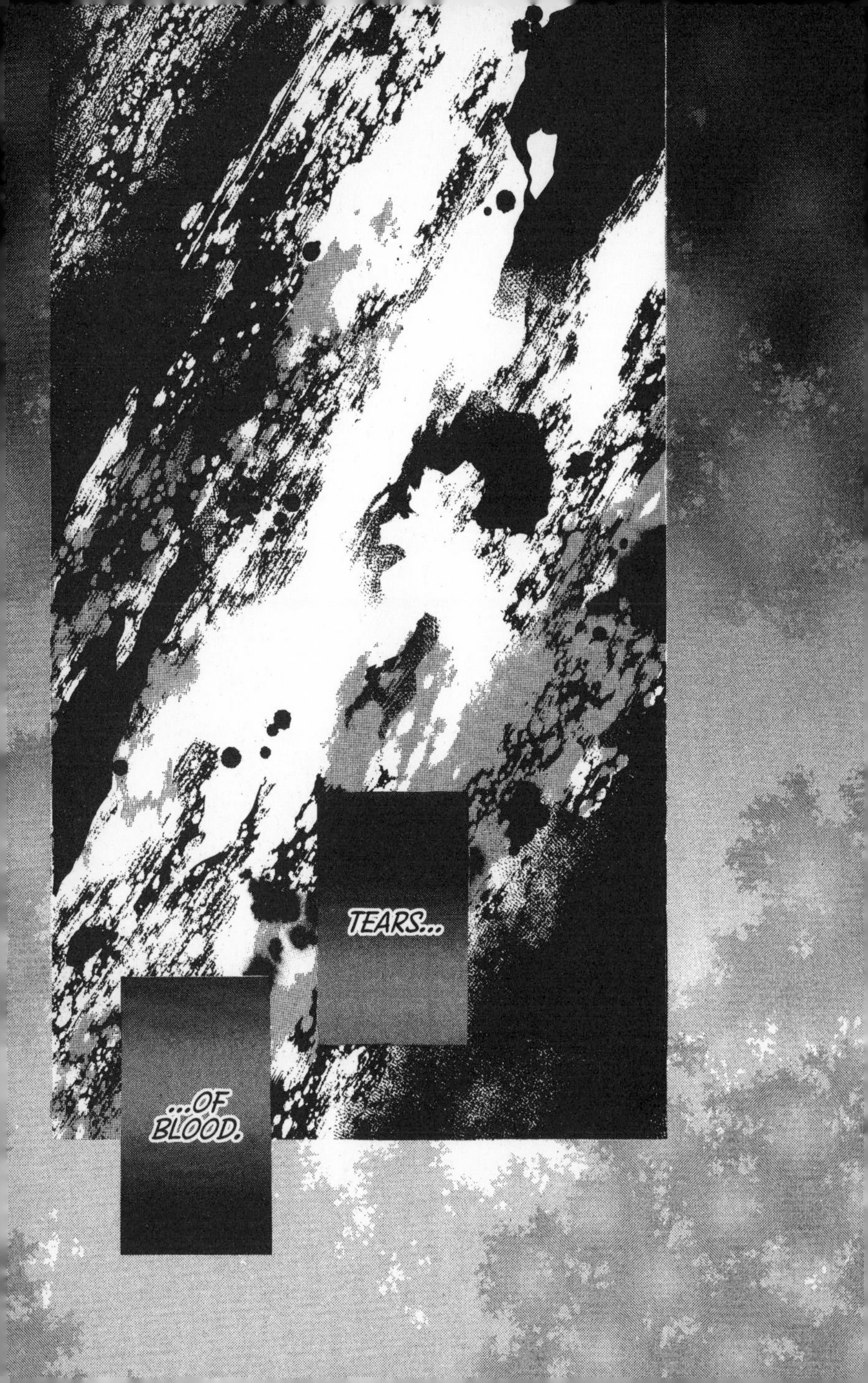
TEARS...
...OF BLOOD.

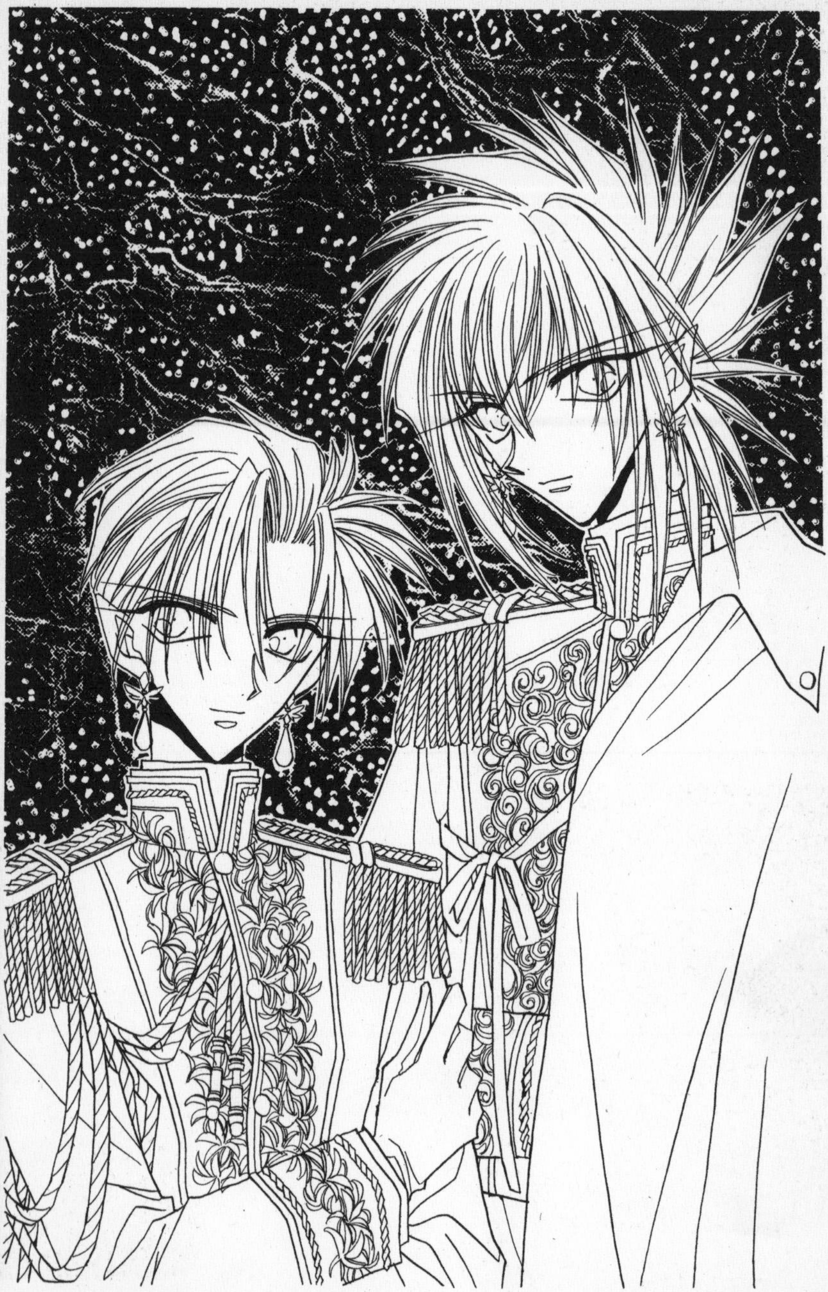

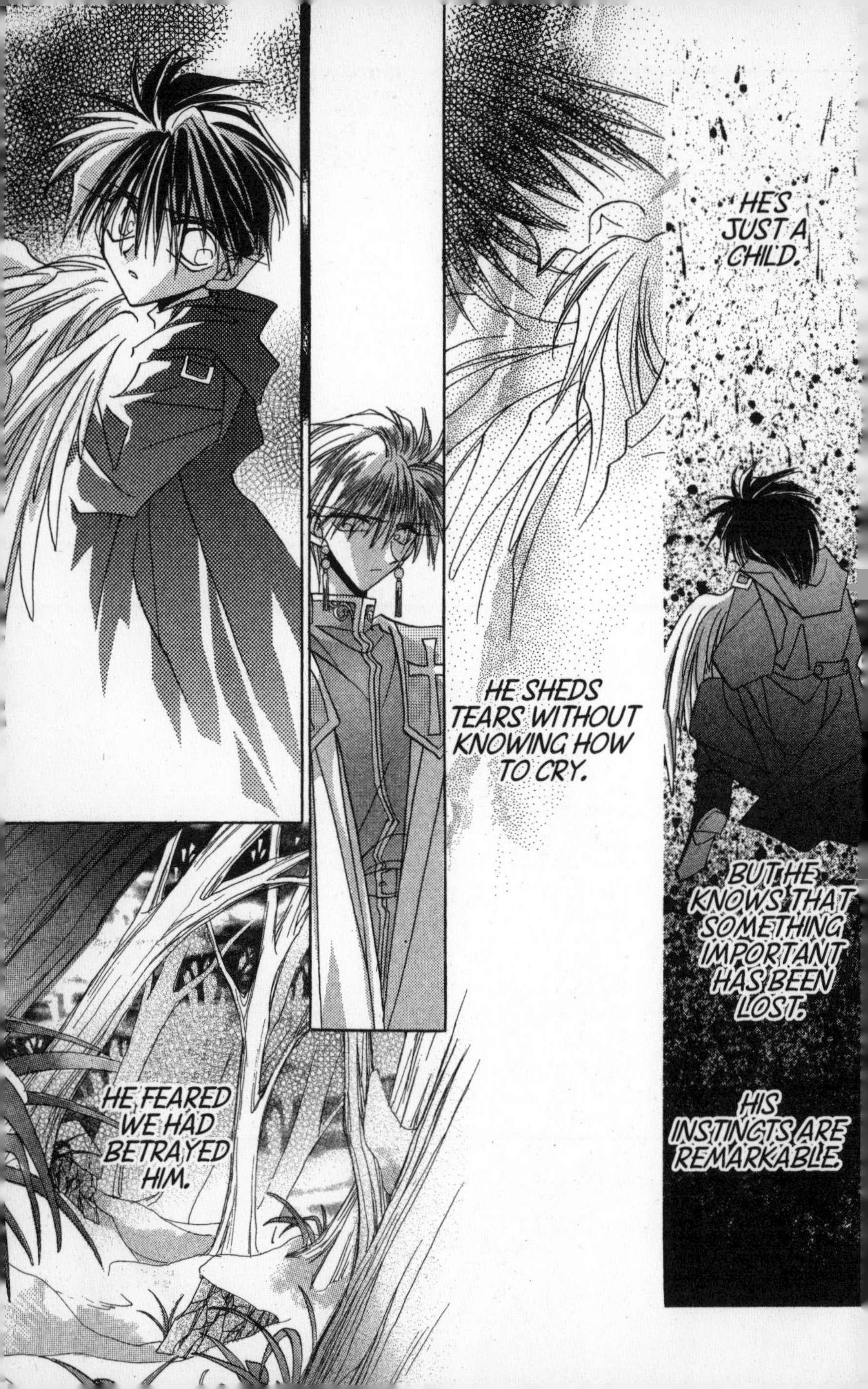
HE'S JUST A CHILD.
BUT HE KNOWS THAT SOMETHING IMPORTANT HAS BEEN LOST.
HIS INSTINCTS ARE REMARKABLE.
HE SHEDS TEARS WITHOUT KNOWING HOW TO CRY.
HE FEARED WE HAD BETRAYED HIM.

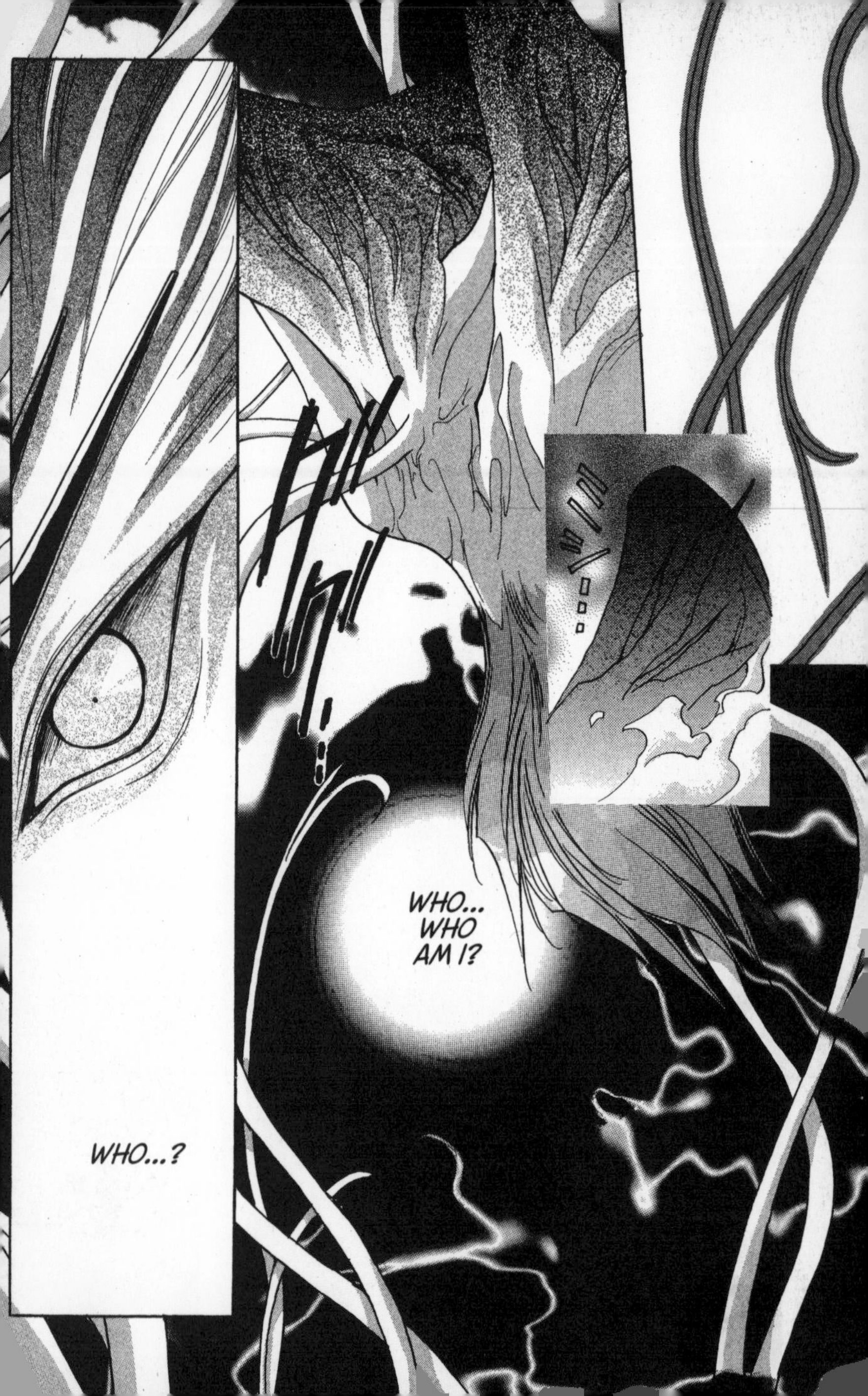
WHO... WHO AM I?
WHO...?

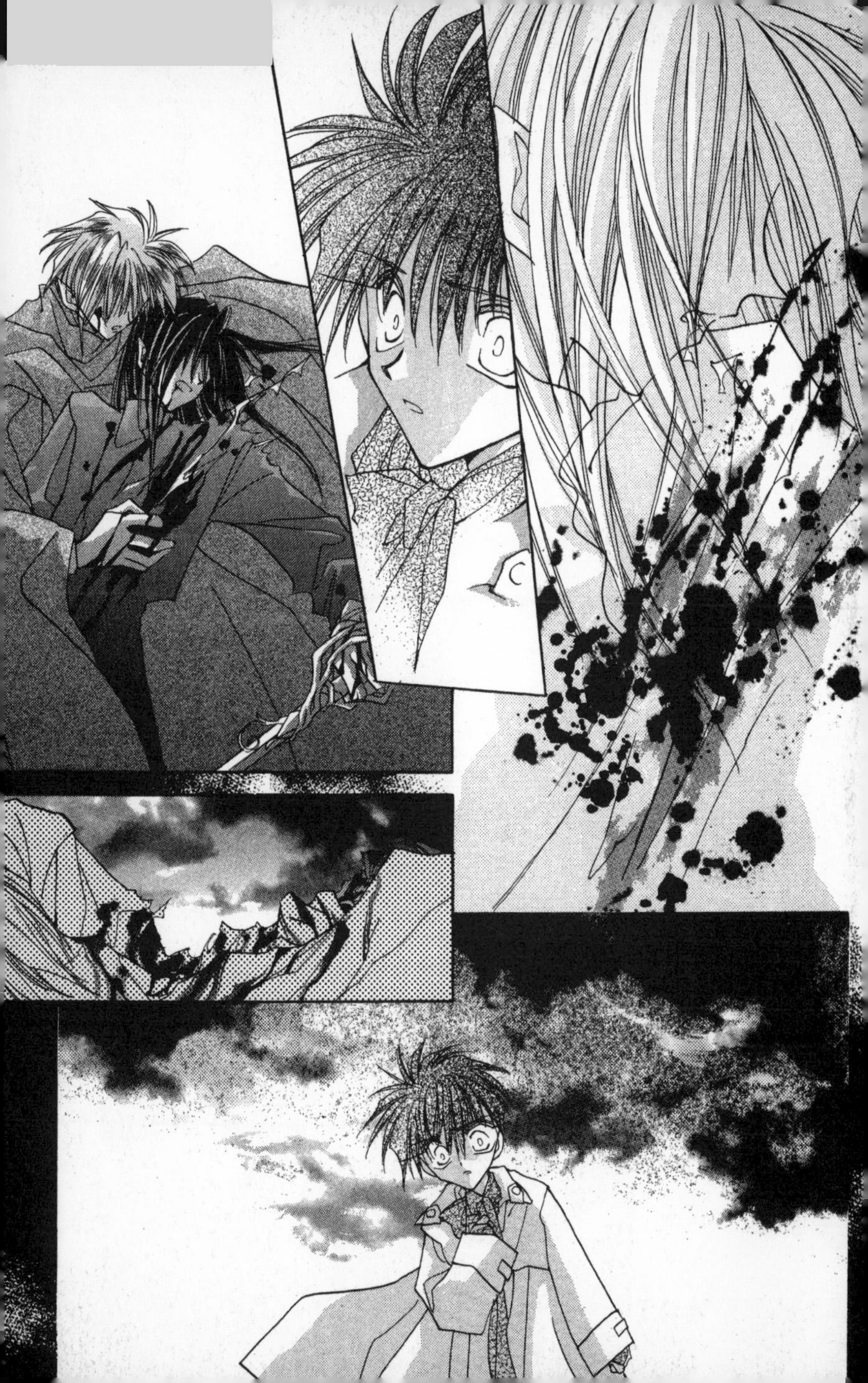

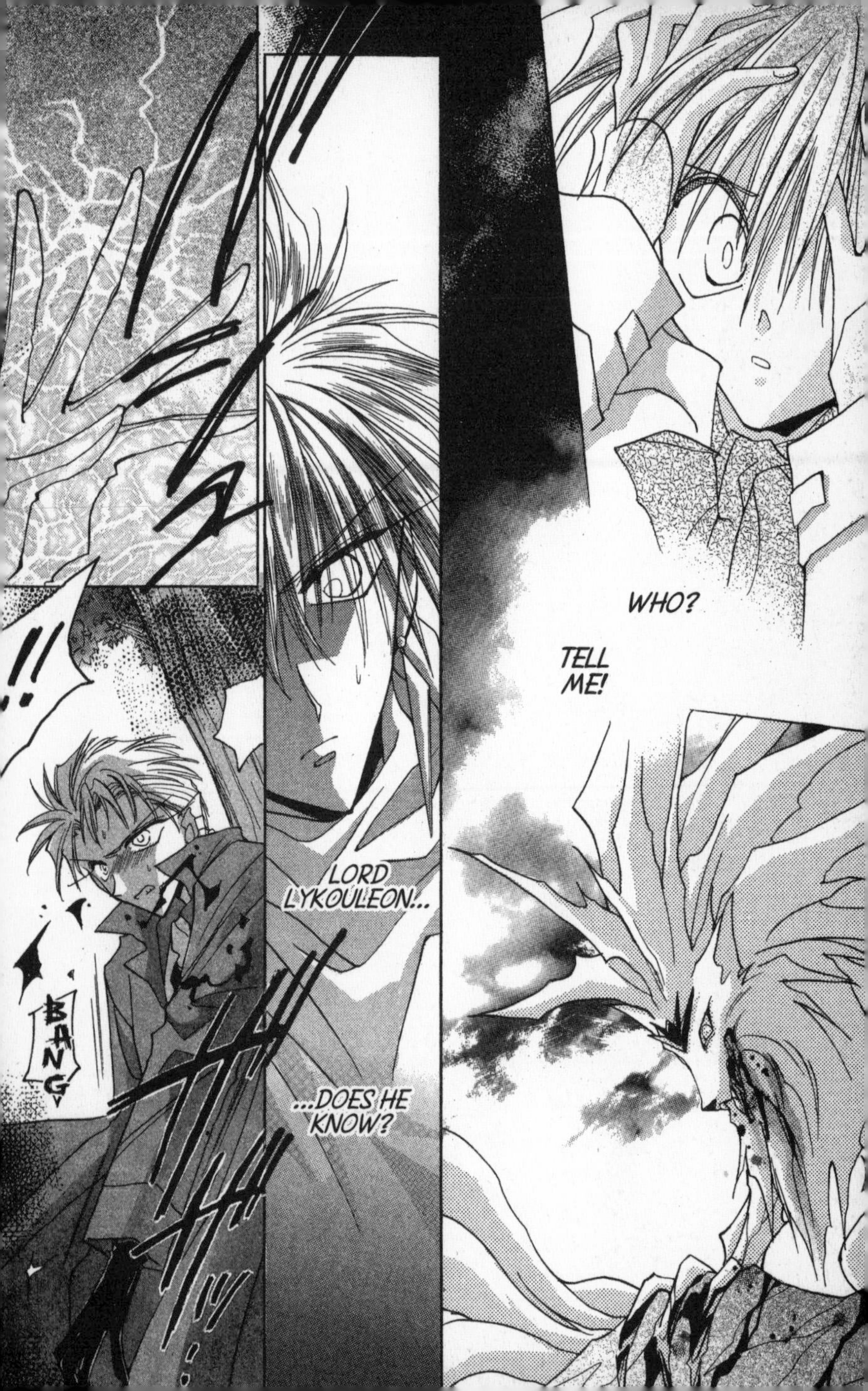
WHO?
TELL ME!
LORD LYKOULEON...
...DOES HE KNOW?
!!
BANG

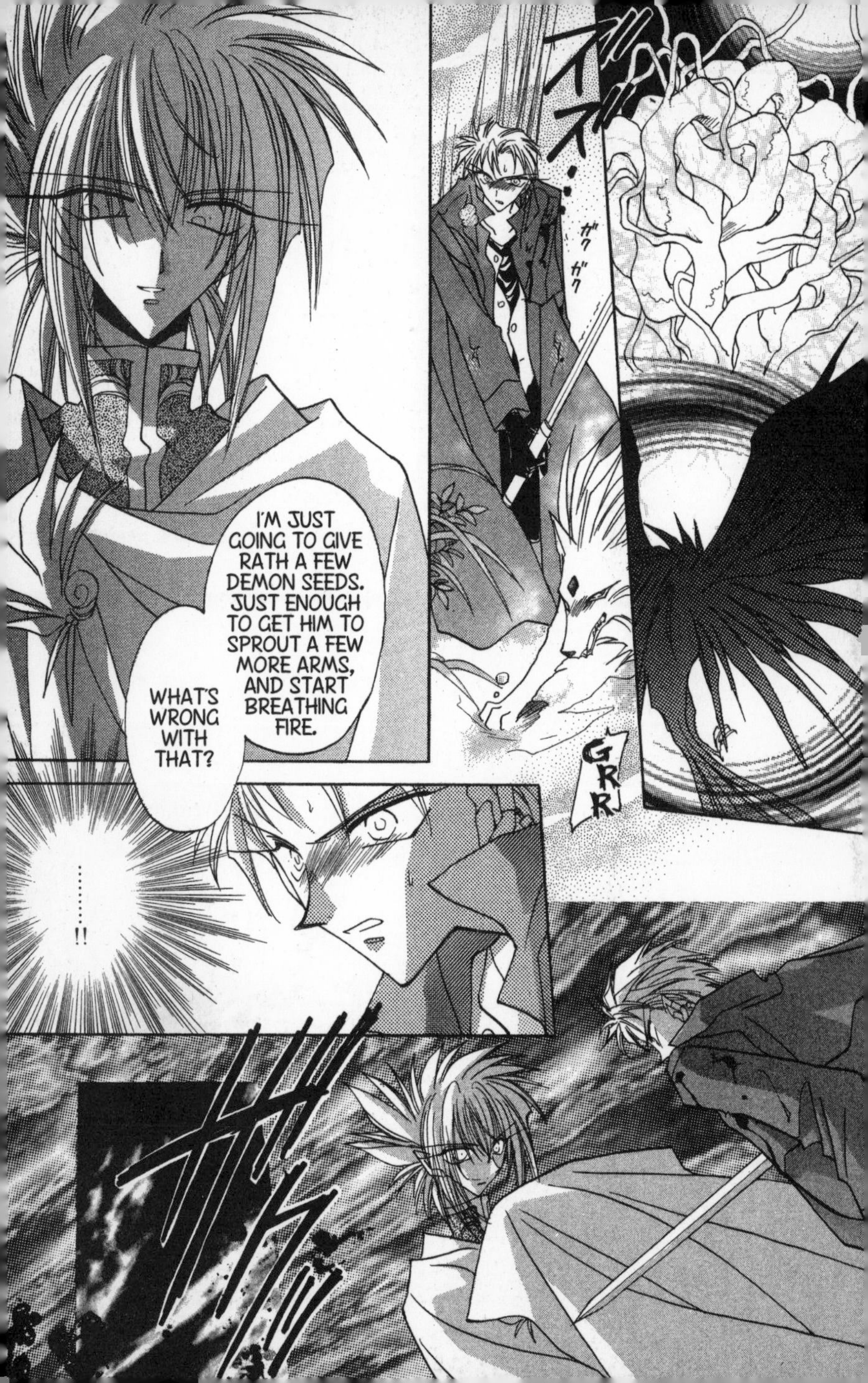
ガク ガク
GRR
I'M JUST GOING TO GIVE RATH A FEW DEMON SEEDS. JUST ENOUGH TO GET HIM TO SPROUT A FEW MORE ARMS, AND START BREATHING FIRE.
WHAT'S WRONG WITH THAT?
......!!

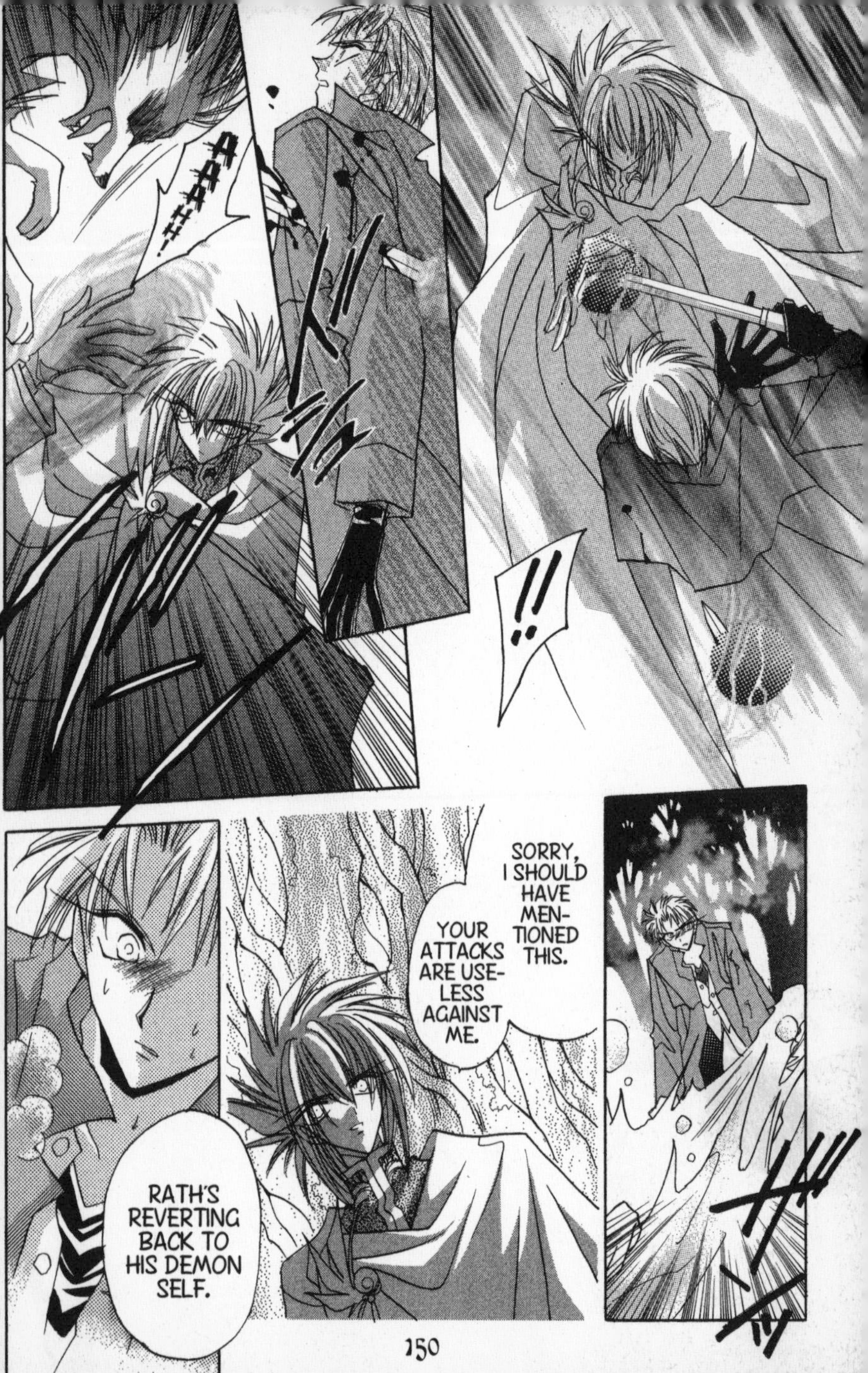
!!
AAAAHH!
SORRY, I SHOULD HAVE MENTIONED THIS.
YOUR ATTACKS ARE USELESS AGAINST ME.
RATH'S REVERTING BACK TO HIS DEMON SELF.

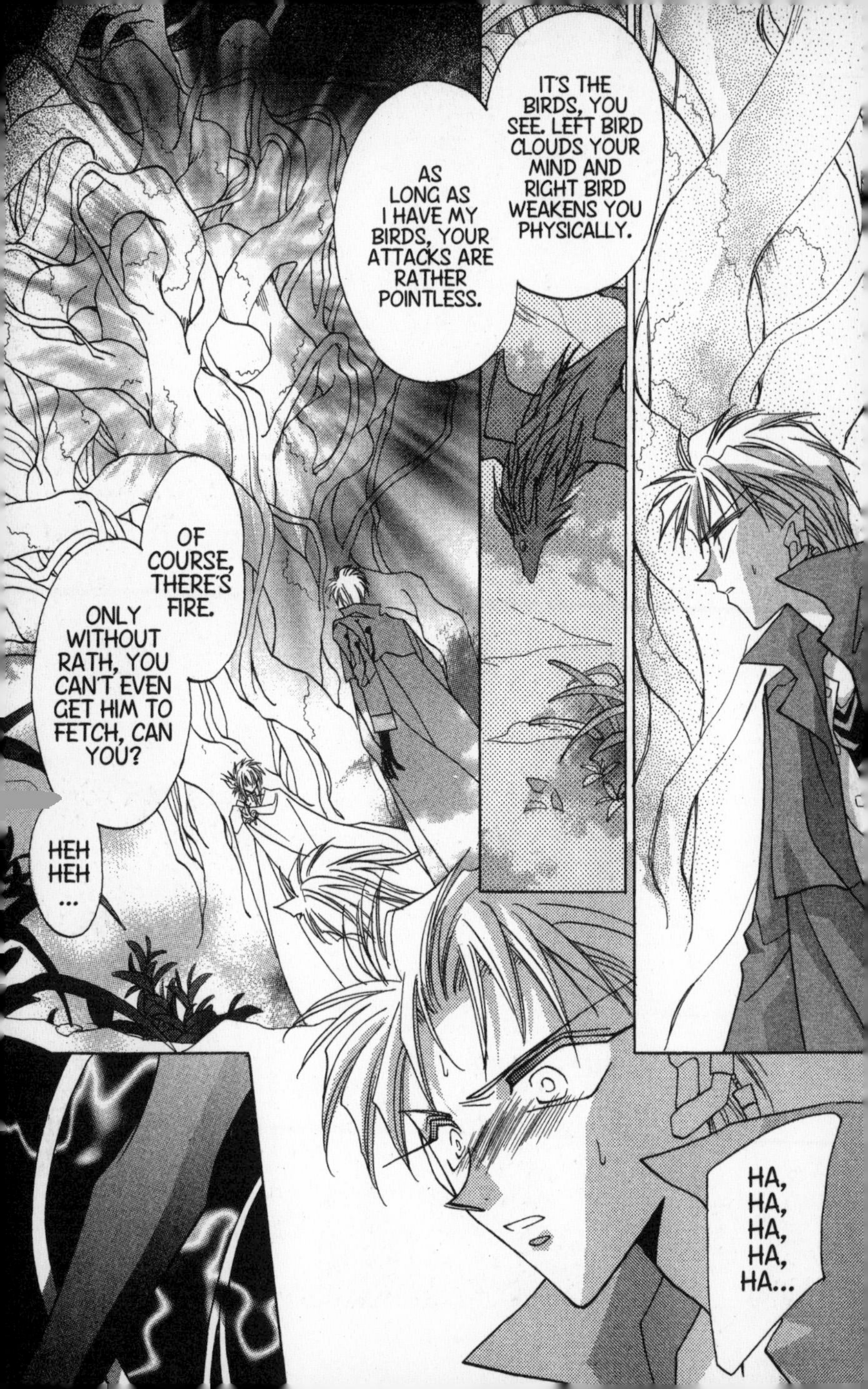
IT'S THE BIRDS, YOU SEE. LEFT BIRD CLOUDS YOUR MIND AND RIGHT BIRD WEAKENS YOU PHYSICALLY.
AS LONG AS I HAVE MY BIRDS, YOUR ATTACKS ARE RATHER POINTLESS.
OF COURSE, THERE'S FIRE.
ONLY WITHOUT RATH, YOU CAN'T EVEN GET HIM TO FETCH, CAN YOU?
HEH HEH ...
HA, HA, HA, HA, HA...

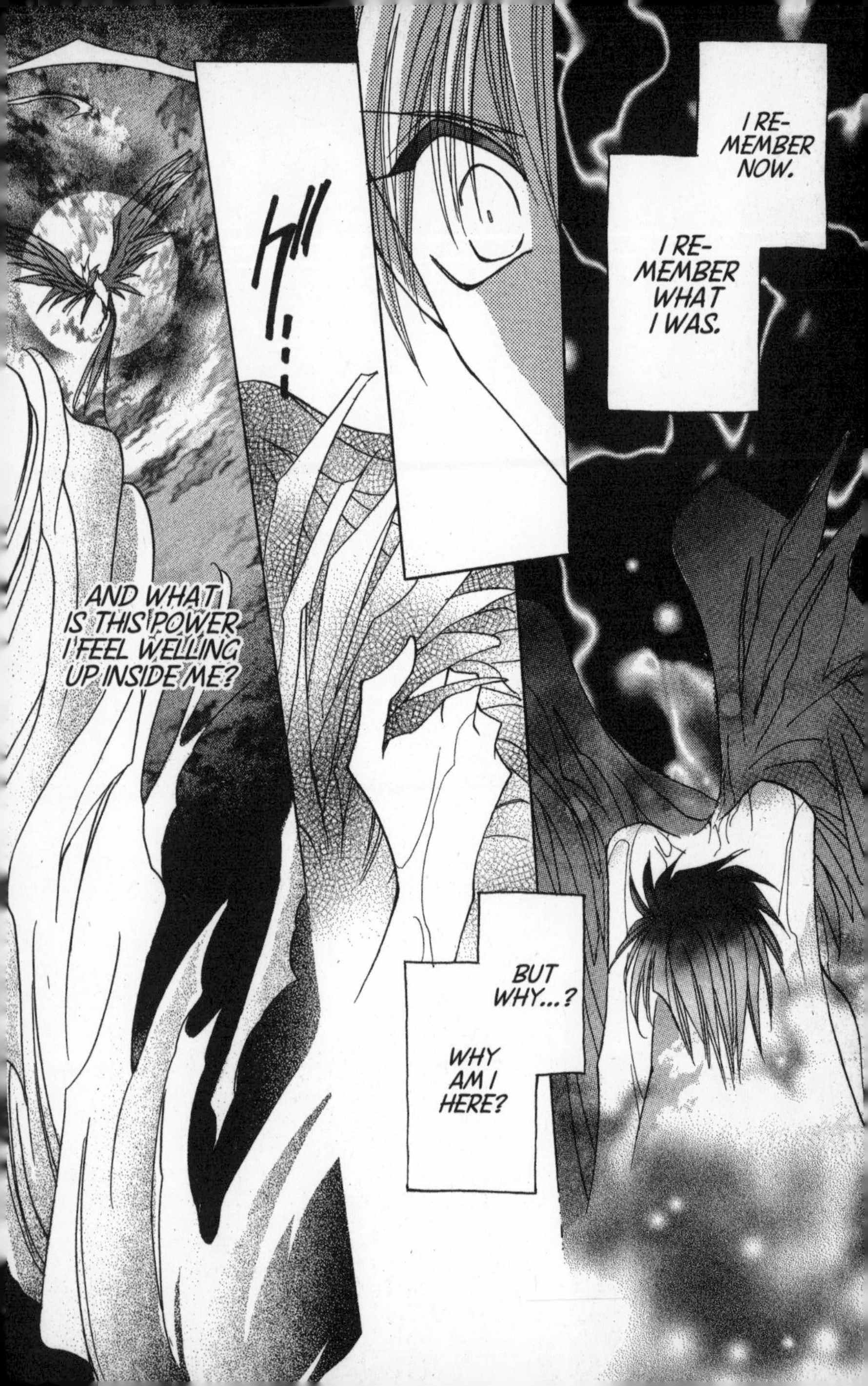
I RE-
MEMBER
NOW.
I RE-
MEMBER
WHAT
I WAS.
AND WHAT
IS THIS POWER
I FEEL WELLING
UP INSIDE ME?
BUT
WHY...?
WHY
AM I
HERE?

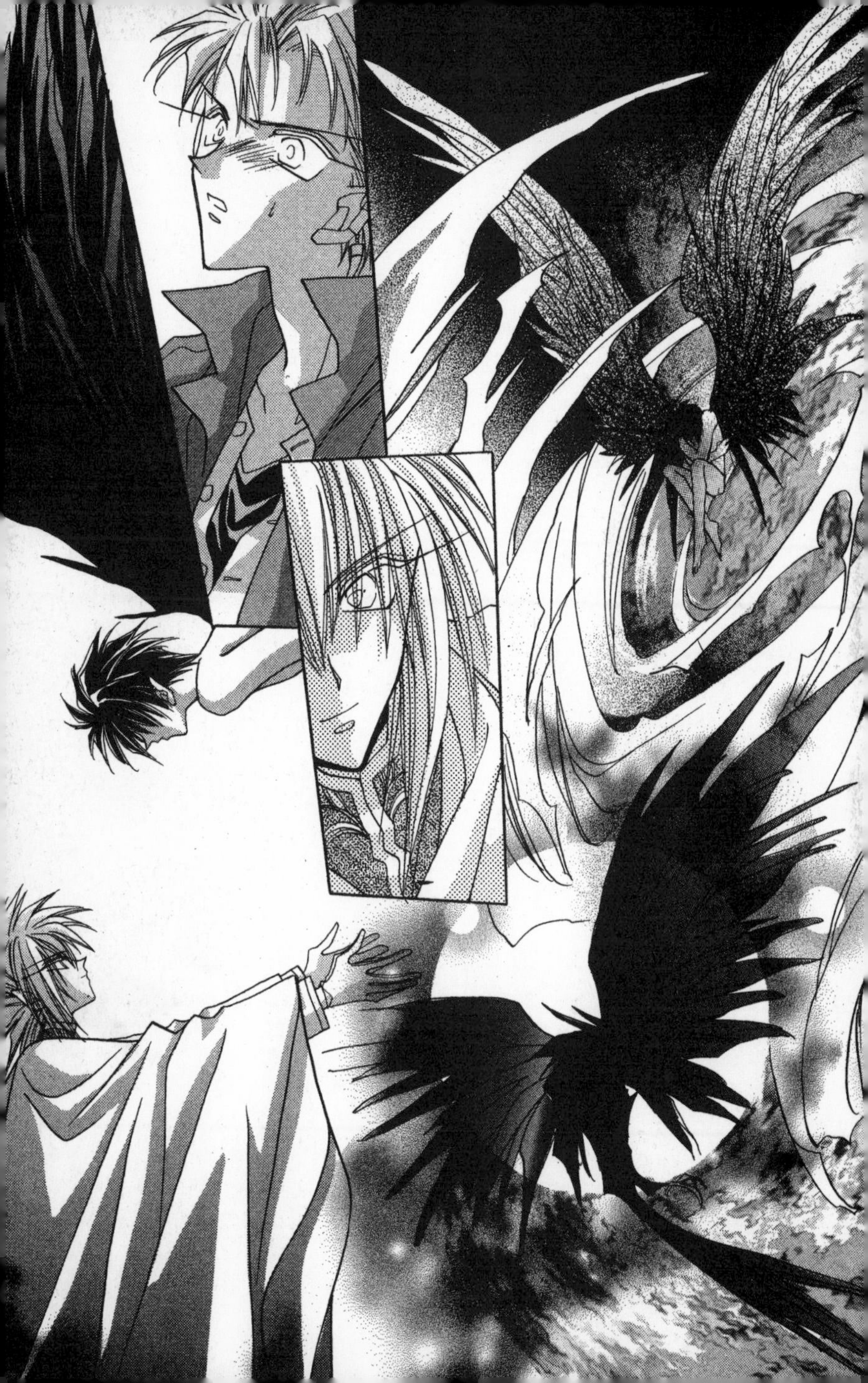

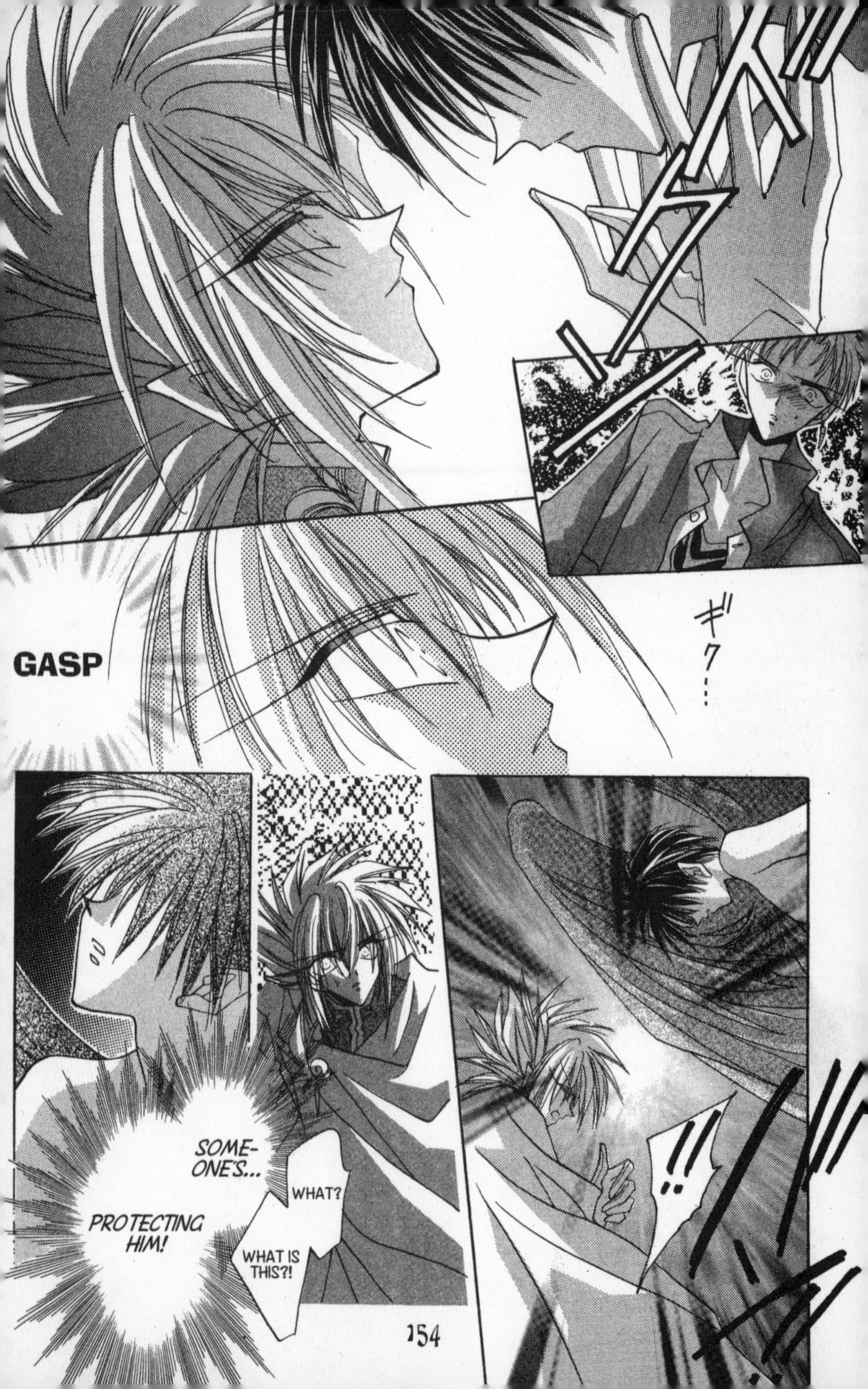
ギク…
GASP
!!
SOME-ONE'S...
WHAT?
WHAT IS THIS?!
PROTECTING HIM!

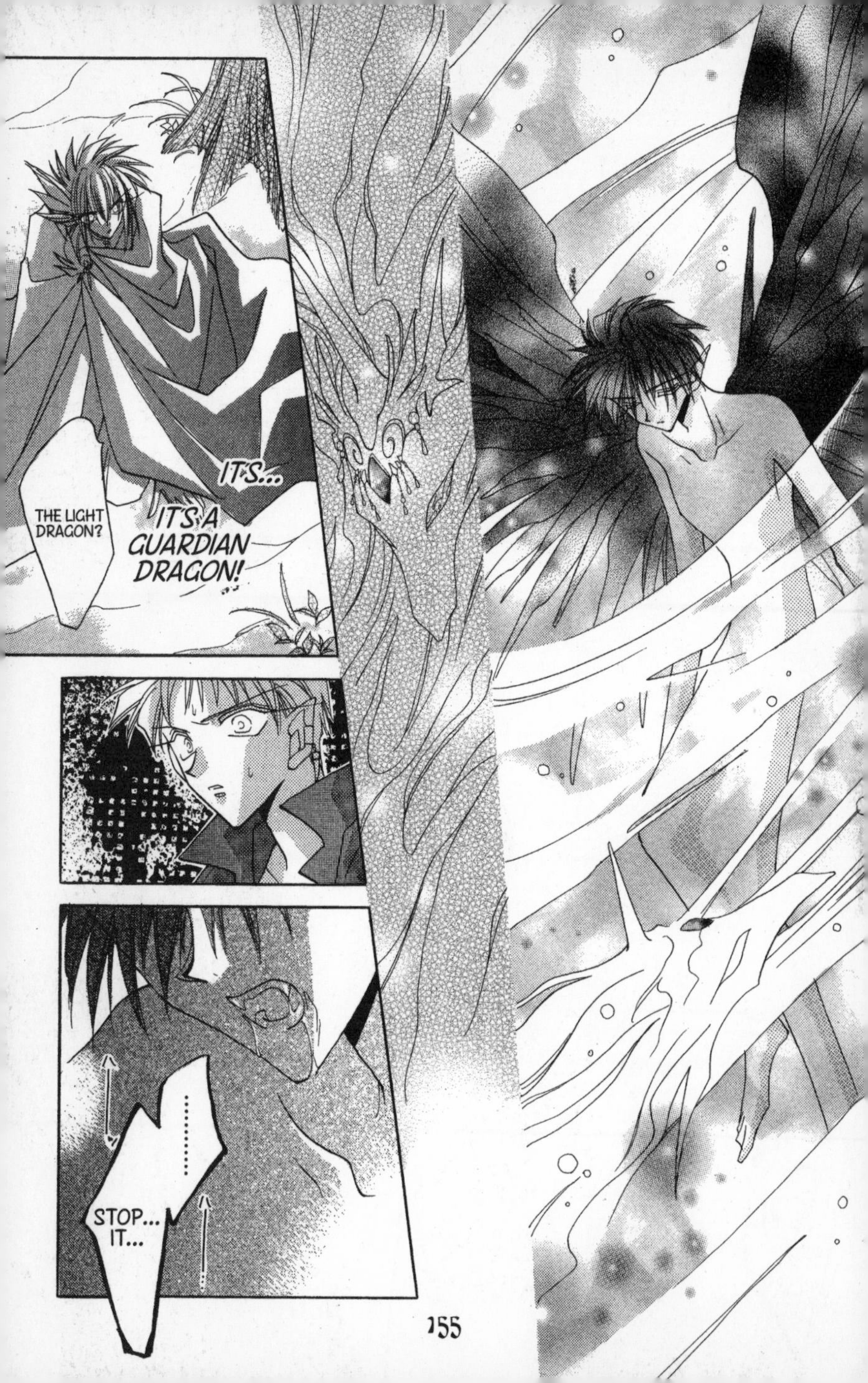
IT'S...
IT'S A GUARDIAN DRAGON!
THE LIGHT DRAGON?
......
STOP... IT...

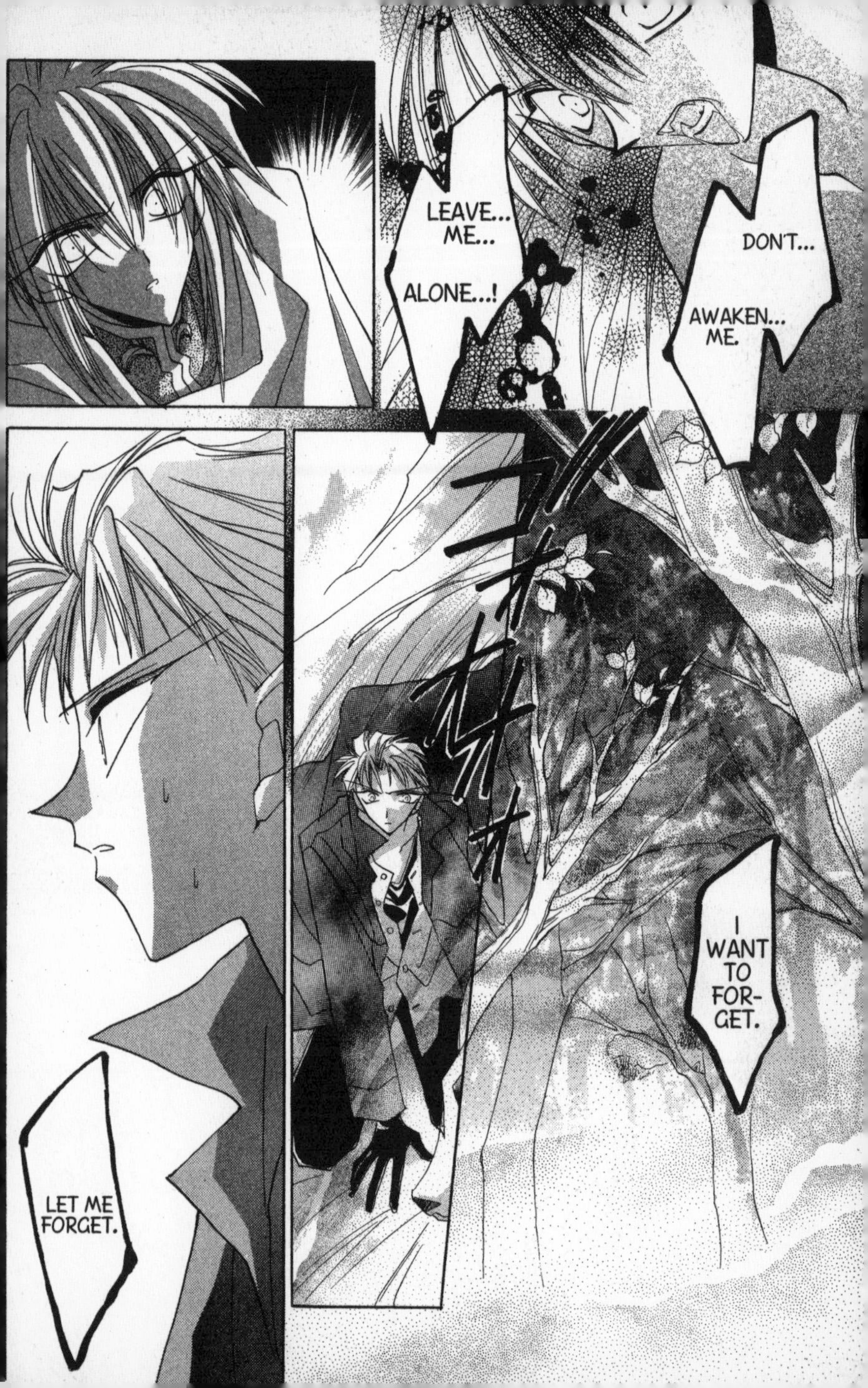
DON'T...
AWAKEN... ME.
LEAVE... ME...
ALONE...!
I WANT TO FOR-GET.
LET ME FORGET.

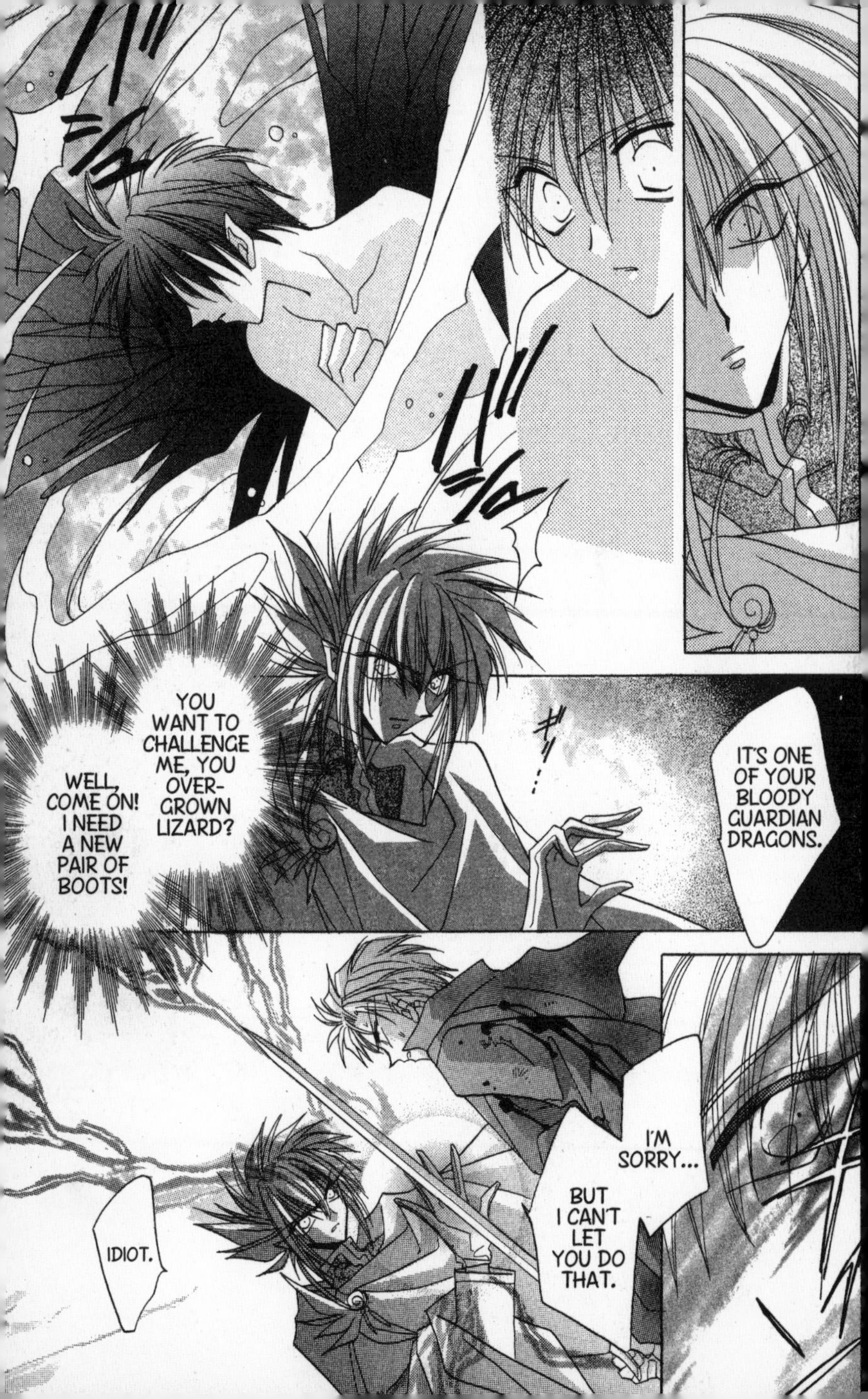
IT'S ONE OF YOUR BLOODY GUARDIAN DRAGONS.
YOU WANT TO CHALLENGE ME, YOU OVER-GROWN LIZARD?
WELL, COME ON! I NEED A NEW PAIR OF BOOTS!
I'M SORRY...
BUT I CAN'T LET YOU DO THAT.
IDIOT.

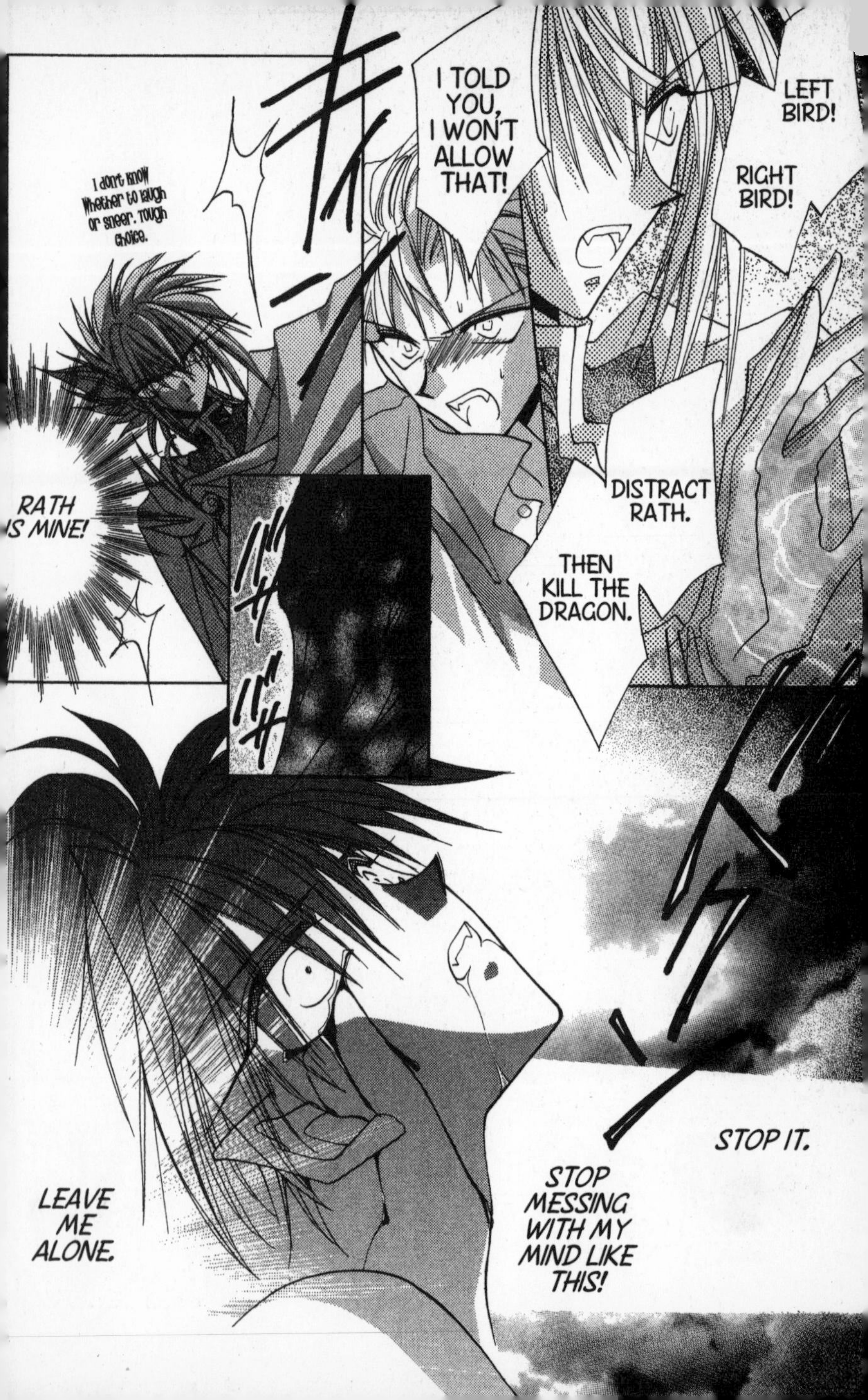
LEFT BIRD!
RIGHT BIRD!
DISTRACT RATH.
THEN KILL THE DRAGON.
I TOLD YOU, I WON'T ALLOW THAT!
I don't know whether to laugh or sneer. Tough choice.
RATH IS MINE!
STOP IT.
STOP MESSING WITH MY MIND LIKE THIS!
LEAVE ME ALONE.

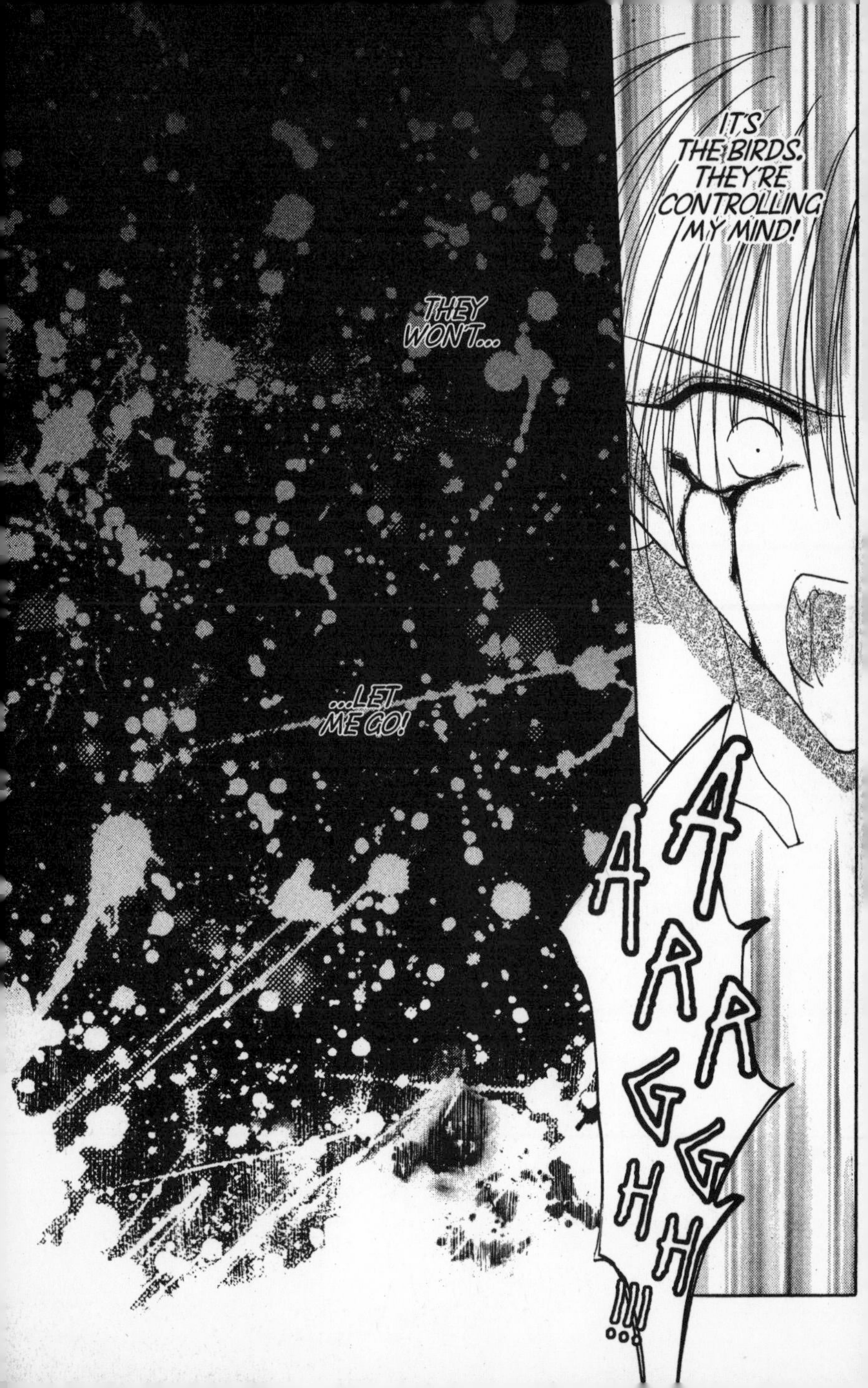
IT'S THE BIRDS. THEY'RE CONTROLLING MY MIND!
AAARRRGGHH!!!
THEY WON'T...
...LET ME GO!

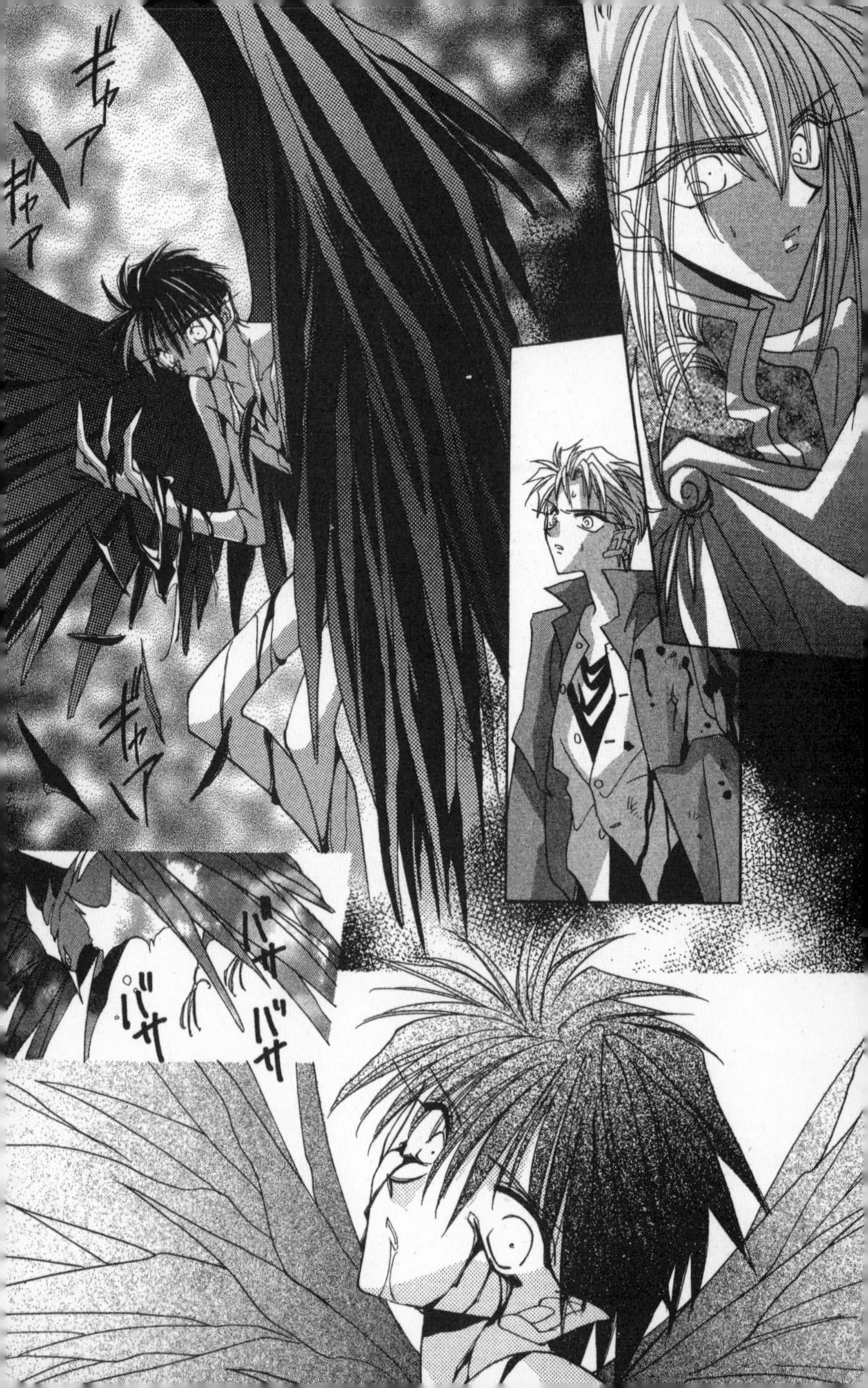
ギャア
ギャア
ギャア
バサバサ
バサ

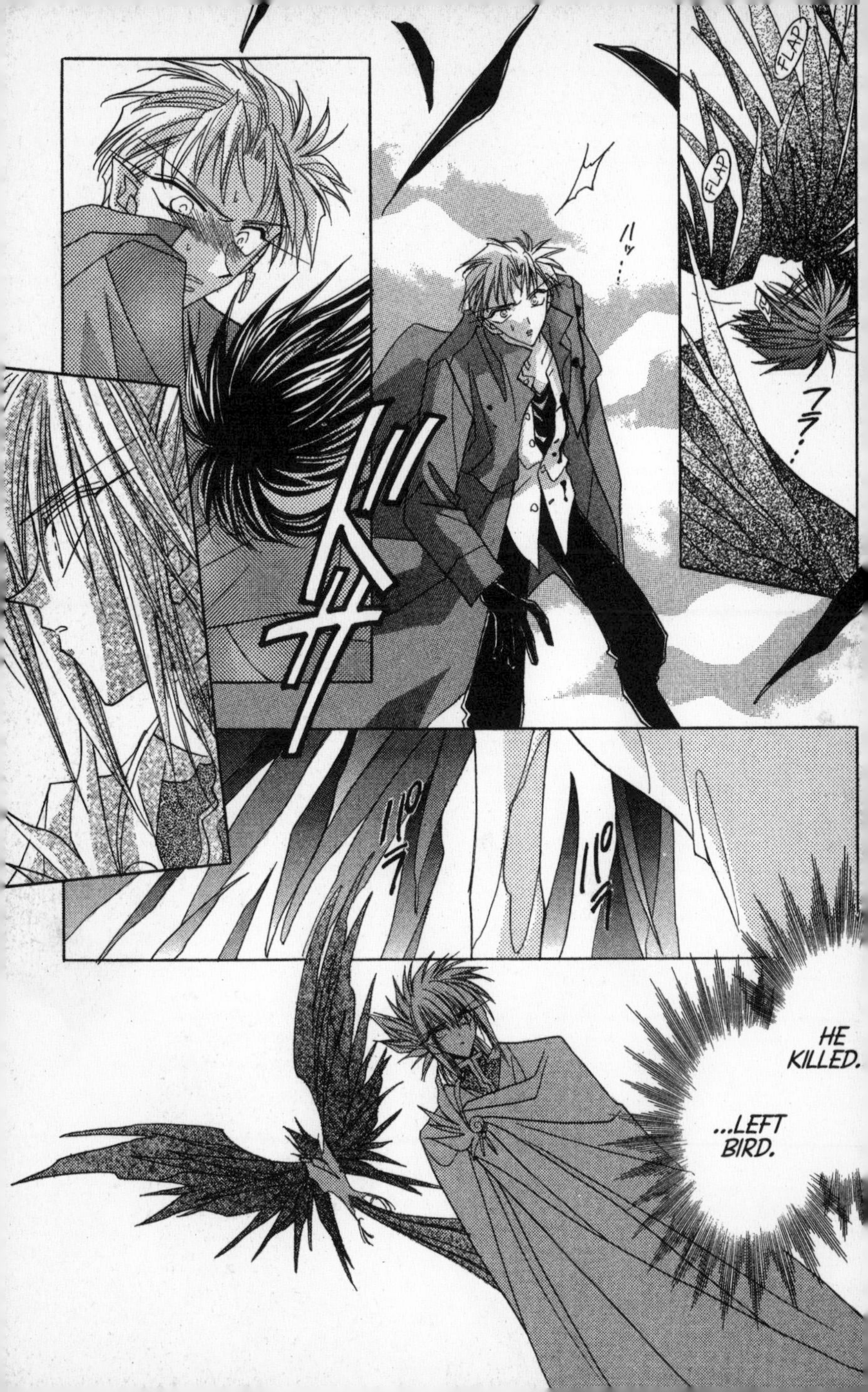
FLAP
FLAP
フラ…
ハッ…
ドキ
パラ
パラ
HE KILLED.
...LEFT BIRD.

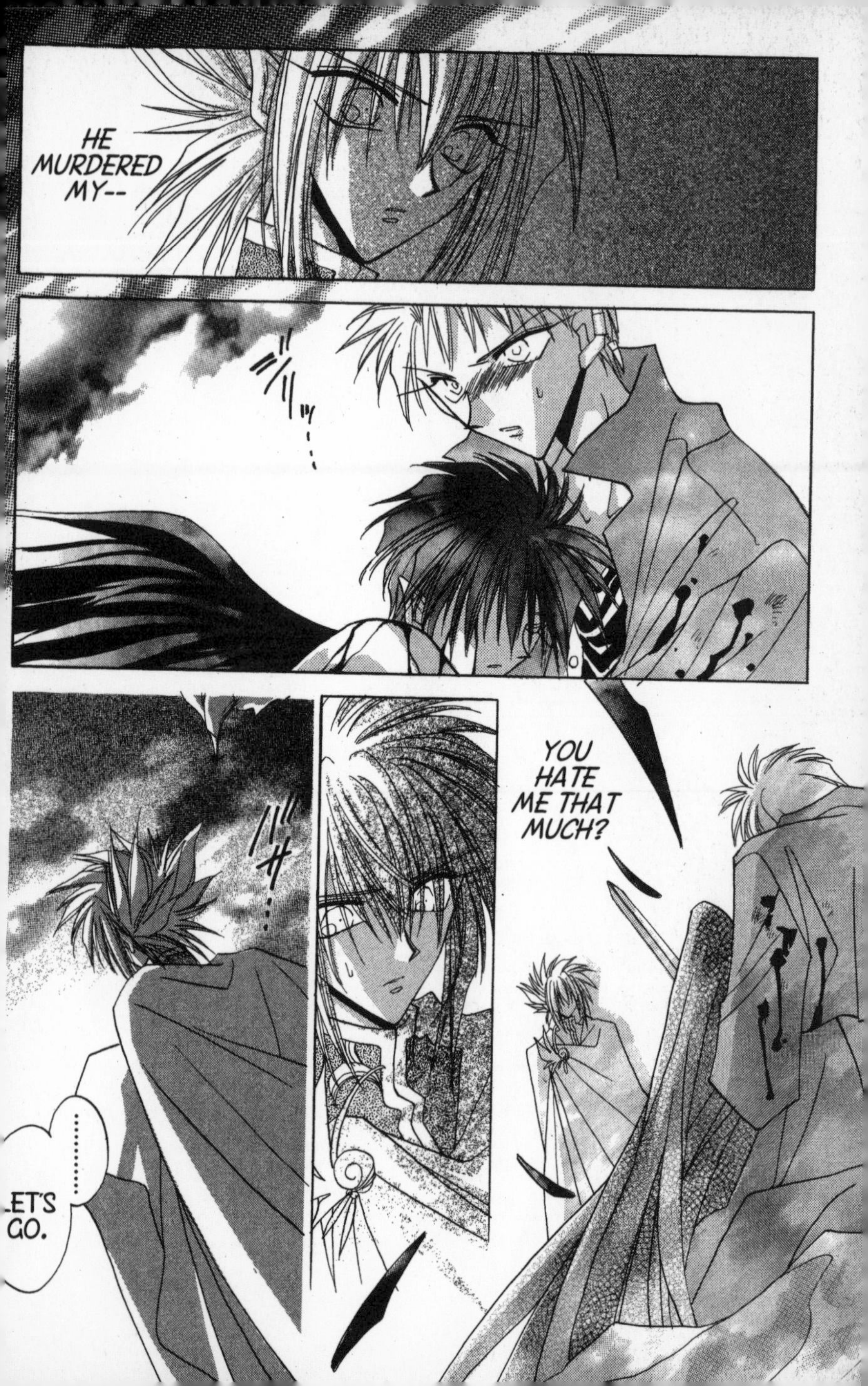
HE MURDERED MY--
YOU HATE ME THAT MUCH?
......
LET'S GO.

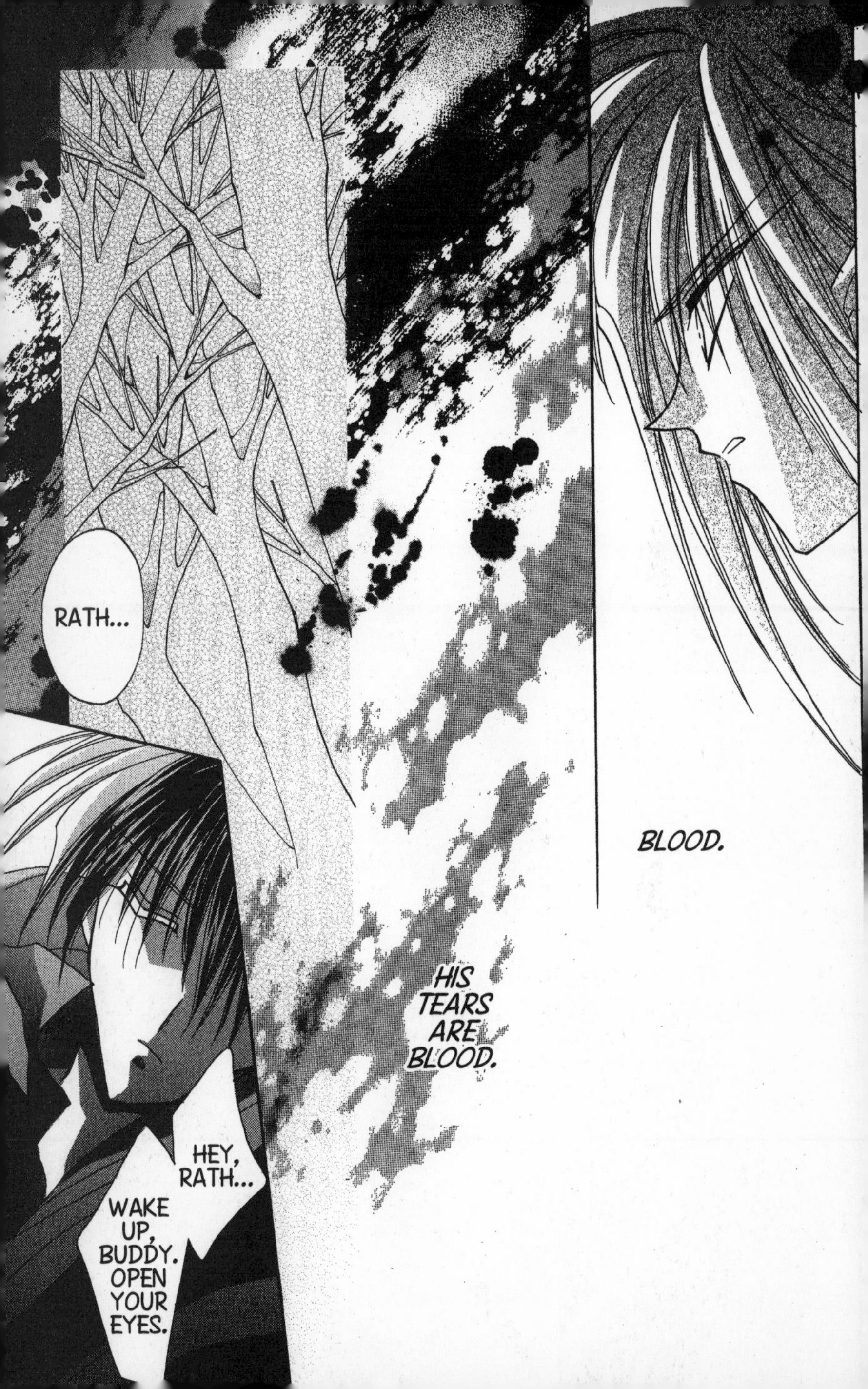
BLOOD.
HIS TEARS ARE BLOOD.
RATH...
HEY, RATH...
WAKE UP, BUDDY.
OPEN YOUR EYES.

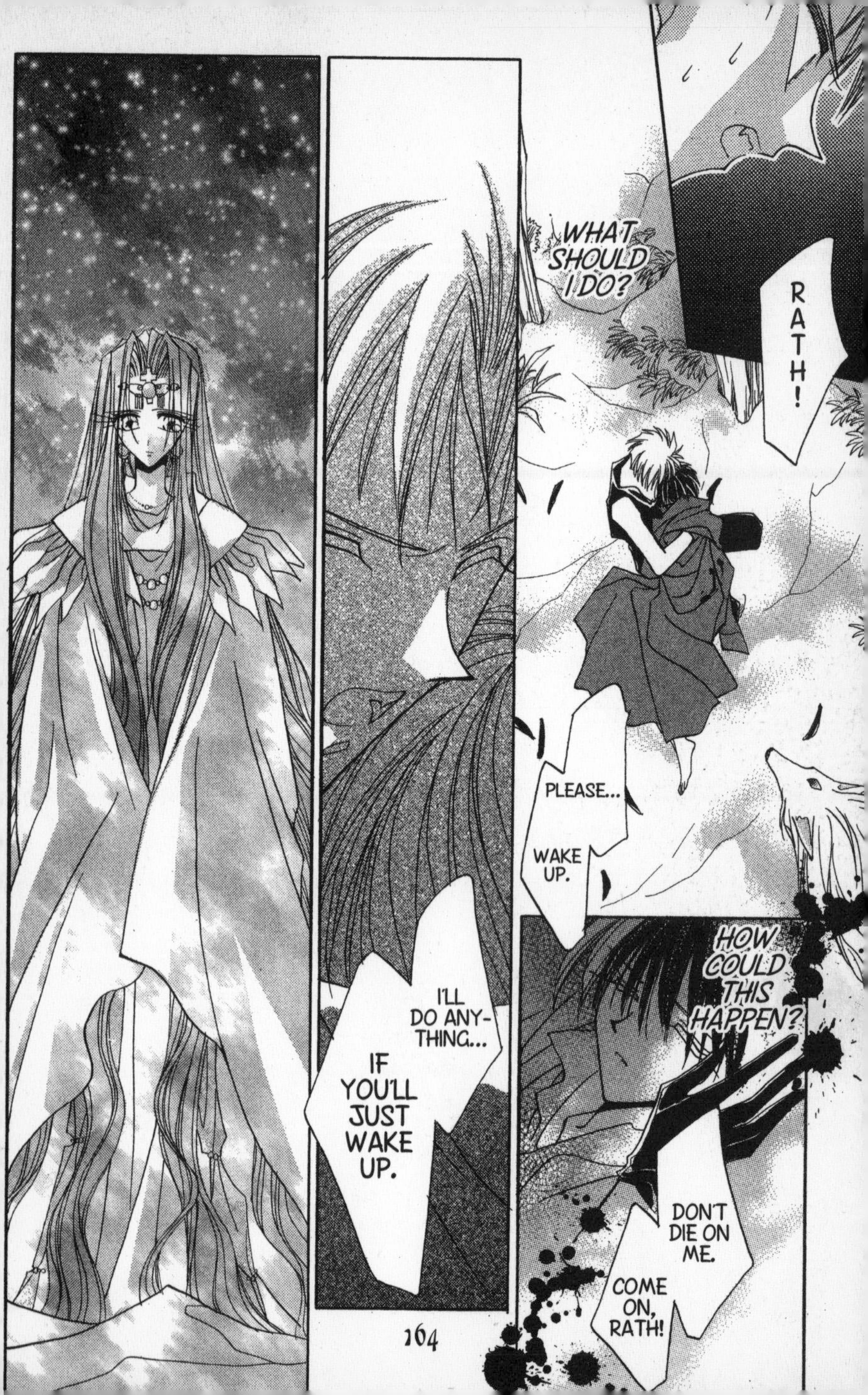
RATH!
WHAT SHOULD I DO?
PLEASE...
WAKE UP.
HOW COULD THIS HAPPEN?
DON'T DIE ON ME.
COME ON, RATH!
I'LL DO ANY-THING...
IF YOU'LL JUST WAKE UP.

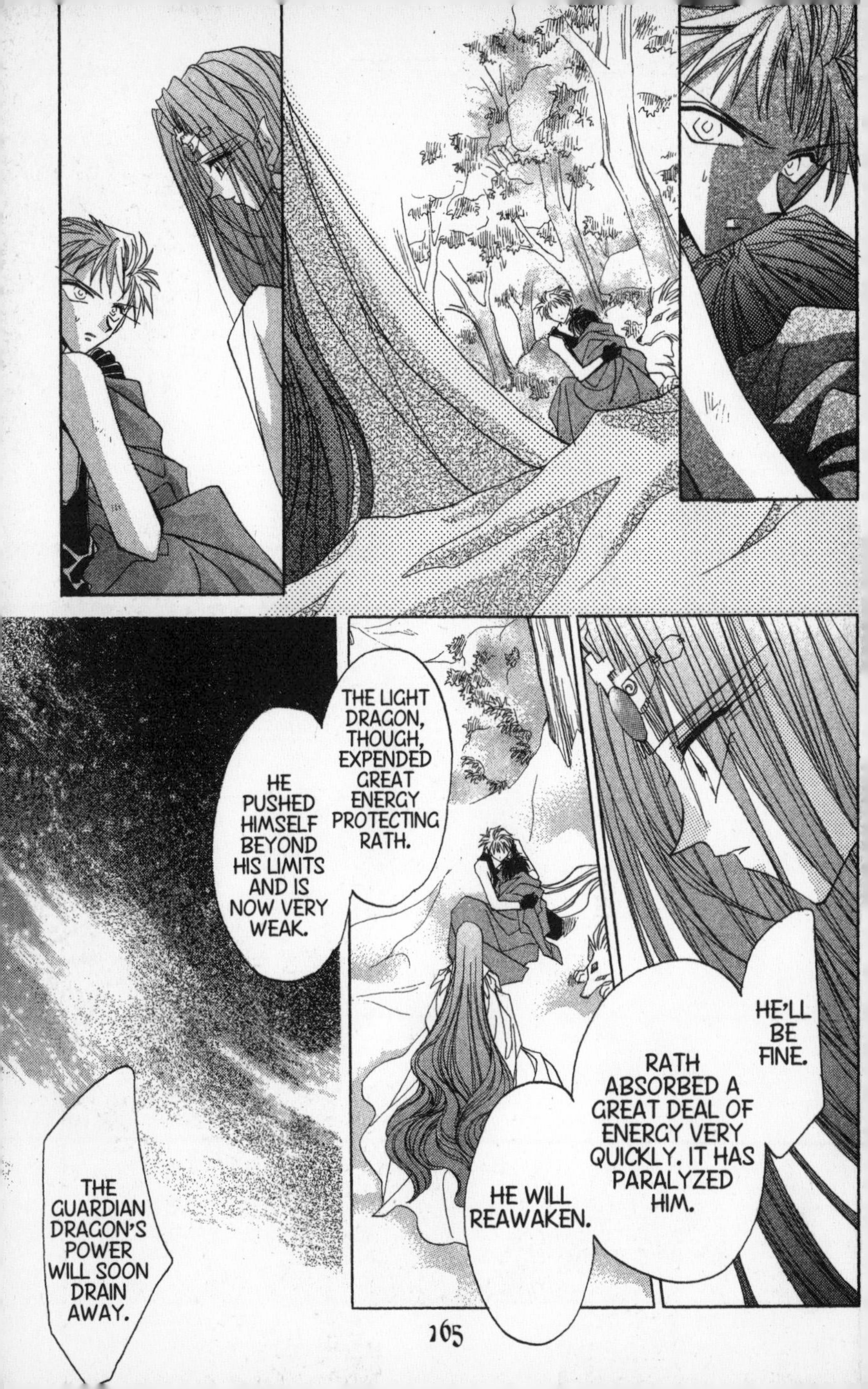
HE'LL BE FINE.
RATH ABSORBED A GREAT DEAL OF ENERGY VERY QUICKLY. IT HAS PARALYZED HIM.
HE WILL REAWAKEN.
THE LIGHT DRAGON, THOUGH, EXPENDED GREAT ENERGY PROTECTING RATH.
HE PUSHED HIMSELF BEYOND HIS LIMITS AND IS NOW VERY WEAK.
THE GUARDIAN DRAGON'S POWER WILL SOON DRAIN AWAY.

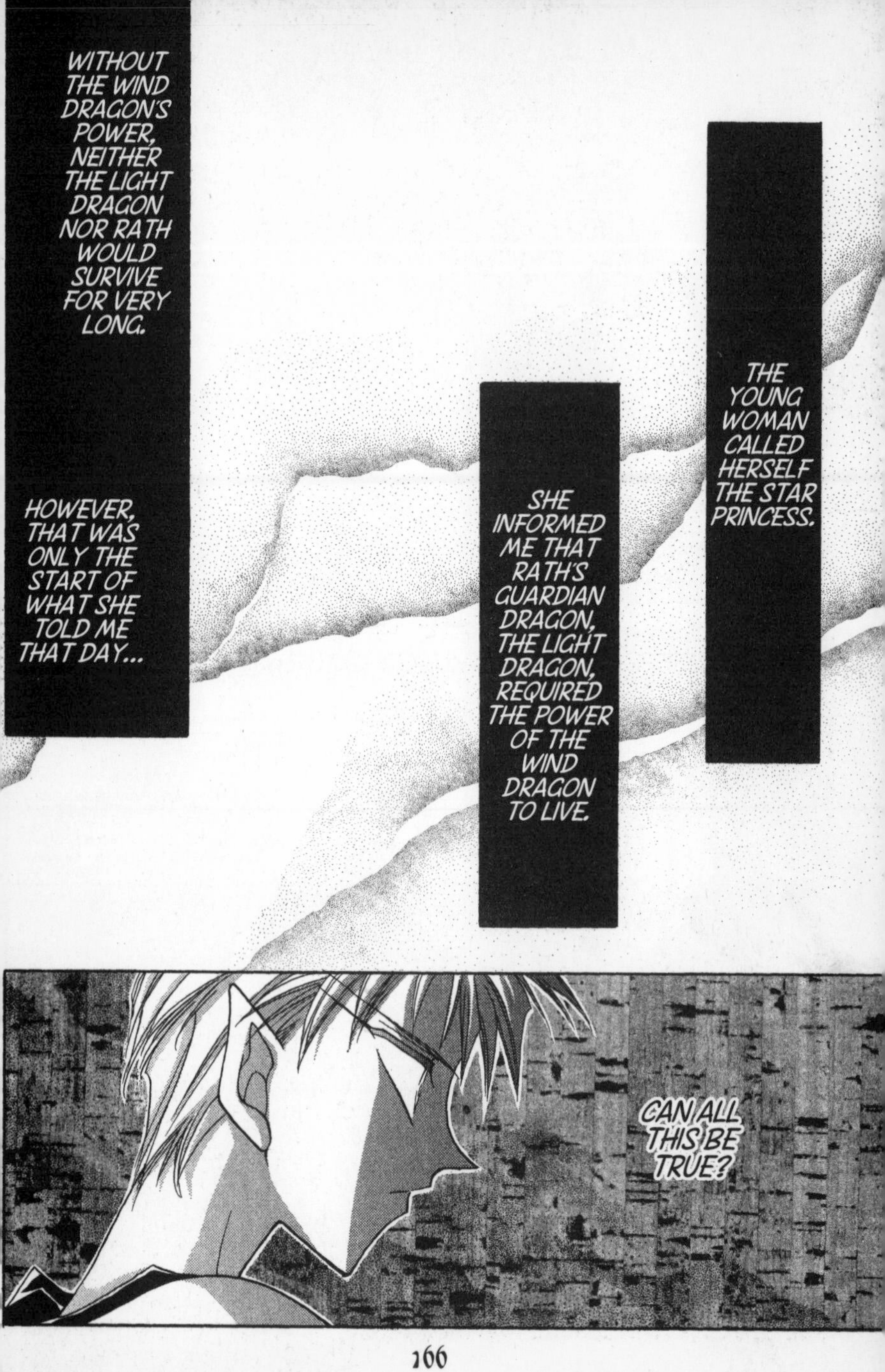
THE YOUNG WOMAN CALLED HERSELF THE STAR PRINCESS.
SHE INFORMED ME THAT RATH'S GUARDIAN DRAGON, THE LIGHT DRAGON, REQUIRED THE POWER OF THE WIND DRAGON TO LIVE.
WITHOUT THE WIND DRAGON'S POWER, NEITHER THE LIGHT DRAGON NOR RATH WOULD SURVIVE FOR VERY LONG.
HOWEVER, THAT WAS ONLY THE START OF WHAT SHE TOLD ME THAT DAY...
CAN ALL THIS BE TRUE?

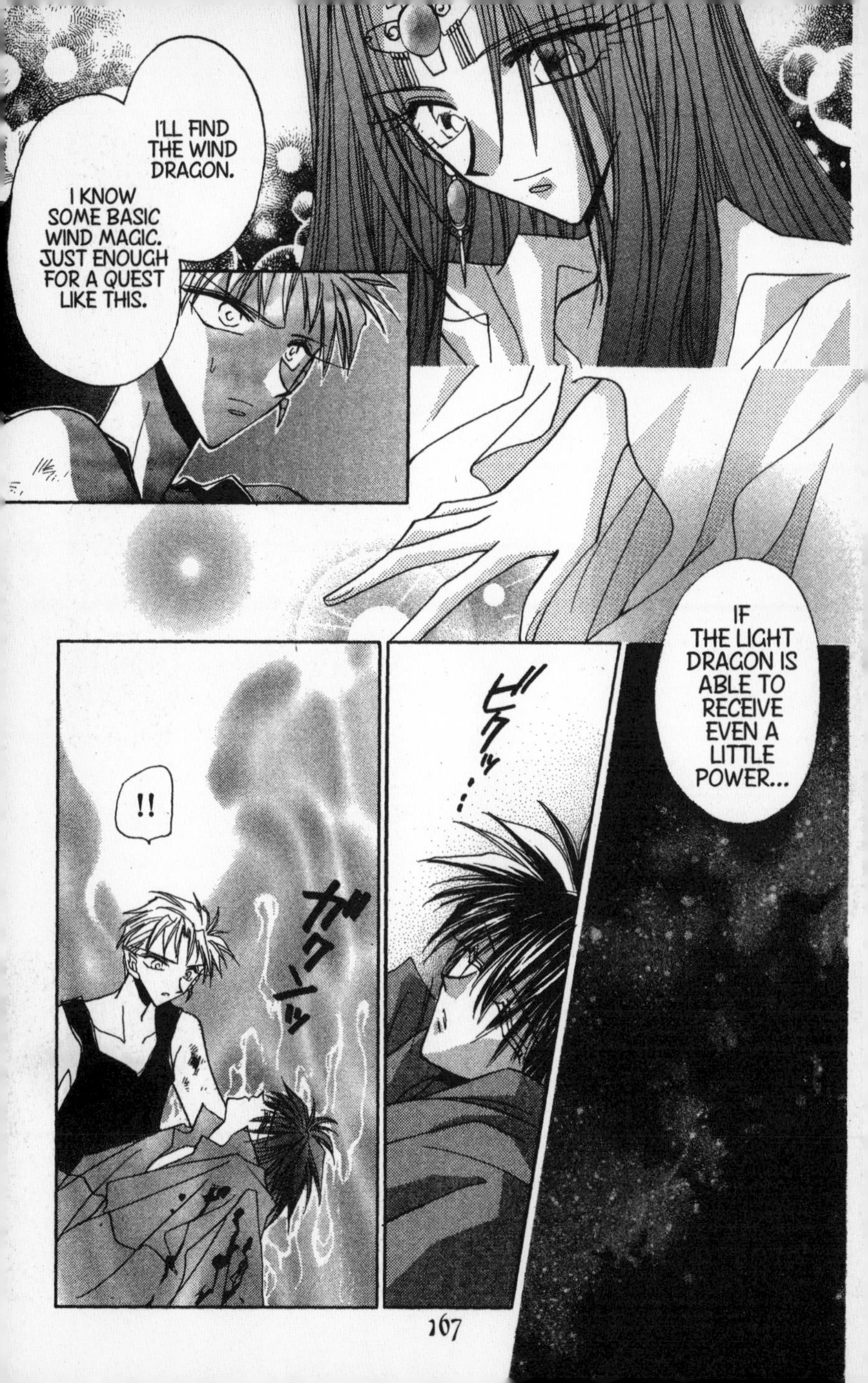
I'LL FIND THE WIND DRAGON.
I KNOW SOME BASIC WIND MAGIC. JUST ENOUGH FOR A QUEST LIKE THIS.
IF THE LIGHT DRAGON IS ABLE TO RECEIVE EVEN A LITTLE POWER...
!!

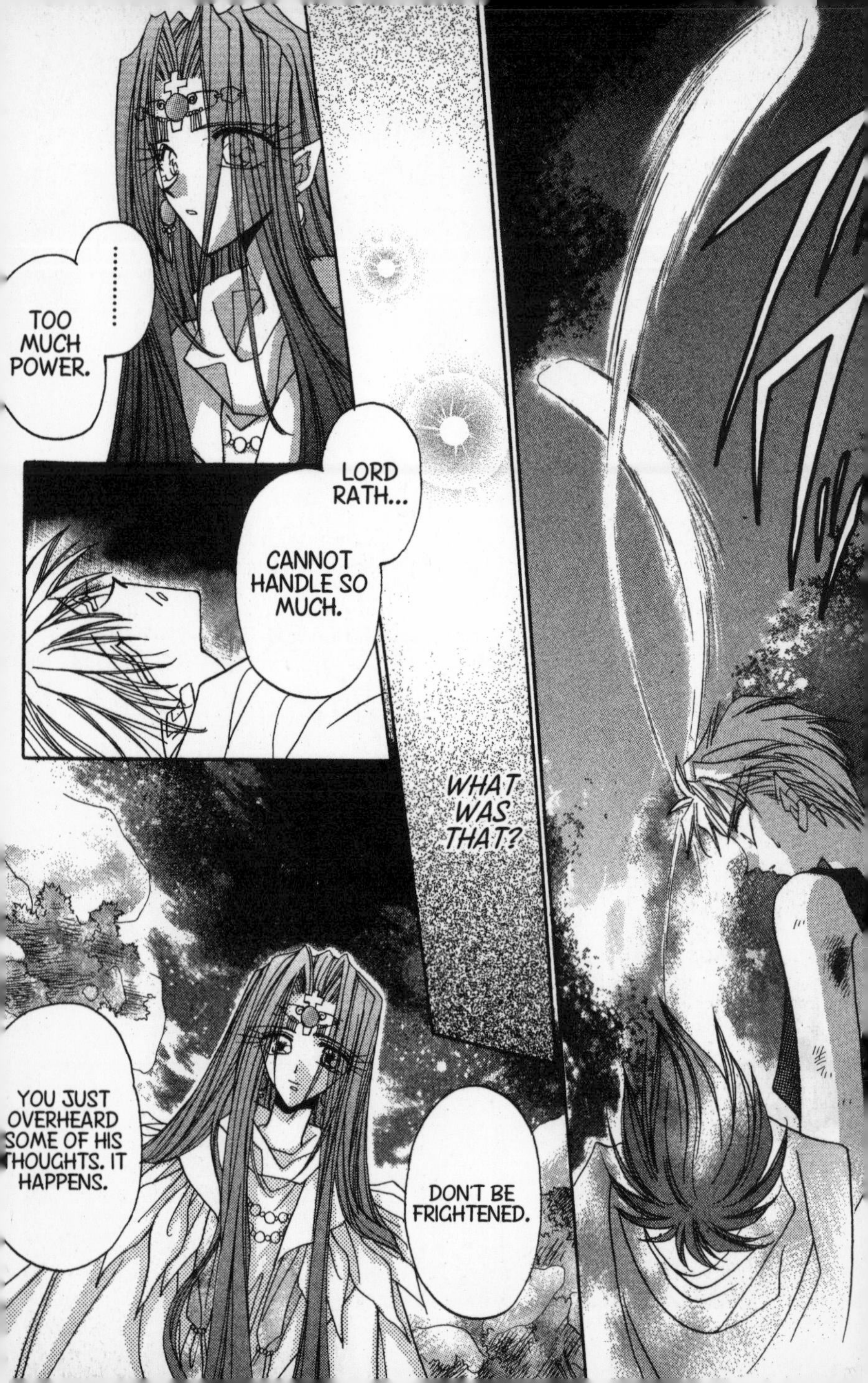
WHAT WAS THAT?
......
TOO MUCH POWER.
LORD RATH...
CANNOT HANDLE SO MUCH.
DON'T BE FRIGHTENED.
YOU JUST OVERHEARD SOME OF HIS THOUGHTS. IT HAPPENS.

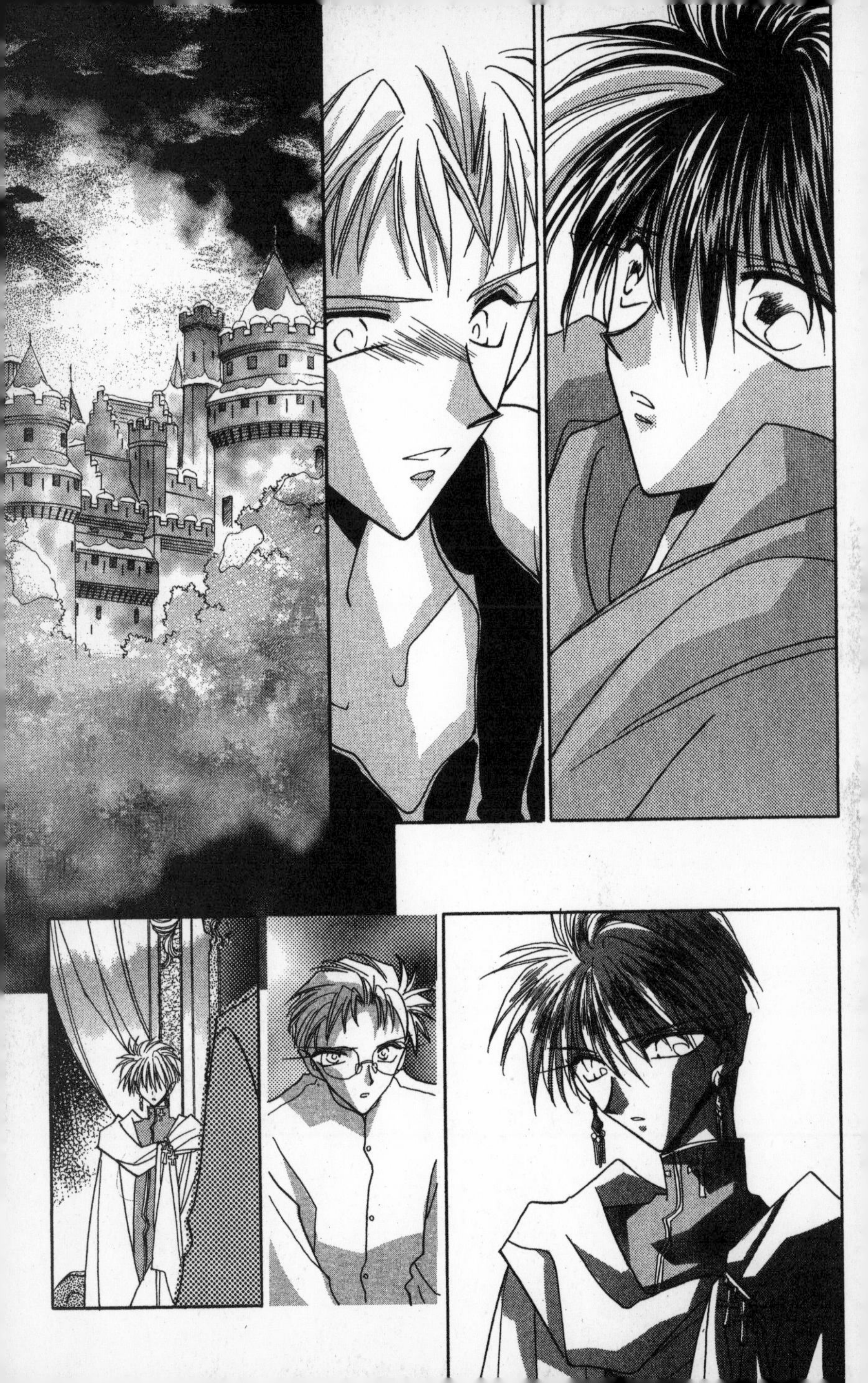

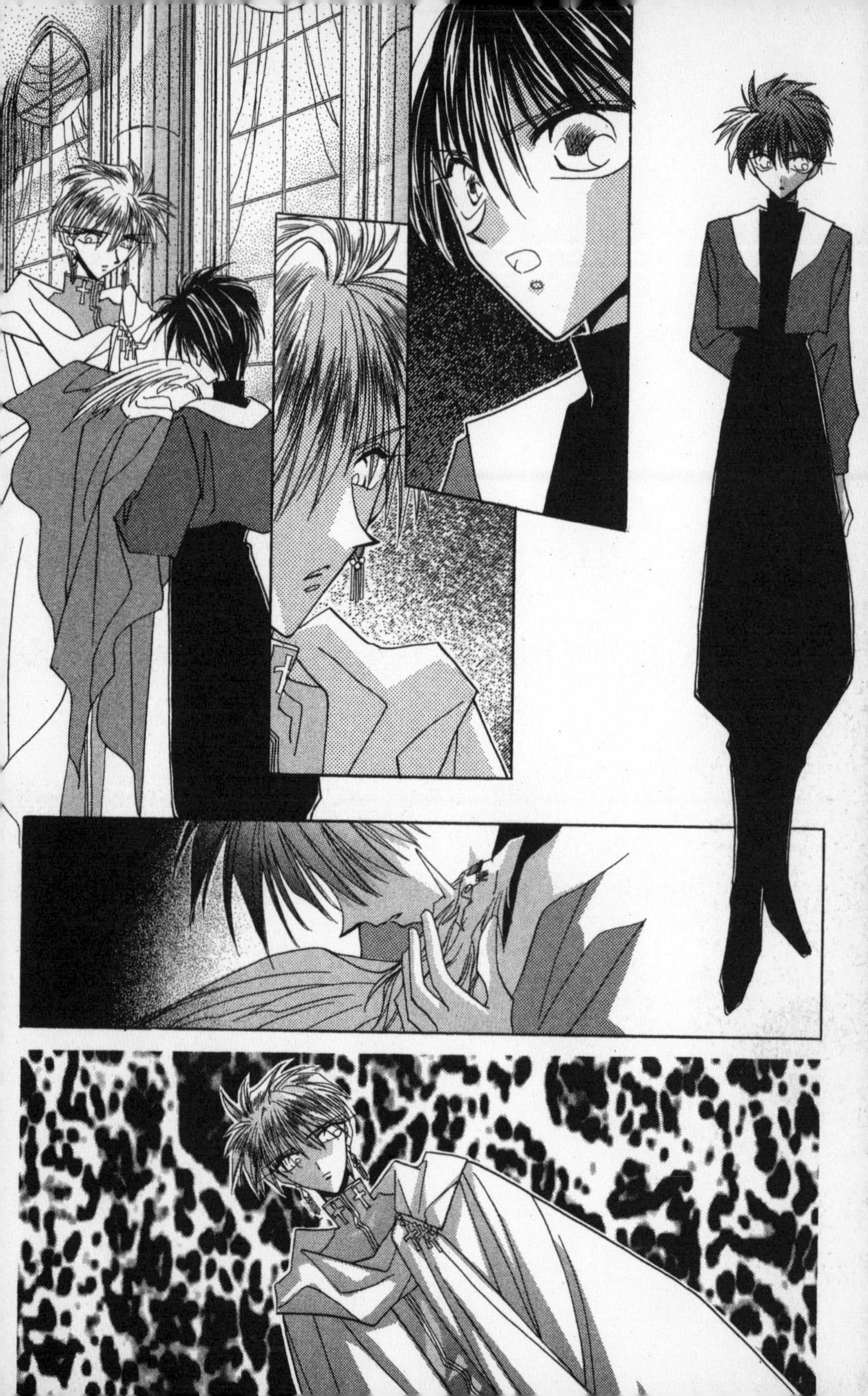

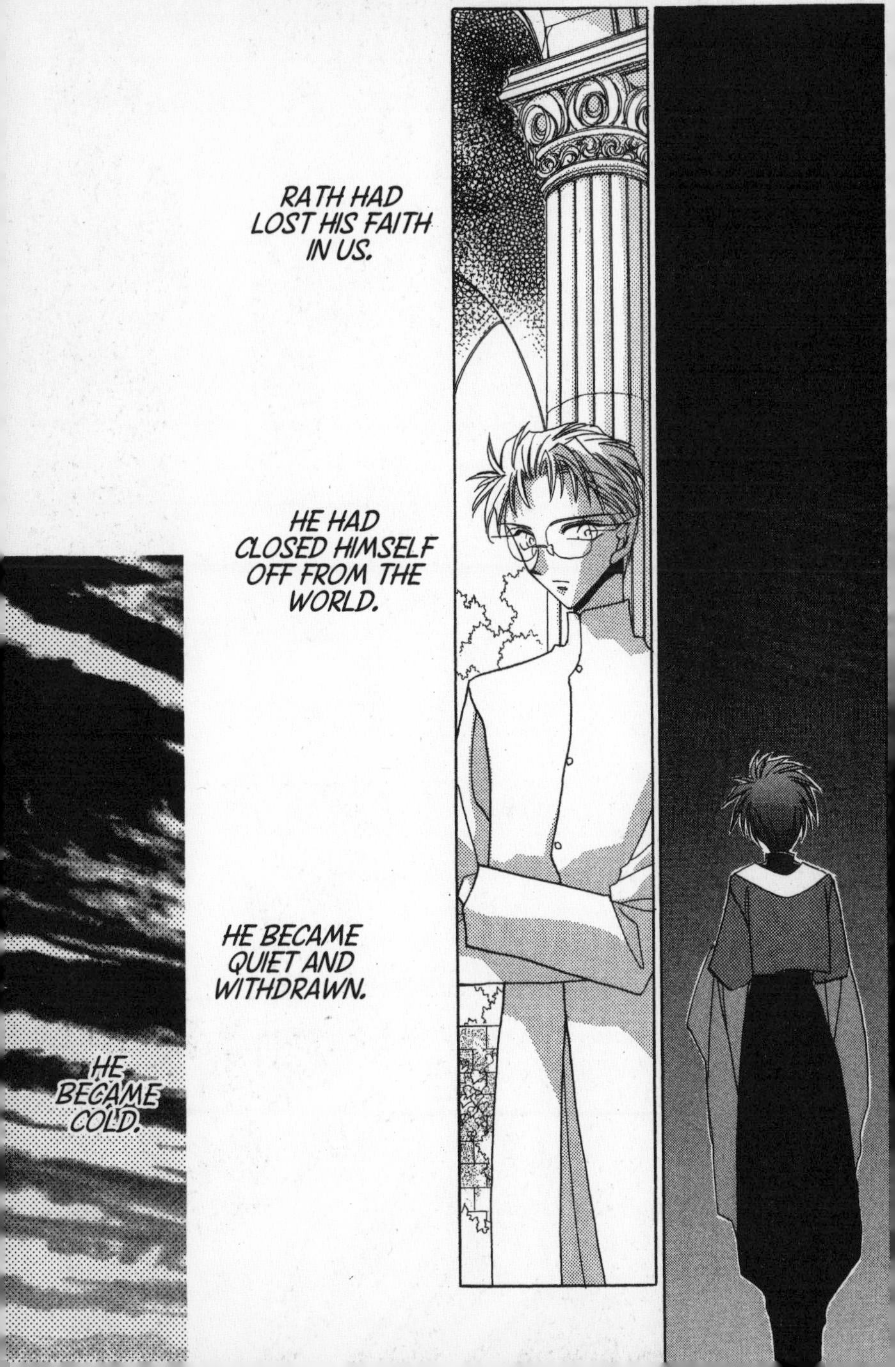
RATH HAD LOST HIS FAITH IN US.
HE HAD CLOSED HIMSELF OFF FROM THE WORLD.
HE BECAME QUIET AND WITHDRAWN.
HE BECAME COLD.

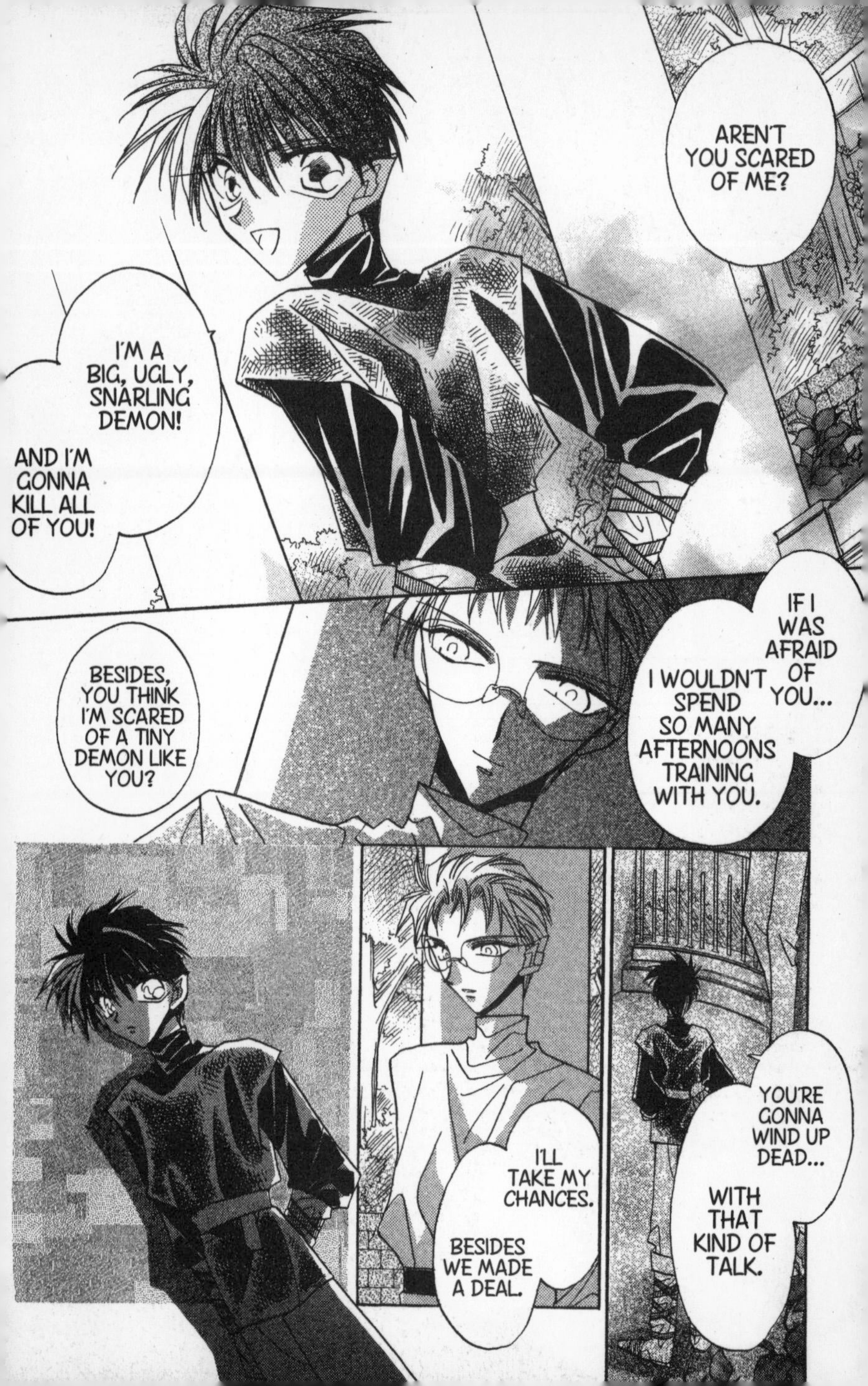
AREN'T YOU SCARED OF ME?
I'M A BIG, UGLY, SNARLING DEMON!
AND I'M GONNA KILL ALL OF YOU!
IF I WAS AFRAID OF YOU...
I WOULDN'T SPEND SO MANY AFTERNOONS TRAINING WITH YOU.
BESIDES, YOU THINK I'M SCARED OF A TINY DEMON LIKE YOU?
YOU'RE GONNA WIND UP DEAD...
WITH THAT KIND OF TALK.
I'LL TAKE MY CHANCES.
BESIDES WE MADE A DEAL.

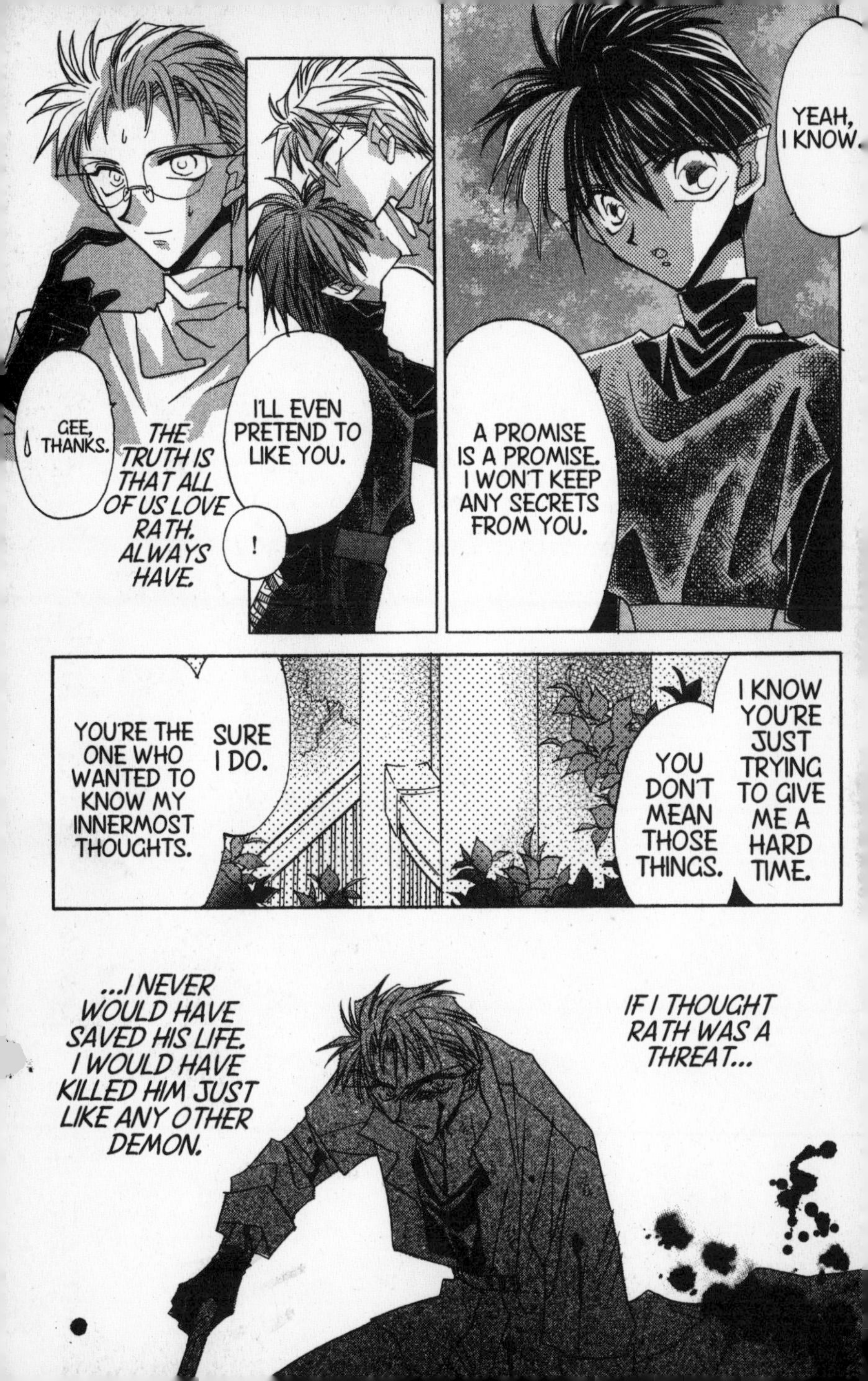
YEAH, I KNOW.
A PROMISE IS A PROMISE. I WON'T KEEP ANY SECRETS FROM YOU.
I'LL EVEN PRETEND TO LIKE YOU.
!
GEE, THANKS.
THE TRUTH IS THAT ALL OF US LOVE RATH. ALWAYS HAVE.
I KNOW YOU'RE JUST TRYING TO GIVE ME A HARD TIME.
YOU DON'T MEAN THOSE THINGS.
SURE I DO.
YOU'RE THE ONE WHO WANTED TO KNOW MY INNERMOST THOUGHTS.
IF I THOUGHT RATH WAS A THREAT...
...I NEVER WOULD HAVE SAVED HIS LIFE. I WOULD HAVE KILLED HIM JUST LIKE ANY OTHER DEMON.

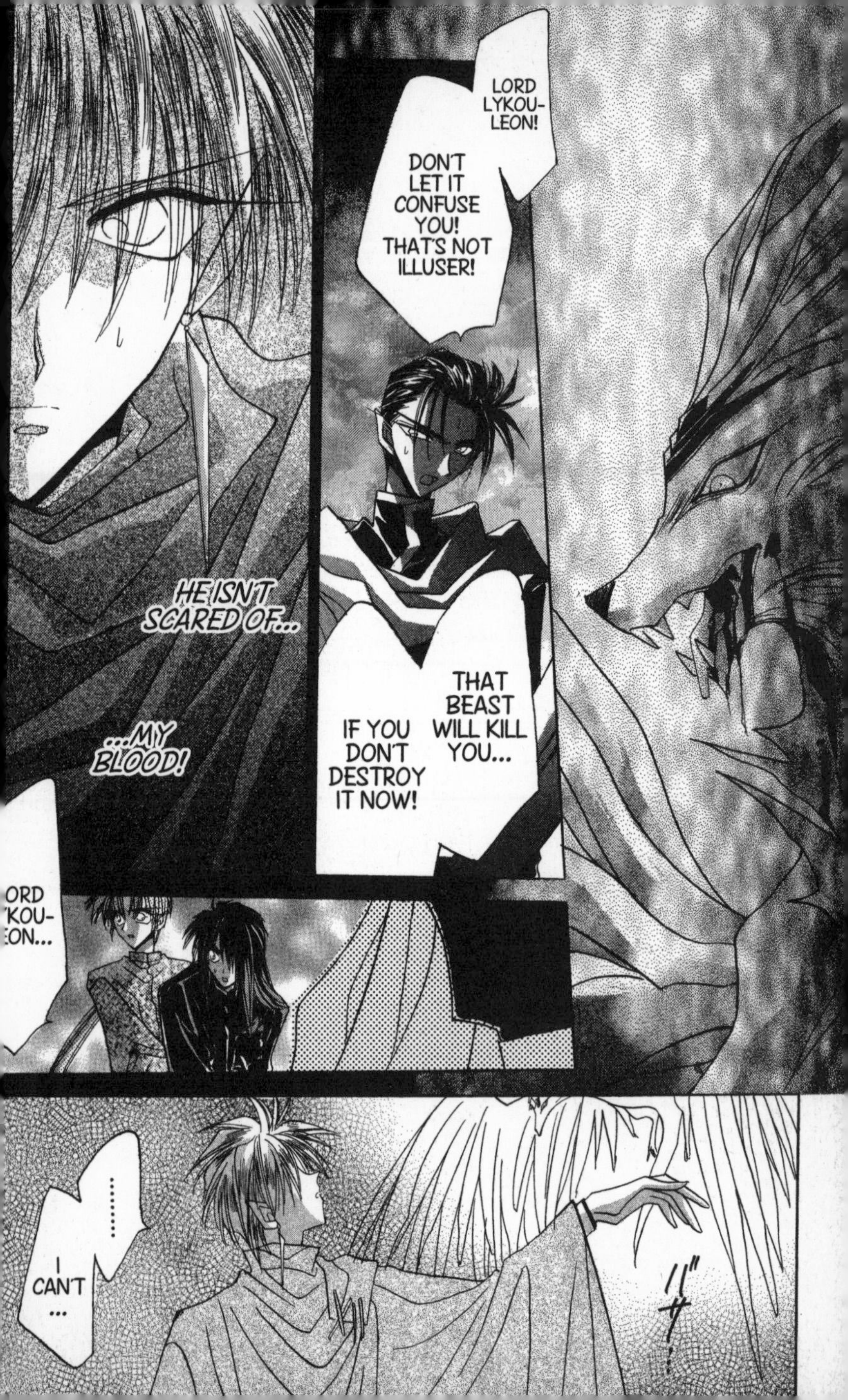
LORD LYKOU-LEON!
DON'T LET IT CONFUSE YOU! THAT'S NOT ILLUSER!
THAT BEAST WILL KILL YOU...
IF YOU DON'T DESTROY IT NOW!
HE ISN'T SCARED OF...
...MY BLOOD!
ORD YKOU- EON...
......
I CAN'T ...
バサ…

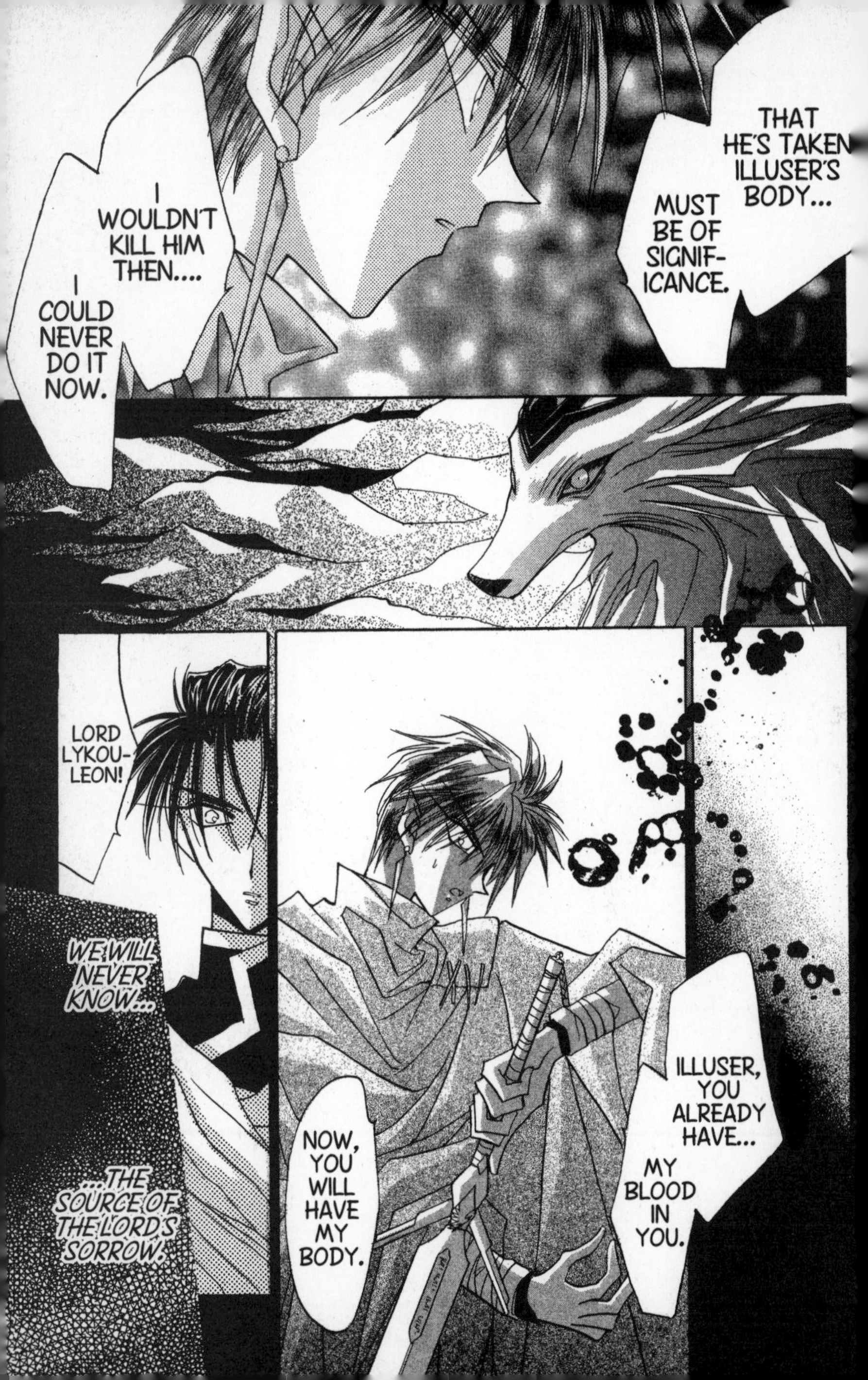
THAT HE'S TAKEN ILLUSER'S BODY...
MUST BE OF SIGNIF-ICANCE.
I WOULDN'T KILL HIM THEN....
I COULD NEVER DO IT NOW.
ILLUSER, YOU ALREADY HAVE...
MY BLOOD IN YOU.
NOW, YOU WILL HAVE MY BODY.
LORD LYKOU-LEON!
WE WILL NEVER KNOW...
...THE SOURCE OF THE LORD'S SORROW.

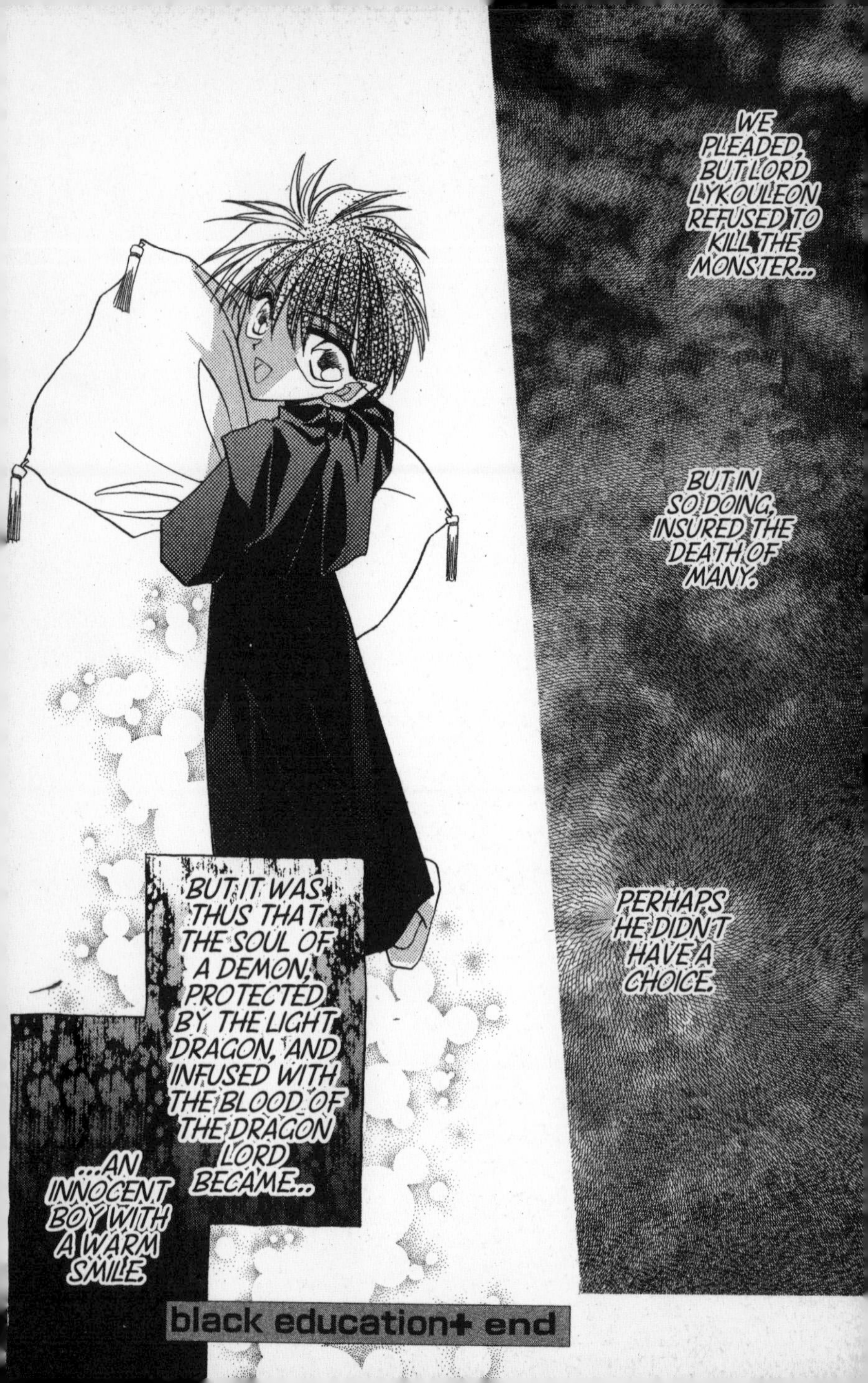
WE PLEADED, BUT LORD LYKOULEON REFUSED TO KILL THE MONSTER...
BUT IN SO DOING, INSURED THE DEATH OF MANY.
PERHAPS HE DIDN'T HAVE A CHOICE.
BUT IT WAS THUS THAT THE SOUL OF A DEMON, PROTECTED BY THE LIGHT DRAGON, AND INFUSED WITH THE BLOOD OF THE DRAGON LORD BECAME...
...AN INNOCENT BOY WITH A WARM SMILE.
black education+ end

Dragon Knights

TOKYOPOP

13

In Volume 13:

Nadil has returned, and life for the Dragon Tribe will never be the same. Nohiro, the young man with the forgotten past, is now aided by three frisky faeries as he searches for more of their kind. But when a call for help leads him to the castle of Kharl the Alchemist, his mission takes a grave turn. Meanwhile, the thief Kitchel and Ringleys, her faerie companion, continue searching for a way out of the cursed Water Cave. With the Three Treasures of Dusis in hand, she must fend off a clan of wolves, a foe from the past, and a truly annoying faerie, however, they're nothing compared to what awaits her outside the cave. Finally, Rath awakens to find Draqueen in shambles, the palace under siege, and Cesia gone. His conscience guilty, he begins a journey that will lead him straight to the heart of the Demon Realm, bringing with it the long-awaited reunion of all three Dragon Knights!

Mineko Ohkami

ALSO AVAILABLE FROM TOKYOPOP®

For more information visit www.TOKYOPOP.com

ALSO AVAILABLE FROM ☺TOKYOPOP®

MANGA

.HACK//LEGEND OF THE TWILIGHT
@LARGE
A.I. LOVE YOU
AI YORI AOSHI
ANGELIC LAYER
ARM OF KANNON May 2004
BABY BIRTH
BATTLE ROYALE
BATTLE VIXENS April 2004
BRAIN POWERED
BRIGADOON
B'TX
CANDIDATE FOR GODDESS, THE April 2004
CARDCAPTOR SAKURA
CARDCAPTOR SAKURA - MASTER OF THE CLOW
CARDCAPTOR SAKURA AUTHENTIC May 2004
CHOBITS
CHRONICLES OF THE CURSED SWORD
CLAMP SCHOOL DETECTIVES
CLOVER
COMIC PARTY June 2004
CONFIDENTIAL CONFESSIONS
CORRECTOR YUI
COWBOY BEBOP
COWBOY BEBOP: SHOOTING STAR
CRESCENT MOON May 2004
CYBORG 009
DEMON DIARY
DEMON ORORON, THE April 2004
DEUS VITAE June 2004
DIGIMON
DIGIMON ZERO TWO
DIGIMON SERIES 3 April 2004
DNANGEL April 2004
DOLL - HARDCOVER May 2004
DRAGON HUNTER
DRAGON KNIGHTS
DUKLYON: CLAMP SCHOOL DEFENDERS
ERICA SAKURAZAWA WORKS
FAERIES' LANDING
FAKE
FLCL
FORBIDDEN DANCE
FRUITS BASKET
G GUNDAM
GATE KEEPERS
GETBACKERS
GHOST! March 2004
GIRL GOT GAME
GRAVITATION
GTO
GUNDAM WING

GUNDAM WING: BATTLEFIELD OF PACIFISTS
GUNDAM WING: ENDLESS WALTZ
GUNDAM WING: THE LAST OUTPOST (G-UNIT)
HAPPY MANIA
HARLEM BEAT
I.N.V.U.
IMMORTAL RAIN June 2004
INITIAL D
ISLAND
JING: KING OF BANDITS
JULINE
JUROR 13 Coming Soon
KARE KANO
KILL ME, KISS ME
KINDAICHI CASE FILES, THE
KING OF HELL
KODOCHA: SANA'S STAGE
LAMENT OF THE LAMB May 2004
LES BIJOUX
LOVE HINA
LUPIN III
MAGIC KNIGHT RAYEARTH I
MAGIC KNIGHT RAYEARTH II
MAHOROMATIC: AUTOMATIC MAIDEN May 2004
MAN OF MANY FACES
MARMALADE BOY
MARS
MINK April 2004
MIRACLE GIRLS
MIYUKI-CHAN IN WONDERLAND
MODEL May 2004
ONE April 2004
PARADISE KISS
PARASYTE
PEACH GIRL
PEACH GIRL: CHANGE OF HEART
PEACH GIRL: AUTHENTIC COLLECTORS BOX SET May 2004
PET SHOP OF HORRORS
PITA-TEN
PLANET LADDER
PLANETES
PRIEST
PSYCHIC ACADEMY March 2004
RAGNAROK
RAVE MASTER
REALITY CHECK
REBIRTH
REBOUND
REMOTE June 2004
RISING STARS OF MANGA
SABER MARIONETTE J
SAILOR MOON
SAINT TAIL

11.20.03 T

PSYCHIC ACADEMY™

You don't have to be a great psychic to be a great hero

...but it helps.

TOKYOPOP®

Available March 2004 At Your Favorite Book And Comic Stores.

TEEN
AGE 13+

www.TOKYOPOP.com

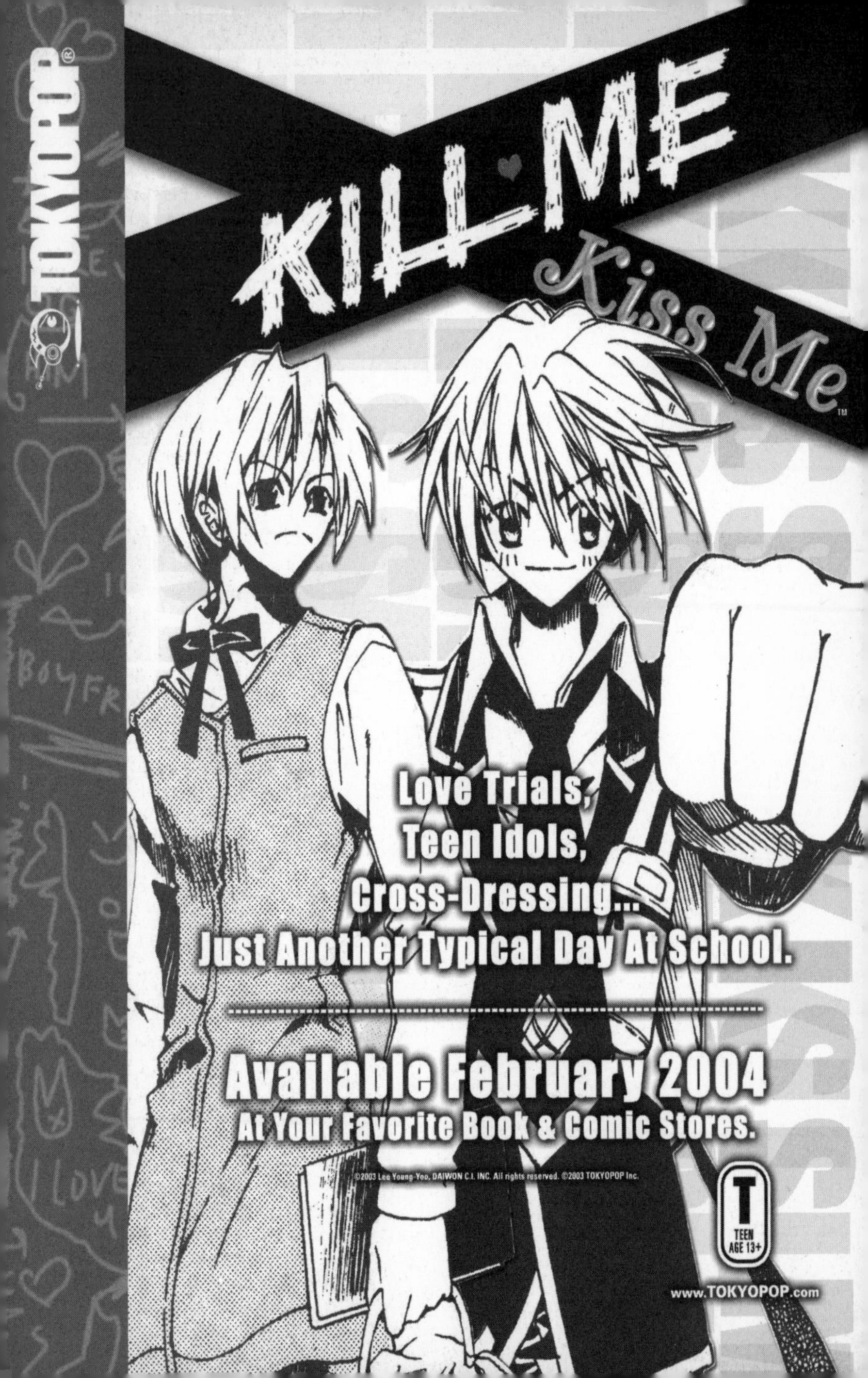
TOKYOPOP®
KILL ME
Kiss Me™
Love Trials,
Teen Idols,
Cross-Dressing...
Just Another Typical Day At School.
Available February 2004
At Your Favorite Book & Comic Stores.
©2003 Lee Young-Yoo, DAIWON C.I. INC. All rights reserved. ©2003 TOKYOPOP Inc.
T
TEEN
AGE 13+
www.TOKYOPOP.com

VAMPIRE GAME
by JUDAL

Reincarnation... Resurrection... Revenge...
All In the Hands of One Snotty Teenage Princess

TEEN
AGE 13+